NEWS AGENCIES
from
PIGEON *to* INTERNET

NEWS AGENCIES
from
PIGEON *to* INTERNET

K. M. Shrivastava

NEW DAWN PRESS, INC.
USA• UK• INDIA

NEW DAWN PRESS GROUP

Published by New Dawn Press Group

New Dawn Press, Inc., 244 South Randall Rd # 90, Elgin, IL 60123
e-mail: sales@newdawnpress.com

New Dawn Press, 2 Tintern Close, Slough, Berkshire, SL1-2TB, UK
e-mail: sterlingdis@yahoo.co.uk

New Dawn Press (An Imprint of Sterling Publishers (P) Ltd.)
A-59, Okhla Industrial Area, Phase-II, New Delhi-110020
e-mail: sterlingpublishers@airtelbroadband.in
www.sterlingpublishers.com

News Agencies from Pigeon to Internet
© *2007, K. M. Shrivastava*
ISBN 1 932705 67 8

PRINTED IN INDIA

This book deals with a very important business in the global communication of news – the news agencies. They were invented because of the desire of newspapers to give wider coverage of news and their limited capacity to do it on their own. The first news agencies started their business when the fastest technology was the combination of telegraph and carrier pigeon. They have survived several technological developments since then and have used these technologies for further diversification of services and revenues. Businesses and governments, besides media outlets, depend on news agencies to keep abreast with the latest developments.

With the advent of the Internet, some thought that the news agencies would go out of business – may end up being dinosaurs of journalism. But as agencies were using digital technologies before the birth of Internet, well-run news agencies found in this threat a new opportunity. Some dying agencies found in it a new elixir of life.

Though there have been some corporate biographies of news agencies and some seminars and conferences, there is no comprehensive analytical work in the past 25 years on this business. This book is an attempt to fill this void in global literature on journalism, media studies, and international communication and business management studies. Besides the students of these academic disciplines, diplomats, policymakers, and all types of communication professionals will find it useful. It will also be a good read for lay readers who unconsciously consume the products of news agencies through all types of media – from newspapers to mobile phones.

My interest in news agencies started in 1978 when I participated as a working journalist, representing the news agency Samachar Bharti in a course for news agency journalists at the Indian Institute of Mass Communication. Mrs. Indira Gandhi, as Prime Minister of India, announced the course at the height of the global debate on New World

Information and Communication Order. Mr. H.Y. Sharda Prasad was then her information advisor. Before the first course was launched, Mrs. Gandhi lost elections and her information advisor was sent to Indian Institute of Mass Communication, as Director. As he had been news editor of Indian Express, he understood the journalistic significance of news agencies; and as information advisor to Prime Minister, he had the political understanding of issues involved. I worked with Samachar Bharti till 1985, when I started my academic career at Punjabi University, Patiala. In 1993, I returned to Indian Institute of Mass Communication to become the course director of the news agency journalism course and since 1995, Professor, News Agency Journalism.

Besides my interaction with news agency professionals during my years of working for Sanachar Bharti, I visited a large number of news agencies headquarters around the world – from Notimex (Mexico) and Prensa Latina (Cuba) to Reuters (London), Vietnam News Agency (Hanoi), BERNAMA (Malaysia) and Australian Associated Press (Sydney), and many more. A large number of agency executives responded to my request for information, among them were those from AP, AFP, and ANSA. Golden Jubilee celebrations of PTI also provided opportunities to interact with professionals from all over the world. I also met almost all scholars working on news agencies at various conferences—Professors Michael Palmer (University of Paris), Oliver Boyd-Barrett (California State Polytechnic University, Pomona), Terhi Rantanen (Media@LSE, London) Elena Vartanova (Moscow State University), Gertrude J. Robinson (McGill University) and S. Jim Kim (Towson University). I am grateful for the inputs. Updates are welcome for the next edition.

K. M. Shrivastava

CONTENTS

CONTENTS

EVOLUTION: THE GLOBAL PERSPECTIVE

*N*ews agency, also called press agency, press association, wire service, or news service, can be defined as an organisation or business that gathers, writes and distributes news from around a nation or the world to newspapers, periodicals, radio and television broadcasters, government agencies, and other users. They have been invisible wholesalers of news and information products to most media consumers—who usually ignore the credit lines in the corner of television screens or in brackets or in small print at the beginning or end of print news stories.[1] Only the radio gave the credit when there was any doubt about the information. Nonetheless, news agencies have been indispensable for those media outlets that wish to give wide coverage to their readers.

Diversification for revenue has been news agency management principle from the beginning. These days diversification has gone to such an extent that any general definition of news agency activities will be incomplete. News agencies are in retail business serving a fragmented media market. They are also in advertising and PR. Some of them publish newspapers, and some have camera crews available on hire, and some are involved in training in media. Like the activities, the ownership pattern is also diverse—private, cooperative, public or state—with different forms of possible management in each category. News agencies have been competing with each other to be first with the news. For this they have been using the fastest communication technology available. In the nineteenth century, agencies used carrier pigeons and now they use satellite phones and the Internet.

Addressing the first meeting of World Association of News Agencies in Moscow on 24 September 2004[2], Director General of Unesco, Koichiro Matsuura said: Editorial independence, unfettered access to information and rigorous professional standards are especially important for news agencies since they provide the news material and footage for so many other media outlets, particularly those lacking the resources to be present in the world's hot-spots, to perform investigative reporting or to cover issues that require large staff deployments or special knowledge. If news agencies did not exist, we would have to invent them!

Pioneers

Charles-Louis Havas (1783 – 1858) was the pioneer of this business. It was he who called it 'agency' (Agence). Before Havas invented news agency business, the main source of foreign news to newspapers were newspapers of foreign countries. Newspapers had employed Havas to translate news from foreign newspapers. In 1832 he set up a foreign newspapers translation bureau and bookshop in Paris. In 1835 it became the Agence Havas, the first worldwide news agency. In 1840, using carrier pigeons, Havas landed news in the news rooms of Paris newspapers—midday news from the Belgian morning press and 3 p.m. news from the same day's British newspapers. No sooner was Samuel Morse's invention, the electromagnetic telegraph, introduced in France in 1845, than Havas started installing Morse machines. Havas also set up an advertising agency in 1852 that created revenue for its newspaper clients and helped them pay for the agency's service. In 1879 the Havas family sold its interests for seven million francs and Agence Havas became a public limited company. In 1940 legislation forced the splitting up of the advertising and newsgathering operations of Agence Havas. The newsgathering operation, now owned by the State, became the Office Français d'Information (OFI, or French Information Office) and in 1944 became Agence France-Presse (AFP), a public corporation.[3]

Two of his employees, rather protégés, were Paul Julius Reuter and Bernhard Wolff[i] who later became founders of news agencies bearing their names in London and Berlin, respectively. The first European news agencies were mostly privately owned by and often—like Havas—named after their founders (Fabra in Spain, Reuters in the UK, Stefani in Italy, Wolff in Germany). However, Joseph Tuwara who started Oesterreichische Correspondenz (Austrian Press Agency) in Vienna was private in name but had the blessings of Alexander Bach, minister of justice and interior. Tuwara, once a revolutionary, wrote to Bach in September 1849 "that the use of a weapon as flexible and long-range as a news agency would be of inconceivable advantage to the government."[5] His private organisation in principle was meant to supply government-controlled news to the Czech, Slovenian, Serbocroat, and Italian language provincial papers taken over by the government to signal unity and preservation of the realm and to contain revolutionary and nationalist voices in parts of the monarchy. It lasted till 31 December 1859, when after the defeat in Italy, Count Agenor Goluchowski replaced Bach as the interior minister and Tuwara was compensated with an annuity of 1200 gulden, as his business was taken over by *k. k. Telegraphen Korrespondenz-Bureau.*

On 28 November 1849, the *National Zeitung*, a Berlin newspaper founded in the previous year as a liberal party paper, announced that it would feature news dispatches from Paris, London, Amsterdam and Frankfurt. Further dispatches were said to come from Hamburg and Stettin in another few days. The day of this announcement was the "birthday" of the "Wolff'sches Telegraphisches Bureau (WTB) which was to become the first and, until, 1933 the most important German news agency. It was named after Bernhard Wolff, manager of the *National Zeitung* and the driving force behind the whole enterprise.[6] Soon, Wolff had the idea of selling his news dispatches to other newspapers—an idea that made the creation of a separate news office necessary. The Wolffsches Telegraphisches Bureau progressed slowly. In 1865, the business was transformed into a joint stock company, the Continental Telegraphen Agentur, which provided for fresh capital. Moreover, the government started to subsidise the WTB. This caused a financial dependency and gave the WTB a semiofficial status. The WTB's new position was made evident by the agency's moving into a wing of the telegraph station building of the post office in Berlin in 1869, which must have been an advantage in the working process. Nevertheless, the dispatches had to be first redistributed to the customers in town by mailmen or the existing pneumatic tube. The WTB remained in the "Reichspost" until 1877. It organised newsgathering in cooperation with smaller news services in other parts of the country. This cooperation, however, was impaired until 1877 by the telegraph charges being graded according to several time zones. In 1893, the WTB opened its first branch in Cologne.

Paul Julius Reuter, the founder of Reuters, the world news and information organisation, was born on 21 July 1816 as Israel Beer

Josaphat in Cassel[7], Germany. He came to England as 'Joseph Josaphat' on 29 October 1845 and was baptised few days later on 16 November as Paul Julius Reuter at St George's German Lutheran Chapel, Whitechapel, London. A week later, on 23 November he married Ida Maria Elizabeth Clementine Magnus, daughter of a banker, at the same chapel. In 1847 he became a partner in a Berlin bookshop, 'Reuter & Stargardt'. In 1848 he had to leave Germany for his radical writings and flee to Paris where he worked as translator for Agence Havas. A year later, he left Havas to set up his own news-sheet. It failed, and he moved to Aachen, where, on 1 October 1849, Europe's first commercial telegraph line opened: the Prussian State Telegraph line from Berlin. He set up the business supplying local clients with the news from the Prussian capital, soon expanding to supply clients in Antwerp and Brussels. When the French opened a line the following spring from Brussels to Paris, he bridged the gap—first with carrier pigeons, and then with horses. In 1850 Reuter was running a news agency in Aachen and had an agreement on 24 April with Heinrich Geller to supply pigeons for service between Brussels and Aachen. The agency operated for over a year, until the telegraph gap closed. As the telegraph network was extended, Reuter preceded it and in 1851, he established himself in London in order to exploit the submarine link between Calais and Dove. He reached London on 14 June 1851, and about four months later, on 10 October, Reuter set up office in two rooms at 1 Royal Exchange Buildings, London. On 13 November 1851 the Cross-Channel submarine telegraph began operating.

The Press Association was founded in 1868 by a group of provincial daily newspaper proprietors in UK to provide a fast and accurate news information service to its members. Its founders sought to produce a more accurate and reliable alternative to the oligopoly of the telegraph companies. Through their cooperation, they wanted to provide a London-based service of news collecting and reporting with correspondents in all the major towns. A committee appointed to make arrangements for the formation of the company said: "The Press Association is formed on the principle of cooperation and can never be worked for individual profit or become exclusive in its character." It is a private company with 27 shareholders, most of whom are national and regional newspaper publishers.

The history of the agencies in Italy began on 26 January 1853 with the foundation of Telegraphic Notiziario Stefani, a week after the inauguration of the telegraphic line Turin-Chambery that allowed the connection with Paris. Owner and director of the Agency was a 34-year-old exile from Venice, Guglielmo Stefani, who had practised journalism at Padova in 1844 –1845, founding two newspapers, the *Euganeo* and the *Pedrocchi Coffee*. Escaping to Turin after the fall of the Republic of Venice in 1849, Stefani began life as a journalist and publisher, also becoming director of the *Piemontese Gazette*, official newspaper of the Reign. It soon became "Agenzia the Stefani - private Telegraphy" with the aid and suggestion of Count Camillo Benso di Cavour (1810 – 1868). Stefani, then formed an alliance with Havas for the international news, covered news from the borders of the Reign of Italy and had subscribers and correspondents in the other Italian states: Florence, Milan, Parma, Bologna, and Rome. It was private property of Gugliemo Stefani and then his successors, got the direct and indirect aids of the Reign of Italy, to influence "an unofficial" organism—the press.

The news agency formula took 35 years to reach Spain from Paris and was first used by Nile Maria Fabra y Deas, a journalist and Catalan industrialist. In 1865 he started an information service Center of Correspondents in Madrid. He himself collected the news, wrote them up and then distributed to subscribers. In 1866, the *Newspaper of Barcelona* requested him to cover the Franco-Prussian war. Fabra accepted the offer, and, in Vienna, came in contact with other correspondents from the great agencies. After the war coverage, he spent few days in Paris, where he met Auguste Havas, one of the children of the founder of Agence Havas. On his return to Spain in 1867, following the guidelines of Havas, he turned the Center of Correspondents into Fabra Agency. Like his contemporaries, Fabra also used carrier pigeons in 1874 and established pigeon houses in Valencia, Barcelona and Palma de Mallorca to have information on ships before their arrival at mainland Spanish ports.

Agence Telegraphic Switzerland (ATS)—the Swiss Telegraphic Agency—was founded on 25 September 1894 in Bern.

Before this, Havas and Wolff had divided the Swiss market. The editors and journalists of Switzerland were not happy with this situation and they created the Swiss Telegraphic Agency in 1894 to secure a source of independent information. The ATS began its activities on 1 January 1895, with eight journalists, from a modest apartment located at Spitalgasse 55, in Bern. In addition to the director, it employed three people in Bern, two in Geneva, two in Zurich and in Basle. By the end of the year, around fifty of correspondents worked for the agency.

The 200 registered shares of 500 francs were subscribed mainly by the newspaper's founders. From start, the founders decided to use the surplus of receipts for the improvement and the development of the service. The number of subscribers increased from 54 in 1895 to 71 in 1900, covering nearly the entire Swiss daily press.

In, 1898 The Bulgarian News Agency (BTA), Bulgaria's national news agency was established by a decree issued by Prince Ferdinand I. Now it is an autonomous national news organization, whose director general is elected by the Parliament. The agency's statute guarantees its independent editorial policy and protects it from any economic and political influence.

Across the Atlantic, the story of evolution of news agency formula was different. In May 1848, 10 men representing six New York City newspapers sat around an office table of the New York Sun. At issue was the costly collection of news by telegraphy. The newly invented telegraph made transmission of news possible by wire, but at costs so high that the resources of any single paper would be strained. David Hale of the *Journal of Commerce* argued that only a joint effort between New York's papers could make telegraphy affordable and effectively prevent the telegraph companies from interfering in the newsgathering process. To get news from the west coast of United States and from abroad, Hale argued, newspapers had to work together if the public was to be served with increasingly wider coverage. Although reluctant at first, the six highly competitive papers agreed to form a cooperative, and the Associated Press was born. Its roots quickly spread, from one correspondent[8] in Halifax, Nova Scotia, to correspondents in the United States in Boston, Philadelphia, Washington D.C. and later to the Midwest. Using the telegraph and the language of dots and dashes known as the Morse code, the AP grew, and in 1875 became the first news organization to secure a leased telegraph wire.

From the beginning, members of AP decided who could join them and who could not. E. W. Scripps, publisher of the Scripps-McRae Newspapers (later Scripps-Howard), had started several newspapers and wanted to be free to start others wherever he wished. He also wanted others to be free to start newspapers because he believed in newspapers as such and in the principle which became the motto of the Scripps-Howard newspapers: "Give light and the people will find their own way." He saw that a single, powerful press association could become such a monopoly in the gathering and distribution of news as to hold the power of life and death over a publisher whose social and economic views might differ from those of publishers who were in control of the news monopoly. Under the restrictive membership rules of the AP as they existed then, such publishers could deny the AP's service to new publishers. His determination to fight this caused him to organise the Scripps-McRae Press Association in the Middle West and the Scripps News Association on the Pacific Coast in the early 1900s. In 1906, he purchased control of the Publishers Press, a small news service in the East, and merged the three services the following year to form United Press Associations. In contrast to the AP practice, he believed that news should be furnished to any publisher who desired it and could pay for it, without regard to competitive interests. He felt that there should be a free flow of information. "I do not believe in monopolies," Scripps said later. "I believe that monopolies suffer more than their victims in the long run. I do not believe it would be good for journalism in this country that there should be one big news trust such as the founders of the Associated Press fully expected to build up."

Government Involvement

Thus the basic reason for the evolution of news agencies was the desire of newspapers to give the widest possible coverage of news. Individual papers were unable to cover the cost of such news collection. There were two options. Either they share the cost of such collection or they pay another enterprise that sells them such collection of news. Third option emerged soon when, like business houses, governments realised the importance of news. Governments soon became involved in agency newsgathering and dissemination. For this they used a variety of means or combinations of methods that included direct ownership, control, tariff concessions for use of state communications facilities, intervention in news content, and overt or covert subsidy or direct financing of news agencies. The first state agency *k. k. Telegraphen Korrespondenz-Bureau* came into existence in 1860, when it started distributing articles to the newspapers published by the Austro-Hungarian Government.[9] Although the State's role varied from country to country, government-run agencies were soon widely acknowledged. Many news agencies that were commonly regarded as private had close connections with their respective governments. Reuters is a case in point: the London-based agency enjoyed significant government support through much of the twentieth century.[10] In India, for example, Reuters functioned as an imperial agency and got government support to eliminate any competition. The Associated Press of India, founded by K. C. Roy in 1910, became a fully owned Reuters's subsidiary in 1919. The Free Press Agency of Swaminath Sadanand, which had made arrangements to take foreign news from other sources, had to face the full might of the British Empire and had to close down.

During World War I, Reuters agreed to disseminate official allied communiqués and news to neutral countries, the British Empire, and the allied troops, while the government financed this service by paying for the transmission costs of the telegrams. Its managing director simultaneously held government office for a period of time. AP in 1930 "lent itself as freely to the uses of government for propaganda services"[11] and in its coverage of American "extraterritorial ventures" the agency "invariably regards every situation through the spectacles offered to it by our officialdom".[12] It was at the suggestion of the State Department that AP made its first entry into the South American market during World War I, although United Press was to be by far the strongest agency there until well after World War II. On the eve of World War II, Reuters received a communications subsidy to augment the volume of its international wireless news services. During the war, Reuters received government finance for the purpose of maintaining the South American bureaus of Havas. The London-based Free French Agency (AFI), later to be one of the founding organizations of AFP, was entirely financed by the British Ministry of Information from 1940 and 1943.

As has been said earlier, the Italian agency Stefani, though private, had the support of Count Camillo Benso di Cavour, the figure who forged the Kingdom of Italy, designed the constitutional structure of the unitary state and served as its first prime minister. The relationship of Stefani with the government became open in 1888, when Stefani (by then it had become 50 percent property of Agence Havas) was at the center of the diplomatic game of Italy, in the operation *potenziamento* of the Triple Alliance. Prime Minister Francisco Crispi started one complex operation in order to detach it from the French and to form one confederation with Prussian and Austro-Hungarian agencies. For months the embassies to London, Berlin and Vienna dealt on the issue with the local ministries; "Stefani", Crispi wrote, "is entirely in our hands and finds morally and also materially from the government." The successive year formalised the agreement: Stefani was detached from Agence Havas, but only formally because the connection would continue through Reuters. From 1900 to 1920, Stefani became a joint stock company with entry of the famous Teodoro Mayer (editor of Piccolo) who possessed one half of it and financier Giuseppe Volpi di Misurata who possessed the other half. Then, with the Fascists, Stefani became the top organ for the propaganda of the regime.[13] The property and the presidency of Stefani went to Manlio Morgagni, former administrative director of the Popolo d'Italia[14], who upgraded it and transformed it to international level. In the evening of 25 July 1943, Morgagni committed suicide for his principles. After 8 September 1943, Stefani moved to the North, having finally become property of the State and an organ of the RSI, ended with its last director, Ernesto Daquanno who was shot dead on 28 April 1945, along with other Fascists leaders.

The St. Petersburg Telegraph Agency (SPTA), the first official news agency of Russia and the predecessor of ITAR-TASS began to operate on 1 September 1904. Three government departments of the Russian Empire—the finance, interior, and foreign ministries—initiated the creation of the first Russian official news agency. A meeting of representatives of the ministries on 4 July 1904, empowered to consider issues concerning the project of a government telegraph agency, adopted the basic documents for the creation and operation of SPTA. The project to launch SPTA was approved by the last Russian Tsar, Nicholas the Second. The agency had to "report within the Empire and abroad political, financial, economic, trade and other data of public interest. Three directors, one from each of the finance, interior and foreign ministries, comprised the panel that managed the agency. On 31 December 1909, the agency was subordinated directly to the council of ministers upon a submission of Prime Minister Petr Stolypin. On 19 August, 1914, one day after Nicholas the Second ruled to rename St. Petersburg into Petrograd, SPTA changed its name accordingly and became the Petrograd Telegraph Agency (PTA). During the Bolshevik revolution of 25 October—7 November 1917, the PTA building in Pochtampt Street was seized by revolutionary Baltic Fleet seamen headed by Military Commissar Leonid Stark. PTA immediately wired the first reports written by Stark about the Bolshevik revolution to the whole world. On 18 November 1917 the Bolshevik government (Sovnarkom) decreed PTA to become the central government information agency. In March 1918, PTA moved to Moscow where it merged in June with the press bureau of the government. On 7 September 1918, the government presidium resolved to rename PTA and the Press bureau into the Russian telegraph agency (ROSTA). ROSTA became the central information agency of the whole Russian Socialist Federative Soviet Republic.

In order to better report the goals and struggles of the newly-founded Republic of Latvia to foreign and domestic news audiences, the provisional government of Karlis Ulmanis (temporarily based in Liepaja) created the state press bureau, Latopress on 4 March 1919. The bureau was relocated to Riga under the authority of the State Chancellery. At this time, Latopress performed functions later to be taken over by the Information Department of the Ministry of Foreign Affairs. In 1919, Latopress concluded partnership agreements with Estonian news agency Estur (now, ETA) and Polish news agency PAT (now, PAP). Cooperation with Poland ensured radio news contact between Riga and Warsaw. On 5 May, 1920 the provisional Cabinet of Ministers created the Latvian Telegraph Agency, renaming it LETA, and appointing Rihards Berzins as its director. Berzins remained at LETA's helm until 1940. An agreement concluded between the telegraph agencies of Estonia, Latvia and Lithuania provided for their close cooperation and authorised LETA to negotiate partnerships with the great world news agencies on behalf of all three. Contracting with Great Britain's Reuters, France's Agence Havas and Germany's Wolff's Telegraphisches Buro, LETA acquired broad and immediate access to world news, for both reception and further dissemination. During this time, LETA established relations with 26 different national news agencies around the world. LETA received authentic and reliable information from its network of foreign correspondents. LETA's Moscow correspondent was a critical source of information to Europe on conditions in Russia, which was closed to foreign journalists until 1925. LETA often rivaled the diplomatic corps in the accuracy and speed with which it delivered important information from foreign posts. LETA staff photographed the arrival and the occupation of Soviet Army in Riga on 17 June 1940, and later transported the documentary materials to Sweden.

Istanbul was occupied by Western powers on 16 March 1920. After the closure of the Ottoman Parliament, Mustafa Kemal Pasha sent a note to the governors and force commanders, asking them to elect delegates to join the Grand National Assembly, which would convene in Ankara. Yunus Nadi (*Abalioglu*), the owner of *Yeni Gun* (*New Day*) newspaper, and journalist-author Halide Edip (*Adivar*), who joined people heading towards Ankara upon this call, met in Geyve on 31 March. Two intellectuals, who got on a train to Ankara, discussed in Geyve-Akhisar station (today called Pamukova) of the necessity that a news agency should be established as a first step. When Yunus Nadi and Halide Edip were discussing how the new agency should be named, they chose "Anadolu" (Anatolia) among other alternatives like "Turk" and "Ankara". Anadolu Agency (AA) was established in April 1920. Mustafa Kemal immediately launched initiatives to herald establishment of Anadolu Agency. By a "historic circular" he sent to the military and civilian authorities throughout the country, he not only mentioned the establishment of Anadolu Agency, but also stressed the importance of making the national struggle be heard inside and outside of the country. AA corespondents were always on the sides of Mustafa Kemal Ataturk in his trips within the country to make his reforms understood well. Anadolu Agency went through a structural transformation in 1925 and got the status of company. With this structuring, which was uncommon even in western standards at that time, Anadolu Agency gained an autonomous status.

On 10 July 1925, the Telegraph Agency of the Soviet Union-Telegrafnoi Agetsvo Sovietskavo Sojuza (TASS) was founded and took over the main functions of the Russian Telegraph Agency as the central information agency of the country. TASS enjoyed the exclusive right to gather and distribute information outside the Soviet Union, as well as the right to distribute foreign and domestic information within the Soviet Union, and manage the news agencies of the Soviet republics. TASS comprised news agencies of all the Soviet republics: RATAU (Ukraine), BELTA (Byelorussia), UZTAG (Uzbekistan), KAZTAG (Kazakhstan), GRUZINFORM (Georgia), AZERINFORM

(Azerbaijan), ELTA (Lithuania), ATEM (Moldavia), LATINFORM (Latvia), KIRTAG (Kirghizia), TAJIKTA (Tajikistan), ARMENPRESS (Armenia), TURKMENINFORM (Turkmenia), and ETA (Estonia). TASS news and photos were received by 4,000 Soviet newspapers, TV and radio stations and over a thousand foreign media outlets. The news agency ran one of the biggest networks of correspondents in the world— 682 offices in the country and 94 bureaus abroad, and employed close to 2,000 journalists and photo correspondents. The current name Information Telegraph Agency of Russia (ITAR-TASS) was assumed in January 1992, after the collapse of the Soviet Union and the proclamation of sovereignty by the democratic Russian Federation. ITAR-TASS has now preserved the status of the central state information agency, but acquired new traits due to democratic transformations in Russia, to changes in information access techniques, new computer and telecommunication technologies.

ATA, Albanian Telegraphic Agency, was founded in 1929, by Mihal Sherko as an indispensable need of the Albanian people to present the Albanian reality of that time. Usually, ATA was identified with Press Office or with Press Department. Since the beginning, ATA had a network of correspondents in the major towns of the country and had at that time connection with foreign agencies like Havas, Paris; Stefani, Rome; Reuters, London; German Press Office, Berlin.

In Spain, Fabra's problem was its international dependency on Havas, which demanded of Fabra the inclusion, in its service, of the news which could be against the interests of Spain, whereas Havas did not have a similar obligation. Many voices were raised against this "Frenchified" dependency since it was the only connection of Spain with the international community; and when a conflict of interests took place, like the war of North Africa, the news reports took the French side. Because of this "French tyranny", Spaniards considered the necessity to create other agencies. Thus Febus, Spes, Iberian and Spain-America were born. The birth of these agencies contributed to the information diversity, but some voices[15] demanded the creation of a Spanish agency with international projection. Journalists and the establishment felt acute necessity of a Spanish agency with international projection during the Civil War (1936—1939). On 3 January 1939, Celedonio de Noriega Ruiz, the Marquess of Torrehoyos and a military man, and Luis Amato de Ibarrola, a journalist, declared before the notary Jose Maria that they have agreed to constitute a mercantile society of anonymous character, with the denomination of Agencia EFE S. A. Both were representing Fabra. Thus, the new agency remained fit for admission to the Club of the Allied Agencies constituted of thirty agencies and in whose statutes it appeared that only one agency from a country could be member of the association. Thus, EFE was born on the ashes of Fabra with the intention to project internationally. It had to spend long years to become the first international agency of the Hispanic world, beating the Anglo-Americans and French in that market. EFE founding document envisaged an "independent and mercantile" agency, yet supported by the government, an "officious" news agency as opposed to an "official" agency.[16]

European Cartel

Due to high telegraph charges, the strategy of cooperation was also applied to international newsgathering.

The first significant agreement was signed between Reuters and Havas in 1856 and was confined to the exchange of news of trade and stocks. The agreement was widened to include Wolff in 1859 and in later years incorporated general news and identified those geographic areas which would be regarded each agency's exclusive markets. For Havas these were to be France, Spain and Italy in Europe; South America; and India and China in Asia. Wolff got Germany, Russia, Scandinavia and the Slavonic countries. Reuters had the British Empire and the Far East. This reduced cost of foreign newsgathering and protected markets. This arrangement has been described as international news cartel.

According to the 1870 agreement, Reuters' territory included England, Holland and their colonies, while Germany, Scandinavia and the cities of St. Petersburg and Moscow belonged to Wolff, and Havas had exclusive right to France, Italy, Spain and Portugal. The Ottoman Empire, Egypt and Belgium were divided between Havas and Reuters, and every other region was declared neutral territory where all the three could operate. Later agreements covered the entire world.

The partners in the post-1870 agreements were to sell their news services only in what by common consent were their own spheres of influence; outside these spheres they would provide news only to other partners.

By restricting Wolff's territorial expansion and making it pay 25 percent of its annual profits, Havas and Reuters succeeded in limiting their partner's activities. The Austro-Hungarian Korrespondentz Bureau was included as new partner in 1887. It had a different status along with Associated Press of United States.

Reuters' official biographer Donald Read has described that in the period 1860 – 1900, Reuters functioned "increasingly as an institution of the British Empire." The government of Bismarck, which wanted to prevent Reuters from taking over the German agency, subsidised Wolff.[17] Several agencies like Stefani, Wolff and Korrespondentz Bureau, with the help of Reuters, sought in 1887 to break the power of Havas. However, the 1889 agreement left Italy as Havas territory; and Korrespondentz Bureau never again achieved either the status of equal contracting party nor the exclusive right to its home country that it held before 1889.

The AP had arrangement with Reuters for foreign news. But the United Press, seeking to gather news abroad, found itself confronted by this cartel "composed of the official and semi-official news agencies of governments in Europe."[18] These "allied agencies" and the Associated Press exchanged news exclusively with each other. They furthermore allotted to each member the right to exploit exclusively certain regions of the world. For example, only the French agency, Havas, could sell its news in South America; while in the Far East, the territory of Reuters, Japanese and Chinese newspapers would have to depend on the British agency for their foreign news. United Press became the first North American news agency to serve newspapers in Europe, South America and the Far East. It established its own bureaus in those areas. Its success in this endeavour led to an invitation in 1912 for UP to ally itself with Reuters, which it did not accept.

At its beginning in 1907, United Press served 369 newspapers in the United States. Its news went to European newspapers through the British agency, Exchange Telegraph. Two years later, in 1909, United Press began a cable service to Nippon Demo Tsushin Sha, the Japanese Telegraph News Agency[19], later merged into *Domei*. This service was to continue until 7 December 1941, when the Japanese attacked Pearl Harbour. By 1914, UP's clientele had doubled. With the outbreak of World War I, newspapers in South America began chafing under the allied agencies' restrictions, which compelled them to get their war news from the French agency, Havas. The South Americans said it was officially subsidised and covered only the allied side of the war. To get the news of both sides, they turned to United Press which began its first news file to South America in 1915. *La Prensa* of Buenos Aires, started using United Press service in 1919. Direct UP service to newspapers in Europe was inaugurated after World War I, in 1921, to clients in Cologne, Frankfurt and Vienna. United Press service direct to newspapers on the Asian mainland followed in 1922, to publications in Peking and Tienstsin. In 1922, the British United Press Ltd., was organised to serve newspapers throughout the British Empire. By 1929, the United Press was serving 1,170 newspapers in 45 countries and territories. United Press merged with the International News Service (founded in 1909 by William Randolph Hearst) on 24 May 1958, becoming UPI.

AP's first challenge to the European oligopoly came in 1902 when a cable service was started to meet requests from Cuba, the Philippines and Central America. A far more serious AP challenge to the European cartel followed in 1919. AP's board of directors, in response to requests from 22 South American newspapers, authorised full-scale service to Latin America. A similar application for the AP news from the Japanese news agency Rengo was approved in 1933. But as a result of the threat UP posed to the cartel, the AP was finally accepted as an equal member of the cartel when it signed a four-party treaty in 1927.[20] This could, however, no longer save the cartel. After the AP had obtained a free hand in South America, it wanted the same in the Far East. The problem was that the Far East belonged to Reuters, which was far superior to Havas as an international agency and which had no intention of surrendering its exclusive control over this territory. Nevertheless, the cartel itself finally collapsed in 1934, with the American agencies, in collaboration with two national agencies, playing the decisive role. One key step was a separate agreement between the Soviet TASS and the two American agencies in 1934, explicitly repudiating the cartel regulations that had prevented such a combination. The other was the national agency Japanese Rengo signing a contract with the AP and thus contravening Reuters' exclusive claim to this territory. Third, and perhaps most decisive of all, was UP once again rejecting Reuters' offer to join the cartel. The era of the European news cartel was over.

After World War

With the end of World War I (1914 –1918) German and Austrian news agencies lost their position on the world news market. In Vienna, the imperial-royal prefix "k. k." was lost and the agency became Telegraphen-Korrespondenz-Bureau and was soon called official news office Amtliche Nachrichtenstelle (ANA). Allies had restricted the overseas activities of German agency Wolff or Continental, after Germany's first defeat. But the Nazis created their own international news machinery: Trans-Ocean, which disseminated by radio, and Deutsches Nachrichten-Büro (DMB), which was a forced merger of previously existing agencies, notably Continental and TU. These affected Reuters and Havas in two ways: they distributed free of charge or at extremely low rates with aid of state funds; and they deprived old European agencies of subscriptions, thus weakening them financially.

Trans-Ocean TO was a news agency founded in 1915 by the "Syndikat Deutscher Überseedienst", a syndicate initiated by the government and financed by the industry and commerce. It aimed at supplying foreign audiences with more and better information about Germany than the Wolffsches Telegraphisches Bureau, the work of which was thought to be insufficient[21]. During World War I, the German foreign ministry used the TO for propagating the German cause. In fact, the TO managed to market its news overseas because agencies like AP, UP, and INS included official German war reports for the purpose of neutral coverage. Apart from that, the TO's successes were small because Germans lacked an understanding of what information was important to the American press. Transocean intensified its international activities in the postwar era and started a daily news service in English, in 1924. Mostly American newspapers in German accepted this service, but rarely did newspapers in English. The main focus of news distribution was again in South America and Asia.

Richard Schenkel founded another news agency in New York. Schenkel worked there as a correspondent of the Berliner Börsen-Courier, a commercial newspaper that was his main customer. In 1913, Schenkel's agency was bought by another German news service. The name of the agency was Telegraphen-Union (TU)[22]. It was largely influenced by the industry and belonged to the conservative right-wing Hugenberg-holding. During the years following the inflation in

Germany, the TU worked on improving its foreign newsgathering. For this purpose, it employed its own staff of correspondents and concluded contracts with other agencies. One of these contracts was concluded with United Press in order to get news from the United States. But the TU failed to establish an independent network of correspondents in the US. It did so not because of technological reasons – the telegraph and the wireless had existed for some time by then – but due to lack of financial resources. The Wolffsches Telegraphisches Bureau continued to depend on the Associated Press for news coverage of the United States in the 1920s. The WTB lost in importance, when the competing agency was founded in 1913. The TU and Wolff-Continental were merged into Deutsches Nachrichten-Büro (DMB) by Nazis in 1934 and functioned till the end of World War II. Nazi Germany's DNB was a private business (limited stock company) even thought the private stockholders were in sympathy with the Government.[23] The DNB was run as a private enterprise to keepup appearances. It was no longer to enter any news exchange agreements with foreign agencies, but, with the help of government subsidies, was to establish its own network of foreign correspondence to ensure complete autonomy and absolute news sovereignty.[24]

The Domei News Agency was established in 1936 with the help of the Japanese government, succeeding Rengo[25] and taking over news and communication operations of Dentsu.[26] The main purpose of the establishment was to send news articles and voices of Japan to the world. It was the only news agency at that time in Japan. From 1931 onwards, Japan has expanded its war fronts towards China, then further into Asia and finally the Pacific area. The Domei News Agency dispatched a large number of war correspondents and photographers to the battlefields and it played a major role in reporting how the war has been going in the Asian and Pacific fronts. Domei News Agency issued almost daily *The Domei Photo News* for the ordinary Japanese people to know how the war was going. *The Domei Photo News* were printed and published approximately 100,000 copies everyday and were delivered to schools, factories, shops and other places in Japan and overseas. They were pinned up on the wall to be widely seen by many people. Domei News Agency stopped its activity at the end of the Pacific War and dissolved in October 1945.

World War II

A wave of establishment or reorganisation of news agencies came with the post-war creation of new governments in various European countries. In all, 24 agencies began operating between 1945 and 1949. However, when virtually whole of Europe was still in Hitler's grip, the Telegrfska Agencija Nova Jugoslavija (TANJUG) was founded[27] on Yugoslav liberated territories on 5 November 1943. It began broadcasting over a radiotelegraph transmitter captured from the enemy. Tanjug started at Jajce, moved to Drvar, then to island of Vis in the Adriatic, and to Aranjelovac before entering Belgrade with the People's Liberation Army on 20 October 1944.

In Italy, National Associated Press Agency – Agenzia Nazionale Stampa Associata (ANSA), was established in 1945, in succession to the Agenzia Telegraphice Stefani (ATS), which had been operating since 1853. ANSA is a cooperative company of 51 publishing concerns. Membership is limited to daily newspapers. Weeklies, periodicals, radio and television can only subscribe to ANSA services without having any vote in the company itself. The agency's aim, according to its statute, is to assure "in the reciprocal interests of its members and in the climate of democratic liberties guaranteed by the Constitution, a broad service of journalistic information to be distributed to Italian newspaper publishing firms as well as to other clients using criteria of rigorous independence, impartiality and objectivity". In Japan, upon the dissolution of the state-owned Domei News Agency at the end of World War II, Kyodo, a non-profit cooperative of Japanese newspapers and Jiji Press Ltd., an independent 100% employee-owned joint stock company, came into existence in November 1945.

On 13 March 1938 when the German troops entered Austria and the Austrian State ceased to exist so did Amtliche Nachrichtenstelle (ANA) – its task being taken over by DNB. But when the Third Reich collapsed, DNB disappeared. ANA resurfaced on 2 August 1945 and was attached to the press department of Federal Chancellery. However, the previous pressure of occupying powers and the boycott of ANA by Anglo-American news agencies forced its end and emergence of the cooperative news agency APA. On 31 August 1946, APA entered in the Vienna commercial court's register of cooperatives after signing a contract with Republic of Austria and buying assets of ANA. The Austria Presse Agentur (APA) was established, as the national news agency owned by 14 different newspapers and the Austrian broadcasting station (ORF).

Deutsche Presse Agentur (DPA), began from scratch in 1949, with its headquarters in Hamburg. It was formed by the amalgamation of three separate news agencies DENA[28], DPD and SUEDENA set up by the United Kingdom, the United States and France in their respective occupation zones.[29] DPA came up as a private, independent agency, owned and managed as a joint venture by the newspapers, radio and television of the Federal Republic of Germany. Among the fundamental obligations of the agency, spelt out in its constitution, is commitment to objectivity and fairness. Merger of DPA with DENA, DPD and SUEDENA was agreed in Goslar on 18 August with a start-up share capital of DM 350,000. The German Press Agency began operating on 1 September 1949.

Wave of Independence

Antara, Indonesia's National News Agency, was founded by Adam Malik, Soemanang, A. M. Sipanhoentar and Pandoe Kartawigoena on 13 December 1937 to serve the struggle for national independence from the Dutch colonisers and Japanese occupation. Antara was the first to announce the proclamation of Indonesian – independence on 17 August 1945. Agencia Telenoticiosa Americana (Telam) was born on 14 April, 1945 as a response of the Argentine government to the control of information by UPI and AP. The Vietnam News Agency (VNA) was founded in September 1945. The first wire service bulletin released by VNA in Vietnamese, English and French carried the Declaration of Independence of the Democratic Republic of Vietnam (now the SRV) read by President Ho Chi Minh at Ha Noi's Ba Dinh Square on 2 September 1945. The Korean Central News Agency (KCNA), the state-run agency of the Democratic People's Republic of Korea was founded on 5 December 1946. It speaks for the Workers' Party of Korea, and the DPRK government with headquarters in the capital city of Pyongyang.

In India the idea of the take-over of Associated Press of India (API) from Reuters was mooted in 1946 at a meeting of the Indian and Eastern Newspapers Society (IENS), a body of newspaper owners of the region, in Lahore. Among those who supported the scheme were Devdas Gandhi of the *Hindustan Times*, Kasturi Srinivasan of the *Hindu* and Tushar Kanti Ghosh of *Amrit Bazar Patrika*. The Press Trust of India, was incorporated in Madras on 27 August 1947. In 1948 the Press Trust of India, cooperative of Indian newspapers, arrived at a three-year agreement with Reuters under which it took over the Associated Press of India and joined Reuters as a partner in the collection and dissemination of news from all over the world. Press Trust of India (PTI) went into operation on 1 February 1949. From 1953 PTI became a free agent, as the PTI board on the basis of experience turned down Reuters' new proposal.

Associated Press of Pakistan (AAP) was established in 1948. Initially it was run through a trust, but it was taken over by the Government through an ordinance on 15 June 1961. In Egypt, the Middle East News Agency (MENA) was established on 15 December 1955 as a joint stock company owned by Egyptian press establishments.[30] In 1960, MENA was nationalised along with other press establishments and was affiliated to the Ministry of Information. In 1978, MENA became a national press establishment affiliated to Shura (consultative) council, like other national press organisations. Pakistan Press International (PPI), a private limited company with Karachi as headquarters was also established in 1956. Prensa Latina (PL), with headquarters in Havana, Cuba, was founded on 15 June, 1959, shortly after the triumph of the Cuban Revolution. Maghreb Arabe Presse (MAP), was created in 1959 in Morocco. Algerie Presse Service (APS) Algeria's News Agency, was founded on 1 December 1961 in the wake of the national liberation war, to be its standard-bearer on the world media scene.

Ghana News Agency (GNA)[31] was established in 1957 as the first news agency in Sub-Saharan Africa, GNA contributed to African and Ghanaian emancipation. Ghana's first President, Dr. Kwame Nkumah, regarded GNA as a counter-weight to biased reporting by international news agencies. After three years of existence as a government department, on 1 July 1960 (the day when Ghana was declared a republic), GNA became a state corporation.

A move was first made in 1957 to start a Nigerian national news agency. The agency was to be a co-operative to be controlled by leading broadcasting and newspaper interests in Nigeria. That move collapsed when the *Daily Times* withdrew from the arrangement.

Three conferences on the development of information media in Africa were sponsored by the United Nations Educational, Scientific and Cultural Organisation (Unesco) in Dakar in 1961, Paris in 1962 and Tunis in 1963. These conferences led to the formation of the Union of African News Agencies. In this wave of agency expansion during 1960 –62, a total of 23 agencies were founded.

OANA (Organisation of Asian News Agencies) was founded in Bangkok at a meeting of Asian news agencies organised under the aegis of Unesco on 22 December 1961. The meeting was participated by Antara, APP, Bakhtar, CNA, Kyodo, PNS, PTI, Orient Press, VP, Information Ministers of Ceylon, Iran, Malaysia and Nepal, Thai Newspapers Association and 20 observers, including AP, Reuters, AFP and various UN bodies and international press bodies.[32]

According to the Unesco Report on World Communications (1975), there were news agencies from 90 sovereign countries of the world. But 40 countries had none and these included 25 countries with populations of more than one million. Agencies were directly controlled by the state in 50 of these 90 countries; in the 40 others, the agencies were cooperatively owned and run by the newspapers and the media. In many of these countries, even where the agencies ostensibly were autonomous corporations, owing to the political set-up, the State cast a big shadow on the news agencies.

On 1 December 1953, the International Press Institute[33], then based in Zurich[34], issued its report on The Flow of the News which was a study done in cooperation with editors, agency executives and foreign correspondents in 10 countries – eight countries from Western Europe and other two from USA and India. This study, performed by the press and for the press, noted the lack of balance in the press picture of another country. It found that news agency coverage was centered heavily on a few major countries—United States, United Kingdom, Germany, France and one or two others—and on international organisations in which these are associated.

The question of adequate and equitable flow of information among all nations, developed or undeveloped, had been reviewed within the framework of the United Nations. The General Assembly at its seventh session in 1952 decided to have a survey made of the state of mass media, and entrusted the task to Unesco. In 1957, the Director General of Unesco conceded the inadequacy of data on this subject and reported that when the factual position was not fully known it was not possible to formulate any programme. Subsequently, several conferences held in different regions brought into focus the need, both to develop national media and to encourage international cooperation in this field, especially in the developing world.

NAM and NWICO

The first official and most important inter-governmental conference of the Afro-Asian Block was held in Bandung, Indonesia, in 1955. This conference is generally seen as the founding meeting of the Non-Aligned Movement (NAM). Most of the 29 participating states had recently been decolonised and the anti-colonial sentiments expressed during the conference were very strong. The Final Communiqué of the Bandung Conference condemned colonialism on various grounds. It called colonialism a 'means of cultural repression' and defined colonialism as 'the subjection of peoples to alien subjugation, domination and exploitation'. When the NAM was launched the area of information was not considered that important. However, we find mention of "cultural development" and "cultural exchanges" in the Belgrade Summit[35] Declaration. The first clear expression of the issues related to the media is found in the Action Program of Economic Cooperation adopted at NAM by the Heads of the State and Government at Algiers (September 5 –9, 1973):

1. The developing countries should get together in the domain of mass communication in order to adopt joint measures to promote the mutual exchange of ideas which are inspired by the following principles:

    (a) Reorganisation of existing communication networks which are inherited from the colonial past and which have prevented them from communicating freely, directly and rapidly.

    (b) An initiative for joint measures to revise current multinational agreement with the aim of revising the tariff for news reports and facilitating faster and cheaper communication.

    (c) Urgent measures to accelerate the process of collective acquisition of communication satellites and elaboration of a code of conduct for the manner of their use.

    (d) Closer contacts between information agencies, universities, libraries, planning and research bodies and other institutions should be encouraged so that developing countries can carry out an exchange of experience and technological know-how and share their ideas.

2. The nonaligned nations should exchange and disseminate information on mutual achievements in all domains through newspapers, journals, radio, television and information media in their countries.

    "They should formulate plans to share experience in this sphere, among other things by organising exchange visits of delegations of specialists in the information media, as well as by an exchange programme of photographs, cultural delegations and art festivals."

In January 1975 news agencies of 12 non-aligned countries, with a common wish for mutual exchange of information, launched the Pool. Among the first reports of the Pool were statements of 17 heads of state or government. Three months later, the Coordinating Bureau of Non-Aligned Countries, meeting in Havana, expressed satisfaction at the initiative, and offered its moral and political support for the development of the Pool. In August 1975, Tanjug reported to the Conference of Foreign Ministers of Non-Aligned Countries in Lima, Peru, that the number of participating agencies had increased to about 40. The conference noted with satisfaction the results achieved in promoting cooperation among the non-aligned countries in the field of mass media, including the establishment of the Pool of non-aligned agencies in January 1975. This conference also decided that a special meeting of representatives of governments and news agencies of non-aligned countries be convened to prepare a draft constitution for Pool members, and accepted India's offer to host it in the following year. Tunisia was appointed as coordinator in this field. The conference also supported the holding of a symposium on mass media in non-aligned countries in Tunis.

In preparation of the meeting of representatives of governments and news agencies of non-aligned countries to be held in India, a workshop of news agencies of India, Tunisia and Yugoslavia was held in Belgrade at the end of January 1976 to draw up a draft constitution for the Pool. This was closely followed in March 1976 by the Tunis symposium on cooperation among non-aligned nations in the field of information.

Three years after Algiers, this Symposium on Communication held in Tunis paved the way for the first Conference of Ministers of Information of the Non-Aligned Countries in New Delhi. Nearly 200 participants, comprising leading personalities from mass media, government representatives and public and scientific workers from more than 50 countries attending the symposium unanimously concluded that the non-aligned and developing countries had unequal position in the international flow of information and the existing systems of communication.

Delegations from 59 countries, led by their respective Ministers of Information and heads of existing news agencies, and seven observers, attended the First General Conference of the News Agencies Pool of Non-Aligned Countries held in New Delhi, India, from 8 – 13 July 1976. Inaugurating the conference, the Prime Minister of India, Mrs. Indira Gandhi, said the non-aligned countries, despite the extraordinary diversity among them, shared a common past, a common present and a common future. They had suffered from colonial rule—economic exploitation, cultural suppression and psychological frustration—and they prized their regained freedom. Yet freedom could not be consolidated without economic strength. The non-aligned countries, therefore, wanted an equitable share of the world's resources and technology and a future free from wars and tension. These goals, she said, made non-alignment one of the most purposive and powerful movements in the world's history. It was based on the positive values of trust, hope and willingness to cooperate. As against that, alignment was negative, in as much as it involved teaming up against others out of fear and suspicion. Mrs. Gandhi pointed out that the non-aligned countries were still handicapped by their colonial past. "The European language we speak itself becomes a conditioning element... We imbibe their prejudices. Even our image of ourselves, not to speak of the view of other countries, tends to conform to theirs."

The conference noted that the serious inadequacy and imbalance in the prevailing world information set-up were the result of concentration of the means of communicating information in the hands of a few news agencies located in certain developed countries. These agencies alone decided what news would be purveyed, and how it would be purveyed, to the rest of the world. The people of developing countries, especially the non-aligned nations, were thus forced to see each other, and even themselves, through the eyes of these news agencies. The international news media misrepresented the efforts of the non-aligned countries for world peace, justice and the establishment of a just world economic order, and also sought to divide the movement.

The non-aligned countries resolved to rectify this situation through greater collective self-reliance. They emphasised that the establishment of a New International Order for Information was as necessary as the New International Economic Order, and that the Pool was an important step towards the establishment of New International Information Order (NIIO). The conference made a Declaration on Information and adopted a constitution for the Pool with a view to facilitating dissemination of correct and factual information about the non-aligned countries.

The Fifth Conference of Heads of State or Government of Non-Aligned Countries, held in Colombo, Sri Lanka, from 16 – 19 August 1976, welcomed and endorsed the Declaration on Information and also the other decisions taken by the New Delhi conference. It described them as an important step towards further cooperation among the non-aligned countries in establishing a balanced and equitable distribution of news and information to the peoples of the world. It said the emancipation and development of national information media was an integral part of the overall struggle for political, economic and social independence. The Statute of the News Agencies Pool of the Non-Aligned Countries was approved by the Colombo Summit. Mrs. Indira Gandhi said in Colombo, "Since Algiers we have been formulating programmes of cooperation amongst the non-aligned. It is now time to pool our resources and our experience. The focus should be on the functional cooperation. The Non-Aligned News Agencies Pool is an example of our determination to be better informed about each other, not just political but also economic level."

The debate about a New World Information and Communications Order (NWICO) tended to focus upon media ownership and upon the contending concepts of information as commodity and information as social good, upon the freedom of information as an individual versus a collective right.[36] The NWICO debate raged throughout much of the 1970s and 1980s in the halls of the United Nations, and particularly within Unesco. NWICO proponents and opponents alike accepted the premise of a link between economic progress and the availability of information.

However, liberal theorists maintained that national cultures and sovereignty were not threatened by information concentration, while structuralists and socialist analysts argued that they were. In particular, the NWICO proponents, mostly drawn from the ranks of non-aligned nations, claimed that Western ownership and control of both the news media and their distribution channels constituted a form of cultural dominance whose covert goal was capitalist economic expansion. This argument, played out in forums such as the Non-Aligned Movement and Unesco conferences, drew support from the Soviet Union, and hostility from Western administrations. It was partly due to fears of the growing "politicisation" of Unesco that the United States and Great Britain withdrew from that organisation in the mid-1980s.

There have been other efforts to create alternatives and most important among such efforts in news agency field is the Inter Press Service (IPS). It was founded in 1964 by a group of journalists including Roberto Savio as a cooperative.

From 1964 to 1968 it served certain Latin American Governments to conduct a dialogue between Europe and Latin America to improve understanding of projects of same political orientation. Between 1968 and 1971, the political situation changed considerably and many IPS offices were closed down. From 1971 onwards, IPS developed into a specialised news agency aiming at becoming a third world agency. IPS had, in the middle of the 1980s, correspondents posted in 50 countries and stringers regularly reported from numerous other capitals.[37] Within three decades IPS services were available through online computer services, electronic databases, printed bulletins or daily teleprinter. It claimed to be the world's fifth largest news agency.[38] With regional editorial and managerial centres in Asia, Africa, the Caribbean, Latin America, North America and Europe, IPS guarantees the cultural diversity of its news report. From the world desk in Amsterdam, The Netherlands, IPS coordinated its global service. Despite financial difficulties, IPS still survives. IPS World Service produces 30 reports a day on events and processes affecting the peoples and nations of the South. Primary languages are English and Spanish. Reports are translated into many other languages and widely distributed. IPS began Internet distribution in 1994, using a website set up by the Norwegian telecommunications company, Telenor. The home page (the Global Gateway), based in Rome, was launched in 1996, with a Spanish-language equivalent added in 1999, produced in Montevideo. IPS leverages its Internet presence through arrangements with several web portals, including One World Online. A keyword searchable archive dates from 1994. Visitors see headlines and the first lines of items; only subscribers can access complete texts. A text-based graphic design accommodates users with slow Internet connectivity. 7,000 hits a day come mainly from the US. IPS also sends customised news packages to over 5,000 subscribers, mostly NGOs, UN and E. U. officials, media and educational institutions and personnel, libraries, trade councils and government ministries.

Distributing via the Internet portals greatly extends the reach of IPS services. IPS, One World and the Panos Institute together are designing Inter World Radio to distribute news scripts to radio stations for reading directly on the air. In the US the main distribution channel is Global Information Network (GIN) daily distributing about 70 English and Spanish language reports to over 300 clients, two-thirds of whom are African-American newspapers, and many of whose readers do not have web access. Some national agencies (e.g. OPECNA, QNA, and WAM) use IPS channels to reach a larger audience. The web also facilitates in-house correspondence among IPS correspondents and bureaus.[39]

In Brazil newspaper groups launched their own news agencies. Agência Estado, of Estado group, distributes information by fax, satellite, FM, pagers and dedicated lines. It was founded in 1970 as part of Grupo Estado: which began with newspaper O Estado de S. Paulo (1875) and now also owns Jornal da Tarde (1966) OESP Mídia Direta (1984) Rádio Eldorado (1958) Agência Estado (1970) and OESP Gráfica (1988). In 1991, the agency started a broadcast service, in 1995 Brazil Financial Wire, in 1998 Release online and in 1998 Infocast. Similarly Agency O Globo,[40] established in 1974, is a division of Globo Organisation, which includes the leading broadcast television network, a publishing company, a radio network, an Internet division and three newspapers. The material distributed by Agency O Globo includes the content of three newspapers *O Globo*, *Extra* and *Diario de S. Paulo,* as well as real time information produced by its Internet division, Globo Online.

Africa and Latin America

Unesco has since early eighties supported the establishment of national news agencies with a view to improving news collection and dissemination within nations and promoting greater diversity of news sources in international news. These projects, CANAD (Central African News Agencies Development Project), SEANAD (Southern and East

Africa News Agency Development Project), and WANAD (West African News Agencies Development Project), collectively, generated or helped to sustain an impressive number of national news agencies in Africa during the 1980s and 1990s (e.g. 13 in the case of WANAD, 12 in the case of SEANAD). However, the projects had not been able to establish any one model of appropriate intervention because the circumstances of each country, each agency, were so different one from another. In Zimbabwe, the national news agency, Ziana, was strong, while in Tanzania; Shihata had almost perished (and is now extinct). In addition to training, the projects also helped supply equipment, ranging from basic start-up technology (even typewriters) to state-of-the-art computers. News exchange was another area of activity. SEANAD supported the design of electronic 'mail boxes' by telephone, a system that was later transformed into software for writing, filing and exchange of news items. The server was based in Zimbabwe, and other agencies were given PCs: the agencies only had to dial the server to offer and collect news stories. There were differences between Francophone and Anglophone African countries. In the territories that had been governed by France, news agencies began life essentially as mailboxes for Agence France-Press, the world's only French language international agency. Other influences were Belgian (e.g. AZAP in Zaire) and Portuguese (e.g. Angop in Angola). Unesco's many initiatives included support for PANA[41] (Africa) and CANA (the Caribbean). From the 1960s to the 1980s, the national agencies typically experienced an uneasy mixture of autonomy and dependence; their editorial content was primed to provide what has been disparagingly referred to as 'protocol' news. Motivated staff was hard to retain. Markets were weak, and subject to government intervention. However, by the turn of the year 2000, it was becoming clear that many national news agencies were in crisis.

In many cases, agency technologies are often obsolete, and in countries whose governments do not appreciate the content that news agencies produce, the agencies are perishing through a mixture of political intervention and inadequate financial support. For example, Zimbabwe Inter-Africa News Agency (ZIANA), founded in 1981, was a rather successful national news agency owned by Zimbabwe Mass Media Trust based in Harare. It has folded up for political reasons; and New Ziana, which has replaced it, is not so successful for lack of funds.

In 1992, there were 48 national news agencies, almost all of which were under the tutelage of public authorities through government institutions such as the information ministries or sometimes directly under the control of the President's office. From the onset, they served as national intermediaries for the distribution of teleprinted news essentially generated by the Western agencies.

Following the acute crisis of the early 1990s, the Pan-African News agency (PANA) kicked off a structural transformation process spearheaded by Egypt and Nigeria who successively occupied the chair of its board of directors. In 1993, a plan of recovery under the aegis of the OAU Secretary General and Unesco was instituted to professionalise the agency and diversify its services.

Finally, with the backing of Unesco, PANA was liquidated in October 1997. In its place, a company, Panapress Ltd., regrouping public and private shareholders was set up with a capital of 12.9 million dollars. It is now a commercial company with 75 percent ownership by African private investors, and 25 percent by African states. With correspondents and stringers in 51 countries, it is committed to "providing accurate, objective, yet fresh view of African people, politics and business climates."[42] It has its headquarters in Dakar, Senegal. Panapress fee-based content can be packaged to suit the content needs of individuals, organisations, print and broadcast media and can be delivered via e-mail or using the Panapress self-service interface www.panapress.com.

Unesco also supported establishment of Caribbean News Agency (CANA), an independent institution serving 13 Commonwealth Caribbean countries[43] from Belize in the north to Guyana in the south.[44] It started operation on 7 January 1976 as a cooperative of 16 media organisations located in six of these countries, headquartered in Bridgetown, Barbados, where it is registered as a limited liability company. It serves over 100 clients with wire, radio, Internet and photo services throughout the Caribbean. The Caribbean Media Corporation (CMC) has evolved from the merger of the commercial operations of the Caribbean News Agency Ltd. (CANA) and the Caribbean Broadcasting Union[45] (CBU). A Chief Operating Officer, reporting to a Board of Directors drawn from the two constituent companies, leads CMC. This demonstrates how in regions of the developing world that share economic and other structures, a regional news agency may have greater viability than isolated national news agencies. CMC combines traditional news agency, Internet and audio-visual operations, and is increasingly commercialising its operations.

Mention should also be made here of Agencia Latinoamericana de Informacion (LATIN) created on 13 January, 1970, by 13 leading newspapers of Latin America.[46] The founders[47] engaged Reuters as managing agent for LATIN with the responsibilities of selecting and training Latin American journalists, management and technical staff for the agency, setting up communication and administrative structure. On 1 July 1971 when the service was launched, it had 44 subscribers; and in December 1977 the number of subscribers was 156. LATIN content combined news from Latin correspondents in Latin America and Washington, world news from Reuters and a summary of the New York Times. It initially transmitted 18 hours a day and in November 1977, it became a 24-hour news service. In May 1981 LATIN ceased to exist.

Post Cold War Era

After the fall of communist regimes in the Eastern Europe and disintegration of the Soviet Union and the later disintegration of Yugoslavia, there was another wave of establishment of new private news agency initiatives and reorganisation of existing news agencies. State agencies have faced reduction in State funds. TASS has become ITAR-TASS, but agencies of different republics can now have independent arrangements with foreign agencies and ITAR-TASS. Tanjug exists but with reduced importance. In Romania, Agerpes, after the reorganisation on 8 January 1990, has become Rompres—Romania's official "mouthpiece" organised as a public institution of national concern. Since the beginning of 1996, the Czech News Agency (CTK) has existed without any state or other subsidy. It covers all its expenses solely from its own commercial activities. Bulgarian Telegraph Agency has closed 50 correspondent bureaus abroad, and is now almost fully dependent on the international and regional agencies for foreign news.

Some private initiatives have succeeded and others have failed. Interfax, founded in 1989 by Mikhail Komissar, with colleagues from Radio Moscow, is a major success story. The Interfax news agency is part of the Interfax Information Services Group which is composed of about thirty companies, including national, regional and specialised news agencies. Baltic News Service (BNS) was founded in Moscow in April 1990, at the height of the Baltic states' struggle for freedom, to bring news directly from the three Baltic countries to Moscow. Since then

BNS has grown fast to be the Baltic region's leading and largest news agency. Now it is a member of Alma Media Group, Finland. Belgrade based BETA News Agency was established in 1992 by nine journalists to provide "full and objective coverage of events in Serbia and Montenegro and Southeast Europe". It calls itself a regional, private, independent news service and maintains the site Clean Hands that deals with corruption in Serbia and Montenegro and its neighbourhood. It is funded by US-based IREX organisation (May 2002 – December, 2004) and Norwegian People's Aid.

Of the leading agencies, which were called Big Four during the NWICO debate, AFP and AP are on sound footing because of their ownership structure. That was not the case with the other two. On the occasion of UP's 50th anniversary, 21 June 1957, *Time* magazine said: "The first major US news service to prosper as a commercial undertaking, the United Press today is the world's most enterprising wire-news merchant." In 1978 UPI served 7,079 subscribers worldwide. It's 2,246 clients outside of the US include more than 30 national and other news agencies which relay its reports to additional thousands of newspapers and broadcasters. In the US, UPI's clients included 1,134 newspapers and other publications and 3,699 broadcasters. In 1982, Scripps family sold UPI. Tennessee entrepreneurs, Douglas Ruhe and William Geissler, took over the news service from the owners of the Scripps Howard newspaper chain. Under their ownership, UPI continued to lose money, eventually filing for Chapter 11 bankruptcy protection in 1985. The company's headquarters moved from New York City to Washington D.C. Mexican publisher Mario Vazquez Rana purchased it out of bankruptcy in 1986. In 1991, UPI was purchased out of its second bankruptcy by a group of Saudi investors and expanded its involvement in the Middle East. In 2000, News World Communications, a media group founded by the Rev. Sun Myung Moon that includes *The Washington Times* newspaper, purchased UPI. Now UPI products include original content in English, Spanish and Arabic. Besides headquarters in Washington D.C, it has offices in Beirut, Hong Kong, London, Santiago, Seoul and Tokyo.

Though it was United Press which started feeding television news clips to television stations, today the market is dominated by Reuters and AP. United Press launched the first international television news film service in 1952 as United Press Movietone News. It had two products—a newsreel that was distributed to theaters and a news film that was distributed to television stations. It became UPI News Films from 1963 to 1967 when ITN joined it to make it UPITN. When ABC purchased it became WTN and was eventually owned by Disney. In the third quarter of 1999, Disney decided that WTN was not part of its core business. It needed cash to meet third quarter projections and it sold the company to AP for $55 million. AP merged it with APTV to make it APTN. Another newsfilm agency Visnews was launched in 1957 as a joint venture of BBC, Reuters and NBC. By 1980, Visnews had about 30 overseas bureaus and 400 freelance cameramen. In 1985, cash-rich Reuters bought Visnews and later renamed it Reuters Television. But the emergence of global television news, led by companies such as CNN and BBC World Television, has to be noted. Though they may subscribe to APTN and Reuters Television, their own channels are distributed by satellite or by cable, or provide news to terrestrial broadcasters and through the Internet.

Charles-Louis Havas, who invented the business of news agencies, would never have imagined the growth and diversity it will achieve in less than two centuries. In that carrier pigeon and telegraph era, who could have imagined about mobile phones and the Internet!

NOTES AND REFERENCES

1. Kent Cooper, General Manager of Associated Press (1925 – 48) narrates an incident in his autobiography: At a large dinner in honour of a renowned New York surgeon, a newly wed, I happened to be seated next to the charming bride. At once she started to shower me with unending praise of her "marvelous, wonderful" husband. While I was politely giving her my undivided attention, the soup course was served. In crescendo she continued to praise her great surgeon. The soup was taken away untouched. The fish course was brought. Still she talked. The fish was removed untouched. By the time entrée arrived, she suddenly became interested in food but asked: "And what do you do?" "Did you ever hear of the Associated Press?" I asked. Balancing a forkful, she exclaimed: "Oh, yes, certainly! My husband takes it. He takes all the newspapers." The lady was just one of millions who could have given no better answer. (Cooper, Kent (1959) *Kent Cooper and The Associated Press: An Autobiography*, New York, Random House p. 3.)

2. World Association of News Agencies in Moscow 24 –25 September 2004 was hosted by Russian agency ITAR-TASS.

3. In 1958, its advertising arm became Havas Conseil, in 1968, it turned into a

corporation, in 1975, it was reconstituted as Eurocom, a holding company; and in 1982, Eurocom was listed on Paris Bourse as a subsidiary of the Havas media group. Later it became part of Vivendi and came out of it. Havas Advertising shifted its global headquarters to New York in 1995. In 2001, it purchased the Havas name from Vivendi Universal for, four and a half million francs and in 2002, at a shareholders meeting changed the group's name from Havas Advertising to Havas.

4. According to Chanan, Michael (1988) all the three were Jews. 'The Reuters Factor', in Sources for the Study of Science, Technology and Everyday Life 1870 – 1950, Vol. 2, ed. Chant, Hodder & Stroughton/Open University. Donald Read in the first edition of *The Power of News: The History of Reuters*, 1992 also says "Like Reuter, Charles Havas and Wolff were Jews" (p. 9).

5. Pensold, Wolfgang (2001) Official Reporting On the History of Government Policies for News Agencies in Austria, APA Symposium on Values in News Agency Journalism, APA, Vienna. (m & z 4/2001 18)

6. Basse, Dieter (1991): Wolff's Telegraphisches Bureau 1849 bis 1933. Agenturpublizistik zwischen Politik und Wirtschaft. München etc.

7. He was the third son of the Provisional Rabbi of Cassel.

8. Daniel Craig opens the first overseas bureau in Halifax, Nova Scotia, in 1849 to meet ships arriving from Europe. This enables the AP to telegraph stories to newspapers before ships dock in New York.

9. Edith Dörfler/Wolfgang Pensold: *Die Macht der Nachricht. Die Geschichte der Nachrichtenagenturen in Österreich*. Wien: Molden Verlag 2001, 15.

10. Read Donald (1999) *The Power of News*, Oxford University Press, Oxford

11. Villard, Oswald Garrison (1930) The Associated Press, The Nation, 23 April, 1942.

12. Villard, Oswald Garrison (1930) The Associated Press, The Nation, 23 April, 1942.

13. During 1938, the difficulties involved in following internal developments in Italy were increased by two government measures. Under the terms of one of these, Italian journalists were forbidden to act as representatives of foreign newspapers. The other provided that the only agency permitted to give out news from the provinces was the official press bureau. The consequence of these new regulations was that the few foreign correspondents left in Italy had their functions virtually reduced to that of receiving official hand-outs from the Stefani Agency and from the official press bureaus of the ministries in Rome, with any attempt to circumvent this procedure likely to be punished by expulsion from the country.

14. Newspaper founded by Benito Mussolini.

15. Among them, the director of the newspaper, the *Socialist*, Julian

Zugazagoitía, and the director of Fabra, Amato Ibarr'' ', wrote to the Government on "the more and more urgent necessity to organise a Spanish informative service for the outside", "to be more kind to its own political interest" that "to consider the absolute veracity of the facts."

16. Kim, Soon Jin (1989) EFE Spain's World News Agency, Greenwood Press, New York, p. 32.

17. Oliver Boyd-Barrett (1998) 'Global' News Agencies: Trends and Issues over 150 years in Boyd-Barrett, O. and Rantanen, T. (Eds.), *The Globalisation of News*, London: Sage.

18. This description of cartel is from the UPI website.

19. History of news agencies in Japan dates back to the late nineteenth century when there appeared several minor news agencies. Many closed down, and mergers ensued in the course of their struggle for survival.

20. As Sir Roderick Jones, general manager of Reuters, put it, "On the question of competition, both Kent Cooper General Manger of AP and I felt strongly that, in order to more effectively counter the United Press, we must place our resources more freely at each other's disposal and confront the United Press as a consolidated unit under a single command, rather than as scattered allies, each adopting more or less his own line of attack." Sir Roderick Jones papers, Reuters Archives/BF3)

21. Klee, Cornelius (1991): Die Transocean GmbH. In: Jürgen Wilke (Ed.): Telegraphenbüros und Nachrichtenagenturen in Deutschland. Untersuchungen zu ihrer Geschichte bis 1949. München etc. p. 135 – 211.

22. Neitemeier, Martin (1991): Die Telegraphen-Union. In: Jürgen Wilke (Ed.): Telegraphenbüros und Nachrichtenagenturen in Deutschland. Untersuchungen zu ihrer Geschichte bis 1949. München etc. p. 87 – 134

23. Kim, Soon Jin (1989) EFE Spain's World News Agency, Greenwood Press, New York, p. 33.

24. Pensold, Wolfgang (2001) Official Reporting On the History of Government Policies for News Agencies in Austria, APA Symposium on Values in News Agency Journalism, APA, Vienna. (m & z 4/2001 p. 26)

25. Japanese news agency Rengo came into being in 1925 with the merger of Kokusai (international news service) and domestic news agency Toho (East), and continued till 1936. Kokusai started in 1914.

26. Dentsu news agency of Japan was established in 1901, having both advertising and news business.

27. Tanjug's founding father was the eminent publicist, artist and political leader Nosa Pijade, later to become president of the Federal Parliament in Belgrade. Tanjug's first director was Vladislav Ribnikar, one the best known anti-fascist journalist and pre-war director and editor-in-chief of the Belgrade daily, *Politika*.

28. On 29 June 1945, the German News Service (GNS) began operation in

Bad Nauheim and was renamed as Deutsche Allgemeine Nachrichtenagentur (DANA) two months later. DANA was under American management for more than a year before it was passed into German hands and was renamed DENA as of 1 January 1947.

29. Deutsche Press Dienst (DPD) agency in the British zone had a news and photo arrangement with Reuters. DENA news agency in the United States zone had arrangement with the International News Service and the International News Photos (INS and INP) not with AP or UP which resumed direct service to German newspapers.

30. In fact, MENA started as an office in 1954 and established itself as a full-fledged news agency on 15 December 1955 in Cairo with a nominal capital of 20,000 Egyptian pounds paid by four publishing houses in Cairo: Al Ahram, Al Akhbar, Dar el Tahrir and Dar el Hilal, each contributing 5,000 pounds.

31. Donald C. Wright, loaned from Reuters, initially headed GNA.

32. OANA Today and Tomorrow in OANA Newsletter Silver Jubilee 1961 – 1986, p. 23.

33. Report on its preface mentioned Zurich, November 1953, but there was an embargo stamp "not for publication before December 1, 1953". A copy with this stamp is in the library of Indian Institute of Mass Communication, Dhenkanal, Orissa, India.

34. Now it is in Vienna.

35. September 1 – 6. 1961.

36. *"The New World Order and the Geopolitics of Information"* by Christopher Brown-Syed originally appeared in: LIBRES: Library and Information Science Research (ISSN:1058-6768) 19 January 1993.

37. In a World of Giants: The role of alternative news services in the struggle for a new information order by Claudio Aquirre-Bianchi and Goran Hedeboro, in Approaches to International Communication, Edited by Ullamaja Kivikuru and Tapio Varis, Publications of Finnish National Commission for Unesco No 35. p. 296.

38. IPS pamphlet 1994.

39. The IPS presentation delivered by Professor Anthony Giffard of the University of Washington and a member of the IPS board in Amman Seminar on News Agencies 2001.

40. Information based on the address of Regina Eleuterio, Executive Manager of O Globo (Brazil) 25 September 2004 at World Congress of News Agencies, Moscow.

41. In 1961, in a meeting of media professionals, it was agreed to create a continental news agency for Africa. In 1977, the first conference of the information ministers, Organisation of African Unity (OAU) 41, was held in Uganda when the debate on NWICO was at its zenith. It was decided to

create a Pan-African News Agency with the aim to ensure a wider flow of information among African countries, as well as between Africa and other continents. Its establishment was formally recognised at the second conference in 1979. But due to financial and technical difficulties, PANA was able to start operation only on experimental basis in 1983.

42. Panapress website, 9 December 2004.
43. History of political and economic cooperation in this region goes back to the 1962 formation of the now defunct West Indies Federation.
44. The Unesco Communication Project in the Caribbean began in January 1972 and in the first few months prevailed upon the governments of the region and got mandate for setting up an agency best suited for the region. Prospective media owners of the agency met and they mandated the Unesco project to negotiate with other stakeholders including governments, telecommunication agencies and international news agencies, with a view to the early establishment of CANA, as Reuters had indicated its intention to terminate its Caribbean service.
45. The CBU, established in 1970, is an association of 25 radio and television stations, plus 20 associate members outside the region.
46. *O Estado de S. Paulo*, Brazil, *El Mercurio*, Santiago, Chile, *El Nacional*, Caracas, Venezuela, *Excelsior*, Mexico, *O Globo*, Rio de Janeiro, Brazil, *El Comercio Lima*, Peru, *Jornal do Brasil*, Rio de Janeiro, Brazil, *Expreso*, Lima, *Peru El Tiempo*, Bogota, Columbia, *El Comercio*, Quito, Ecuador, *La Tercera de la Hora*, Santiago, Chile, *La Verdad*, Caracas, Venezuela, *Diario Popular*, Sao Paulo, Brazil.
47. In 1973, Reuters, *Excelsior*, Costa Rica and Hoy, Bolivia became shareholders of LATIN in the same proportion as founders.

NEWS AGENCIES IN INDIA

The first newspaper to publish news from Reuters by mail in India was the *Bombay Times*. On 21 March 1866, Henry Collins[1] landed in Bombay to set up Reuters operations in India. Representing the interest of Reuters in India and the Far East, he set up his two-roomed office on Hornby Road in Bombay. The purpose was to catch the big newspapers by feeding commercial intelligence about the eastern as well as foreign markets to businessmen and speculators in India and abroad. Political stories filed from the sub-continent were in great demand abroad. Herbert Reuter remarked at the outbreak of the Anglo-Afghan War in 1878, "this Afghan War has created such an interest in India that we cannot afford to let Indian politics drop". The output initially was 77 words a day from India, and the rate was one pound sterling per word.

In fact, Reuters followed the British cable system to extend its own empire. News from England and the news from the rest of the world as viewed from London, was received promptly enough through the telegrams of Reuters ever since the establishment of electrical means of communication on 23 June 1870 when the London-Bombay submarine telegraph cable was inaugurated. It was only in 1885 that the emphasis began to shift towards Indian news. In those days, Reuters was essentially a part of the British scheme of things. With the appointment of Edward Buck as the Reuters correspondent, the agency started expanding and consolidating.

API

Keshab Chandra Roy[2], a journalist from Calcutta went to Simla, the summer capital of the Government of India, and became special correspondent of several Indian newspapers. As early as 1908, Roy saw the possibilities of starting a national news agency. He learnt in 1906 that England had adopted the multi-address telegraph system, enabling newspapers to sent press telegrams and receive them at special rates. Along with some British journalists, he persuaded the viceroy, Lord Minto, to institute a similar system in India which proved a boon and paved way for syndication of news messages. Roy was an admirer of the AP and dreamt of starting a similar agency in India. In 1910 he launched an agency – the Press Bureau, with offices at Bombay, Calcutta and Madras. He argued that Indian newspapers could not pay separate telegraphic rates and so correspondents' messages to The Press Bureau offices would be copied and distributed. By 1913 the Press Bureau had worked for three years and was in red because the Indian newspapers were not paying the bills. Its subscribers included the *Statesman* and the *Madras Mail.* Roy had to sell his property to keep the agency going.

About this time, Edward E. Coates, the representative of the *Statesman* of England and Reuters, was persuaded by the Finance Member of Viceroy's Executive council to start an Indian news agency as he could know of failure of a bank in Madras full one week later. This agency supplied Indian news to about a hundred officials all over the country and entered into an agreement with Reuters for the supply of foreign news. Sir Roderick Jones, Reuters' chairman persuaded Roy to amalgamate his agency with Coates and form a new one, which he called Eastern News Agency.[3] It was, however, called the Associated Press of India (API)[4]. Coates sold his interest and retired while Roy took charge of the news operations in 1919 under the overall control of the Reuters general manager based in Bombay.[5] Roy is credited with great persuasive skills. The Indian Telegraph Act was amended, at Roy's instance, to secure for registered news agencies the facilities available to registered newspapers. It was again Roy who persuaded Hugh Keeling, the chief engineer, to allot to the agency the site in New Delhi's Parliament Street on which the Press Trust of India building was to come up many years later.

Reuters' outward service from India was supplemented by Reut-Buck providing amplification of certain messages, which the Government was interested in and Globe-Reut provided for similar amplification worldwide. The British Government started the British Official Wireless, compiled by the British Foreign Office. Messages were relayed on wireless between Rugby in England and Kirkee in India.

These were also distributed by Reuters. By the early twenties, Reuters and its subsidiary, the API, were well under official control. Payment to Reuters/API was shown in the budget under the heading, "Miscellaneous-Subscription to periodicals". Invariably reply to questions on the payment in the legislative assembly was that it was not a subsidy to Reuters or the API but payment for the services rendered.

The teleprinters were introduced in 1937 by the general manager of Reuters in India, W. J. Moloney. It revolutionised the system of transmitting news and made it possible to provide agency service at reasonable rates to small newspapers throughout the country. Moloney, who also ran the API from 1923 to 1937, said, in a memorandum to the Board of Reuters in 1944, "Of my work in India, the most important features were the substitution of Indians for Europeans in the various branches... the supply of Reuters news to the vernacular newspapers to none of whom in virtue of our contracts with the English newspapers could Reuters deliver any service. The contracts were renegotiated so as to permit of a service to the vernacular papers. Another development during my time in India was the establishment of the 'Reuterian' Wireless Commercial Service from Rugby direct daily to our office in Bombay within a couple of minutes of the quotations on the New York and Liverpool exchanges. The year 1937 saw the inauguration of the teleprinter service. The first circuit was from Bombay to Calcutta direct; the full service of our other branches was not completed till 1938."[6]

The Free Press

The combination of Reuters and the Associated Press meant official control and this became apparent in the early twenties with Gandhi's movements.

S. Sadanand launched the Free Press Agency (FPA) in 1927. He said in his statement of objects and reasons that public opinion was moulded entirely by news supplied from day to day and it was "difficult if not impossible to mould healthy public opinion owing to the monopoly held in the supply of news by subsidised news agencies."

The FPA had a foreign section as well. Cables of some of the leading news agencies of the world were selected and pooled by the London office and sent out to India. Reuters often lost this race.

The full weight of the imperial authority was deployed to thwart this enterprise. Official pressure was exerted on Sadanand's fellow directors and four of them resigned in 1929 and the fifth did so in 1930. The Press Ordinance of May 1930 came down with a heavy hand on newspapers publishing FPA news. The Free Press telegrams were subjected to a strict censorship and newspapers grew reluctant to publish news supplied by the agency for the fear of offending the Press Ordinance or other emergency press laws. API also exerted pressure by insisting that its service would not be available to newspapers subscribing to the other agency.

Sadanand sought other ways of continuing the battle, and he started the *Free Press Journal*[7] as a morning daily in June 1930 from Bombay; associated newspapers were started[8], publishing Free Press news exclusively. In 1930 a smuggled copy of the *Free Press Journal* was the cause of much concern in the Reuters office in Bombay and cables were sent home of Reuters being beaten by the opposition. Important FPA scoops included the Chittagong armoury raid case in February 1933. K. Rama Rao, one of the most respected journalists of his times, dug up the background of the case and printed the story of the arrest of Surya Sen, the leader.

There was a protest against a news agency running newspapers, and when his directors arrived at an agreement with the Associated Press, Sadanand had to give up his chain newspaper enterprise. In 1935, when his newspapers' securities were confiscated, Sadanand had to close down his agency. Sadanand went bankrupt through the forfeiture of the heavy securities he had to pay repeatedly for the violation of the imperial code. Penalty had to be paid for an editorial entitled "Swaraj is the only remedy" in the agency's paper *Free Press Journal* and for publishing extracts from an article by Mahatma Gandhi and for a report of Vithalbhai Patel's speech in New York.

If Mohandas Karamchand Gandhi was a freedom fighter, journalist Swaminath Sadanand was a journalist freedom fighter. He fought for the freedom of the press not only when the British were ruling India but also after independence when he could warn about the dangers of dominance of the world news by a few news agencies. He did not invent the phrase "new world information and communication order" but he could see the problem from which the world is suffering even today.

In his early journalistic career, Sadanand worked with Reuters (rather, its subsidiary Associated Press of India) for a while. Hardly anything is available on that period but it is clear that his desire to have an independent Indian news agency was born during that time. He had also been to Burma before coming back to Bombay to launch Free Press of India News Agency. S Trikannad, a former Assistant Editor of the *Free Press Journal* has this to say: "He had started his career in a low paid job in the Associated Press of India (API), then gone to Allahabad and joined the *Independent* the very day Pandit Motilal Nehru[9] was arrested, then migrated to the *Rangoon Times*. It was there that his ambition was first fired to start a news agency of his own that would present Indian news to the world at large."[10]

There are different versions about the beginning of Free Press of India (FPI) but Sadanand himself wrote, "Free Press of India is an independent national news agency planned in 1923, founded in 1925 and in active existence till 1935... Free Press of India had the support of the entire national press of India while it was functioning. It maintained a comprehensive internal service. It was the first Indian news agency which organised and maintained an efficient world news service to the press of India during the years 1932 – 35."[11]

Started a few years before the Second Round Table Conference, the Free Press news service provided many scoops during the conference but even nationalist papers were afraid of publishing Sadanand's reports. Some did pay subscription but refused to print any of his news. It was then that he started a chain of newspapers in many languages, which would make use of his news service.

K. Rama Rao wrote about Sadanand, "The honours of the freedom fight of 1930 – 1933 went equally to Swaminath Sadanand and the *Free Press Journal* on the press front. The paper was waging an epic fight against the Government; in fact, it was the head and front of the journalistic onslaught. Sadanand was in high mettle and in much affluence too then. The *Journal* was the dauntless bark he sailed and he was the pilot who weathered myriad storms. The bark was often near going down but he somehow held it on its course. Sadanand is dead, but he has left behind him a legendary fragrant reputation for gallant audacity and several institutions firmly established and exceedingly useful to the country."

Rao worked with him in that fateful period and having seen him from close quarters had given a description of the character of the man, "Made of tempered steel he did not have an atom of fear in him. He was courageous to the point of being inventive and original to the point of being unpredictable. Security after security was forfeited for defiance of law; blow after blow fell, but he did not bat an eyelid; he did not budge an inch from the firing line. With head bloody but unbowed, he went on attacking. No risk was too big, no adventure too reckless. He reveled in crises, some self-created. A soldier every inch of him, now he fought and won, now he fought and lost; but he never ran away from danger or difficulty."

About the Free Press Agency, Rao wrote, "The Free Press news agency, which he founded in 1927, was intended to cover the nation's political activities, which the Associated Press, with its pronounced official bias and peculiar affiliations could not do or was neglecting to do. The agency did good patriotic work during the time it lived; it made revelations inconvenient to the Government; it fought bitterly against the ruinous ratio fixed between the rupee and the pound sterling and the Ottawa agreement. The agency died in 1935 for want of support, the opposition of the foreign Government of the day and of the vested interests. Sadanand's gallant attempt to establish an Indian news agency also included a foreign section parallel to Reuters. It certainly deserved to succeed but did not. Even apart from the service it provided, the sheer brilliance of his *modus operandi* should have earned it the enthusiastic loyalty of the entire Indian press. Cables of some of the leading news agencies of the world were bought by the London office and pooled, and the choicest of them were sent out to India. Often, Reuters was left standing. A smuggled copy of the dak edition of the *Free Press Journal* caused daily pain and hourly perturbation in Hornby Road and doleful cables went home of being beaten by the "opposition". It proved its worth as I can vouch from personal experience. But the Indian press did not support him and Sadanand ruined himself bearing the burden."

Sadanand wrote, "By combined action on the part of the alien Government, Reuters and the loyalist press and public-men, the activities of Free Press of India and *Free Press Journal* were brought to an abrupt end in July 1935. The *Free Press Journal* resumed publication in December 1937, soon after the advent of the popular ministries in the Provinces. Free Press of India resumed its activities in 1945. It paid considerable attention to the collection and dissemination of world news to the Press of India. Free Press of India deputed special correspondents and opened offices in Nanking, Cairo, Singapore, Batavia, London and New York in implementation of its plans for a world news service primarily for India and secondly for the world press."

Sadanand was given an assurance that teleprinter lines would be leased to the Free Press of India but later this facility was denied. "On 30 April 1947, it was made clear to Free Press of India that it could not rely on receiving the facility of leased teleprinter channels for its news agency activities. Free Press of India, thereupon, suspended its activities until such time as the policy of the Government of India crystallised and was implemented."

Sadanand was a member of the negotiating team of Indian Press for negotiations with Reuters. In his minute of dissent[12] to the Indian and Eastern Newspaper Society, dated 23 July 1949, one finds clarity of his mind:

> "A news agency is the machinery which collects and disseminates world news to India and which makes available news of India to the World Press. Freedom of Information, namely the right of free access to news and equally free access to the machinery for the distribution of the news, has engaged the attention of the best minds of the world. A series of international conferences have been held and vital decisions have been taken in regard to the fundamental principles of collection and dissemination of news. India is a party to the conventions adopted by the International Conference on the Freedom of Information. . . . The control of wireless and the teleprinter channels in India, to regulate and influence the operations of indigenous and foreign news services by Britain before the advent of a National Government and by the National Government after it came into power, is the subject of criticism in the responsible circles of the world press."

The story about why S. Sadanand failed to get leased teleprinter lines for Free Press of India was written years after Sadanand was dead and gone. B. C. Dutt, a Naval Mutiny man, whom Sadanand gave a job at Free Press Journal, did a story on movement of armed forces after independence. Other newspapers reproduced that scoop. Next day, the editor, S. Natarajan, did not congratulate B. C. Dutt but said, "Our hero has known only naval prison. This time he has earned himself a few years in a civil jail." Then looking at him, Natarajan smiled, "Don't worry. I shall keep an eye on you there. Being the editor, I shall be GOI's[13] guest first, then you." In all innocence, Dutt asked, "What have I done, Boss? No one can repudiate the story."

"Yes, Sardar Patel, the Home Minister, did not actually say your story was wrong. But the correct spellings of names of all ships, of the army units and the ranks of senior officers taking part, have given your identity away." For, only an ex-fighting force man could have the names and ranks right. Dutt was the only one.

"Sardar has found that out. He only wanted to know who leaked it to you." Natarajan continued: "He's furious that we published the news about the armed forces without official clearance. The phone almost burnt-up by the time he hung up on Sadanand last night." However, nothing happened to Dutt or Natarajan. Dutt wrote in his Golden Jubilee contribution to the Saga of the *Free Press Journal*, "Many years later, when I was no longer a journalist and Sadanand was no more, Natarajan told me the consequences of my scoop. Sardar cut Sadanand dead. He refused him all facilities to launch his news agency Free Press of India. This shocking news Natarajan himself learnt much later. According to Natarajan, long after the Sardar had black balled him, Sadanand mentioned casually, 'Free Press Journal will go on even after I am gone, but FPI will remain unborn.' He did not blame anyone or me. That was the man, Sadanand."

United Press of India

The United Press of India was started from Calcutta in 1933 by B. Sen Gupta, who had resigned from the Free Press. Sen Gupta was the Managing Director and Dr. B. C. Roy, Chairman of Board of Directors. The news agency had financial and other difficulties from the beginning. The competition was with the Associated Press with its speedy teleprinter transmission. When Dr. Rajendra Prasad inaugurated the United Press teleprinter services in 1948, the news agency had a fresh lease of life. The agency finally closed down in 1958, as newspapers were unwilling to keep it alive. C. Raghavan wrote about the collapse in 1977, "At that time, on behalf of the Indian Federation of Working Journalists, I repeatedly met the Home Minister, the late Govind Ballabh Pant, in an effort to prevent the closure. Pandit Pant was willing to declare a moratorium on UPI's debt to the Post and Telegraph Department—quite a substantial sum—provided he was assured by the owners and newspapers that they would meet the other debts, including the Provident Fund dues of employees, and assure that the service could be run economically. The newspapers were unwilling and the owners were unable to do anything. And so the United Press of India (UPI) collapsed."[14]

Press Trust of India

The run-up to independence had also thrown up ideas of running free India's own national news agency as an objective disseminator of information about a resurgent nation, freed of the foreign yoke. "The evolution of the concept of a national news agency was the direct consequence of the spirit of independence that swept the country since the days of the Quit India Movement. The desire to shake off the imperial domination in the field of news supply was at the heart of this evolving thought," said Ramnath Goenka, a former chairman of PTI.

After two years of consultations and planning among senior journalists, newspaper proprietors and national leaders like Pandit Nehru and Sardar Patel, free India's first national news agency, the Press Trust of India, was incorporated in Madras on 27 August 1947. This was within a fortnight of what Jawaharlal Nehru described as India's "Tryst with Destiny" at the historic central hall of Parliament on the night of 14 – 15 August .

In 1948, Indian newspapers formed the Press Trust of India, on the basis of cooperative ownership.[15] It arrived at a three-year agreement with Reuters under which it took over the Associated Press and joined Reuters as a partner[16] in the collection and dissemination of news from all over the world. At the end of four years, the agreement was ended and the Press Trust of India began purchasing Reuters' services in bulk and distributing them to its subscribers in India.

The idea of the takeover of API from Reuters was mooted in 1946 at a meeting of the Indian and Eastern Newspapers Society (IENS) in Lahore. Among those who supported the scheme were Devdas Gandhi of the *Hindustan Times*, Kasturi Srinivasan of the *Hindu* and Tushar Kanti Ghosh of *Amrit Bazar Patrika*. Meanwhile, the Labour government which had come to power in England in the wake of the Tory defeat in 1945, had sounded Reuters to come to terms with the Indian newspapers about the transfer of its interests. Reuters were reluctant to give up its monopoly in India even at a time when the British had decided to transfer the power to Indians. While agreeable to the handing over of the business of the internal agency, API, to the national news agency, Reuters wanted to retain control over the foreign news service. Then Reuters could manipulate the Indian and Eastern Newspaper Society (IENS) to get into a post-independence arrangement favouring Reuters all the way.

The deadlock was finally resolved through the intercession of Sardar Vallabhbhai Patel, the Member for Home and Information of the Government of India. He insisted on the total transfer of Reuters's Indian interests to the Indian news agency, Press Trust of India, failing which the Reuter teleprinter line license due for renewal in July 1947, would not be renewed. Sardar Patel asked the IENS president to inform the Reuters that a new agreement be made for the immediate transfer. Reuters promptly agreed to a total transfer and invited an Indian newspaper delegation to visit England to negotiate a new deal, as the teleprinter line license of Reuters was due to be renewed in July 1947 and there was a government resolution that future licenses could be given only to Indian agencies. The new partnership deal was approved by IENS on 27 July 1948. The agreement was finally announced on 21 September 1948. On 14 January 1949, PTI remitted the required money and became a partner of Reuters with effect from 1 February 1949. Thus, the Press Trust of India (PTI) which had been registered as a company in August 1947, went into operation on 1 February 1949.

PTI began as a non-profit venture. According to the Memorandum and the Articles of Association of the company, shareholding was restricted to newspapers regularly published in India, which subscribed to its services. The shareholders could not be paid any dividends, with the income being invested solely on the promotion of professional activities originally set out for it. Its Constitution had also provided that "control shall at no time pass into the hands of any interests, group or section." Administration was the responsibility of a general manager and a Board of 14 directors, of whom 10 were from the newspapers and 4 were public men. A chairman was elected annually.

To direct the Indian desk in Reuters' headquarters in London, the PTI chose G. Parthasarthi, who has been assistant editor of the Hindu since 1936. K. Gopalan, a senior member of staff from API days was assigned to assist him. They reached London on 20 April 1949 to discover that the India desk consisted of six men. Five had no knowledge of Indian conditions and even Indian geography. The sixth had a distant connection with India by virtue of having been a sub-editor of the *Statesman* in Calcutta about twenty years ago. But he was long past the age of retirement.

Reuters violated the agreement by sending representatives to territories marked for PTI in the agreement, without prior consultation as envisaged in the agreement. Reuters also went for an agreement with Eastern News Trust of Pakistan. Another irritant was appointment of a British correspondent in New Delhi on a regular basis. Reuters also wanted an alteration in terms of agreement: In clause 3, in 'restatement of principles' forming the basis of partnership, it said, "The whole is greater than the part and any rights or privileges of one part should not directly or indirectly affect the whole."

On 13 August 1952 Dr B. V. Keskar, Minister for Information and Broadcasting in the Government of India, wrote to K. Srinivasan, editor of the *Hindu*, "The Government expects the PTI to stand more and more on its own legs, not subservient to other international agencies but equal to them and not also forming a subsidiary part of any international cartel. If we find that PTI has entered into an agreement which derogates from the position that we expect it to have and becomes subservient to any foreign and/or international network, we might have to think seriously how far we can continue to give the PTI the facilities and cooperation that we have been extending to it until now."

Prime Minister Nehru[17] wrote to Srinivasan, "I am reluctant as Prime Minister to interfere in the partnership arrangements between the PTI and Reuters. That is the primary responsibility of the members of the PTI. But naturally, I am greatly interested in this matter because of its wider implications. I should like national news agencies to develop in India and I would like to judge every proposal from that point of view." The basic difference between PTI and Reuters, he thought, was reflected in the foreign policies of the two countries. The agreement seemed to suggest that Reuters did not like PTI to give publicity to the Indian view in international affairs, especially in Asian countries, and also wanted to increase control over PTI. This aspect of the question had not been considered when the original agreement had been drawn, since India's foreign policy had not been developed then. The Prime Minister went on to explain that Indian policies in the Middle East and South East Asia—the Indian area allotted to PTI—caused apprehension to Reuters who attempted to neutralise or lessen PTI activities in this area. They had even sent a correspondent to India and there had been tendentious propaganda by a Reuters man in Pakistan. Nehru did not see much advantage in PTI being able to control news going out of India, "I am a little more interested in news that goes to and comes from the places like Cairo, Baghdad, Tehran, Rangoon, Singapore and Djakarta." The new formula proposed by Reuters was rejected by the PTI board on 20 September 1952, thus putting an end to its partnership with PTI. "When PTI emerged a free agent in 1953, we felt as happy as Jawaharlal did at the end of the interval between India's attainment of dominion status and its emergence as a sovereign republic – an interval during which he chafed at having to couch communications to His Majesty in the phraseology of a subject addressing his liege."

The 30,000 km long teleprinter network that PTI inherited from API in 1949 had grown to 55,000 km by the end of 1975. Starting with 30 bureaus, the PTI had 70 bureaus spread over cities and towns. The number of teleprinters linking the bureaus was 1150 in 1970, 1160 in 1972, 1180 in 1974, and 1200 in 1974 – 1975. It had a total staff strength of 1251 in 1975, of which 181 were journalists, 268 stringers and 801 non-journalists. The available data indicate the rise in PTI revenues from Rs. 1.52 crores in 1971 to Rs. 1.90 crores in 1975. These figures do represent growth but the margin of growth, over time, was not substantial.

PTI operations abroad could not match the scale of its coverage within the country, due primarily to financial constraints. The number of foreign correspondents went down from 12 and 9 at various stages, and finally, by 1975 only 5—for United Nations, Moscow, Kathmandu, Colombo and London. Earlier, there were correspondents on the news trail not merely in Cairo, Belgrade, Kuala Lumpur, Tokyo, but also nearer home in Dacca, Karachi and Rawalpindi.

In 1959, PTI's exclusive partnership with Reuters for the purchase of Reuter news ended. PTI kept its windows on the world scene open through arrangements for exchange of news with 14 foreign news agencies – Reuters (UK), AFP (France), UPI (USA), Tanjug (Yugoslavia), Antara (Indonesia), Polska Agencja Prasowa (Poland), Allgemeiner Deutscher Nachrichtendienst (German Democratic Republic), BSS (Bangladesh), Novosti (USSR), Bernama (Malaysia), Prensa Latina (Cuba), Agerpress (Rumania).

United News of India

The 25-year-old United Press of India (UPI) had collapsed in 1958 and the void had to be filled. The Press Commission Report (1952 – 1954) had spoken of the need to have "at least two news agencies each competing with the other and also acting as a corrective to the other".

The newspapers shared this feeling. The United News of India (UNI) was sponsored by eight newspapers, *Hindu, Times of India, Statesman, Amrit Bazar Patrika, Hindustan Times, Hindustan Standard, Deccan Herald and Aryavarta*. It was registered as a company on 19 December, 1959.

On the first day of its operations, 21 March 1961, the UNI sent out just 2 messages to its subscribers from its cabin in the IENS building: a message from Dr. B. V. Keskar, the Minister of Information and Broadcasting and another one from Mr. Alfred Charlton, former editor of the *Statesman*.

For some time the agency had to make do with old UPI teleprinter machines, rusted through disuse. From this modest start, the UNI grew into an important rival agency within a decade. The number of UNI subscribers in 1961 was 13. It had risen to 50 by 1964, 109 by 1967 and to 223 in 1971. In 1971, UNI had 249 teleprinters and 43 centres. By 1975, the 53 UNI bureaus across the country had been linked up by 408 teleprinters. Within 10 years of its existence, the UNI was earning a revenue of Rs. 54.31 lakhs. It registered an increase from Rs. 67.73 lakhs in 1974 to Rs. 87.14 lakhs in 1975. It was a five-man office when UNI began. By 1975, it had a staff of 697, which included 139 journalists, 392 non-journalist and 166 stringers. The pace of growth was rapid in the case of UNI, but in absolute terms and in relation to the country's requirements, its coverage was still inadequate.

The UNI had launched a number of specialised services. In 1968, it introduced a weekly backgrounder service of well-documented, in-depth backgrounders on current topics. In 1970, the UNI Agriculture News and Feature Service was launched, a pioneering effort in the field of agricultural journalism. The financial and commercial service provided trend reports on Indian and foreign markets. The last in the series was the UNI Airmail News Service (1971) designed to ensure a steady flow of processed and factual information on a variety of themes to periodicals. UNI was also the first to venture into the field of science reportage with a full-time science correspondent.

For world news, the UNI had arrangements with the Associated Press (USA), Deutsche Press-Agentur (West Germany), Agenzia Nazionale Stampa Associata (Italy), Agerpress (Rumania), Ceteka (Czechoslovakia), Jiji (Japan), the Eastern News Agency (Bangladesh),

Rashtriya Sambad Samiti (Nepal) and Tanjug (Yugoslavia). The UNI had four stringers, one each in Hong Kong, Singapore, Kabul and Colombo and one staffer each in Dacca and Kathmandu. To supplement foreign agency coverage, it had a radio monitoring unit to pick up the news from the major world radio networks.

Hindustan Samachar

India's first multilingual agency, the Hindustan Samachar, was set up in Bombay as a private limited company in 1948 by S. S. Apte. Its avowed aim was to educate the masses to take part in national development and to strive for national integration through the promotion of all Indian languages. This early effort was limited to the distribution of news among local newspapers through Devanagari telegrams.

The situation improved somewhat with the advent of Devanagari teleprinters (teleprinter service was inaugurated by Purshottam Das Tandon in 1954), but the heavy transmission costs forced Mr. Apte to hand over the agency to a cooperative society of workers. In 1957, it became a society called the Hindustan Samachar Cooperative Society, with its headquarters in New Delhi. Being workers' cooperative, it remained free of the control of both the government as well as the big newspaper proprietors.

In 1975, it had a teleprinter circuit of 14, which connected its network of 21 bureaus. It also had at one time bureaus in Nepal, Sikkim and Bhutan. Financially, it was better off than Samachar Bharati. The agency's revenue rose from Rs. 7.96 lakhs in 1971 to Rs. 10.77 lakhs in 1975. It had a staff of 162, of whom 74 were journalists, 68 non-journalists and 20 stringers.

The agency fed news to its more than 135 subscribers in 10 languages – Hindi, Gujarati, Marathi, Punjabi, Urdu, Bengali, Oriya, Assamese, Telegu and Malayalam. It had teleprinter services in Hindi and Marathi. Copies filed by correspondents to headquarters would be put out after editing to the regional centres where they would be translated into local languages for transmission to local subscribers.

It ran special feature services to tap additional sources of revenue and explore new fields in reportage It used to bring out a year book in Hindi entitled *Varshiki*.

A monthly feature service named *Yugvarta* was also brought out containing a minimum of 15 news features on themes of topical interest.

Samachar Bharti

The second language agency, the Samachar Bharati, was registered as a company in 1962, was inaugurated on 2 October, 1966, and commenced commercial distribution of news to newspapers from January 1,1967. In 1970, the agency was converted almost into a government company with the State governments of Bihar, Gujarat, Rajasthan and Karnataka holding more than 50 percent of the company's shares. Its first chairman was the governor of Bombay, Sri Prakasa. Jayaprakash Narain served as its chairman for several years. In spite of its heavy share-capital, the Samachar Bharati remained financially weak. Even in 1976, its salary arrears came to Rs. 1.60 lakhs, in addition to the uncovered liabilities of Rs. 9.57 lakhs. Its revenue during 1975 was Rs. 5.50 lakhs only. The number of teleprinters stood static at 49 between 1971 and 1975, connecting a network of 13 bureaus. There had been no marked increase in the strength of the staff, either. In 1975, it had 138 employees. Of these, 40 were journalists, 48 non-journalists and 50 stringers. In 1971, the staff had numbered 141, including 41 journalists, 50 stringers and 50 non-journalists.

However, despite the financial handicaps, the agency rendered valuable services in supplying news to the language papers, most of them small and medium newspapers, not merely in Hindi but also in Marathi, Gujarati, Kannada, Urdu and Punjabi. Among its subscribers were 50 newspapers, the AIR and state information agencies. In 1973, it started an annual reference manual in Hindi called *Desh aur Duniya*. It also had a feature service – *Bharati*. The agency had at various times organised seminars and workshops to give professional training to language journalists and stringers.

Samachar

The four agencies, PTI, UNI, Hindustan Samachar and Samachar Bharti merged their separate identities into what came to be known as "Samachar" in February 1976.

The decision to "restructure" the four teleprinter news agencies had been taken by Prime Minister Indira Gandhi at a meeting held in her office on 26 July 1975. The minister of Information and Broadcasting, V. C. Shukla, discussed several times with the heads and representatives of the four agencies his proposal for all the agencies merging together to form a single agency.

In December 1975 the Government considered a proposal to set up, under an Act of Parliament, a corporate body which would take over the four agencies. The governing council was to be nominated by the President of India. Since the finances of all the agencies were in the red, they were not entitled to any compensation but only to a solatium. The proposal to incorporate the news agency under an Act of Parliament was not approved by the Cabinet which instead discussed "other methods" to bring about a merger of the four agencies. It was decided subsequently that a registered society should be created.

While efforts were made to 'persuade' the heads of the agencies to agree to the merger, several other steps were taken by the Government. The All India Radio, then a government department, on 2 January 1976, served notices on PTI and UNI that the subscription would cease with effect from 1 February 1976. The formal agreements had expired as far back as 1973, and thus, there was no legal problem in serving such notices. The teleprinter services taken by different government departments and at the residence of ministers were terminated. The type of response from the agencies varied although under the circumstances each one had to fall in line.

The employees' unions of the four agencies passed resolutions accepting the idea of a single national news agency. The employees legitimately believed that belonging to a larger size all-India body could in no way be disadvantageous to them. Indeed, there is a section of opinion which holds that the country should have only one major news agency; such an evidence was laid before us by several eminent journalists, including some who had themselves suffered during the Emergency as a result of the creation of Samachar.

On 21 January 1976, V. C. Shukla made a statement in the Lok Sabha saying that the Government welcomed the initiatives taken by the news agencies towards merger. As against the proposal for a statutory corporation owned by the government, which had been considered in December 1975, a society was registered under the Societies Registration Act, 1860, on an application signed by seven persons on 24 January, 1976. The applicants were: G. Kasturi, P. C. Gupta, Dr. Ram S. Tarneja, Abid Ali Khan, Dr. L. M. Singhvi, N. Rajan and B. K. Joshi.

The credit line of Samachar had started appearing from 1 February 1976, following an agreement signed by the four agencies on 29 January 1976. Thereafter, the agencies gave power of attorney to the Samachar

Managing Committee to transact all business on their behalf; their general bodies approved this in due course. With effect from 1 April 1976, the Managing Committee of the Samachar started functioning and carrying on business, which had belonged to the four agencies.

Non-Aligned News Agencies Pool (NANAP) came into existence in 1976. Samachar was the Indian partner in the arrangement. Before the initiation of the Non-aligned Pool idea, the Samachar relied for the bulk of its international news on Reuters (UK), AP (USA) and AFP (France). In addition, it had bilateral agreements with the following TASS (Soviet Union), PAP (Poland), ADN (GDR), CETEKA (Czechoslovakia), Kyodo (Japan), Agerpress (Romania), ANSA (Italy), PRENSA LATINA (Cuba), Antara (Indonesia), VNA (Vietnam), Tanjug (Yugoslavia) and BSS (Bangladesh), the last five being national agencies of non-aligned countries.

After the New Delhi Conference in July 1976 and the acceptance of the News-Agencies Pool Scheme, the Samachar started arrangements for exchange of news with the following nine news agencies from the non-aligned world: QNA (Qatar), INA (Iraq), SUNA (Sudan), ALPRESS (Algeria), MAPRESS (Morocco), KNA (Kenya), ENA (Ethiopia), ZANA (Zambia) and BERNAMA (Malaysia). In course of the year 1976 – 1977, "arrangements" were started with another seven news agencies of non-aligned countries – MENA (Egypt), ARNA (Libya), GNA (Ghana), SHIHATA (Tanzania), NOTIMEX (Mexico), RSS (Nepal) and SLBC (Sri Lanka).

Samachar reorganised the Hindi Wing and recruited more staff for this purpose. It started offering a complete service to the subscribers, and many Hindi papers which were earlier taking the English service switched over to the Hindi service. A Marathi service was also launched.

Samachar became a major issue in 1977 elections, and after the defeat of Indira Gandhi, the fate of this entity was sealed.

Kuldip Nayar Committee

The committee to examine the structure of Samachar as news agency and suggest its reorganisation was appointed by the Government of India, Ministry of Information and Broadcasting through Resolution No. 30/14/77-Press dated 19 April, 1977. Kuldip Nayar chaired the committee. Members were D. R. Mankekar, C. R. Irani, A. K. Sarkar, K. R. Malkani, Rahul Barpute, Ishrat Ali Siddiqui, K. Chathunni

Master, Nikhil Chakravartty, S. G. Munagekar, R. Rajagopalan and L. Dayal (Member – Secretary). The committee submitted its report in August 1977.

It recommended the restructuring of Samachar into two agencies—one to provide service in English and the other in Indian languages, and both to organise jointly an international agency. "We recommend that Samachar should be dissolved and in its place there should be two news agencies: Varta and Sandesh. They in turn should set up jointly an organisation for international services which may be called NEWS INDIA. The new arrangement, according to our recommendations should be brought about by Parliament through a charter which should be reviewed after 10 years."

The committee said the purpose of creating the news agency set-up under a statutory charter from the Parliament is three-fold: (1) to provide safeguards for the qualitative attributes of objectivity, adequacy and independence; (2) to preserve the structure of the agencies; and (3) to extend statutory protection to the process of conversion of existing agencies into the new set-up. "We recommend that in the Act of Parliament provisions should be made to the effect that the collection and dissemination of news would be free from any slant, pressure or interference exerted either by government authorities or by any other source and that the news coverage would be fully impartial, objective and independent."

In effect, the Committee retained the basic structure of Samachar, giving different names to its English, Hindi and foreign services and making them separate entities.

A note of dissent by C. R. Irani and A. K. Sarkar to the report of the committee suggested, "Samachar should be broken up into two fully competing news agencies, primarily in the English language, for the simple reason that this is the language in which the service is demanded. This is fully supported by the evidence placed before us. PTI and UNI achieved a high reputation, both domestically and overseas, before they were forcibly taken over and there is no reason why the two agencies to replace Samachar should not be given back those names. Both agencies should be left free to develop Hindi and regional language services, as each may consider best. If competition is important in the English language, it is equally important in other languages. I am strongly opposed to giving Varta a monopoly of Hindi and regional language services which, in my view, will not be in the interests of subscribing newspapers in those languages. Both agencies should be free to take the services they choose from overseas. I am totally opposed to granting a monopoly to News India of international news coverage. It would certainly be possible for both agencies to work out a limited sharing arrangement between themselves, but they must be left free to do so." They pointed out that a separate Hindi agency "is not viable today and is not going to be viable in the fairly distant future." The report took no account whatever of the overwhelming evidence from major and minor newspapers published in the various Indian languages that they would rather have service in English than have translations from Hindi into the various Indian languages.

Indian Federation of Working Journalists (IFWJ) published a booklet *Slaughter of Samachar*[18] compiling views on the report and the issue of news agencies in India. It pointed out, "All seasoned agency executives in India concede there really was not any competition as such between the PTI and UNI. The competition is and should be between newspapers. Before Samachar was brought into being, the PTI and UNI had an aggregate of 383 subscribers among newspapers. Of these only 81 subscribed to both. In other words, over 300 newspapers were not fascinated by the competition when the two services were available to them. And ironically enough, our champion freedom fighter and crusader for competition, Curshow Irani[19] was one of the very first to cut off the UNI service, even though his paper was one of the eight distinguished sponsors of that agency."[20] This publication also had a report on a four-hour seminar on Samachar held on 13 October presided over by C. Raghavan, former Editor-in-Chief of PTI. Its consensus was "the retention of Samachar with a suitably restructured set up and having an editorially independent Indian language wing would be in the best interests of the nation having regard to the need to have a strong, economically viable news agency which would cater to the ever increasing and varied demands of subscribing newspapers and readers belonging to all strata of a developing society."[21] The IFWJ booklet also reproduced an article by C. Raghavan from National Herald in which he said that the UNI was "formed neither for competition in news nor because the PTI has become lethargic. It was merely an attempt to prevent the Government and Parliament from implementing the recommendation of the Press Commission vis-a-vis the PTI and to have another agency in their pocket to counter the employees' strike threat."[22] Press Commission (1954) recommended the transfer of PTI's management to a public corporation to be set up by a Parliamentary enactment.[23] By the time the Press Commission reported in 1954 the share capital of PTI was almost wiped out mainly because newspaper subscribers, who were also owners, never paid enough subscriptions to meet the cost of news service.[24]

In the Lok Sabha (House of People) debate on the subject C. M. Stephen, Vayalar Ravi, Sugata Roy (all Congress) P. G. Mavalankar (Independent) and Parvati Krishnan (CPI) drew the Government's attention to the fact that the four news agencies were in poor shape before the merger. While Stephen suggested a levy on circulation, Mavalanker suggested that some newspapers who paid as much as 10 paise as commission to venders out of the sale price of 35 paise per copy and less than a paisa for agency services must raise their prices by one or two paise, telling their readers that the increase in the price is to be regarded as "freedom-of-the-press-levy". Mavalanker was emphatic that the price for freedom must be paid by the press and commended the policy of the AP, the cooperatively owned and operated news agency of American newspapers, "which even to this day refuses to sell its services even to USIS"[25].

The report was examined by a cabinet sub-committee[26], which favoured a return to the position as it obtained before the formation of Samachar. L. K. Advani, the minister for information and broadcasting, in a statement made in both the houses of Parliament announced this decision of the Government on 14 November 1977: "The former Government had not only actively assisted the formation of Samachar but had also guided the managing committee of Samachar in their policy decisions. Samachar was in this sense, a product and symbol of Emergency and indeed, an aberration arising out of Emergency. Government has, therefore, come to the conclusion that at the moment the Government's role in the matter should be limited simply to the setting right of this aberration. News agencies forced to merge under pressure and against their will during the Emergency should be allowed to function independently as they were earlier. It would then be open to them if they were to cooperate or come together in order to ensure that they are able to play more effectively the pivotal role expected of them in the press set up. The Government feels that having created a climate of freedom, it should leave the development and expansion of news agencies to the Press and the agencies themselves."[27] T. R. Ramaswami, the president of IFWJ said that in taking this decision the Government not only ignored the opinion of the bulk of news agency employees but also competent professionals. "In the name of competition, there will be duplication now as has been the case before, frittering away the limited resources. As for foreign coverage, the restoration of *status quo ante* will further increase India's dependence on transnational news agencies."[28]

The *status quo ante* was restored and the four agencies resumed functioning separately as before Samachar from 14 April 1978. At the time of breakup of Samachar, the Government offered them financial assistance on a tapering basis for six years, besides non-recurring rehabilitation grant and development loans to restart separate operations once again. India Desk of Non-Aligned News Agencies Pool is operated by PTI. Hindustan Samachar[29] and Samachar Bharti[30] were once again in financial trouble within a decade.

Goenka Committee

The minister of state for information and broadcasting convened a meeting of the leading editors and proprietors of language newspapers for the purpose of obtaining consensus for formation of an Indian language news agency for dissemination of news in Indian languages on 25 – 26 June 1985. At the outset the minister made it clear that the government did not propose to start any agency nor did the government want to get involved in the management or functioning of any agency.

The consensus at the meeting was that there is a need for an Indian language news agency to meet the requirements of newspapers in Hindi and other Indian languages. The participants also recognised that there is no possibility of reviving Hindustan Samachar and Samachar Bharati.

The meeting was of the unanimous view that it is for the proprietors and editors of newspapers themselves to operate such a news agency service. The proprietors and editors agreed to examine the possibility of raising resources for setting up a viable news agency service in Indian languages. It was also agreed at the meeting that if it was not considered possible to raise adequate resources to set up a separate Indian language news agency, an alternative could be for the existing English language news agencies to start services in Indian languages also.

Consequent thereto, a committee of eminent newspapermen, under the Chairmanship of Ramanath Goenka, was constituted to examine the various aspects of the matter. The following were the members of the committee: Ramanath Goenka (convenor), K. Narendra, Ramesh Chandra, Narendra Mohan, P. Mohapatra, Somasundaram and S. M. Agarwal.

The committee found[31] that the creation of a full-fledged news agency with adequate technological backup would require at least Rs. 3 crores for capital expenditure and, in addition, recurring expenditure of Rs. 1 crore per year. The Indian language newspapers were not at all in a position to raise even 50 percent of this capital. Further, the running cost of Rs. 1 crore per year could not be recovered from Hindi/Indian language subscribers.

On the other hand, if Indian language service is added to the infrastructure of an existing news agency, the additional annual cost would be only Rs. 50 lakhs per year. There would be practically no capital cost. This level of annual expenditure could be managed both by newspapers and other subscribers like AIR and Doordarshan. If, however, there is still any deficit, the news agency concerned could bear it.

Recommendations of the Goenka Committee led to the death of Hindi agencies, both Hindustan Samachar and Samachar Bharti. Goenka then was Chairman of PTI. UNI already had launched a Hindi service UNIVarta in May 1982. PTI launched its Hindi service *Bhasha* in April 1986.

PTI 2005

At the beginning of 2005, PTI subscribers include 450 newspapers in India and scores abroad. All major TV/radio channels in India and several abroad, including BBC in London, receive the PTI service.

With a staff of over 1,300, including 400 journalists, PTI has over 80 bureaus across India and foreign correspondents in all major cities of the world including Bangkok, Beijing, Dhaka, Jerusalem, Johannesburg, Islamabad, Kathmandu, Kuala Lumpur, London, Moscow, New York, Washington DC and Sydney. In addition, about 400 stringers contribute to the news file.

It has arrangements with the Associated Press (AP) and Agence . France-Presse (AFP) for distribution of their news in India, and with the Associated Press for its photo service and international commercial information. PTI exchanges news with nearly 100 news agencies of the world as part of bilateral and multilateral arrangements, including Non-Aligned News Agencies Pool and the Organisation of Asia-Pacific News Agencies PTI Services:

English News Service

Available in two forms, the 'core' service covers major developments in diverse fields in a compact form. A more comprehensive segmented service allows papers to pick additional inputs from segments of their choice: national, regional, economic, commercial, international, and sports. Core service puts out about 40,000 words and the full-segmented service up to 100,000 words per day.

Bhasha

Bhasha is the Hindi language news service of PTI. With its own network in the Hindi-speaking states and drawing on PTI files, *Bhasha* puts out about 40,000 words per day.

Stock Scan

Screen-based services providing stock market information from main stock exchanges of the country.

News Scan

Displays news in capsule form on video monitors. Major developments in the country and abroad are covered.

Data India

A reference weekly, provides a digest on the happenings in India, in a user-friendly alphabetical listing.

Economic Service

A fortnightly journal providing analytical reports on the state of the Indian economy and trends in the corporate world.

PTI Mag

A weekly package of 11 special stories on topics ranging from arts to business to science. Available through the wire service as well as through mail.

Science Service

Reports on the developments in the fields of science and technology with particular reference to India in a fortnightly journal.

PTI Graphics

A weekly mailer package of 14 graphics. Covers all major developments. On special occasions like the budget, graphics are distributed by satellite.

PTI Feature

A package of four weekly features on topical, national, international and general events.

PTI-TV

Provides spot coverage and makes corporate documentaries on assignment basis.

Photo

Available in two packages to suit the needs of small and big newspapers. PTI Photo provides pictures on the national, foreign and sports scenes via satellite, dial-up and hand delivery. The full colour service of the Associated Press of America (AP) is also made available through PTI.

Asia Pulse

An online data bank on economic developments and business opportunities in Asian countries. Formed by PTI and four other Asian media organisations, Asia Pulse International is registered as a company in Singapore.

UNI 2005

At the beginning of 2005, UNI claims to serve more than 1000 subscribers in more than 100 locations in India and abroad. They include newspapers, radio and television networks, websites, government offices and private and public sector corporations. Its communication network stretches over 90,000 km in India and the Gulf states. It has more than 325 staff journalists around the country and more than 250 stringers, covering news events from remote corners of the country. UNI claims to have correspondents in major world cities such as Washington DC, London, Dubai, Colombo, Kathmandu, Islamabad, Dhaka, Singapore, Sydney and Vancouver, bringing to subscribers, stories of interest to Indian readers.

UNI has collaboration agreements with several foreign news agencies, including Reuters and DPA, whose stories it distributes to media organisations in India. It also has news exchange agreements with

Xinhua of China, UNB of Bangladesh, Gulf News Agency of Bahrain, WAM of the United Arab Emirates, KUNA of Kuwait News Agency, ONA of Oman and QNA of Qatar. UNI launched its own Gulf operations in 1980.

UNI also developed diverse services for different clients. As stated earlier UNI launched a full-fledged Indian language news service, UNIVARTA, in Hindi in May 1982. Now it is serving nearly 300 newspaper and non-newspaper subscribers in several states across India. Besides spot news, UNIVARTA provides news features on a wide variety of topics, including art and culture, science, agriculture, economy, heritage and India's neighbours.

This was followed a decade later (in 1992) with the launching of an Urdu service on teleprinter for the first time in the world. From just six subscribers then, it now reaches more than 50 subscribers in different parts of India. This wire service covers all important news developments with special emphasis on the Muslim world, particularly West Asia. It reports all major Urdu cultural and literary events.

UNI's Financial Service (UNIFIN) launched in January 1979 is a comprehensive wire service giving global coverage of the financial and commodity markets, from Wall Street and NASDAQ to European and Asian markets. It provides near real time reports on trading in Bombay Stock Exchange and other leading exchanges in the country, along with reviews. For international markets it depends on arrangements with Reuters and Bridge News. UNIFIN also puts out reports on the Indian economy and various segments of the industry and finance, such as banking, insurance, oil and gas, energy, automobiles, telecommunications, information technology and fast moving consumer goods. It also regularly covers all the apex industry and business organisations. The UNIFIN package includes important political stories that have an impact on the financial world and also coverage of the bullion, food grains, sugar, oil, oilseeds and the other markets in India.

UNI launched a national photo service way in 1987 and plans to take it into the digital age and also widen coverage to more areas and topics. It also delivers news pictures from around the world to subscribers through collaboration arrangements with AFP.

UNI Direct is a service that brings the latest news stories from India and all over the world directly into a subscriber's desktop computer.

Subscribers in select cities in India no longer need to depend on teleprinters and will be saved the bother of handling paper rolls and ribbons. Subscribers can see the latest news story coming live in a box on their computer screen, 24 hours a day, seven days a week. They can access the entire day's file in the "Arrival Log", where the stories are saved, sorted by time. They can also go to different "baskets" such as foreign, political, stocks, parliament, regional, sports, elections and so on. Thus, they can focus only on topics of interest to them. With UNI Direct, subscribers can also have access to stories of the past 30 days. The stories can be searched by topic, date or take numbers.

UNI Graphics was launched in March 1991, and has now firmly established itself as an integral part of Indian newspapers. Graphics are sent out in both English and Hindi. For the benefit of newspapers in other languages, blank copies of the Graphics are sent, along with the text in English, which can be superimposed by the newspaper in the language they want. UNI Graphics service made its mark with the 1991 Lok Sabha elections, when newspapers were flooded with about 400 graphics in a period of about 45 days. They include maps of individual states with a graphic representation of the 1989 results and the electoral history since 1971 of about 350 constituencies. Economic reforms have given boosts to this service. Sports, accidents and an increasing number of other topics find place in graphics with an ever increasing data bank.

In July 1986, UNI started its television wing UNIdarshan to provide news features, news clips and documentaries for Doordarshan and other organisations.

Another specialised service run by the news agency is UNISCAN, a news service fed into television sets for hotels, top government officials and corporate clients

United News of India has a number of mailer services, the oldest of them being backgrounders launched in 1968 in English and in 1982 Hindi, in are issued once a week. Other mailer services are UNI Agriculture Service in English launched in July 1970, UNI Economic Service launched in 1979 and UNI Energy News Service, launched in September 1980.

Asian News International (ANI)

Visnews Bureau Chief in India, Prem Prakash, launched Asian News International (ANI) as a separate business when Reuters took over Visnews. While he became Chief of Reuters TV in India, his son Sanjiv

Prakash took charge of ANI, which supplied South Asian stories to Reuters.

ANI has now developed into South Asia's leading multimedia news agency with over 50 bureaus in India and across the globe. Its range of products encompass loosely edited news feeds and customised programmes for television channels, audio bytes for radio stations, live webcasting and streamed multimedia/text content for websites and mobile carriers and wire services for the print section. ANI also provides a range of facilities for foreign and domestic channels to package their reports in India and uplink by satellite. These include provision of professional crews, editing and post-production facilities, access to our archives, which are the most comprehensive collection of South Asian news videos anywhere in the world, uplinking facilities and providing fixers, coordinators, producers and correspondents, if required.

ANI delivers 3 subcon (subcontinent news) feeds via Reuters all over the world. About 18 top stories of the day from the subcontinent are cut to 3 minutes duration each with natural sound track. Scripts with translations are provided instantaneously.

A full ANI TV Service is also put together in New Delhi which include about 25 other news and feature items which may not figure in the subcon. These are longer duration cuts and include interviews with experts, features from remote corners of the subcontinent along with translations and detailed scripts. These items are delivered via tape two or three times a day depending on the individual client's requirements. Subcon and TV service of ANI is picked up by almost every broadcaster in Asia including BBC, CNN, NHK (Tokyo), CNA (Singapore), MBC (Middle East Broadcasting), Doordarshan and PTV (Pakistan TV). The shelf life of many of the feature items is for weekend programming use and hence the service is picked up by many ethnic television channels in the US and UK. *Multimedia News Service* has customised product offering for the web publishing community to offer their visitors a rich experience of video, audio, text and picture content. It is ideally suited for horizontal and vertical portals, corporate/niche websites, online editions of newspapers and magazines and TV channels, who seek to provide their visitors, a rich multimedia experience in news and general interest features. Breaking news events as well as other happenings in the spheres of culture and entertainment, sports, lifestyles or business are digitally captured, processed and provided to the websites as fully voiced-over capsules for an enhanced user experience. The processing can be in Real media, ASF or Quicktime formats in various speeds, tailor-made to the requirements of varied clientele. The streamed files are delivered via the FTP route to the client's end. The content is continuously updated and offers a comprehensive view of news and events as they happen.

ANI also provides high quality "live webcasting" facilities of events from Delhi.

ANI has also introduced its SMS/MMS services, comprising text and video content for use in mobile applications, aimed at keeping users visually informed, even while on the move.

ANI has a number of ready to air weekly programmes on a variety of subjects for audiences interested in trends and happenings in South Asia. Some of the programmes are specific in subject like business and industry, which would deal with stock markets, product launches, joint ventures, interviews with visiting delegations; or entertainment, which would deal with film launches, music videos, restaurant launches, fashion, etc. They come anchored and voiced-over. These can be dubbed and anchored in Hindi or Punjabi. The shows can also be anchored with client specific chromakey background and/or microphone logo. These ready-to-air shows are cost effective as they are tailored to suit broadcaster needs without the broadcaster having to make any changes. Some of the programmes available are: South Asia Newsline – a 5 days 15 minutes anchored news bulletin available via satellite in UK; US Correspondent Notebook – a 10-minute report anchored in English with specific logo, twice a month; Dateline Punjab – a half hour anchored weekly feature based programme in English and Punjabi; India's World a – half hour English programme on features from India; This Week in India – a half hour round up of issues of Indian interest; Kashmir Now – features and news from Indian Kashmir, available in Hindi and Kashmiri; Dateline South Asia; – half hour in English, round up of week's events in South Asia; Hello Bollywood – an anchored half hour programme on Hindi films and film stars. Balle Punjab – Anchored half hour programme on Punjab in Punjabi; Ghoomta Aina – an anchored half hour Hindi programme on features and investigative reports, *ANI Text News.*

ANI text news targets newspapers, websites and radio stations as its primary clients. The ANI wire service offers wide ranging content on politics, social issues, science, health, business and entertainment besides unique features that bring out the extremely interesting, yet unknown richness of the South Asian cultural tapestry. To add depth to its coverage in today's business conscious global economy, it offers commodity prices as well as frequent news analysis of major events in India and overseas.

The hallmark of the ANI wire service is its flexibility. It enables users to request a unique tailor-made package, to suit their editorial needs. Once the parameters are laid, ANI seeks to meet those and offers its subscribers the desired customised content.

To provide a global view, ANI has it's correspondents and representatives based in strategic locations across South Asia, Europe, the Middle East and America, while its vast domestic network enables it to churn out unique national content from across India.

The ANI wire service is delivered as per the specific requirements of the subscribers through e-mail or FTP.

Crew Hire

Asian News International (ANI) TV has crews in more locations in South Asia than any other news agency or television channel. There are over a hundred well-equipped camera crews in strategic locations in South Asia who can move quickly to cover news. This also includes remote corners of the region which are difficult to access and expensive to reach. It makes better business sense to use ANI crews for facilitating coverage. Many foreign broadcasters send their reporters to New Delhi and further to other parts of the region using local ANI crews. This service is made very inexpensive for ANI-TV subscribers which include BBC, NBC, ZEE TV, CNN, PBS (USA), NHK, ZDF.

IANS

Indo-Asian News Service (IANS), formerly India Abroad News Service, was conceived by Gopal Raju, founder of the *India Abroad* weekly newspaper, in 1986, to enhance the flow of news and information between India and North America. As a multinational and multilingual wire service, it has carved a niche in reporting India and South Asia and events of interest to this region around the world.

Every major newspaper group in India subscribes to the service. IANS has subscribers in many countries, including the United States,

Britain, Australia, South Africa, Pakistan and Gulf countries like the United Arab Emirates, Oman, Qatar, Bahrain and Saudi Arabia.

In the next few months and years, the IANS network will spread wider, enabling more countries to access news, features and analytical writing from India and other South Asian countries.

IANS reporters have broken numerous headline-grabbing stories and done many sensational interviews.

In 1995, IANS started a Hindi service. Today its subscriber base encompasses all leading newspapers in Hindi. IANS has a Gujarati service and has plans for other languages as well.

It is perhaps the only South Asian media organisation to have an Arabic website—www.alhindelyom.com—that helps to bridge the information gap with a region that has a large Indian and South Asian population.

The IANS service offers media organisations a cost-effective support system in comparison to more expensive news bureaus. News, features and insight from the subcontinent can also serve as powerful information backup for non-media organisations, international bodies, multinational companies and think tanks with an interest in this part of the world.

IANS gets news from all over South Asia, North America, Europe, Australia and regions from where newspapers have rarely got India-relevant news in the past.

Newspaper production

IANS has entered a new area of business activity not usually associated with a news service: newspaper production. IANS is now not only geared to provide content to newspapers outside India but has the expertise and the technology to produce entire pages, even entire newspapers, outsourced to it, at a fraction of the cost. The division was producing newspapers (four in the United States and two in Britain) in three languages – English, Gujarati and Punjabi – at the end of 2004.

TV Division

A natural progression of its growth has been the addition of an audio-visual dimension: IANS TV. The TV division produces quality documentaries that tell unusual and riveting Indian and South Asian stories for audiences in the country and abroad.

IANS Solutions

IANS Solutions is a newly formed unit of the organisation that provides all solutions needed for the development of an Internet strategy. IANS Solutions blends design, technology and marketing expertise to create a Web presence that delivers the results you are looking to achieve. Its talented Web designers collaborate with our technology group to create a personalised website that is graphically superior and functionally sound.

NOTES AND REFERENCES

1. Henry Collins (1844 – 1928) was aged 22 only when he was posted to Bombay as the first general manager for Reuters, India; from 1878 until his retirement in 1909, he was Reuters' general manager in Australia. (Read, Donald (1999) *Power of News: The History of Reuters*, Second Edition, Oxford University Press, p. 33)

2. The first Indian to function as a political correspondent at the British imperial capital, Roy was a high-school dropout who made a success of the journalistic career and rose to be a nominated member of the Central Legislative Assembly as a distinguished journalist. Working for more than one newspaper at a time, including the *Tribune* of Lahore, the *Indian Daily Mail* of Bombay and the *Amrita Bazar Patrika* of Calcutta, Roy found it easy to have a news pooling arrangement with European journalists to carry on with his work. It was from this experience that the idea of a news agency grew in Roy's mind. Soon he collaborated with three of his professional colleagues – Usha Nath Sen, Durga Das and A. S. Iyengar – to float and run the API. Though the exact time of API's birth is somewhat hazy, according to the book *Reuter's Century: 1851-1951* by Graham Storey, it was started in 1910. (PTI website, 1 December 2004).

3. K. C. Roy finally gave up in 1919 his brave effort to run an Indian-owned domestic news agency, and Reuters became the sole supplier of foreign and domestic news to the Government and to the newspapers of India. The London-based Eastern News Agency, owned by Reuters, merely used the name Associated Press of India. API was to be registered as a private limited company, wholly owned by Reuters, much later in September 1945. (PTI website, 1 December 2004).

4. Read, Donald (1999) *Power of News: The History of Reuters*, Second Edition, Oxford University Press, pp. 176 – 177: The Eastern News Agency, started by Reuters in 1910, had absorbed the Associated Press of India (API). API had been launched by the Indians as a domestic news agency to collect news about India or the Indian press; but it was never

financially viable. Its moving spirit, K. C. Roy, was an able journalist and a nationalist, who advanced his cause through charm and moderation. Roy joined Reuters at the takeover and became head of the news department. He served loyally, without compromising his opinions, until his death in 1913. The API kept use of its own name within the Reuter organisation.

5. Another version (K. Rama Rao/M. Chalapathi Rau): K. C. Roy was the dominant figure in the formation of the first Indian news agency. In scenting news, in getting it from the highest sources in the land, and in transmitting it, he was considered exceptionally agile and intelligent. To compete with Howard Hensman of the *Pioneer* which carried great weight with the official world, Edward Coates of the *Statesman,* Edward Buck of the *Englishman* and Dallas of the *Indian Daily News* set up the Associated Press of India. When Roy, who assisted them, claimed a directorship and was refused, he formed the Press Bureau along with Usha Nath Sen. When Roy was made a director, he devoted himself to strengthening the Associated Press. Branches were opened in Calcutta, Madras and Bombay; each subscribing newspaper was charged Rs. 350 per month, and the Associated Press paid the telegraph bills. In 1919 before the outbreak of the First World War, Roy accepted amalgamation with Reuters because of financial difficulties. Roy also started the Indian News Agency, a news bulletin of two typed foolscap pages, for civil and military officials at Rs. 60 per copy; it continued till 1947. The news summary was supplied to newspapers also, and when it was stopped, the small newspapers suffered.

6. Read, Donald (1999) *Power of News: The History of Reuters,* Second Edition, Oxford University Press, p. 176: In an autobiographical note dated 11 July 1944, Moloney listed the most important features of his work in India: "(1) The closer association of Indians with the management of the branches (there were no Indian managers in Reuters on my arrival in India), (2) The merging of the staffs of the Eastern News Agency and of Reuters, which led to great economies, (3) The supplying of Reuters news to vernacular newspapers, (4) The successful resistance to the tendency to sell out in India as we had done in Australia, Japan and South Africa.

7. Sadanand saw the limitations of the press under the repressive laws of the British Empire. Though his news agency, the Free Press of India, supplied well-authenticated reports of official excesses, the papers of the day could not make use of them. Sadanand decided that if the newspapers did not carry the Free Press of India despatches, it should have its own newspaper to publish them. But, the Free Press Agency had no press of its own. So, Sadanand decided to bring out a cyclostyled news bulletin, calling it *Free Press Bulletin.* The first dummy was actually produced on a duplicator! By then, Sadanand had already built up a rare reputation as a reckless and fearless journalist. He had his admirers, too. *Free Press* continued for a while

as a cyclostyled newspaper when Mr. R. B. Lotwala, proprietor of the *Advocate of India* offered to hire out some old machinery of his press. Thus was the printed *Free Press Journal* born on 13 June 1930.

8. In fact, Sadanand purchased the *Indian Express* in 1932 from Dr. P. Varadarajulu Naidu who had started it a year earlier. Sadanand ran it for some months. On the recommendation of C. Rajagopalachari, Sadanad made K. Santhanam, who had just been released from prison, its editor. The *Indian Express* became a morning paper and wrote for the Congress. It was sold at half an anna, in line with Sadanand's innovative seal. Very soon a sister Tamil daily, the *Dinamani*, was added, and in a short time this daily outstripped its rivals. The *Indian Express*, however, fell into a financial crisis and it finally passed into the hands of Ramnath Goenka who later became a newspaper baron. Sadanand wanted to start a paper in every province of India. In 1932, he started an evening newspaper: the *Free Press Bulletin* in Bombay and a Gujarati daily, *Nav Bharat*. He also started a Marathi daily in Bombay—*Navshakti*. *Free India*, an English daily which he began in Calcutta, had a very short life.

9. Father of Jawaharlal Nehru. He left his legal practice to join the freedom struggle on the call of Mahatma Gandhi.

10. Trikannad, S. (1948) "The Free Press Fever" in *The Saga of A Newspaper and the City it Grew With*, Indian National Press, Bombay.

11. Sadanand, (1948) S. *Facts About Reuters: Indian Agreement*, Sadanand, Bombay.

12. Sadanand was prophetic when he said in this note of dissent: Dramatic developments are in offing in the international world. It is a question of months or a year or two before the world divides itself into a series of armed camps. India has chosen to pilot an independent foreign policy. The countries of the world would prefer India to align with one or more groups now coming together to face all the contingencies. India, it is clear, cannot today determine her foreign policy except as óne of independent effort to promote world peace. The organisation and development of a world news service by India does not offer considerable difficulties. It is realised that only Britain and the United States of America have their own world news services. India will have no difficulty in concluding agreements with one or more news services which help her considerably to build up a national news service.

13. Government of India (GOI).

14. IFWJ (1977) *Slaughter of Samachar,* New Delhi. p. 22.

15. The seven men who subscribed initially to the shares of PTI were K. Srinivasan, Editor, *The Hindu*, Madras, Khasa Subba Rau, Editor, *Swatantra*, Madras; S. S. Vasan, Editor, *The Anandavikatan*, Madras; S. Sadanand, Managing Editor, *Free Press Journal*, Bombay; C. R. Srinivasan,

Editor, *Swadesamitran*, Madras; A. A. Hayles, Editor and Director, *The Mail*, Madras; and S. V. Swamy, Editor, *Free Press*, Madras.

16. Recalling PTI's takeover of the news operations of the erstwhile API, Goenka wrote: "Sadanand and I were happy that PTI eventually took over the operations of API from February 1, 1949. We were, however, unhappy with the package in terms of which PTI became a junior member of Reuters which retained its monopoly of distributing international news to Indian newspapers.

17. There were some instances of Reuters' bias or news manipulation. Reuters' report on the Green Pamphlet "The Grievances of the British Indians in South Africa" (1896) nearly killed Gandhi as it exaggerated what he had said. The provocative report read: "A pamphlet published in India declares that the Indians in Natal are robbed and assaulted and treated like beasts and are unable to obtain redress. The *Times of India* advocates an inquiry into these allegations. The Natal Advertiser wrote, 'A perusal of Mr. Gandhi's pamphlet recently published in Bombay, leads to the conclusion that the telegraphic description of its objects and contents was considerably exaggerated. True, Mr Gandhi complains of a certain amount of ill treatment. . . but there is nothing to warrant the statement that he alleges that the Indians in Natal are robbed and assaulted and treated like beasts.'"
On January 13, 1897, Gandhi was attacked by white workmen several times on his way from the ship to the house of Parsi Rustomji. Refusing to prosecute his attackers, Gandhi wrote to the Attorney-General, "I do not hold assailants to blame. They were given to understand that I had made exaggerated statements in India about the whites in Natal and calumniated them. The leaders and you, if you will permit me to say so, are to blame. You could have guided the people properly but you also believed Reuters and assumed that I must have indulged in exaggeration."
Jawaharlal Nehru ridiculed Reuters' "Riga Correspondents" who sat in London or Paris and concocted stories denigrating the infant Soviet State. On his return from the Soviet Union, he said "The question most frequently asked me has been about alleged nationalisation of women!"
In the spring of 1942, there was a Reuters gaffe about the supposed death of Subhas Chandra Bose in an air accident. The whole nation was shaken with grief. The congress President and Gandhi sent telegrams of condolence to the aged mother of Bose. When the allegedly dead Indian leader broadcast a talk from Radio Berlin, there was an effort to disclaim responsibility for the report. Reuters thus did not command any respect from Prime Minister Nehru.

18. IFWJ (1977) *Slaughter of Samachar*, New Delhi.

19. C. R. Irani, one of the dissenting members of Kuldip Nayar Committee.
20. A. Raghavan (1977) Kuldip Nayar Committee Report, IFWJ publication *Slaughter of Samachar*, IFWJ, New Delhi, p. 9.
21. IFWJ (1977) *Slaughter of Samachar*, New Delhi, p. 14.
22. IFWJ (1977) Slaughter of Samachar New Delhi, p. 23.
23. IFWJ (1977) *Slaughter of Samachar*, New Delhi, p. 9.
24. IFWJ (1977) *Slaughter of Samachar*, New Delhi, p. 21.
25. IFWJ (1977) *Slaughter of Samachar*, New Delhi, p. 42 – 43.
26. Headed by Jagjivan Ram, who was a Defence Minister in the Janata Government and a minister in the Indira Gandhi government during Emergency but formed a new party, Congress for Democracy, just before the 1977 general elections.
27. Statement made by Information and Broadcasting Minister L. K. Advani on 14 November 1977 in Lok Sabha and Rajya Sabha (the two houses of Indian Parliament).
28. IFWJ (1977) *Slaughter of Samachar*, New Delhi, pp. 52 – 53
29. In 1983 it claimed to serve in 13 languages: Hindi, Marathi, Gujarati, Urdu, Punjabi, Bengali, Oriya, Assamee, Telugu, Kannada, Malayalam, English and Nepali, and had correspondents in Kathmandu, Thimpu and Port Louis. (Contribution of A. N. Bal, News Editor, *Hindustan Samachar*, to *Media Problems and Prospects* published by National Media Centre, New Delhi, pp. 123 – 124.
30. In 1983 it claimed to serve 150 subscribers in 10 Indian languages. (Contribution of Krishna Kant, News Editor, Samachar Bharti, to *Media Problems and Prospects* published by National Media Centre, New Delhi pp. 124 – 125).
31. Answer to Rajya Sabha question No. 1147 on 02 August 1985 by V. N. Gadgil, Minister of State Information and Broadcasting.

NEWS AGENCY VALUES

*T*o be first is a journalistic pride. News agencies have been competing with each other to be first with the news at the desk of subscribers. Charles-Louis Havas, considered the first founder of a news agency, had already understood that rapidity was an essential factor in the transmission of news. For that reason he installed his agency in a street next to the post office. The technique has improved infinitely since 1832. Thanks to advances in communication technologies, agencies now talk of realtime coverage of important events. Agencies could beat their rivals first by days, then hours and minutes, and now seconds. With 24-hour news channels and the Internet, there is rush to break the news among different media, particularly, news agencies who serve all different types of media.

Unesco said in *News Agencies: Their Structure and Operation* (1953): "Under systems of government which respect freedom of information, the very purpose of an agency places it under an obligation to observe the most rigid objectivity and impartiality, without which the organisations it supplied with news cannot rely on having the right of choice which is implicit in freedom of expression."

The First Press Commission of India (1952 – 54) observed: "The basic function of a news agency is to provide news reports of current events to the newspapers and others who subscribe for its service. As would be apparent from this description, it acts only as an agent for collection. It is, therefore, expected to have integrity and disinterestedness." The Press Commission emphasised that, as in the case of justice, a news agency should not only possess integrity but should be seen to possess it. The need for objectivity arises from the character of the news agency as the supplier of bulk and basic news to the large variety of news outlets, with different hues and attitudes. This only can contribute to a sense of proportion in disseminating different points of view and reflecting various facets of life. The Indian Press Commission even remarked that "a news agency should not have any specific editorial policy of its own in the sense in which the term is generally understood."

Proclaimed Values

News agencies themselves swear by certain principles and values. These are placed in their corporate websites and any write up on themselves. Here is an assortment of such statements by different news agencies:

Reuters

Reuters[1] is most eloquent in such statements. It says:

Reuters news operations are based on the company's Trust Principles[2] which stipulate that the integrity, independence and freedom from bias of Reuters must be upheld at all times.

Reuters is dedicated to preserving its independence, integrity and freedom from bias in the gathering and dissemination of news and information. Under the constitution of the Reuters Founders Share Company, the directors of Reuters Founders Share Company are required to act generally in accordance with the Reuter Trust Principles, and to endeavour to ensure, as far as they are able by the proper exercise of the powers vested in them, that the Reuter Trust Principles are complied with. The constitution of Reuters Group PLC requires Reuters directors, in the performance of their functions, to have due regard to the Reuter Trust Principles in so far as, by the proper exercise of their powers and in accordance with their other duties as directors, those principles are capable of being observed.

The Reuter Trust Principles are:

- that Reuters shall at no time pass into the hands of any one interest, group or faction;
- that the integrity, independence and freedom from bias of Reuters shall at all times be fully preserved;
- that Reuters shall supply unbiased and reliable news services to newspapers, news agencies, broadcasters and other media subscribers and to businesses, governments, institutions, individuals and others with whom Reuters has or may have contracts;

- that Reuters shall pay due regard to the many interests which it serves in addition to those of the media; and
- that no effort shall be spared to expand, develop and adapt the news and other services and products of Reuters so as to maintain its leading position in the international news and information business.

AFP

The AFP represents editorial quality and reliability, a reputation built since the agency was founded in 1835. AFP is fully independent from outside influences, be they political, corporate, ideological or religious. It guarantees total objectivity and an ability to provide specialty or customised products.

AP

The AP has a mission statement:

The Associated Press is in the information business. Its fundamental mission is to provide state, national and international news, photos, graphics, broadcast and online services of the highest quality, reliability and objectivity to its domestic owners as economically as it can. The AP is a member-driven company.

News bearing the AP logotype is expected to be accurate, balanced and informed. AP feels that unrestricted access to the sources of news is essential if those standards are to be met by the AP and other news organisations.

Its legendary General Manager Kent Cooper used to say, "true and unbiased news – the highest original moral concept ever developed in America and given to the world."[3]

UPI

United Press claimed to have established two new principles in news agency operation. One was that a news organisation could cover the news of the world independently. The second was that newspapers anywhere could buy this news. Newspaper publisher E. W. Scripps combined three regional news services to form the United Press Associations. UP's announcement on 15 July 1907 said: "It is announced that the United Press will not be run on narrow or monopolistic lines, but will seek to give fair and impartial service to all legitimate newspaper publishers in the field." Scripps later said: "I regard my life's greatest service to the people of this country to be the creation of the United Press," because the competition provided by UP prevented the Associated Press from having a monopoly in determining what news was provided to the public. In a recent press release, UPI writes about itself, "Since 1907, United Press International (UPI) has been a leading provider of critical information to media outlets, businesses, governments and researchers worldwide. Covering a wide range of topics, UPI's journalists provide in-depth reporting of major news events and offer unique analysis of global issues affecting business and policy decisions. UPI products include original content in English, Spanish and Arabic. Headquarters are in Washington DC with offices in Beirut, Hong Kong, London, Santiago, Seoul and Tokyo."

AAP

Australian Associated Press (AAP) has a mission statement:

"To provide the Australian media, private and public sectors with a cost effective, unbiased, reliable, comprehensive news and information resource". Another, later version, "Our mission is to deliver high-quality, timely and impartial news, analysis and information to our customers."[4]

It also claims to adhere to some principles:

This mission statement is supported by a number of principles that guide the way AAP operates:

AAP's news and information services are available to all the Australian news media.

The AAP news service (pictures and text) is always sold to the Australian media on a non-exclusive basis.

There should be no cross subsidies between one customer group and another.

AAP is a wholesaler of information and does compete with its media customers

In addition we try to avoid conflicts by maintaining regular contact with our customers at all levels of their organisations.

Finally, probably the two biggest areas of potential conflict to avoid at all costs are ones involving price and quality of service. When disputes arise in these areas, they are very difficult, time-consuming and often expensive to resolve.

Providing a quality, impartial, timely and comprehensive news service at a competitive price is therefore critically important.

Some others

Agence Telegraphic Switzerland (ATS) says, "Our company, old of more than one century, rests on three basic values which are the independence, the solidarity and the capacity of innovation, which constitute the base of the hotlines of the ATS."

Italian ANSA claims to stick to the values: Timeliness, Objectivity, and Authority. Press Trust of India (PTI) talks of authenticity, accuracy and speed while United News of India (UNI) claims an enviable reputation for fast and accurate coverage. Associated Press of Pakistan (APP) remains committed to excellent journalistic traditions by objective, credible and accurate reporting.

Jiji Press of Japan says: In keeping with the motto "Bringing World News to Japan and News about Japan to the World," Jiji Press enjoys a solid reputation in Japan and abroad for its reliable, fair and objective reporting based on independent management made possible by being 100 percent employee-owned.

Chinese agency Xinhua claims, "With truthful, objective coverage of domestic and international events, and its espousing of Third World interests, Xinhua News Agency will continue to be a voice that the world cannot afford to ignore."

Here is post-cold war statement from a state run national agency: The main task of the News Agency of the Slovak Republic is to gather, compile, archive and provide versatile information on events in Slovakia and abroad that fulfil the requirements of objectivity, trustworthiness and quick access, in accordance with Act 81/1996 (statute on periodic press and other means of mass information).

Armenpress news agency in Armenia has adopted the motto of securing accurate, unbiased and speedy information.

Mediafax the largest independent news agency in Romania has the following "company values":

1. *Clients are the most important.* Answering to the clients' expectations is always targeted
2. *Professionalism and integrity.* Mediafax is the News Agency that provides objective, equally distant and prompt information.
3. *Quality.* The quality of its services has turned the clients of Mediafax into faithful customers. Quality is the only field where Mediafax does not prove flexibility. Mediafax has also undertaken

the mission of providing the companies in Romania with the realtime connection with the required information

ITAR-TASS successor to Soviet TASS says in 2005: As the very nature of news production continues to evolve, the agency are using the latest available technologies in order to make realtime news distribution faster and more efficient. "We closely cooperate with authorities, political parties and movements, public and humanitarian organisations, government ministries and business structures. The potential of our news agency can quench any information thirst." ITAR-TASS motto is "realtime, reliable and quality news"!

All this is fine. But what is reality? Do agencies really adhere to these proclamations? There is no problem with speed. These days the aim is to give real time- reports as events are happening. But should there be a conflict between speed and accuracy, then accuracy has to be preferred. If mistakes are made, they should be corrected promptly. But objectivity, independence, fairness and bias are debated endlessly.

Objectivity

The problem of objectivity is the concern of all news media, but more particularly of the news agency whose primary responsibility is collection of news and its distribution to a wide range of subscribers holding diverse opinions. The agency's judgement of news, selection, arrangement, and presentation of facts must satisfy all its subscribers. Where it tilts heavily on one side to the detriment of others, it not only abdicates but also betrays its function, and thereby loses its credibility; and once any news agency loses its credibility, its effectiveness, social as well as professional, is undermined. Competing agencies claimed their rivals to be subsidised and not independent and therefore their news not being fair and objective.

A government may choose to force a news agency to disseminate such information as it thinks should reach the population and nothing more. In such a situation, it may feel secure against any subversion of its regime by way of dissemination of information. But the very logic of its action in curbing the normal function of the news agency will impair the credibility of the news agency as also of the Government in the eyes of the public. And once its credibility is lost, no news agency can mould public opinion. This way, one of the major instruments of obtaining public consent, tacit or explicit, can be destroyed, and in final analysis, the discrediting of the channel of information works against the interest of any democratic system.

However, there is as yet no clear-cut definition of objectivity. It does not have same meaning for everyone. In the socialist camp, partisanship, so long as it favours classes and forces considered to be "progressive", is objective. This is based on the premise that class and social bias are inherent in any evaluation of events, statements, or theories. Theoreticians in the non-socialist camp will not accept this. They will say the journalist's mission is to know, to seek the truth. Despite the controversy, both the camps accept objectivity as the norm of news agency work.

In introduction to *News Agency Journalism* published by the International Organisation of Journalists, two Czechoslovakian journalists, Slavoj Haskove and Jaroslav First, dismiss as "false" the concepts of "absolute objectivity" and "perfect impartiality". They contend that no serious news-writer can completely divorce himself from a partisan approach to social and political developments. But they add: "A different concept of objectivity, however, which is possible to achieve, is the methodical factuality of balanced news reporting. This means, in general, that news reporting should be as near to reality as possible: that facts and figures introduced into news items should be checked and double checked; that evaluative terms should be used with utmost care, and only where it is possible to support them with proofs and reasons, where they are well-founded on facts.

"It means that the presentation should not be one-sided and emotionally exaggerated, but well-balanced. It means also, that all sources should be quoted if possible, and handled accurately, and that their evaluations and points of view should not be mixed up with those of the news-writer himself. His own personal observations, if included, must be clearly distinguishable from any second-hand information he incorporates in his news item, after checking its veracity.

"In this professional and methodical meaning of the word, news agency objectivity, of course, is obtainable and desirable. It may even form an indispensable solid basis for a more outspoken partial treatment of news in individual papers, radio, or by individual news commentators and analysis."

But Herbert Brucker in his book *Communication is Power: Unchanging Values in Changing Journalism* published by the New York

Oxford University Press (1973) says, "It is nonsense to say that there can be no such thing as objectivity. Any newsman qualified for his calling and tempered by experience can tell the difference between a slanted story and a fair one. Objective reporting is nothing more than what good reporting has always been: the work of a disciplined professional who has tried his damnedest to get the whole story, and then to present it accurately and honestly without letting his own bias creep into it."

Committee on News Agencies headed by Kuldip Nayar reported in August 1977, "The days of mere stenographic reporting are a thing of the past all over the world. While important statements and pronouncements have to be accurately covered – since accuracy is an essential component of objectivity – the need for a perceptive, in-depth approach to information concerning problems facing the community as a whole, cannot be over emphasised. A catalogue of data does not make an effective news item. The staff of the news agency today, whether belonging in the reporting or the editorial section, has to be equipped with an understanding of the problems and developments they have to handle. This is not possible without a modicum of specialisation since the complexities of a modern society undergoing technological revolution cannot be transmitted to the lay public without the transmitting agency itself having a grip over them."

The requirements of source made the agency reporter an "objective interviewer." He was content with reproducing expressed opinions accurately. He was not concerned with his own assessment of their truthfulness. It might have helped him to free himself from responsibility, from the need for extensive knowledge of things. But it did not help objectivity. For, taken in with the widely respected maxim that news value depends on who tells it, the passive role of the reporter led to subversion of the truth. A telling example of it is the way Senator Joe McCarthy in the United States was able to capture headlines day after day with accusations which everyone knew were wrong but no one knew how to stop from reporting. This contributed in some measure to a reassessment of the rules of objectivity in the West. Interpretation, background, and analysis came to be accepted as an essential part of objective reporting with the obligation cast on the reporter to indicate the validity of his data and the accuracy of his attribution. The path had been cleared for this change earlier in 1947 by the US Commission on Free and Responsible Press under the chairmanship of Robert Hutchins, then Chancellor of the University of Chicago. The first of the five requirements of press in a free society the commission listed was: "A truthful, comprehensive and intelligent account of the day's events in a context which should give them meaning." The commission observed, "It is no longer enough to report the fact truthfully. It is now necessary to report the truth about the fact."[5]

A news agency can adhere strictly to all the requirements of objectivity and yet produce an impression on the readers, which is not justified by the reality. Two agencies reporting the same story may convey contrary impressions. It is here that the spirit of objectivity is more important than the observance of formal rules. A newspaper may "play up" a story or "play down" another reflecting the news judgement of the editor or the policy of the paper. A news agency can have no larger "policy" than meeting the interests of the community as a whole. As the first Press Commission of India observed in 1954, "As purveyors of news, agencies should not merely keep themselves away from bias and follow strictly the principles of integrity, objectivity and comprehensiveness in the coverage of news, but it should also appear clear to the newspapers, and to the public, that the news agencies are maintaining such a course."

The news agency, therefore, has to be careful about what point of a story it takes for a lead, for that will become the yardstick of its objectivity. The lead will not only influence the "copy-taster" and the sub-editor in the newspaper but also the reader. The lead will influence the structure of the story and provide an angle of view. As with the lead, so too with the choice of details, selection of quotations, use of descriptive words, and in the technique of presenting background, news agency copy should consciously strive to be in appearance and in substance non-partisan and fair.

The test of objectivity is whether a report presents both the sides of a case. Is it dispassionate and fair to all concerned? Does it openly or otherwise endorse a point of view? Objectivity does not of course mean uncritical acceptance of things at their face value. It is essential in a democracy that dissent should get adequate coverage. Much in the same way, a news-agency has to guard against the danger of being identified with or dominated by any vested interests, economic, social, communal or political, or even by what is called the 'establishment' in any walk of the community's life. While the main responsibility, therefore, is of the

State, the strength and vitality of the news agency itself is also a protection against interference. The best guarantee for a news agency's efficiency is the existence, within the agency, of persons of caliber. Many news agencies of the world have evolved different techniques of internal checks and supervision, so that any lapse is immediately noticed and a constant evaluation of the work is done.

Bias

However, there is another school of thought that there is no such thing as objectivity. It is just a journalistic myth, which is claimed but cannot be achieved. No matter how much one may try to ignore it, human communication always takes place in a context, through a medium, and among individuals and groups who are situated historically, politically, economically, and socially. This state of affairs is neither bad nor good. It simply is. Bias is a word that identifies the collective influences of the entire context of a message.

Bias stems, among other things, from (1) national interest, (2) the social and political structure within which an agency operates, (3) the nature of the news source, and (4) the background of the "gatekeeper" or copytaster. Slant is more evident in interpretative reports. But even "straight" news reports are not immune from it and it is here that national interest as well as the interest of the bulk of clients determines the angle of view.

This is very well illustrated by the example of how a US news agency on which most of the Latin American countries depended for their news reported the attainment of freedom by the South American colony, Surinam, in 1976. For Latin America and for the rest of the world, the event was of historic significance as it marked the removal of the last outpost of direct colonial rule from the continent. But since the US was interested in Surinam solely as a supplier of bauxite, the news agency led its story by saying that export of that commodity to the US would be unaffected by Surinam's independence from Dutch rule. The US agency, in this case perhaps cannot be faulted because the angle was appropriate to the US interests. But must national interest be allowed to determine the global news value of an event? The example is perhaps a case of unintended bias, which an agency claiming to be an international one should in any case have corrected in its copy meant for destinations other than the US.

Distortion resulting from the commercial concept was illustrated by Juvan Somavia, now the Chief of ILO as quoted in a Unesco document prepared for the International Commission for the Study of Communication Problems in 1978. According to him, "The commercial concept of news (has) a built-in systematic discrimination against those events that cannot be sold—which are not news because the controlling market has no interest in them. At the same time, there is a tendency to distort by projecting those aspects of events that make them more marketable." The end product is "an out-of-context message whose content is determined by the logic of the market." News content is thus shaped by preferences that dominate a news organisation. The news report will conform to all the norms of objectivity in a formal way but the impact will be conditioned by obvious and subtle, intended and unconscious bias.

Another important source of bias is the sociopolitical and economic structure within which an agency operates. News judgement will inevitably reflect the values upon which this structure rests. The gatekeepers or copy-tasters have, therefore, become significant in debate on bias in news. The nature of newsgathering and processing operations often gives rise to bias. Different people see the same event variously. It is like the six blind men "looking" at the elephant. Each had his own "perception" depending upon which part of the elephant's body he had felt. But together they did not make an elephant. Similarly, when news has to be gathered from different sources, the final report may still not present a truthful or a full picture.

Foreign News IPI Study

There were several studies on objectivity and bias during the controversial debate on New World Information and Communication Order (NWICO) in 1970s and 1980s. But in the 1953 International Press Institute[6] (IPI) study on News Flow, which was by the press and for the press, there are some views, assessments and advice about foreign news coverage, which may still be relevant. This study looks at issues like bias from a professional angle.

Like the American editors contributing to this study, editors in Western Europe used equivalents for the English words *interpretation, background* or both, to mean the kind of writing that is designed to put the news into its proper perspective. Only a few European editors are opposed to the principle of explaining the significance of a foreign event, but fewer European editors than American ones stress the importance of interpretive writing in the news agency reports. In discussions of the subject of interpretive writing at the London Assembly of the IPI[7] in 1953, it was suggested that newspaper editors in Europe were more accustomed than their American colleagues to the blending of *interpretation* with so-called "straight news" and traditionally more tolerant of the presence of *editorialising* in news stories.

The majority of European editors contributing to a discussion of explanatory writing in foreign coverage accept it as essential. "Facts are limited in value," said a German editor. "The full value of the news can be estimated only when it is seen in its proper perspective; it must be interpreted on the basis of background."

A British editor complained that "a good deal of agency news has to be discarded because there is not sufficient interpretation, and a bald statement of the facts is often incomprehensible to the ordinary reader." About one-fifth of the European editors, questioned on their views of interpretation by the agencies, believe that it should be separated from "straight news." Explanatory writing from the news agencies is useful, some European editors pointed out, even when there is not space to use the stories in question. It educates the editor and his staff; it provides the basis for editorial comment.[8]

However, some European editors who wanted explanatory material could see a risk of bias or editorialising in agency interpretation of foreign news events. There can be, believed a Belgian editor, even "bias in good faith." The minority of editors who say they did not want explanatory material at all were chiefly apprehensive about the possibility of bias or editorialising. "We are skeptical about all interpretation, even our own sometimes, in this age of psychological warfare," said a Dutch editor, typical of a few in each country.

The editor of a London newspaper was against any interpretation by agencies on three counts: (1) every agency is dominated by the nationalistic view of one country; (2) agency interpretation is generally interpretation from anonymous sources; (3) agency interpretation is often interpretation supplied by "small-town newspapermen" who just happen to be "attached to a world-renowned agency."[9] A Swiss editor said he found "that almost every foreign correspondent runs the risk of becoming biased. He is almost bound to lose his capacity to view the whole picture objectively, and he will often give a one-sided picture of political events as seen from his place of assignment."[10] National prejudice, in the eyes of one editor in Belgium, operates in two ways on the correspondent; "If the special correspondent enjoys total liberty of expression, he is often exposed to a dual nationalistic pitfall-prejudice in favour of his own country and of the country in which he is stationed."[11]

The IPI study found that European editors, much more than Americans, believed that improvement was needed in the accuracy of agency dispatches. Some editors also talked of sensationalism even in the reporting of so-called "straight news." Good many examples given of both shortcomings point to the translations of agency reports in the offices of local bureaus and national agencies and some European editors discussed this problem specifically. A French editor said that the copy "teems with inaccuracies" and even gives "opposing meanings" to identical words used in different sentences. Other editors say the problem is one of translating for their readers agency copy written in the perspective of foreigners.[12]

The competition for "exclusives" is taken to account for instances of sensationalism. "Exclusive stories are rare," said the editor of a Paris daily, "and have sometimes to be invented."[13] A French editor says the agency bureaus are "overfeeding" their subscribers and that what newspapers primarily want are digested and tailored reports.[14] A Dutch editor, typical of the others, said that agency correspondents often "write for Americans and not Europeans; sometimes they write for Anglo-Saxons and see Europe from the outside."[15]

The study found that a distinguishing characteristic of Indian press coverage of Western countries was that relatively little of it is covered by Indian journalists.[16] Mr. Robert Trumbull[17], the *New York Times* correspondent based in India, analysing the picture of his country given in the Indian press, found the picture of the United States in the press of India as "bizarre" as the average American's impression of India. "If the average Indian's impression of the United States is formed by the newspapers, he must think of Americans as a race of hustling dollar-grabbers, fantastically efficient in working hours, but obsessed in leisure time with comic books, night clubs, the crueler sports and vicarious sex. The place of cultural activities, religion and family life in the United States gets insignificant publicity, while racism, snobbery and material ambition are overexposed."[18]

Taya Zinkin of the *Manchester Guardian*[19] commented on the picture drawn of the United Kingdom in the press of India in the IPI study. "The coverage of England in the Indian press," Mrs. Zinkin said, "is, in general, of very high quality. The educated Indian understands England; indeed, on many subjects his mind works in the same sort of way as does the English mind . . . (If) Indian reporting on England is lopsided, it is hardly ever distorted."[20] The reporting is sometimes "lopsided" because the Indian attitude toward Britain is partisan in the same way as the attitude of many Britons is partisan. "Some subjects," Mrs. Zinkin said, "are always covered, others never. . . There is a great concentration on 'colonial' and 'semicolonial' issues; even the cold war gets far less space than the Anglo-Iranian Oil Company or the Suez Canal dispute, Mau Mau and Central African Federation. England arouses interest neither as a European nor as an Atlantic, but as an Imperial power; even its place in the Commonwealth is assumed rather than reported."[21]

Exposing Competition

Business rivals always study each other and do not miss opportunity to expose each other to score a point when needed. News agencies are no exception to this phenomenon. Agencies have been charging each other of bias and dependence on governments.

For example, in its early days, United Press was confronted by a cartel composed of the official and semi-official news agencies of European governments. Those "allied agencies" and the Associated Press exchanged news exclusively with each other. Further, they allotted to each member the right to distribute exclusively in certain regions of the world. Only the French agency, Havas, for example, could sell its news in South America. In the Far East, the territory of Reuters, Japanese and Chinese newspapers had to depend on the British agency for their foreign news.

In its competition with the monopolistic alliance, the United Press established two new principles in news agency operation. One was that a news organisation would cover the news of the world independently. The second was that newspapers anywhere could buy this service. As a result, United Press became the first North American news agency to serve newspapers in Europe, South America and the Far East. At the same time, it established its own bureaus in those areas with correspondents instructed to report the news objectively and without government or political bias.[22]

In 1905, Reuters and Havas "repeatedly, and politely but pointedly" told their Russian official counterpart the *St. Petersburg Telegraph Agency* (SPTA or "Vestnik") how to "compress dispatches, and write them for their respective British, French and imperial customers: Vestnik dispatches proved wanting on several counts—speed, accuracy, news values and presentation."[23]

Kent Cooper wrote in *Barriers Down*[24] (1942):

> While many of the European agencies endeavoured to maintain accuracy, they were subject to outside influence in the matter of bias. Moreover, they were really not press associations of the type of the Associated Press, which served only newspapers. They had commercial interests, including banking: news was more or less secondary. Some of the smaller of them paid no attention to news whatever, excepting the "handouts" that came from government offices or the major agencies. Many of these proprietary agencies were under government control and were used for the distribution of propaganda at home and abroad. Some found this line of endeavour much more profitable than the collection and dissemination of ordinary news.

In his autobiography, Kent Cooper wrote, "Reuters was the instrument that through its news reports undertook to weld Britain's dependencies exclusively to the mother country. With the same restraint, it kept all other members of the cartel from sending news to the heavily populated areas of western Pacific, including China and Japan. England's dominance in trade and influence of all these vast territories was supported by pro-British news delivered to them by Reuters. Reuters had done more for England in that respect than either England's great navy, which ruled the seas, or its shipping, which then led in carrying on the commerce of the world."[25]

Michael Nelson[26] prepared an internal paper for Reuters General Manager Gerald Long in 1976, regarding incomes derived from governments of home countries. It calculated that AP and UPI derived, 2.2 and 1.6 percent of their income respectively, from the US government, while Reuters was having it at 2 percent.

The System

Some bias rolls in because of problems and attitudes within the system as J. Herbert Altschull pointed out in the Preface to his book *Agents of Power* (1984)[27]

The time was 1957 and I was working as chief correspondent of the Associated Press in the West German capital of Bonn. The Christian Democratic Union (CDU) of Konrad Adenauer had just been returned to power in an election in which, for the first (and still only) time in German history, a single political party won an absolute majority of the seats in parliament – the Bundestag.

My story ought, I was told (by desk in New York), to emphasise that the Adenauer victory was a "defeat" for the Communists, who had actively campaigned against CDU in favour of the SPD, the Social Democratic opposition. "No," I told the desk" in a return message. "That was an incorrect assessment. The Soviet Union actually wanted Adenauer to win: the Russians were more comfortable dealing with bonafide conservatives (p. x ends) whom they could attack as imperialist warmongers. To deal with SPD leadership, specially at that time, was embarrassing to the Soviet Union because both the Communist Party in the Soviet Union and the SPD in West Germany traced their lineage back to Marx, and differences between them had to be painstakingly (and usually inadequately) justified. The campaign against Adenauer," I told New York, "was designed not to defeat Adenauer but to gain votes for him from anticommunist Germans."

The dialogue then came to an end. Power resided at the other end of the wire, and I was instructed to follow orders and write a story declaring that the Adenauer victory was a defeat for the Communists. I had two choices: to follow orders or to turn in my resignation. My wife and children would likely not favour any romantic heroism, so I swallowed my pride, and convictions, and wrote what I was asked to write. Left to me only was the consolation of requesting that the story be dispatched without a byline. "Keep my name off it," I declared with a touch of bravado.

The story illustrates the nature of news in international setting. It is inevitably reported as *Us* versus *Them,* as the "good guys" versus the "bad guys". The essence of "news" is conflict, and it is difficult for individual journalist to paint the shadings of gray or even to point out where *Us* and *Them* agree and share the same goals and values. The notion that news has a kind of independent character or that stories tell themselves is simply wrong, just as it is incorrect to think that reporters and editors somehow stand apart from the political, economic, social, and cultural system that has shaped them. Conflict between Us and Them is driven into the belief system of journalists as thoroughly as it is into that of their fellow citizens. It is part of their ideology. To imagine that journalists are a breed apart, somehow able to be "objective" about the world around them in ways that others cannot is to believe in a logical absurdity.

Mort Rosenblum is forthright in his book on functioning of AP, "Coups & Earthquakes -Reporting the World for America" which he published when he was editor of the *International Herald Tribune*. He describes how differently an earthquake in Italy will be treated to one in Guatemala:

> But if thousands are killed in Guatemala, the reporting is different. The dead, are vague round numbers. Emphasis is likely to be on American aid for the victims rather than on victims themselves. And the story generally is given less play. This double standard exists partially because Italy is easier to cover than Guatemala and more reporters are easily available. But it is mainly because Italians are seen as individuals with physical and cultural characteristics familiar to Americans ... Guatemalans are seen, on the other hand, only as faceless residents of underdeveloped world. The standard is part of the unwritten but well-developed sliding scale: a hundred Pakistanis off a mountain in a bus make less of a story then three Englishmen drowning in the Thames.[28]

In the internal editorial magazine of Reuters, *Highlights,* for April 1990, Gay Dinmore wrote, "Are we really a 'world information agency', as we rather pompously like to claim? Or at least in its news coverage, is Reuters still very much a Western-based, Western-looking organisation? Whose views do we express? Watching events unfold in Eastern Europe, I could not help but sense sometimes that elation in our reporting has crossed that hazy boundary into glee." Dinmore then turned to coverage of his own territory, China, "the end of seven weeks of celebration of people's power in Peking was a sobering experience." He thought pro-Western bias led to too much optimism about the outcome. "The sources we often quoted—diplomats or otherwise- were as much betrayed by their own wishful thinking as we were. Analyses we wrote at the time, saying this must be end of the Deng Xiaoping era, were at least premature. I wish I could go back and insert a few more 'But on the other hand ...'"[29]

Another problem of the system is major dependence on stringers or part-time correspondents by the news agencies. Sometimes stringers exaggerate or even cook up things for improving chances of use of their copy. On the other hand, the copy from a stringer may be so limited that it has to be improved at desk thousands of miles away by persons who may not have the right background and may therefore introduce mistakes. Once, reporting a train accident in Assam on the eve of new year, Reuters said that the train was overcrowded because people were coming to new Delhi to celebrate the New Year. In fact, people of Assam and other North Eastern States working in Delhi go to their homes for Christmas and New Year. Several stringers and their competitive approach resulted in huge exaggeration in the number of dead in this accident.

Some Real Examples

It is impossible to understand the importance and reality of the bias and distortions of various kinds without looking at few real examples:

Tourists Kidnapping

I had the opportunity to study how the story of kidnapping of foreign tourists in Jammu and Kashmir was covered by Reuters and AP for media outside India. I could get Reuters and AP copy as supplied to media in London on the day of kidnapping, 6 July 1995, through BBC computer which receives from a large number of news agencies in London but could be accessed from terminals at Delhi office. Both, AP and Reuters, used bylines of Indian stringers who had filed basic information. Use of the byline will give credibility to the story and would also pass on the responsibility for anything wrong to the stringer.

Here is the AP copy:

00370 ———

AP-3Bk11HBC-India-Kashmir Kidnapping, 03830Bk11H

3Bk11HBC-India-Kashmir Kidnapping, 03830Bk11H

3Bk11HSoldiers Search for British, U. S. Tourists Kidnapped in OBk11H

Kashmir

3Bk11HBy QAISER MIRZAOBk11H

3Bk11HAssociated Press WriterOBK11H

SRINAGAR, India (AP)—Hundreds of soldiers fanned out across a mountainous region of Kashmir on Thursday to search for two Americans and two Britons held hostage by separatist militants.

A little-known Muslim rebel group, Al-Faran, said it kidnapped the tourists two days ago to force the Indian government to release six guerrilla commanders from jail, police said.

Several other foreigners hiking with the tourists were freed by the militants Wednesday night and turned over to UN observers in Srinagar, the summer capital of the state, police said.

News reports said the freed captives may have included women children and an elderly man, but that could not be confirmed.

Police were questioning two Kashmiri guides who accompanied the tourists and reported the kidnapping Wednesday night.

It was the third time since June 1994 that Western tourists have been kidnapped by Kashmiri militants in India. All of them were eventually freed unharmed, but one incident involved a shootout and other the murder of a negotiator.

The rebels have been fighting for independence since 1989. More than 11,600 people have died in the conflict in Jammu-Kashmir, the only Muslim-majority state in the mostly Hindu India.

The two Kashmiri guides said that the tourists captured on Tuesday evening were taken hostage at Aroo village, near the tourist town of Pehalgam, 65 km (40 miles) south of Srinagar.

Police identified the two Americans as John Donald and Donald Freid, and the two British nationals as Paul Well and Kelly Megan. Their home towns were not immediately available.

In June 1994, two British tourists were kidnapped near the same place in Jammu-Kashmir and released unharmed 17 days later by Harkat-al Ansar, a little known guerrilla group that wants the state to become part of neighboring Islamic Pakistan.

In October 1994, Kashmir militants kidnapped three British and one American tourists in New Delhi and held them captive for 10 days. They were freed during a predawn shootout with Indian police that left two policemen and one of the kidnappers dead.

And here is the Reuters copy of the same story on the same day:

520 (RWS) DEL000243

BC-KSHMIR-TOURISTS 2NDLD (PVS LONDON)

Kashmir militants kidnap British, U. S. tourists

(Changing dateline, updating with details)

By Ashok Pahalwan

JAMMU, India, July 6 (Reuter) – A previously unknown militant group has kidnapped four foreign tourists – two Britons and two Americans – in the strife-torn northern Indian state of Jammu and Kashmir, officials said on Thursday.

Officials of the state tourism department told Reuters that the Al Faran group kidnapped seven tourists and their two guides while they were trekking near Pahalgam, some 90 km (60 miles) east of Srinagar, the state's summer capital.

The group is demanding the release of guerrilla leaders captured during a five-year-old revolt in predominantly Hindu India's only Moslem-majority state in which police and hospitals say more than 20,000 people have been killed.

It later freed three tourists – two women and an older man –and two guides, keeping just four, who they identified as Paul Wells and Cathy Manjin from Britain and Americans John Dorrel and Don Freud Hatching.

Relatives said in London that Wells, a 23-year-old photography student, was on a six-week trekking holiday in India.

"They were walking in the Kashmir hills in Indian Kashmir and a military group overran them and took four of them off," a British Foreign office spokesman earlier said in London.

Indian officials said the tourists were on their way to Pahalgam from Baltal, in the foothills of the Zojila peak, the gateway to Buddhist Ladakh region, when they were picked up.

The Press Trust of India (PTI) said the militant group was demanding the release of guerrilla leaders like Master Ahsan Dar, the self-styled commander of the Moslem Mujahideen group, held in a government jail.

It also demanded the withdrawal of all cases against Javed Ahmed Mir, the military leaders of the Jammu and Kashmir Liberation Front (JKLF) freed on parole by the government as part of plans to revive a political process, PTI said.

India says it plans to hold elections by the end of the year for a new Jammu and Kashmir state assembly, which was dismissed shortly after the rebellion broke out in Kashmir in January, 1990 and the state was placed under direct rule from Delhi.

India rules two-thirds of Kashmir and Pakistan the rest of a region over which the two countries have fought two of their three wars since their independence from Britain in 1947.

Some of the many militant groups fighting India rule of the Himalayan region have kidnapped Indian officials and businessmen. Several have been killed.

Foreigners have been seized three times and an Israeli tourist was killed in a bungled hostage taking attempt.

A year ago, the Harkat-ul-Ansar militant group kidnapped the 16-year-old son of British journalist and businessman David Housego and a friend when they were trekking near Pahalgam.

Kim Housego and David Mackie were later released after several Kashmiri groups condemned the kidnapping and appealed to Harkat-ul-Ansar for their early release.

In these reports, the kidnappers and their imprisoned leaders were described as rebels, militants and guerrillas and not as terrorists. This qualifying word would be reserved for World Trade Center bombers or 9/11 perpetrators. As background, AP writes "The rebels have been fighting for independence since 1989. More than 11,600 people have died in the conflict in Jammu-Kashmir, the only Muslim majority state in mostly Hindu India." Similar background by Reuters on the same day for the same story was, "The group is demanding the release of guerrilla leaders captured during a bloody five-year revolt in predominantly Hindu India's only Muslim-majority state in which police and hospitals say more than 20,000 people have been killed."

The figures of dead have such a vast difference and the reports give the wrong impression as if so many people have been killed by Indian forces, while the fact is that the majority of those who have died in Kashmir have been killed by the other side. Both described Kashmir as only Muslim majority state in mostly Hindu India, forgetting that the name of the State is Jammu and Kashmir and it has three regions: Jammu is Hindu majority, Ladakh is Buddhist majority and Kashmir valley is Muslim majority. Also forgetting the fact that India is home to more Muslims than any other country of the world except Indonesia.

Police and hospitals and also PTI have been quoted for credibility but any journalist who knows can easily sense lies and distortions without difficulty. Police and hospitals never give joint figures as the quotes indicated in the reports. If any such data were available, the two agencies would not have given such different figures. Careful analysis of these examples shows how by using background and loaded words bias is built into a story that appears very objective and professional at first glance. However, sitting thousands of miles away, other media organisations will go by what these agencies say and would lend their own credibility to the distortions and bias. The lay consumer of media is thus at a further disadvantage.

Vietnam War Girl

Another interesting example is provided by some stories on Ms. Kim Phuc, which were filed by AP and reproduced worldwide. Examples here are taken as reproduced by the Asian Age, New Delhi. Following is the story put out by the AP on 12 November 1996 from Washington DC:

Girl in Famous Vietnam war photo pleads for peace

By Harry F. Rosenthal

Washington, Nov. 12: The little girl in one of the most famous photographs to come out of Vietnam war is pleading for "real peace, no fighting, and no hostility."

Ms Phan Thi Kim Phuc, whose plight helped turn Americans against the war, made a rare public appearance on Monday, laying a wreath at the Vietnam Veterans Memorial as part of Veterans Day observance.

The picture of Ms. Kim Phuc running naked and terrified down a Vietnamese highway won a Pulitzer Prize for Associated Press photographer Nick Ut. He now works for AP in Los Angeles.

"I have suffered a lot from my physical and emotional pain," Ms. Kim Phuc, now 33, told a hushed crowd of veterans and their families. "Sometimes, I thought I could not live, but god saved my life and gave me faith and hope." Ms. Kim Phuc and her family had taken refuge in a Buddhist pagoda that day, June 8, 1972, when the village of Trang Bang came under a fierce napalm attack from the South Vietnamese. The village, in Tay Ninh province 40 km west of Saigon was considered a Viet Cong stronghold.

The pagoda took a direct hit. Two of Ms. Kim Phuc's brothers died instantly. The jellied gasoline burned the clothes off her body and she ran out of the pagoda with her brother Phan The Ngoc, screaming with pain and fright. He is the one in the left foreground of the picture.

"If I could talk face to face with the pilot who dropped the bomb, I would tell him we cannot change history but we should try to do things for the present and for the future to promote peace," Ms. Kim Phuc said.

Ms. Jan Scruggs, founder of the memorial, nearly wept as she introduced the young woman who is now married, has a child, and lives in Toronto.

She described Ms. Kim Phuc's suffering, "when an American commander ordered South Vietnamese planes" to drop napalm. "Napalm is a very terrible weapon," Ms. Scruggs said. "It burns through the skin down to the bone." Ms. Kim Phuc has had years of skin grafts and still suffers other after effects of her injuries.

The Vietnamese summoned her in 1984 to Ho Chi Minh city to be used in propaganda films. In 1986 she went to Cuba to study pharmacology and met Huy Toan, who became her husband. The two accepted an invitation to spend their honeymoon in Russia and successfully sought asylum as refugees when their jet stopped for fuel in Canada on way back to Cuba.

"I did not think that I could marry nor have any children because of my burns," Ms. Kim Phuc told the audience. "But now I have a wonderful husband, a lovely child and a happy family, thank God." (AP)

Now let us look at another story filed on her by AP from Toronto on 6 June 1997:

Naked little Vietnamese girl forgives, forgets

By David Carry

Toronto, June 6: She's best known to the world as a naked little girl, screaming in pain and terror on a highway in Vietnam. She looks so different now, a proud mother trading grins with her 3-year-old son.

On June 8, 1972, Ms. Phan Thi Kim Phuc and her family had taken refuge in a Buddhist pagoda when their village was hit by Napalm bombs dropped by South Vietnamese warplanes acting on US orders. One bomb struck the pagoda killing two of Ms. Kim Phuc's brothers and setting her clothes on fire. Ripping the cloths off, she ran down the road.

The photograph of the nine-year-old girl fleeing in agony won a Pulitzer Prize for Associated Press photographer Nick Ut and helped turn American public opinion against the war.

Though that photograph remains one of the most indelible images of war, Kim Phuc, who now lives in Toronto with her husband and son, has committed herself to preaching forgiveness.

"Even though I suffered physically and emotionally, I'm happy, because I'm living without hatred," she said in an interview.

Her life has taken several twists since the attack on her village of Trang Bang.

In 1984, Communist officials summoned her to Ho Chi Minh city to be used in propaganda films. In 1986 she went to Cuba to study pharmacology and met Huy Toan, who became her husband.

The two accepted an invitation to spend their honeymoon in Russia and successfully sought asylum as refugees in 1992 when their jet stopped for fuel in Canada on way back to Cuba.

They lived on welfare for two years, but now are making do with Huy Toan's earnings as counselor for handicapped adults. A book project is in the works and Kim Phuc is an active member of a Baptist church. She is expecting a second child in August, and for now is kept busy her son Thomas, a cheerful boy who speaks Vietnamese, English and a smattering of Spanish. Her parents still live in Trang Bang, and she would like to find the money to bring them to Toronto for a visit.

During her first two years in Canada, Kim Phuc kept a low profile, but she returned to the public eye last year, laying a wreath at the Vietnam Veterans Memorial in Washington a part of Veterans Day observance.

"If I could talk face to face with the pilot who dropped the bomb, I would tell him we cannot change history but we should try to do things for the present and for the future to promote peace," she said then.

After the ceremony, the American who ordered the attack on her village emerged from the crowd, embraced Kim Phuc and sobbed, "I'm so sorry."

"It's all right," she told John Plummer. "I forgive, I forgive." (AP)

When we look at these stories, how do we categorise them? Is it human interest or propaganda or both? The Washington dateline story says she was summoned by Vietnamese "to be used in propaganda films." But successfully seeking asylum as refugees when the jet stopped for fuel in Canada on way back to Cuba is human interest! How easy is it to get asylum in Canada? Or can we call it kidnapping of a Vietnamese propaganda resource and using it for the same purpose by the kidnappers? Or is it a good example of how to manage events for media?

Refugee Market

In 1994, the United News Of India (UNI) used to distribute AP news to its India clients. In a hotel lobby, on September 5 that year, I looked at a UNI teleprinter and found for my class of news agency journalism course what looked to be a good example of bias. Another reading gave me a feeling that the story could be a fake one, just concocted at the desk without real fieldwork. The story was full of quotes, to increase the credibility, but the content was suspect because of the way it was presented. Another evidence that the quotes could be fake was supplied by a journalist from Cape Verde, Fernando Rui Tavares Ortet, who was attending the class. He told the class that the names used in the story were hybrids of names of Cuban patriots, like Jawaharlal Gandhi or Mohandas Nehru for India. Here is the AP story as circulated by UNI:

ZCZC

FN 11

CUBA-REFUGEE MARKET

WANNA BUY A RAFT? PRIVATE ENTERPRISE THRIVES ON HAVANA'S SHORES

HAVANA, SEP 5 (AP) FOR SALE: HOME MADE RAFT OF OIL DRUMS, MAST AND CLOTH SAIL INCLUDED, GUARANTEED TO FLOAT YOU AT LEAST AS FAR AS THE NEAREST U. S. COAST GUARD SHIP. PRICE: 3,000 DOLLARS.

"THIS BOAT WILL NOT ONLY GET YOU TO MIAMI. IT WILL TAKE YOU TO CANADA OR JAPAN AS WELL," SAID ERNESTO AGRAMONTE, SIPPING RUM AND COCA-COLA IN THE SHED OF THE VESSEL HE AND HIS FAMILY SPENT A WEEK BUILDING.

AGRAMONTE'S SALES PITCH MAY BE EXAGGERATED. BUT HE HAS SOMETHING OF A CAPTIVE MARKET: THE THOUSANDS OF CUBANS WHO WOULD RATHER RISK THEIR LIVES AT SEA THAN SUFFER HUNGER AND POVERTY ON THE COMMUNIST ISLAND.

HE IS ONLY ONE OF MANY CUBANS TRYING TO MAKE MONEY OFF THE DAILY EXODUS OF REFUGEES FROM HAVANA'S SHORES. SO FAR THIS YEAR, MORE THAN 31,000 CUBANS HAVE BEEN INTERCEPTED AT SEA.

"THERE IS A LOT OF EXPLOITATION. IT'S CRIMINAL" COMPLAINED RAFTER ANGEL CUSTODIO GONZALEZ. "THE PRICES ARE 20 OR 30 TIMES HIGHER THAN THEY SHOULD BE." MORE AP YJ CB AT 1050

DELHI 11:07

NNNN

ZCZC

FN 12

CUBA-REFUGEE MARKET TWO LAST HAVANA

THESE DAYS A WOODEN OAR FETCHES TWO DOLLARS, A USED INNER TUBE —A STAPLE OF THE MAKESHIFT VESSELS – ABOUT 25 DOLLARS, AND A SIMPLE COMPASS FROM 30 DOLLARS. READY-TO-SAIL RAFTS, SOME EQUIPPED WITH MOTORS, REGULARLY SELL FOR THOUSANDS OF DOLLARS.

AGRAMONTE DECIDED TO SELL HIS RAFT AFTER RELATIVES IN SPAIN ADVISED HIM NOT TO FLEE FOR FEAR COAST GUARD CUTTERS WOULD HAUL HIS FAMILY OFF TO THE U. S. BASE AT GUANTANAMO BAY. AT LEAST IN CUBA, AGRAMONTE SAID, HE COULD STAY IN TOUCH WITH HIS RELATIVES BY TELEPHONE

ABOUT A DOZEN PROSPECTIVE BUYERS SHOWED UP TO ASK AGRAMONTE ABOUT THE RAFT. WOULD BR RAFTERS USUALLY POOL MONEY AND RESOURCES TO GET THE VESSEL THEY NEED, AND TRADE IN AMERICAN DOLLARS BECAUSE THE CUBAN PESO HAS LITTLE VALUE.

"THERE ARE PEOPLE WHO HAVE SOLD THEIR HOUSE, THEIR CLOTHES, EVERYTHING," SAID JUAN BRUNO SOTO, WHO WEARS A COMPASS AROUND HIS NECK AS A GOODLUCK CHARM. "IF I HAVE A BOAT, AND YOU HAVE A COMPASS, WE CAN MAKE A DEAL."

NEARBY, HALF A DOZEN MEN LOUNGED AROUND A 100 DOLLARS RAFT OF THREE INNER TUBES LASHED TOGETHER WITH A "FOR SALE" SIGN ON THE MAST. IGNACIO ZIMENEZ STROLLED UP.

"ANYBODY HERE INTERESTED IN TYRES? THEY ARE NEW—10 DOLLARS" HE SAID. "I'VE GOT BEER AS WELL."

NO TAKERS. UNDISCOURAGED, ZIMENEZ MOVED ON. AP YJ CG AT1055

DELHI 11:07

NNNN

The first character of the story, Ernesto Agramonte, bears the hybrid name of Ignacio Agramonte, the Cuban patriot of 1871 and famous Ernesto "Che" Guevera, and the last character quoted in the story,

Ignacio Jimenez, is the hybrid of Ignacio Agramonte and 1950 patriot Alvare Jimenez. Was it just an effort to find some Cuban names to cook up the story or a deliberate insult to the heroes of Cuban history? But sitting thousands of miles away people will believe it to be a good human-interest story and use it as the UNI staff did.

These examples have been selected because they are so clear and relate to some incidents that are very well known around the world. Local media in most countries used these stories and gave them their own credibility, as most consumers are not aware or bothered about how the news is gathered or how the system is used and manipulated. These examples also show it is easy to claim to be unbiased than being really unbiased.

Those who are responsible for manipulating news have more resources than the reporters who gather the news. How the news agencies and other media function is much better known today than earlier and events are staged to suit the requirements of media. Basic human instinct of laziness exists in reporters as well and this is exploited to the hilt by media managers who are more professional and better paid than the reporters on the beats.

The individual reporter and the agency must constantly ask themselves whether they have found out the other side of the story and whether they are being "used" by anyone. Reporters and editors must be careful while using adjectives and background, where usually bias creeps in unnoticed.

NOTES AND REFERENCES

1. Under the founder Paul Julius Reuter and his son Herbert, objectivity had not been pursued as an avowed high purpose, to be set alongside the initial commitment to accuracy, speed and impartial distribution. It was added as a fourth aim by Roderick Jones who reconstructed Reuters as a private company, Reuters Limited, in 1916, with the help of the British Government, after Herbert Reuter shot himself (18 April 1915). And yet, he contrived objectivity with patriotism. In an interview on 24 October 1915 at the time of his appointment as general manager, Jones said, "At the same time, as a British agency, when we are dealing with international affairs, we naturally see them through British eyes." Objectivity, therefore, did not exclude reporting the news from the British point of view. It only excluded taking sides within the British point of view. (Read, Donald (1999) *The Power of News*, Oxford: Oxford University Press, pp 129-133)

2. Reuter Trust was formed to "safeguard the neutrality and independence of Reuters" in 1941. The preamble to the 1941 agreement of trust referred to the national interest in wartime. "The Press Association and the Newspaper Proprietors Association, recognising the present national emergency and the uncertainties of the future render necessary special precautions to ensure in the national interest that Reuters be so established and consolidated that in every event it shall preserve its position as leading world news agency, have mutually agreed to enter into this agreement." The preamble was omitted in the postwar version. (Read, Donald (1992) *The Power of News*, Oxford: Oxford University Press, p. 244)

3. Cooper, Kent (1959) *Kent Cooper and The Associated Press: An Autobiography*, New York: Random House, p. 11.

4. About AAP at corporate website as seen on 10 April 2005.

5. *A Free and Responsible Press*, Chicago: The University of Chicago Press 1947.

6. International Press Institute (1953) *The Flow of the News,* Zurich.

7. The International Press Institute is a global organisation with members in 115 countries dedicated to the promotion and protection of press freedom and the improvement of the practices of journalism. IPI's membership is made up of editors, media executives and leading journalists working for some of the world's most respected media outlets. It is now headquartered in Vienna.

8. IPI Report, p. 163.

9. IPI Report, p. 164.

10. IPI Report, p. 166.

11. IPI Report, p. 167.

12. IPI Report, p. 165.

13. IPI Report, p. 165.

14. IPI Report, p. 168.

15. IPI Report, p. 167.

16. IPI Report, p. 175.

17. In India since 1947, also responsible for Pakistan, Afghanistan, Ceylon and Nepal.

18. IPI Report, p. 178.

19. Taya Zinkin has been correspondent in Bombay since 1951.

20. IPI Report, p. 183.

21. IPI Report, p. 184.

22. From the UPI chapter in the 1981 edition of the *Scripps-Howard Handbook* — under a section called: "Some Scripps-Howard Institutions."

23. Michael Palmer: *What Makes News*, In: Oliver Boyd-Barrett/Terhi Rantanen (ed.): *The Globalisation of News.* London: Sage 1998, pp. 177-190, 181

24. IPI Report, 20.
25. Cooper, Kent (1959) *Kent Cooper and The Associated Press: An Autobiography*, New York: Random House, p. 263.
26. General Manager of Reuters from 1976 to 1989.
27. J. Herbert Altschull (1984) *Agents of Power: The Role of News Media in Human Affairs*, New York Longman: (IPI Report page xi).
28. Rosenblum, M (1979) *Coups & Earthquakes – Reporting the World for America*, New York: Harper and Row, p. 124.
29. Read, Donald (1999) *The Power of News The History of Reuters*, Oxford: Oxford University Press, pp. 469 – 470.

TECHNOLOGY AND DIVERSIFICATION

One of the strengths of the news agencies has been the use of the latest available communication technologies. Telegraph, telephone, teletype, radio photo and satellite transmission, all expensive technologies of their times, were keeping news agencies in a privileged position. News agencies could bring news and pictures from far-away places, even to small local newspapers that could otherwise never to afford it on their own. With the development in technologies, it was possible for news agencies to develop new services. Some agencies even invested in technologies to be ahead of others, and some entered into joint ventures with technology companies and even forged some strategic alliances with rivals to beat other rivals.

Pigeons and Telegraph

In 1849, Paul Julius Reuter found that the best available technology was a fleet of 45 pigeons that would deliver news and stock prices between Brussels and Germany within two hours, beating the railroad by six hours. He quickly moved on to exploit the potential of telegraphic cables. In 1851, Reuter made use of the first undersea cable between England and France, providing an opportunity for much quicker exchange of both news and stock prices between London and the political and business centres of Europe.

In 1858 the first news from Europe arrived in the US directly by transoceanic cable. Addressed to the AP, the cable contained 42 words summarising five stories in headline form and concluded: "Mutiny being quelled, all India becoming tranquil."

In *History, Theory and Practice of the Electric Telegraph,* by George B. Prescott, published in 1860,[1] (pages 385 – 387) there is description of how the AP functioned:

"Some ten years since the leading journals in New York associated themselves together for the purpose of collecting, and sharing the expense of telegraphing, the most important items of news from all parts of the world. A general agent was appointed to superintend the practical operations of the system to be introduced whose headquarters are in New York. Other agents are located in all the principal cities of the United States and British America, and in some of the European cities. Subsequent to the formation of the New York association, nearly all the daily newspapers in the United States became associated with it. Everything of interest occurring in any part of this country is telegraphed at once to the general office in New York, copies being dropped at all intermediate points on the route, and the other parts of the country being supplied from the central office. The annual expense of the press reports for the United States is about $200,000, of which the New York press pays about one half, and the remainder is divided among the different members of the association in other sections of the country—the larger cities paying the bulk of the expense, while the country papers are only taxed some $30 or $40 per month each. The larger share of the press reports comes over the wires during the night—commencing about 6 p.m. and concluding generally about 1 a.m. but not infrequently, continuing as late as 4 o'clock, and sometimes all night."

Between 1863 – 1866 Reuter continued investing in technology by building telegraph lines. He built a line within Ireland that sped transatlantic news to London eight hours ahead of his rivals and additional lines to improve communications with Continental Europe. AP did not build its own telegraph lines but became, in 1875, the first news organisation in the US to secure a leased telegraph wire. In 1882, Reuters started using the column printer to transmit news electronically to clients replacing the messenger delivery. AP achieved conversion from Morse transmission to teleprinter[2] in 1914. In 1923, Reuters used radio to transmit news internationally in Morse code. By 1939, about 90 percent of Reuters' news was transmitted by short-wave radio. In 1927, Reuters introduced teleprinter to transmit news to London newspapers.

AP Photo Service

The AP in 1927 started a fledgling news picture service. A small band of photographers was assigned to key cities, and pictures were sent from bureau to bureau primarily by train, sometimes by air, from abroad by ocean liner. On rare occasions, the AP would use the AT&T picture transmission system to send a picture of special urgency from its origin to a distribution point. In virtually every instance, however, delivery could take up to 85 hours. When the ocean liner Moro Castle caught fire off the New Jersey coast in 1934, an AP photographer flew over the vessel and took shot after shot of the scene. The negatives were then processed in New York and original negatives sent via airmail to key distribution centers in Chicago and Los Angeles. The pictures were printed and redistributed by train and mail. The AP used to pay train conductors two dollars for delivering packages to messengers. The system in the early 1930s became increasingly adept at handling pictures in this combined air-sea-and-rail network. AP General Manager Kent Cooper, despite opposition and serious technical barriers, adopted the AT&T system to the particular needs of the newspaper industry. The system transmitted pictures from one city to another. But Cooper wanted many cities to receive photos in one transmission, so AP engineers and telephone company operatives went to work. On 1 January 1935 the AP WirePhoto network was born; its first photo was a view of an airplane crash in upstate New York. The AP network grew rapidly from its start of 47 papers in 25 states, and regional networks were developed. During World War II, less than 10 years after the birth of AP WirePhoto, AP staff photographers covered the battle fields of the world and their pictures, handled through pool operations in London and Guam, brought photos home in record time.

When Marines landed on Iwo Jima to fight Japanese forces in February 1945, the AP's WirePhoto service transmitted photographs to newspapers less than a day after AP photographer Joe Rosenthal made them. Rosenthal's now-historic photograph of victorious Marines raising the American flag on Mt. Surabachi was one of a group of pictures he took of the landing, battle and aftermath. The photos were flown to Guam and sent by Navy radio to San Francisco where they were transmitted over AP's WirePhoto service 17 1/2 hours after the Marines landed on Iwo Jima.

"It seems almost incredible that newspapers reporting the first landing on Iwo Jima could simultaneously publish pictures of the landing itself," the *New York Times* said. Systems that received photos without the need for human attention gradually replaced the manual reception of pictures.

The AP Wirephoto success prompted the start of two other wire photo picture networks – Acme (later known as United Press Newspictures) and International News Photos (later to merge with UP and become United Press International).

In Europe, independent networks began providing photos to European newspapers that received AP news. By the 1950s, these networks traded pictures via radio circuits across the Atlantic. In the 1960s, an undersea cable linked the networks. AP made agreements in some areas with national picture agencies; in some areas, AP setup its own picture network built on the US model. By the end of the 1960s, AP sat astride a picture network that was linked solidly from Tokyo, through the US, into Europe and on as far as Moscow. Colour began appearing in the world's newspapers, and AP photographers and darkroom technicians transmitted full colour via wire. New technologies appeared to enhance the quality of the AP WirePhoto network—the most revolutionary was LaserPhoto. Using a photo paper processed with heat instead of chemistry and a laser light source instead of the decades-old lamps system, LaserPhoto brought a new, higher-quality picture to American newspapers. A few years later, AP introduced a second network, LaserPhoto II, which used satellite technology to transmit primarily colour news pictures.

But it was clear that the days of analog transmission—the telephone wire transmission of pictures that had existed since the turn of the century and had served WirePhoto since its inception — were limited. New news technologies had speeded up word transmission, increasing the number of available stories. Analog telephone lines became more and more limiting because of the demand for quicker delivery of more pictures including colour. It took 40 minutes to transmit one colour photo on the analog system. The answer was digital photo transmission.

The process toward better transmission began in the 1970s, and by 1978, AP had introduced a new photo tool, a technical marvel that used digital technology to handle pictures, the AP Electronic Darkroom. The system was used primarily to receive pictures, store them digitally and then retransmit them without loss of quality. Picture enhancement by computer was possible in the darkroom and substantial improvements in photo quality were achieved, especially in the handling of foreign photos. By the late 1980s, electronic darkrooms were at work in New York, Chicago, Washington DC and Los Angeles. Electronic darkrooms were built and assigned to London, Frankfurt and Tokyo, the major international control points for pictures. And soon after, electronic darkrooms were utilised at major stories, such as political conventions and Olympic games.

By the time AP photographers were shooting all pictures in colour, the Leafax scanner was created. A picture-transmitting device that also scanned photographic negatives and created digital pictures, the Leafax took the time-consuming and messy chemical printing out of the news picture distribution workplace.

The final step in a new picture system was yet to come—the design and implementation of a full digital system.

In 1989, AP announced that it would install at member newspaper sites the AP Leaf Picture Desk to receive photos. The old WirePhoto network would be abandoned; the LaserPhoto II network would come down. Full colour pictures were transmitted on a large satellite circuit at speeds of about 15 seconds per photo, as compared to 40 minutes on the analog lines. And because AP was shooting all colour, all photos would be in colour, high-quality colour preserved by the digital system in a way analog could not match.

The new system required significant changes in the way pictures were handled by newspapers' operations departments. Pictures were viewed on a computer screen; there were no more prints. Digitised pictures could be enhanced by newspaper editors to meet the exacting requirements of their individual publishing systems, and passed digitally into the prepress and press rooms.

A team of AP technicians was dispatched to help newspapers wire their newsrooms, and a team of AP trainers showed editors how to operate the equipment. Because colour quality from the wire was now easily controlled, the use of colour increased and papers printed colour as never before. Their own local pictures, likewise, were handled through the system.

Two final steps completed the digital evolution. On 28 January 1996 AP photographers used a new electronic camera, the NC 2000, to shoot the Tempe, Ariz., Super Bowl XXX entirely without film. The camera, a joint development of AP and the Eastman-Kodak Company, made digital pictures on electronic chips built into the camera. Today, photographers at the AP and many of its member newspapers routinely use the next generation of digital cameras, the Nikon-based Kodak DCS

620 and the Canon-based Kodak DCS 520, to shoot high-quality pictures that can be transmitted in seconds.

The development of a digital photo archive in New York was the next step in AP's digital evolution. Today, the AP Photo Archive holds some 700,000 photos. Any user anywhere in the world can enter the archive via the Internet, browse the picture file by utilising search criteria and download selected pictures in a matter of minutes.

The Associated Press operates the most sophisticated picture collection distribution system of any news organisation—the black magic of the classic film and chemical photo process has been replaced by the equally magical process of digital picture handling. There is no place on earth too remote for same-day news picture transmission.

Broadcast Services

The United Press Association grew up as a newspaper service, distributing its dispatches in written form to be set in type. In 1935, however, it became the first news service to make its reports available directly to radio stations. It established a radio newswire for which dispatches were written in a different style so that they could be read into the microphone—for the ear rather than the eye. It started out as UPI Audio in 1958, and became the UPI Radio Network in 1983. The UPI Radio Network, nee UPI Audio, ceased operations at 12:32 PM EDT Thursday, 19 August 1999. UPI's remaining 400 broadcast contracts were sold to the archrival Associated Press.[3]

The United Press started a newsfilm syndication service, UP Movietone[4], in 1948[5], with 20th Century-Fox[6]. Afterwards the United Press acquired the International News Service in 1958, adding the "I" to "UP," that became "UPI Movietone" and later still, UPITN when it was part owned by ITN of UK. Later, with Disney as Worldwide Television News (WTN) agency, it was also finally sold to AP in 1998.

In 1941 nearly 1,000 commercial radio stations operated in the United States. United Press, INS and Transradio Press served limited amounts of news to some. Others received no news service. State or regional copy only made the news agencies' radio wires if it was considered sufficiently important to be of general interest. And most broadcasters didn't gather local news for their own use.

The AP changed that by launching a separate round the-clock-broadcast wire called Circuit 7760. On April 1, 1941, the wire "officially" signed on Atlanta station WSB, and New York's WQXR,

WOR and WNYC. "Specialists" wrote news stories for the wire in a new kind of style meant for the ear.

Just one year after its official launch, AP's broadcast wire was serving more than 200 stations in 120 cities, broadcasters were beginning to gather local news and 110 employees were on the broadcast payroll. In 1947, the AP board of directors elected the first group of radio stations—456 in all—to associate membership.

Throughout the 1950s and 1960s, AP continued to gain broadcast members and in 1974, launched AP Radio Network at their request. It provides hourly newscasts, sportscasts and business programmes to member radio stations and eventually became the first radio network in the world to be delivered via satellite. The same year, AP added an audio service that provides voice feeds and actualities to supplement the broadcast wire. Today the service reaches nearly 1000 AP broadcast members.

By 1979, The Associated Press Broadcast Wire was the single longest leased circuit in the world. The same year, the APTV wire, the first newswire designed specifically for television stations, was introduced. In 1980, AP Radio became the first radio network in the world to be delivered via satellite.

In 1983, the AP moved its broadcast operations from AP's New York headquarters to AP Broadcast News Center in Washington D.C. On 4 May the AP transmitted the first broadcast from its new location.

By 1988, AP's broadcast services outlets reached more than 5,000.

The 1990s have been a decade of explosive growth in AP's radio and television services. AP introduced low-cost newsroom software, AP NewsDesk, designed for radio stations, the first in a series of affordable software products that made member newsrooms more efficient.

AP gave its members the tools to manage the increasing flood of information available on AP wires and other information sources. In 1994, AP NewsCenter, a newsroom system for television stations, was launched. And in 1997, AP introduced ENPS the Electronic News Production System, designed for the British Broadcasting Corporation.

AP also introduced GraphicsBank, the first online archive of television graphics, which serves more than 300 US television stations.

In 1994, the AP launched APTV, an international video news service based in London. APTV in 1998 became APTN—Associated Press Television News—when AP purchased video agency WTN from its parent companies, ABC News of the United States, ITN of Great Britain and Channel 9 of Australia. APTN provides video of the day's top news stories by satellite to major news organisations worldwide from 83 AP bureaus in 67 countries. APTN puts strong emphasis on enterprise journalism and telling the whole story in narrative form at critical moments in different international time zones.

Also in 1994, AP launched AP All News Radio, a 24-hour-a-day fully packaged radio newscast. ANR makes it possible for stations in all market sizes to carry the popular and profitable all-news format. More than 70 radio stations are now ANR affiliates and easily insert local news and advertising into the ANR format.

In 1996, APTV, in a joint venture with Trans World International (TWI), launched SNTV, a sports news video agency. The partnership has claimed market leadership, drawing on the strengths of the world's largest newsgathering organisation and the world's largest independent supplier of sports programming. SNTV currently serves more than 100 broadcasters worldwide.

Satellite and Computers

In 1953, Reuters opened a new listening station at Green End on the outskirts of London. Broadcast monitoring became an increasingly important method of receiving up-to-date information, particularly from Communist countries. In 1962 Reuters sent its first satellite news report to the US via Telstar, making it the first private company to venture into space communications. AP created a large scale news agency CRT (Cathode Ray Tube) news writing and editing system, starting in 1971. AFP used satellites for transmissions from 1st August 1971. AP started satellite transmission of news in 1980, but in 1984, it became the first news organisation to own a satellite transponder. The first video editing system was also introduced in Reuters' New York office in 1973, and journalists used VDUs instead of typewriters to write and transmit news. Reuters also become the first company to use the Intelnet 1 satellite service provided by INTELSAT to transmit news, pictures and market quotations.

The AFP board of directors decided to computerise AFP in October 1973, but it was not until November 1975 that an agreement on computerisation was reached. The Latin-American desk of AFP was the first to be computerised in March 1976. Agora, a databank of AFP news items was launched on 1st January 1981. In AFP, the Hong-Kong desk was computerised on 1 January 1982 and the Asia-Pacific region now has its own headquarters. On 15 October 1984 AFP launched its audio service and on 1 January 1985 its launched the international photo service. From January 1986, AFP started transmitting its services on the Minitel. The Polycom subsidiary was set up and the satellite transmission network implemented. On 1 October 1988, AFP launched its graphics service. In 1991, AP Graphics Bank became the first online graphics archive for television, using standard telephone lines.

Reuters Financial Services

In the 1960s Reuters recognised the need to diversify when commercial TV began to eat into the profits of the national newspaper groups who owned half of it. Reuters started to focus on building electronic financial products to subsidise its unprofitable news arm. In 1964, Reuters acquired Ultronic Systems, a computer company that provided it with links to stock markets in London and New York. Thus in 1964, Reuters pioneered the use of computers to transmit financial data internationally with the launch of its Stockmaster.

The collapse of fixed interest rates after the dismantling of the Bretton Woods agreement and the financial turmoil that followed the oil crises of the Seventies gave Reuters huge leverage as markets depended more on realtime market information. In 1973 the Reuter Monitor Money Rates service started screen-based foreign exchange trading to the world. It enabled trades to display up-to-date rates for currencies on screens, which were till then were depending on telephone and telex. Reuters' 'green screen' Monitor product was a must-have for brokerage houses by the mid-Eighties, and the company's turnover went from £17. 5m to £242m in a 10-year period.

In 1981 the Reuter Monitor Dealing Service was launched enabling dealers in foreign currency to conclude trades over video terminals. This service cut the time of an average transaction from 40 seconds to 2 seconds. In 1986, Reuters acquired Instinet, which was to become world's largest electronic brokerage firm, serving the equities and fixed income markets. Instinet helped clients find the best prices by giving them instant access to global liquidity, enhanced efficiency and greater opportunities to reduce transaction. In 1987, Reuters launched Reuters Equities 2000 quotations service on IDN; the Reuters News Picture terminal, an electronic picture editing system and Pocket Monitor, a mobile financial information service.

In 1992, Reuters launched Dealing 2000, the first international computerised matching service for foreign exchange and GLOBEX, the global after-hours electronic trading system for futures and options. In 1993 it launched Equity Focus, a UK equities service to challenge the London Stock Exchange's traditional product. In 1994: Reuters acquired TIBCO, which became a world leading developer of software for the Internet. Reuters' also launched the interactive business service—Business Briefing—and Reuters Financial Television Service. In 1995, Reuters Greenhouse Fund was set up to invest in hi-tech start-ups, giving Reuters early access to new technologies. In 1996, Reuters launched the 3000 series, a package of Securities, Treasury and Money products. New innovations included access to new databases, a secure email facility, a new multimedia news package and a Netscape browser. The Reuters.com website went live.

Reuters used Microsoft's latest web browser to launch Business Briefing as an Extranet service in 1997.

In 1998, Reuters launched Reuters Mobile providing customers with access to Reuters products via the Internet, PocketReuters, a pager service carrying global 24-hour realtime financial data, and Newsbreaker, a multimedia news-on-demand product. It was the first service of its kind to combine video-led multimedia format with full interactivity. Reuters photographers, principally those covering major sporting events used Wavelan, a new leading edge technology that enables pictures to reach a publication's newsdesk within 5 minutes of being taken.

In 1999, Reuters launched the 3000 Xtra service, the latest generation of 3000 products that used the latest developments in desktop technology and the Internet capabilities. Reuters Inform, the company's first realtime e-commerce information product delivered through the public Internet and Reuters Online Report PLUS providing online daily news, video, text and video content was also launched.

In 2000, Reuters embarked on joint ventures with Multex.com, forming a new company, Multex Investor Europe, with Equant forming Radianz and with Aether Systems forming Sila Communications. In Multex Investor Europe, both companies combined their leading Internet technologies to offer a financial Internet portal for European private investors. Radianz was established with the aim of developing the world's largest Internet Protocol network for financial markets. Sila

Communications provided wireless access to Reuters content and Internet information.

In 2002 Reuters launched Reuters Messaging, a reliable, high-security, high-speed instant messaging service developed specifically for the global financial services industry. Developed by Reuters and Microsoft and more than 30 financial institutions, the service allows financial professionals to communicate instantly with their colleagues and customers.

AFX

On 4 February 1991, AFP launched AFX News, an English-language economic subsidiary. In April 1995, AFP-Direct was launched enabling personalised transmissions of AFP services. In February 2000, ALCATEL and AFP teamed up on Mobile Internet Content. In March 2000, AFP purchased the Financial Times Group's 50% holding in AFX. In September 2000, Rex Features joined ImageForum, and in September 2001, new partners joined for AFP's online image bank service. In February 2002, AFP[7] joined forces with Visiware[8] a leader in interactive TV in a partnership to develop interactive television news services on an international scale.

dpa

The German Press Agency dpa, which could begin operation on 1 September 1950, was not far behind in using technology and diversification. In 1956, an extraordinary shareholders meeting endorsed decision to expand dpa services abroad, and in 1957, the dpa European Service began long wave transmissions. However, the dpa Overseas Service in English transmissions used five short wave channels. In 1958, the dpa Bildfunk picture wire replaced postal distribution with long wave transmission. In 1959 the dpa Spanish Service started. In 1967 the dpa German Service and picture service were transmitting round-the-clock. The Middle Eastern Service in Arabic went on air, the Latin American Service expanded from 6 to 12 hours a day and the English-language service also expanded.

In 1973, the first generation of ERNA (electronically steered news switching installation) was commissioned into service and the dpa journalists began editing texts on computer screens.

In 1979, dpa introduced a standard news item format and the dpa customers are able to receive and process news items on screen. In 1980, dpa European Service began transmitting 24 hours a day. In 1981 the dpa's economic desk began operation. In 1983, Photo Service was equipped with electronic picture desks. In 1984, the dpa Selection Service was introduced after extensive trials so that customers receive tailor-made selection of news items and work began on the dpa Databank.

In 1985, dpa became a partner in founding the EPA European PressPhoto Agency B. V. The Hague/Frankfurt.[9] After almost two decades of documenting the defining moments of recent European history, the European Pressphoto Agency in May 2003 launched its own, independent worldwide picture service.

In 1986, dpa broadcasting services began operation and gms, Global Media Services GmbH, is founded as a dpa subsidiary. In 1988, dpa bought the Globus Kartendienst GmbH and expanded its range of graphic material. Now dpa stopped using partner agencies to help supply its international customers and worldwide coverage is provided exclusively via dpa's own foreign correspondent network.

The year 1989 was eventful when dpa started unrestricted reporting from the German Democratic Republic. dpa and the East German "ADN Allgemeiner Deutscher Nachrichtendienst" Berlin, agreed to cooperate on distribution and technology. Also dpa and five other agencies set up "mecom Medien Communikationsgesellschaft mbH" to undertake satellite transmission of their services.

In 1990 the *Thueringer Allgemeine* newspaper in Erfurt became the first paper in East Germany to subscribe directly to the German Service. By the end of the year, 41 newspapers along with radio stations and television in the new federal states had signed up as customers of the dpa. Setting up of 100 percent dpa subsidiary, dpa-Agenturdienste GmbH, Berlin took charge of activities in eastern Germany. Services were set up in the five new federal states with 14 regional bureaus and a central office in Berlin.

In 1991, dpa acquired a 75 percent holding in the ZB-Fotoagentur Zentralbild GmbH, Berlin. In 1994 dpa increased control of ZB-Fotoagentur Zentralbild GmbH to 100 percent and introduced digital picture transmission via satellite. dpa subsidiary "Global Media Services GmbH took over "news aktuell GmbH", Hamburg. In 1995, dpa Picture Service went to full digital production, using databank-based library.

In 1996, Hamburg operations of the international Spanish Service were transferred to Madrid where the dpa Agencie de Prensa Alemana SL is founded. It produces the Spanish service together with the editorial department already based in Buenos Aires. In 1997 the dpa Agenturdienste GmbH, Berlin was absorbed into dpa as a whole. An editorial department was set up in Nicosia, Cyprus and began producing the dpa international service in Arabic from January 1997. An editorial desk was established in Bangkok to deal with news from Asia. The dpa-MedienServer (MES), a reception system for dpa's Picture Service, dpa-Online, dpa-Graphic and the dpa/RUFA broadcasting services was introduced. Test phase of dpa-Online began in February. April marked the introduction of dpa's rapid picture transmission service, which offers all images in colour. Another milestone was the purchase of RUFA Rundfunk-Nachrichtenagentur GmbH.

In 1999, dpa's German Service and European Service editorial departments were reorganised and a new general/soft news desk was created. A joint venture (dpa share 50 percent) with AFP subsidiary AFX, the dpa-AFX-Wirtschaftsnachrichten GmbH started work on July 1, 1999.

In 2000, dpa's new Berlin central office was inaugurated and a subsidiary dpa-info.com started while dpa-Photo Databank contents were made available via the Internet. International Service in English was restructured and from August 2002, the main editorial desk was based in Cork/Ireland. In 2002, dpa Picture Alliance GmbH was also established to distribute via an Internet portal images provided by dpa-Bilderdienste and other leading photo agencies.

Joint Ventures

Agencies have been looking for ways to expand global reach and diversify portfolio and in this there could be strategic alliances and joint ventures even with the competitors. Here are a few example:

Factiva

Factiva® — a Dow Jones and Reuters company — provides the world's best collection of global information.

Founded in 1999, Factiva®, provides world-class global news and business content to organisations worldwide, including Dow Jones and Reuters newswires and The Wall Street Journal—unduplicated in a single service elsewhere. Factiva offers the only single content solution with multiple-language interfaces and multilingual content covering nearly 9,000 sources from 153 countries in 22 languages.

Factiva's products and services help companies integrate news and business information into their daily workflow to increase organisational intelligence and leverage external and internal content within the knowledge-management function. Factiva's content management and integration services are used by leading organisations around the world.

Built on industry standards and open architecture, Factiva products deliver flexible, extensible, customisable solutions to enable easy integration and use in the enterprise. Editorial and technical consulting, taxonomy application, integration expertise and e-learning programs reflect Factiva's innovative approach to delivering solutions beyond the content.

CNBC

Founded in 1997, CNBC is a service of NBC Universal and Dow Jones, offering audiences in the US, Asia and Europe business-news programming. Dow Jones produces content for business television through its global alliance with NBC Universal, the No. 1 US television network. Dow Jones co-owns with NBC Universal the CNBC television operations in Asia and Europe, and also provides news content to CNBC in the US. Dow Jones has helped make CNBC the leader in business television, breaking major stories and providing up-to-the-minute market information, analysis and interviews. CNBC is available to nearly 207 million households worldwide.

Launched on 12 January 1998 CNBC Europe is produced and broadcast in London, and has 45 bureaus across Europe, the Middle East and Africa, including Berlin, Dublin, Madrid, Moscow, Rome, Zurich, Amman, Jerusalem and Johannesburg. It spans 61 nations across this region and is seen in 85 million households.

Launched on 2 February 1998 CNBC Asia is headquartered in Singapore and has four bureaus: Hong Kong, Sydney, New Delhi and Tokyo. It is seen in 27 countries: American Samoa, Brunei, Cambodia, China, Hong Kong, Indonesia, Macau, Malaysia, Maldives, Palau, Papua New Guinea, the Philippines, Saipan and Guam, Singapore, South Korea, Taiwan, Thailand, Vietnam, Bangladesh, India, Nepal, Pakistan, Sri Lanka, Japan, Taiwan, Australia and New Zealand.

SmartMoney

Launched in 1992, *SmartMoney*, The Wall Street Journal Magazine of Personal Business, is a joint venture of Dow Jones & Company with Hearst Corp. and provides vital personal-finance information and advice to money-wise consumers in the US. It was started to service the need for personal-finance information among the group of professional and managerial Americans who, while affluent and sophisticated, are overworked and overwhelmed. *SmartMoney* promises to answer the tough questions of those seeking clarity in today's confused times. In doing so, it has established a new standard in personal-finance publishing and virtually redefined upscale service journalism. It presents practical ideas for saving, investing, and spending, plus regular coverage of technology, automotive and lifestyle subjects including such areas as upscale travel, fashion, fine wine, music, food and more.

Vedomosti

Founded in 1999, *Vedomosti* (The Record), a joint venture of Dow Jones, Pearson plc and Independent Media, is the independent business newspaper for the new Russia. *Vedomosti*, a Russian-language business daily, is a two-section (front and Companies & Markets) "broadsheet" with 16 pages which employs the resources of more than 2,000 journalists worldwide. *Vedomosti* targets top and middle managers, professionals and entrepreneurs. Its audience represents the top level of society: affluent people in decision-making positions. *Vedomosti* puts a strong emphasis on companies and markets: consumer markets, finance, communications and technologies, oil and gas, industry, Russian and international market data, commodities data, real estate, and career and management.

STOXX

Launched in 1998, STOXX Ltd., a joint venture among Deutsche Boerse AG, Dow Jones and SWX Group, provides and services the Dow Jones STOXX^{SM} indexes, Europe's leading regional equity indexes.

The Dow Jones STOXX^{SM} indexes were launched in February 1998 in advance of the European Monetary Union, the launch of the euro and the creation of the Eurozone on 1 January 1999. The indexes cover the European equity markets in several complementary ways, i.e., by region, by size, by sector, and now also by style.

The design, development and delivery of these indexes ensure that they are investable, tradable and transparent—key factors that underlie their commercial success.

The Dow Jones STOXX^{SM} and Dow Jones Global Indexes methodologies are consistent and, therefore, the indexes from both index families are comparable.

STOXX Ltd., is a joint venture of Deutsche Boerse AG, Dow Jones & Company and SWX Group. Together, these three joint venture partners provide STOXX Ltd., with all the necessary expertise: international credibility, considerable index calculation and equity-market experience, and technological synergies.

F. F. Soucy

Formed in 1963, F. F. Soucy, Inc., and its majority-owned subsidiary, F. F. Soucy Inc. & Partners, Limited Partnership (formed in 1974 with Dow Jones & Company and Rexfor), produce approximately 250,000 metric tons of newsprint and specialty printing paper annually.

Utilising two newsprint machines with the ability to produce both recycled and nonrecycled paper, F. F. Soucy is a division of Brant-Allen Industries, Inc.—a producer of high-quality newsprint suitable for full-colour printing with mills located in both the US and Canada. It is headquartered in Quebec.

AFP has diversified through subsidiaries and joint ventures as well: AFX Financial news; AFP GmbH German language subsidiary Text graphics and Internet products; Sports-Informations-Dienst (SID) German language sports service; Fileas Satellite data broadcasting (with France Cable et Radio, a subsidiary of France Telecom and ParisBourse); Company news, corporate press releases and financial statements in French (with the Agefi financial news company); Inedit Editorial Engineering: integration of information technology for media companies.

AAP Image

Australian Associated Press (AAP), in association with Wildlight Photo Agency[10], brings to corporations and individuals an extensive range of quality Australian images. The launch of this service on the AAP network allows the many users of AAP Image to now acquire the most amazing and poignant images that capture Australia at its finest. AAP Iimage is Australia's leading online image library with more than

800,000 digital images. The archive is a rich and diverse collection of images ranging from creative, celebrity, sport and travel to daily news images.

AAP New Media headlines can be seen on larger than life digital news tickers. These tickers are located at The Channel Seven Sydney Studio in Martin Place, Sydney, and on top of the Young & Jackson hotel on Flinders Street in Melbourne. The news is constantly updated with the latest breaking news headlines, thanks to AAP priority news streaming feed. These news tickers are an addition and also an extension of the Channel Seven website that also displays the very same breaking news headlines. Channel Seven and AAP bring the news to Australians on the move.

Besides the above joint ventures, AAP itself provides some interesting examples of diversification. Thanks to one of the nation's most detailed racing databases, at the punch of a button, AAP can generate race form for any horse racing in Australia and New Zealand. Results, fields, jockeys, betting markets, ratings – AAP supplies them all, along with news coverage from all major metropolitan and regional race meetings. AAP New Media, among several telstra i-mode® sites accessed using an i-mode mobile handset, has three interesting sites: the AAP lottery service, The World Game, and the Urban Cinefile.

PA PR Services

Many agencies in their hunt for revenue have diversified into public relations services. The Press Association of UK offers a wide range of services specifically designed for PR agencies and in-house PR departments. PA's unique position at the centre of the media industry in the UK enables it to provide support for many PR and marketing campaigns and media-based activities. The Internet-based breaking news feed, PA Newsfile provides a continuous news monitoring service to agencies and press offices, keeping them one step ahead of the headlines. More than 1,000 stories a day are transmitted on PA Newsfile - including political, city and home news. Added features include the capacity to submit press releases directly to The Press Association news desk as well as a fully searchable 28-day news archive.

Many PROs also subscribe to the PA Morning Bulletin, a free e-mail service supplying details on the events of the coming day, which are likely to make the news. PA Sportsfile provides an online breaking sports news service for any organisation that needs access to all the latest sports data, news and reports.

PA's press release and picture distribution services – PA Mediapoint and PA Picselect—allow organisations to get their messages and images straight into the newsrooms of the UK's media and beyond and can also host complete virtual pressrooms, carrying text, pictures, audio and video clips. The Press Association distributes press releases directly into editorial newsrooms through the same lines and satellite links as its editorial. This means that PA Mediapoint—news and sport and customers' press releases—can be seen on thousands of editorial screens across the UK. This service has been selected by the government News Network[11] to deliver more than 6,000 releases every year from Government departments, official agencies and the Royal Family. One cannot buy this service direct from PA. Instead, press release distribution companies sell it on PA's behalf. These companies are: PR Newswire[12]; Business Wire[13] and na Europe[14]

PA Broadcasting offers TV interview training as well as studio and crew hire. Its TV and radio studios can connect to anywhere in the world, and camera crews can be booked to cover corporate events on location. Television News Release (TNR), part owned by The Press Association, provides customers with media and marketing services including video and radio news releases, corporate videos, media training, and, the latest initiative, a range of marketing services.

The Press Association has developed a wide range of PR support services designed specifically for the film distribution industry. PA's contract publishing division can produce high-quality promotional features, newspaper supplements and bespoke magazines to assist a media campaign. Promotional supplements containing a variety of content including features, photographs, puzzles, competitions and entertainment listings can be designed and distributed to the press for publication. PA can design, build and host virtual pressrooms to hold any film publicity material from press releases and photographs to downloadable video and audio for use by print, online and broadcast journalists. PA also offers broadcasting services to film clients, including camera crew hire and editing facilities for coverage of launches, interviews, premieres or parties. With links to the BT tower, PA can transmit electronic press kits and other material to broadcasters worldwide and PA can alert every major UK broadcaster to the availability of footage via the PA wire service. PA photographers are available to cover major film premieres and parties. Depending on editorial value, pictures may be transmitted on the PA picture wire. Photographers can also be hired to provide high quality pictorial coverage of any promotional event or press call.

Asia Pulse

But this does not mean this kind of diversification is limited to Europe and US. Formed in 1996, Asia Pulse Pte Ltd is a joint venture company which draws on the resources of Asia's major news and information providers, including: Australian Associated Press (AAP), LKBN ANTARA (Indonesia), Nihon Keizai Shimbun Inc. (Japan), Oman News Agency, Pakistan Press International Information Services Ltd, The Philippines News Agency, The Press Trust of India Ltd, Vietnam News Agency, Xinhua News Agency (People's Republic of China), Yonhap News Agency (South Korea), Central News Agency (Taiwan), Islamic Republic News Agency (Iran) and sources in Malaysia and Singapore. Asia Pulse is the realtime commercial intelligence and news service for the Asian region. If a change in the industry impacts on business, Asia Pulse will cover it in 30 countries and 50 industry categories.

Asia Pulse creates a continuous flow of updated information that gives a competitive advantage in doing business in Asia. It provides an in-depth source for researchers requiring coverage of Asian companies, industries, infrastructure, investments, joint ventures and trade opportunities. Its profiles of key industries such as automotive, construction, iron and steel, oil, coal, gold, banking, information technology, textiles, telecommunications, footwear, beverages, chemicals, consumer goods and tourism are continuously updated as major changes in the industry take place. There are some other products and services, such as the *Asia Pulse Business Etiquette Guide* to help the business traveller understand subtle cultural protocols and avoid common misunderstandings when conducting business in this region.

Then there is AsiaNet news distribution network via 14 Asia-Pacific news agencies and five worldwide affiliates which connects communications professionals managing a multinational audience with delivery channels to international media for their media releases and images. Formed in 1995, the consortium taps into the established infrastructure of its news agency and affiliate backbone to reach over

5000 media outlets across 34 countries and regions. Clients choose a circulation—package, circuit or single-country destination—and the time they wish to distribute their news. Narrow industry-targeted options or broad general news selections are available, with precision delivery guaranteed. Translation services - often handled by agencies' in—house journalists—are provided inclusive, optimising access for companies whose media relations could otherwise be handicapped by language and cultural barriers. Instantaneous, electronic delivery supersedes any geographical and temporal barriers to communication. AsiaNet Members are: Australian Associated Press: AAP MediaNet; United News of Bangladesh (UNB); Xinhua News Agency, N. C. N. Limited (NCN), a wholly owned subsidary of the Xinhua News Agency; Press Trust of India; ANTARA National News Agency (Lembaga Kantor Berita Nasional ANTARA), Indonesia; Kyodo News JBN, Kyodo News PR Wire[15]; BERNAMA PRWire Malaysia Global; The New Zealand Press Association (NZPA); Pakistan Press International (PPI); The Philippines News Agency; Yonhap News Agency, South Korea; InfoQuest Ltd,[16] Thailand; Vietnam News Agency (VNA).

ITAR-TASS

ITAR-TASS has also diversified a lot using latest technologies. The 2004 ITAR-TASS catalogue contains a large number of information products, besides full news service and photo service, to meet different demands of mass media, non-government and state organisations both in Russia and abroad. It gives news round-the-clock in six languages – Russian, English, French, German, Spanish and Arabic. It offers real time news services, bulletins, dossier, references and information on order. Daily volume of transmitted information is about 200 newspaper pages from over 200 correspondents in Russia and abroad.

Here is assortment of different ITAR-TASS products:

ALL NEWS: All News cycle is the main and most complete news wire of ITAR-TASS. It is regularly updated with about 400 daily reports from Russia and the world on domestic and foreign policy, activities of the presidents and bodies of authority, international developments, economy, society, culture, religion, armed forces and combat activities, law enforcement and crime, emergencies and natural calamities, and sport. Available online and in hard copy, round-the-clock in real time. Volume: 600 Kb.

WORLD SERVICE WIRE: In English language, about 200 daily reports, wired online round-the-clock in real time. Volume: 350 Kb. In French, Spanish, German and Arabic languages, 150 daily reports each, Wired online daily from 09:00 to 01:00 hours Moscow time. Volume: 250 Kb.

RUSSIAN NEWS: All news from Russia and about Russia from abroad, about 250 daily reports, Available online and in hard copy. Wired daily in real time. Volume: 375 Kb.

WORLD NEWS: All news from abroad, about 200 daily reports, Available online and in hard copy, wired daily in real time. Volume: 350 Kb.

TOP STORIES: Only most urgent news about important developments in Russia and the world, round-ups of ongoing events, comments and views, almost 50 daily stories online, news and comments wired round-the-clock in real time, round-ups wired at 11:00, 15:00, 19:00 hours Moscow time on business days. Volume: 75 Kb.

MOSCOW NEWS: All news from the capital and the region, about 30 daily reports, wired online round-the-clock and in real time. Volume: 45 Kb.

CIS AND THE BALTIC COUNTRIES NEWS: All news from the Commonwealth of Independent States and the Baltic countries, about 40 daily reports, available online and in hard copy, wired round-the-clock in real time. Volume: 60 Kb.

NEWS FROM AUTHORITIES: The president and his administration, the government and parliament, all bodies of authority and key political events in Russia, 50 daily reports, wired online round-the-clock and in real time. Volume: 75 Kb.

FOREIGN POLICY NEWS: Russian foreign policy activities, about 80 daily reports, statements of foreign ministry officials, official comments and off-record assessments, briefings and press conferences, versions and comments, international cooperation, references and biographies, wired online round-the-clock and in real time. Volume: 120 Kb.

RUSSIAN FEDERAL DISTRICTS: News in regional breakdown, 20 daily reports in each program, available online and in hard copy, wired round-the-clock and in real time. Volume: 20 Kb.

ECONOMIC NEWS: Important business, economic, financial news from Russia and foreign countries, 50 daily reports, wired online round-the-clock and in real time. Volume: 75 Kb.

CULTURE NEWS: 25 daily reports, first nights, shows, festivals, books, cinema, theatre, tournees, pop stars. Based on reports from ITAR-TASS correspondents in Russia, wired online round-the-clock and in real time. Volume: 40 Kb.

RELIGION NEWS: Traditional confessions, state-church relations, charity, religious holidays, public statements of church hierarchs, 10 daily reports, based on reports of ITAR-TASS correspondents in Russia, wired online round-the-clock and in real time. Volume: 15 Kb.

CRIME AND EMERGENCIES: 30 daily reports from the office of the Prosecutor General, the Interior ministry, the Federal Security Service (FSB), statements and comments of top law enforcers, major trials and investigations. Reports on emergency situations, fires, accidents, natural calamities, rescue work, reports of the Emergencies ministry. Based on reports of ITAR-TASS correspondents in Russia, wired online round-the-clock and in real time. Volume: 45 Kb.

AVIATION, SPACE and ARMS NEWS; FIVE CONTINENTS' NEWS-1: Reports from abroad in more detail compared to All News wire. Contains 20 rubrics, including scientific and technical developments, medicine, culture, army and navy, press reviews, etc. 80 daily reports. Available online on business days from 09:00 to 20:00 Moscow time.

INTERNATIONAL EXPRESS INFORMATION: 30 daily reports on political developments abroad, major events, statements by foreign leaders, response to developments, major documents and resolutions of international organisations, summits, conferences and negotiations, changes in governments, brief biographies of politicians, reports on visits of Russian officials abroad and their statements there, comments and forecasts of foreign media, political analysts and experts. Available online on business days from 09:00 to 20:00 Moscow time. Volume: 45 Kb.

ARMY AND SPECIAL FORCES: 25 reports each Tuesday, Russian armed forces, foreign armies, navies, secret services, military hardware and armaments, strategic development guidelines, military doctrines, international military contacts, special operations. Available online. Volume: 40 Kb.

CULTURE: 25 reports every Tuesday, world cultural life, first nights, shows, festivals, books, cinema, theatre, tournees, archaeological discoveries, international cultural ties, elite life, life of pop stars. Based on reports of ITAR-TASS correspondents in Russia. Available online. Volume: 40 Kb.

RELIGION AND SOCIETY: 20 reports every Wednesday, activities of various confessions, traditional and non-traditional confessions, religious holidays, relations between various confessions. Based on reports of ITAR-TASS correspondents in Russia. Available online. Volume: 30 Kb.

SCIENCE AND TECHNOLOGY: 25 reports every Tuesday, latest achievements of the Russian and foreign science, most promising research guidelines, new horizons and hazards for humanity. Available online. Volume: 40 Kb.

MEDICINE: Latest research, achievements and promising guidelines in Russian and world medicine, sanitary and epidemiological situation in Russia and abroad, non-traditional health care. 25 reports every Tuesday. Available online. Volume: 40 Kb.

ECOLOGY: Ecological situation in Russia and abroad, current research, comments and recommendations of ecologists. 20 reports every Wednesday. Available online volume: 30 Kb.

KALEIDOSCOPE: 20 reports each Tuesday and Thursday, records, adventures and mysteries, historic and cultural monuments, natural preserves and parks, useful advice. Available online. Volume: 30 Kb.

HOROSCOPES Eastern: 3 pages every Wednesday. Available online and in hard copy. Volume: 6 Kb. *Business British* 3 pages every Thursday. Available online and in hard copy Volume: 6 Kb.

French: 5 pages a month. Available online and in hard copy. Volume: 10 Kb.

INFORMATION PACKAGES ON ORDER: Information packages on various topics are produced from selected news of daily cycles and databases of ITAR-TASS and its partners. They can also be prepared by ITAR-TASS correspondents in Russia and abroad.

There is separate BUSINESS WIRE and its off-line variant Financial News and a large number of specialised products like: Banks and finances; stock market; fuel and energy news; commodity markets and foreign trade; metallurgy; communications information systems and databases; banking services; etc.

Then there are many daily, weekly and monthly bulletins dealing with different specific subjects like:

CARD-ONLINE (in Russian language): Russian plastic card and travelers' check market. Russian issuers and international payment systems. Bank tariffs and ratings. Review of laws on plastic card market. Analysis of plastic card expansion to the regions. New services of processing companies, technological firms, equipment suppliers. Available online on business days. Volume: 10 reports.

ECOTASS-WEEKLY (in English language): News and analysis of the Russian economic development. Based on ECOTASS-DAILY bulletin. Available online. Volume: 30 pages

PENSION BULLETIN: The state and trends of the pension market. New laws. News from the Pension Fund. Review of state and non-state pension markets. Pension reform in Russia. Quarterly analysis of the Pension Fund activities. Available online and in hard copy twice a month. Volume: 10 pages.

Similarly there is SPORT NEWS wire and specialised packages and then there is PHOTO NEWS. Real-time pictures about major events in Russia and the CIS. About 50 – 100 pictures daily. Portraits of state leaders, political party and public leaders, outstanding sportsmen, cultural workers, etc. Transmitted in the JPEG (*. jpg) format 2048 x 1680 pixels daily and in real time. There is PHOTO ARCHIVE with over one million photos, negatives and slides. The biggest Russian history chronicle fund. Over 160,000 digital photos. Permanent update.

PHOTO SERVICES: Shooting pictures on orders in Russia and the CIS, pictures of visits and other events in Russia. Photo studio for experts and companies interested in photo advertising (65 square meters). Printing up to the 2 x 3 meter size. Reproduction. Developing on E-6 and C-41 processes. International Kodak Q-lab certificate. Negatives from slides and vice versa. Large-sized slides (1 x 2 m) for outside and inside advertisements on the basis of "Duratrans" plastic. Photo accessories and equipment: mini-labs, processors E-6, slide and negative copying facility, printing and developing equipment, etc.

ITAR-TASS: Photo Agency is Russia's oldest agency specializing in photo news. Known as Photochronica TASS for decades, the agency was and remains to be the leader in photo coverage of political, social and cultural life in Russia. The origin of Photochronica TASS dates back to 1926, when, under the Russian Telegraph Agency, then named ROST, there was set up a cliché shop, a small unit providing the national central press with photographs. Gradually the small shop grew into a world photo agency.

ITAR-TASS original graphics and Reuters graphics in Russian language are produced and supplied to clients in Adobe Illustrator format. There is an electronic archive of ITAR-TASS graphics since April 1997 with unique illustrations for retrospective publications with selection on orders.

There is large number of publications based on information gathered from all over the world in shape of reference volumes and reviews.

Distribution of press releases, statements and addresses in Russia and abroad are possible through ITAR-TASS channels, as well as through its partner – PR NEWSWIRE (USA). ITAR-TASS television bureaus are at the largest cities of the world: Washington D.C., New York, Tokyo, London, Beijing, Rome, Teheran, Stockholm, Ankara, Tel Aviv and Prague, ready for partnership.

The ITAR-TASS print shop with five-colour and four-colour printing equipment can produce leaflets, booklets, catalogues, magazines, calendars, posters, and other advertising materials with various finishing options, printing and post-printing services. Also takes up direct mailing in Russia, the CIS and abroad according to ITAR-TASS address base or by the address base of the customer.

It also has the oldest training center in Moscow that offers fast and effective training to foreign languages (any level), Russian (practical literacy), work on a personal computer (all programs), typewriting. ITAR-TASS also runs:

"PUSHKINO" rest house, comfortable rooms, attentive staff, full board, sauna and swimming pool, billiards, sport facilities and children's room, library, convenient drive-in, 37th kilometer of Yaroslavl highway; and

"TASS-CLUB" RUSSIAN CUISINE RESTAURANT: Delicious Russian cuisine, reasonable prices and high service level and a comfortable banquet hall.

Russian News & Information Agency, RIA Novosti: Besides diversity in its main information services has commercial printing, translation and advertising services. It runs a real estate agency, a travel agency, can organise and carry out the video recording of theatre productions and also rents premises of its Cultural Centre.[17]

Problems at Reuters

Diversification may also have some problems. Reuters discovered it after the bust of the dot.com bubble, as it ran into its first loss in its 151-year history in 2002. In 1984, the company floated on the stock market, generating £50m for itself and a windfall for the newspaper groups, which still owned shares. But the financial boom put pressure on the company to drive its products forward technologically. So a policy of growth through acquisition of technology companies was aggressively pursued, with mixed results. Some, such as the purchase of Rich Inc, were a major hit. Rich allowed the company to provide news feeds to multiple hubs and the product swept through the trading floors, helping Reuters to revenues of over £160m a year by the end of the Eighties. Instinet, an equities-trading product that enabled blocks of shares to be traded 'off-market', thus minimising the danger of destabilising share prices, was another huge success.

During the late Eighties and early Nineties, Reuters management was confronting growing threat from a new rival—Bloomberg—set up by former Salomon Brothers broker Michael Bloomberg. The Bloomberg product was initially inferior to Reuters. But it did have one key advantage: it allowed bond traders to refer to historical trades, allowing a degree of price analysis over time that Reuters could not provide. But Reuters' attempts to compete with Bloomberg led to financial disaster and a series of lawsuits.

In 1989, the company hired a former Smith Barney executive, Stephen Levkoff, to devise a bonds analysis database to rival Bloomberg. But the product, released as Decision 2000, was regarded as a technological disaster and cost $10m after Levkoff sued. Another lawsuit, from brokerage house Cantor Fitzgerald, followed over a failed joint venture through which Cantors would provide Reuters with a live feed of US Treasury securities prices. Even worse was to follow with Reuters' next project, code-named 'Armstrong', an ambitious attempt to correct what it had failed to achieve with Decision 2000—fusing realtime market data with legacy information. Armstrong proved to be another huge disaster and cost the company some $20m.

By the time Peter Job took over as chief executive of the company in 1991, Reuters had arguably lost its focus. Job also failed to articulate a coherent plan for Reuters to take on the looming threat of the Internet.

By the time Reuters embraced the Internet in 2000, other information providers had already stepped into the breach. Reuters' approach was haphazard and hampered by slow decision-making. And its project to bring its systems into the Internet age, code-named Gazelle, met with the same fate as Armstrong. Shortly after announcing its Internet investment, the company created Reuterspace, a business division into which it put all its non-core businesses, including TV and business-to-business services.[18]

Such was the strength of the nineties bull market that many of Reuters' fundamental weaknesses were not exposed until after the dotcom crash, by which time Job had been replaced by Tom Glocer in 2001.

Reuters announced on 24 July 2001, alongside the reorganisation, that it intended to save £150m by 2003. As a result,[19] 1,100 members of staff lost their jobs. Reuters saw its share price dive 90 percent, to little over 100 percent, in less than three years. Its problems took a turn for the worse with a dramatic decline in business from customers— primarily cash-strapped investment banks had axed thousands of staff. Leaner banks needed fewer Reuters terminals and services, which convey information about shares, bonds and currencies to city dealers.[20]. With continued sluggishness in financial markets and competition from Bloomberg News and other financial data services, growth remains elusive for Reuters. Tom Glocer, Reuters' chief executive, said sales in the core subscription businesses might not turn positive until 2006.[21] Under Reuters' Fast Forward programme for recovery which is seeing 3,000 job cuts overall, some 200 jobs worldwide, half of this work force now in the US is migrating to Bangalore, with another 200 workers to be recruited locally among Indian graduates. Reuters is following in the footsteps of other British companies such as BT in relocating to India, where English-speaking workers cost a fraction of their British counterparts.[22] The group expects its three-year Fast Forward programme to save £440m by 2006, reducing its workforce from 15,500 to about 13,000.[23] Reuters sold the ORT SAS group, based in Paris, to Coface a subsidiary of Natexis Banques Populaires. The divestment, completed on 31 March, 2004, was part of Reuters aim to reduce non-core holdings and focus on its core businesses under Fast Forward.[24]

This does not, however, mean that there is a full stop to new projects. The Reuters Channel, a video news service to consumers, became the first news service available on a new media centre service launched by the software group Microsoft in the United States in October 2004. The availability of the interactive service in consumers' homes represents a departure for Reuters, which earns some 90 percent of its revenues by providing financial information to investment banks, brokers and currency traders.[25] Earlier Reuters had decided to pull its licensed business content from various websites in order to drive more traffic to its news portal. Dow Jones pulled its news feed from Yahoo Finance, and only gives headlines to Yahoo from The Wall Street Journal's site to drive traffic and paid subscriptions. Conversely, AP Digital jumped into the vacuum with a new expanded business—news service.[26] The battle continues!

On 14 March 2005, CME (Chicago Mercantile Exchange Inc.)[27], the largest US futures exchange and the largest regulated marketplace for foreign exchange (FX), and Reuters launched CME FX on Reuters. The launch of CME FX on Reuters paves the way for more dynamic and efficient markets as the first major linkage between sell-side traders in the interbank FX market and the electronic CME FX futures markets, where hedge funds and other major buy-side participants play a major role. Diversification continues!

For weak national agencies, diversification using new technologies is a generally recommended solution and they can take a leaf out of the experience of the big and more successful ones.

NOTES AND REFERENCES

1. Here is an interesting anecdote on newsgathering by a newspaper in this book. One of the earliest feats, after the extension of the telegraph lines west to Cincinnati, was brought about by the agency of the *New York Herald*, before any regular association of the press was formed in New York. It became known that Mr. Clay would deliver a speech in Lexington, Ky., on the Mexican war, which was then (1847) exciting much public attention. From Lexington to Cincinnati was eighty miles, over which an express had to be run. Horses were placed at every ten miles by the Cincinnati agent. An expert rider was engaged, and a shorthand reporter stationed in Lexington. It was dark by the time they had prepared Mr. Clay's speech. The

expressman, on receiving it, proceeded with it for Cincinnati. The night was dark and rainy, yet he accomplished the trip in eight hours, over a rough, hilly country road. The whole speech was received at the Herald office at an early hour the next morning, although the wires were interrupted for a short time in the night near Pittsburg, in consequence of the limb of a tree having fallen across them. An enterprising operator in the Pittsburg office, finding communication suspended, procured a horse, and rode along the line amidst the darkness and the rain, found the place and the cause of the break, which he repaired, then returned to the office, and finished sending the speech. The expense of forwarding the speech by express and telegraph amounted to about $500.

2. C. F. Carter wrote an interesting article "Within a tick of the news" in *Technical World Magazine*, April 1914 (pages 262 – 264): Fifty years ago, the word "ticker" was coined in a broker's office somewhere, and to the whole United States that name very quickly meant a device which printed hieroglyphics on a strip of paper, the whole unintelligible to the layman. Today the ticker prints its news on a strip of paper about five inches wide, in language that can be understood. To supplement it, messenger boys from the bureau carry bulletins to give more details on the stories which have been summarised and printed on the ticker. The organisation is a wonderfully large and perfect one. Reliability being the fundamental feature, no statement is sent out without verification. Of equal importance is speed. Once a bit of news is secured, the point is to get it to subscribers with the least possible delay. Two editors are always on duty during business hours on the same principle that some ocean liners carry two captains, so that the bridge may never be without the presence of a commander. At the same big desk sit four expert typists who take news over the telephone from reporters. The Stock Exchange man has his own typist who is not permitted to leave his desk even for a moment without calling someone to take his place. For long-distance messages, there are telephone booths equipped with typewriters and a slot through which the typist hands the message, a line or two at a time. From the typewriter, the item goes to the editorial desk where it is summarised and then passed on to the telegraph operator. Instantly, the message is on its way to hundreds of receiving instruments in banks, brokers' offices, newspaper offices, hotels, and elsewhere. The "local staff" for this system of news gathering and news distribution consists of seventy-six reporters, each of whom is a specialist on some one subject. To each of the great railroad systems and each of the leading industrial concerns a man is assigned, whose sole duty it is to study that one property and write about it. European news is supplied by a London company, which is the largest news distributing agency in the world, with correspondents all over England and the continent. For seven hours a day, the news ticker spins out

a moving picture of important events of the world as they occur. The "Street" always knows when anything happens long before it is generally known, because the "Street" is thickly peppered with tickers.

The new ticker is merely a form of the printing telegraph, which has furnished more contributions to the scrap heap than any other invention. While inventors have tinkered at the printing telegraph for more than fifty years, less than five million dollars worth of such machines are in use in the whole world. Most printing telegraph instruments for long-distance transmission are to be found in Europe. The special form for serving individual patrons is also found chiefly in Europe. In London, especially, the news-ticker service is well-developed—financial, sporting, political, and religious items being furnished to various classes who desire special fast service in news reports. The old service from the Stock Exchange was badly handicapped by a poor receiving instrument, but the machine now in use is a complete regeneration of the old device. Instead of weights and springs for motive power as in the first one, storage batteries that need renewal only once in eight days have been substituted. Instead of crow's foot batteries, a three-horsepower generator at the main office supplies the electric current that keeps the system going. Instead of a paper roll that ran out just before the news item you particularly wanted came along, there is a roll that needs renewal but once in nine days. This paper is specially made for the purpose to insure uniform thickness, and absorbent, so that it will take ink readily. Also, the machine has been speeded up to double its former capacity, and its noise has been suppressed. The essential mechanical feature of the present news ticker is a type wheel, bearing on its periphery the letters of the alphabet. The wheel revolves in one direction only. The sending machine has a keyboard like a typewriter with a key for each letter connected with tiny electric motor. The pressure of a key stops all the type wheels on all the receiving instruments at the corresponding letter while a bar presses the paper against the type, thus making the impression. When the key is released, the wheel automatically slides along on its shaft one space. At the end of the line, the printing wheel is thrust back to the left side of the page ready to begin a new line, while at the same instant the paper is pulled up one space. The printed lines are five and one-quarter inches long. The service gives out news to the "Street" where it is most needed, for without an up-to-the-minute knowledge of what the outside world is doing, rumour is much more likely to affect the sensitive market. The newspapers with their hourly editions do not come often enough. The news must come hotter and faster than these possibly can.

3. Tom Foty, "End of UPI Radio" *Radio World*, IMAS Publishing, 15 September, 1999.

4. In late 1925, William Fox's brother-in-law, Jack Leo, ushered Fox into a studio projection room where he found himself watching, and hearing, a caged canary singing, and then, a Chinese man singing while playing a ukulele. The new method involved a photographic recording of the electronic soundwaves themselves and placing the narrow images onto the film beside each frame. For the first time ever, both sight and sound could be recorded together while the camera was rolling on a soundproof stage. Playback required the film passing across a sensor inside the film projector, which then translated the soundwaves' images into electrical impulses that came out through the loudspeaker, like a phonograph or radio speaker. For one million dollars, Fox bought the rights for what become the "Movietone" sound-on-film system. He invested about six million dollars developing the process, building a soundstage in his New York studios at 54th Street and Tenth Avenue. Fox research labs worked on cleanly recording sounds in the field, too. By spring 1926, Fox witnessed a talking picture of a Jersey Central railroad, train screeching past him with its whistle wailing for all the world to hear. The Warners beat Fox to market with the first talkie, *The Jazz Singer*. Fox replied with the first talking newsreels for the news "Fox Movietone News."

5. On 16 February 1948 - NBC-TV aired its first nightly newscast, "The Camel Newsreel Theatre," which consisted of Fox Movietone newsreels.

6. In 1935 Fox Film, Fox Theaters and Twentieth Century merged as Twentieth Century-Fox.

7. AFP's 1,200 reporters, 200 photo-reporters and 2,000 stringers based in 165 countries provide a 24/7 wordwide multilingual and multimedia news coverage. Paris-based AFP produces daily 400,000 to 600,000 words, 700 photos, 50 news graphics, as well as video, sound and multimedia content. Languages used are French, English, German, Spanish, Italian, Portuguese, Arabic, Mandarin Chinese.

8. Visiware creates, develops, markets and manages interactive TV services worldwide: digital program guides, portals and browsers, enriched-TV services, interactive TV ads, home-shopping services, etc. Paris-based Visiware exercises editorial responsibility over two international, interactive game-oriented TV channels: LudiTV (now Playin'TV) and Fox Kids Play (in partnership with Fox Kids Europe).

9. epa was established in 1985, created by Europe's foremost national news and photo agencies just as the landscape of the international news picture industry began to change with new faces replacing old. epa's early shareholders ANP, APA, ANSA, belga, dpa, EFE, KEYSTONE and LUSA are still with it in 2005 and along with newer shareholders pap (the national Polish agency) and (Greek news agency) ANA, continue to provide the

most comprehensive photo coverage of western and central Europe available.

10. Founded in Sydney in 1985, the agency has firmly established itself as one of Australia's leading photo agencies. Wildlight avails a network of photographers of the highest standard for photographic assignments, and offers the resources of international partners in France, Germany, Italy, Japan and the US. Wildlight maintains an archive of 300,000 original colour transparencies and several thousand black and white photographs in formats ranging from 35mm to 6 x 17cm.

11. The GNN is the regional arm of the Government Information and Communication Service (GICS) and serves all the English Regions, Scotland and Wales. It was formerly the regional network of COI Communications and moved to GICS in the Cabinet Office in April 2002, following a recommendation from the COI's five-yearly agency review.

12. Established in 1954, PR Newswire has offices in 14 countries and routinely sends its customers' news to outlets in 135 countries and in 30 languages. Utilising the latest in communications technology, it provides electronic distribution, targeting, measurement, translation and broadcast services on behalf of some 40,000 corporate, government, association, labour, non-profit, and other customers worldwide who seek to reach a variety of critical audience including the news media, the investment community, government decision-makers, and the general public with their up-to-the-minute, full-text news developments. PR Newswire's leading brands include ProfNetSM, eWatch™, Online MEDIAtlas™ and MultiVu™. PR Newswire is a subsidiary of United Business Media plc of London.

13. Business Wire disseminates full-text news announcements from thousands of companies and organisations worldwide (our members) to news media, financial markets, disclosure systems, investors, information websites, databases and other audiences. With more than four decades of experience and leadership, Business Wire enables companies to fulfill the disclosure requirements in many countries, including the US, UK, Canada, France and Germany as well as reach financial audiences around the globe. With access to more than 60 leading news agencies throughout the world, in addition to its own proprietary network technology, Business Wire ensures that news is delivered to audiences in each market via their preferred manner and in their preferred language.

14. *na europe* is the largest and first truly dedicated European newswire service for corporate and marketing communications professionals. A division of news aktuell, the distribution arm of dpa, the national news agency in Germany, *na europe* harnesses the power and reach of major national news agencies in the UK, Germany, Switzerland, Austria, Belgium, France, Italy and Spain among others. With more than 25 partner news agencies

worldwide, the service can reach the widest possible spectrum of media across the United States, Latin America, Asia, Africa and the Middle East.

15. Kyodo News PR Wire is the first full-scale press release news agency in Japan, which was established in September 2001 as the affiliate of Kyodo News JBN, to expand the press releases distribution service both for domestic and foreign media.

16. InfoQuest Limited is the leading provider of multi-lingual information management solutions in Thailand—delivering both the infrastructure software that lets companies collect and manage information within the organisation.

17. Catalogue of RIA Novosti, 1995.

18. Mooney B. and Simpson B. (2003) *Breaking News: How the Wheels Came off at Reuters,* Capstone: John Wiley.

19. Dan Milmo, 'Jobs go as Reuters restructures' 2001, *The Guardian*, 24 July.

20. Richard Wachman, 'Hogg to step down from Reuters' City Editor, *The Observer*, 6 April 2003.

21. Eric Pfanner, 'As Reuters struggles, shares fall' *International Herald Tribune*, 28 July 2004.

22. Chris Tryhorn, 'Reuters jobs bound for Bangalore' *The Guardian*, 17 September 2003.

23. Dan Milmo, 'Reuters' US sales mark recovery milestone' media business correspondent, *The Guardian* 22 April 2004.

24. Reuters sold the ORT group to Coface, Reuters Press Release dated 1 April 2004.

25. Jane Martinson, 'Reuters takes its news into the home' media business editor, *The Guardian*, 6 October 2004.

26. Mark Glaser, 'Reuters, AP Follow Different Paths in Search of Revenues' *Online Journalism Review*, 4 May 2004, The University of Southern California.

27. CME, a wholly-owned subsidiary of Chicago Mercantile Exchange Holdings Inc, offers futures and options on futures primarily in four product areas: interest rates, stock indexes, foreign exchange and commodities.

5

THE INTERNET

News agencies were born when carrier pigeons[1] were the fastest and more reliable to carry the news along with telegraph. Now they are facing new types of challenges that have been brought about by the rapidly changing global IT environment, particularly the Internet and broadband communications. These two revolutionary tools have provided diversified formats and means of communications. Increasingly, news agencies are being required to change the roles they play in society from their traditional role of swiftly communicating news and information to the print media to one of providing all forms of news and information including images, graphics and voice feeds to a broad spectrum of users.

Internet is an international network of interconnected computers that enables millions of people to communicate with one another in "cyberspace" (invisible space in which the Internet operates) and to access vast amounts of information from around the world. Unlike online services, which are centrally controlled, the Internet is decentralised by design. Each Internet computer, called a host, is independent. Its operators can choose which Internet services to use and which local services to make available to the global Internet community. There are a variety of ways to access the Internet. Most online services offer access to some Internet services. It is also possible to gain access through a commercial Internet Service Provider (ISP).

The Internet is at once a worldwide[2] broadcasting capability, a mechanism for information dissemination, and a medium for collaboration and interaction between individuals and their computers without regard for geographic location. The invention of the telegraph, telephone, radio, and computer set the stage for this unprecedented integration of capabilities. The Internet represents one of the most successful examples of the benefits of sustained investment and commitment to the research and development of the information infrastructure. It was also in 1972 that the initial "hot" application, electronic mail, was introduced, and the World Wide Web came out of the lab to be available on the Internet at large, in the summer of 1991.

The Internet is a vast data Network and is built for high resilience against failures. It is available throughout the world, almost everywhere. It is relatively cheap for data transport services and is fast compared to traditional connections. However, it is basically insecure, hostile and prone to loss of data and hacking. No "quality of service" is guaranteed in Internet applications. However, Internet connections can replace traditional expensive lines. The Internet impacts on all areas of technology: Base technology such as Networking Systems and Information Architecture, Application Process Interfaces (API), Graphic User Interfaces (GUI), and Information Technology Standards. There is hardly any area in information technology where the Internet has no impact.[3]

As news agencies found the death of distance because of the Internet, there was fear of extinction of news agency business. This business constitutes the very basics of news gathering and distribution. News agencies are first of all providers of news stories and also of pictures, graphics, radio and video reports and other information to media. News agencies generally prepare news products that can be used by other news organisations with little or no modification, and then sell them to other news organisations and non-media subscribers like government departments, corporations, individuals, analysts, etc. Telegraph, telephone, teletype, radio, photo and satellite transmission, all expensive technologies of their times were keeping news agencies in a privileged position. News agencies could bring news and pictures from far away places, even to small local newspapers that otherwise would never be able to afford to do it on their own. The Internet changed all this. Using the Internet, mobile technologies and digital photography, anybody from practically any place on the globe can instantaneously send e-mail, SMS message, a picture or even a video. It is not difficult and it costs less and less. Thus the basic model of news agency business was challenged.

News agencies individually and collectively discussed the Internet and evolved strategies to deal with it. As early as 1999, in the Golden

Jubilee celebrations of Press Trust of India[4], Monique Villa, Director, Development and Business, Agence France-Presse said about the Internet:

> Once upon a time, life used to be simple for those of us who work in the international news business. Then along came the Internet and—virtually overnight—the simple and uncomplicated life we once knew disappeared into cyberspace. We quickly discovered there is a big difference between our traditional clients—that is newspapers, magazines, radio and television—and the portals and web publishers which we know as the New Media."

Giving some details of how AFP is handling the situation, Villa said,

> "For news providers, the Internet is a two-edged sword. We can't afford not to be on the Web, but equally we can't afford to show everything we've got. Or for that matter to give away our product, which is what some Web publishers seem to expect. Thus we have embarked on a policy of packaging news products aimed specifically at Web publishers, and at the same time we are moving quietly into the world of electronic commerce."

In 2001 a workshop on News Agencies in the Era of the Internet organised by Unesco[5] brought together in Amman, Jordan, the representatives of 13 news agencies from Africa, Asia, the Caribbean, Eastern and Central Europe, and the Middle East. These also reflected a broad range of different kinds of news agencies, including both national and regional agencies, those whose ownership was either public or private or a mixture of both. A technical expert[6] pointed out, "Current national agency strengths include valuable accumulative corporate knowledge, years of local experience, and valuable local content. Weaknesses are often to do with technology (related to existing channels of delivery, etc.) and marketing (e.g. poor brand identity and weak market positioning). Opportunities include expansion of market size through introduction of new services, capitalisation of accumulative knowledge, and expansion in channels of delivery. Threats include competition from international news agencies, local portals, and from local private and commercial agencies. Responses include the deployment of a knowledge Management system; survey, categorisation and evaluation of knowledge; expansion of delivery channels (Internet portals, mobile phones), new services and multimedia presentation."[7] The Press Trust of India (PTI) presentation pointed out, "Many agencies took a century to develop brand reputations for authenticity, accuracy and speed. The Internet enables newcomers to construct brand in far less time, in competition against established players."[8]

The Inter Press Service (IPS) presentation[9] assessed the Internet's threats and opportunities for news agencies. Distributing via Internet portals greatly extends the reach of IPS services. IPS, OneWorld and the Panos Institute together are designing InterWorld Radio to distribute news scripts to radio stations for reading directly on the air. In the US the main distribution channel is the Global Information Network (GIN), daily distributing about 70 English and Spanish language reports to over 300 clients, two-thirds of whom are African-American newspapers, and many of whose readers do not have web access. The web also facilitates in-house correspondence among IPS correspondents and bureaus. "On the downside, the Internet has undercut IPS carrier services, which previously generated a third of revenues. Demand for technical services has dwindled since technical advances, deregulation and privatisation slashed the cost of telecommunications and undercut other services. Savings from lower telecommunications rates have been offset by the cost of developing and maintaining websites. Not all clients have high bandwidth access or the appropriate hardware and software, so IPS still has the cost of dedicated data circuits and satellite feeds, in addition to its websites. The Internet intensifies competition and gives direct access to sources once available only through news agency services. Clients resist paying for categories of information that many regard as a social right, particularly when they concern development. Funding from potential donors, an alternative or complementary source of revenue is drying up. Furthermore, the Internet is not ubiquitous. Calls from rural Africa, for example, are expensive. Local connectivity between ISPs is not universal. Calls across Africa must still sometimes be routed via Europe or the U.S.A."

The Caribbean Media Corporation (CMC), evolved from the merger of the commercial operations of the Caribbean News Agency Ltd. (CANA) and the Caribbean Broadcasting Union (CBU), disclosed its plans about Internet. "A new division, the Global Services Division, will tap the potential of the Internet. CMC has two contracts to supply proprietary data to companies, as well as maintaining websites. The CANA online web-site includes top stories from the CANA Wire Service, which draws on Reuters for international news. Other available online services include an electronic news retrieval (dial-up or email) service; a public relations wire service; CANA Radio, including a daily 15-minute news programme; CANABusiness$$ Interactive; and Internet training for government and private sector executives; Caribbean Newspaper Clipping Service; Caribbean News online for websites; and an online photo service for newspapers and websites."[10]

The Internet has moved, within the space of a few years, from being a perceived threat to news agencies, to being a central core of strategies for growth and profit in the case of at least some major and not-so-major agencies. Throughout the world, news media (and other organisations) are developing websites that include news. The news may come from the news media themselves, or it may come from news agencies. But the net effect is one of proliferation of both news sites and news sources, and this presents a major competitive challenge to traditional national news agencies. A significant part of this process is the reductions in cost that the Internet affords for the development of online news services. News becomes cheaper to collect, process and disseminate, all the more so where there is no strict observance of international copyright agreements. Increasingly, therefore, the critical competitive edge is quality: the scope, immediacy, relevance, accessibility of the news that is collected, the availability of multi-media links and background as required, and the clarity and visual attractiveness of display. But most important of all is the realisation that the central business model that has underwritten news agency operations for over one hundred and fifty years, namely the principle of news agencies as 'wholesalers' selling primarily to 'retailers' (though sometimes to other 'wholesalers') is itself under threat. 'Retail' media such as CNN and the BBC are increasingly hawking their news products to other media as well as to retail end-users, individual news consumers. And established news agencies themselves are increasingly looking to the potential growth of direct news provision to news consumers, bypassing the traditional 'retailer' route. The Web allows a new form of publishing and any new form of publishing is in competition with old forms. Agencies who publish directly on the Web are no longer "wholesalers", but are in collision with the business model of their customers.

The very existence of a news agency depends on its ability to prove that it can deliver products that the customers need and are willing to pay for. Customers that depended on news agencies now sit on the bank of a vast lake of information of all kinds and forms—text, photo, audio, video— with a virtual fishing rod in hand that enables—them to chose and pick what they want. In this new environment, news agencies should not look at the new information technologies with fear but turn the situation around by taking advantage of these technologies. In fact, the Internet changes *everything* and it changes *nothing*. Everything because in the way information is produced, processed, delivered and consumed, the Internet is changing every element. And nothing; because basics of good journalism have not changed – clear, crisp, reliable, accurate reporting, good photography, strong television camera work, and, on the top of it all, good editing and analysis.

When the first Internet portals emerged in Poland, their managers wanted to do the news on their own. They hired scores of journalists but were soon confronted with economic realities. It did not take long for them to realise that buying news from Polish Press Agency PAP is definitely a better solution for both sides. Similarly, some mobile telephone companies decided to rely on PAP as a source of news. The Internet also turned out to be a very useful tool in the Polish Press Agency's successful entry into the field of financial and business information. In a relatively short period of four years, PAP has been able to become a major player. When it comes to business news in Poland, PAP economic service is now present in almost all banks and brokerage firms in Poland. As the economy in Poland expands, PAP is planning to develop information products that will address the growing needs of large and medium size companies for information that can strengthen their competitive edge.[11]

Internet has given a big boost for global communications by making compatibility of technical systems much easier. Thanks to the Internet, content is structured and separated from presentation and presentation formats can be generated individually. TCP/IP protocol is a worldwide standard for network access. The Internet has produced platform-independent technologies. The Internet has produced the "wirelessly connect always-on" news consumer. The individual and global access of users to the Internet allows creation of new information products. And many such products from news agencies are available in HTML, XML and TEXT with IPTC topic codes to indicate subject matter. Content is delivered via FTP pull or push, email or via the Web.[12]

The ease with which new technologies allow for transmission of data has already had an impact on the area of press photo. Digital photography, inexpensive transmission, and capacity of the Internet to display pictures online has changed the environment a press agency has been working in into a far more difficult one than ever before. The days of press photo coverage in the form of daily photo service may be over sooner than we can imagine. How long will newspapers' photo editors stay satisfied with a set of pictures selected by an editor sitting at an agency's desk? There is unlimited supply of all kinds of pictures available online, ready at one click of the mouse. They want to be in charge, to make their own selection, and now they can.

On the other hand, the technological development provide new opportunities for press photo departments of news agencies. As vast collections of archive pictures are being gradually digitalised at great expense, news agencies do not need to limit themselves to providing for day-to-day needs of the press. As their pool of digitialised pictures increases, they will have more and more unique pictures from the past to offer to publishing houses, PR agencies and others on a commercial basis. Important developments that can help strengthen the position of the national news agencies can come from close co-operation between them. EPA, the European Pressphoto Agency is an excellent example of such co-operation. Member agencies cover their own territory for others, and all members help finance coverage of countries or places where their photographers are not present. The EPA experience is an excellent example of benefits arriving from close co-operation between several national news agencies. Digital photography allows agencies to illustrate news development on the Web within minutes of a story breaking while agency photo databank offers publishers the flexibility of personally picking pictures from huge archives, via the Internet. The Japanese news agency, Kyodo, also maintains a bilateral mutual technical cooperation exchanges with Xinhua of China and Yonhap of South Korea and has established special methods for mutual use of the photo database using Internet technology.[13]

New products can be created from sub-sets of the agency. For example, AAP (Australia) has the Radio and Television Service (RTV). This service is comprised of a shortened version of the main stories from the Comprehensive Wire written in broadcast style. This service enables radio and television broadcasters to create scripts for their newsreaders or to simply read the service directly to air. There is significant potential to exploit this service further, firstly as a cost-effective way of creating the Internet and digital content, and secondly, to meet the growing demand from newspapers for short summaries of news stories. For example, AAP provides a news Shorts Message Service (SMS) alert service to major news customers, (e.g. editors and news directors) alerting them to the very biggest breaking news stories 24 hours a day. A new area of business is the supply of content to the third generation (3G) mobile phones. AAP has three distinct services to these 3G customers: text and pictures created from AAP's news and picture content; original video material created in AAP studios; content syndicated on behalf of APTN and Australian broadcasters Channel 7 and Channel 10. Complementing these news and information services to mobile phones, AAP also provides a range of SMS products. For example, AAP partners with a TV sports show to provide viewers with regular updates on their favourite sports. AAP news is available on a variety of platforms, including at-seat monitors on Qantas the Australian national airline. Qantas, carries an AAP text news service that is regularly updated during the flight via satellite. AAP news even appears on screens set into restaurant table tops, which is certainly one of the more unusual uses of content.[14]

Even before the Internet databanks turned around, at least one news agency—the Austrian news agency (APA) which was in "red figures" for almost 40 years, from 1947 until 1987—it is paying regular dividends to its owners, as it has developed into an "integrated information company". APA enlarged its business profile by implementing database information as an integrated part of its information products and by combining that with its traditional real time news service. APA has developed an Integrated Information System called AOM – APA OnlineManager, which combines (a) the push service, the general news service, with (b) the pull service, the databases. The agency can now be described as a database-driven company, which enriched the traditional "transmitting" function of a news agency with a second main functionality, the "storage" function. The most advanced and successful products the APA offers in the last few years are electronic press clipping services based on the newspaper content stored in the databases. The articles and other contents, including pictures and videos, are offered in HTML format as well as in full page via FTP.

Since 2003 the APA produces transcripts of Austrian R/TV network-broadcasts including the related video streams, a highly accepted product.[15]

A news agency's business today, according to the International Press Telecommunications Council (IPTC)[16], is adding value to content of various media types, and selling and delivering customised content to various types of customers in the process of news gathering, news distribution and building/providing a news repository. The advent of new technology and new platforms provides a fabulous opportunity for news agencies, to grow new profitable revenues from a completely new group of customers. With it comes the chance to invest in the quality journalism that is at the very heart of news agency business.

With the huge increase in new outlets for news services, well-run news agencies that focus on their core news activity can look to the future with confidence.

Tom Curley, the new president and chief executive officer of The Associated Press, told 82nd annual meeting of the New York Newspaper Publishers Association on 27 August 2003 about his plans. "We are transforming the AP from a wire service, which we've been for 150 years to an interactive database and news network that connects us, and not just connects us technically, but more importantly connects our common business and journalistic goals." Curley said that to increase revenues, the AP must expand its foreign presence, photo services, and revenue from the Internet, while increasing anti-piracy protection from those who would use AP's product without paying for it.[17] The news service would be offering member newspapers tools for customising how they use AP products and greater access to prepackaged news pages covering everything from sports update to financial news. The AP is looking at ways to market photos and news from member newspapers to foreign outlets and other buyers. AP's news operations — from print to broadcast to broadband — would be merged into a single unit that could deliver a multimedia product. "We see eAP as a giant leap forward," he said. John Reid, AP's director of services and technology outlined six elements of eAP: [18]

- *eAP Central:* A common database repository for all AP content.
- *eAssign:* A new system within AP for making, coordinating and tracking assignments; elements can be made available to members and other customers as well.

- *eCategorise:* A software engine to categorise, index and search.
- *ePackage:* Tools for editors to build multimedia packages that are easy to use as part of a newspaper page, website, television presentation or wireless device.
- *eDistribute:* Providing AP content through the Internet that is tightly integrated with customers' systems.
- *eSolutions:* AP's use of all the advancements to provide technology or technical services to customers.

The Japanese government has promoted IT strategy specifically aimed at increasing the number of household users of broadband communications services to 20 million by 2005. In Japan, the number of mobile phone users has been growing by 10 million annually since 1996. And most of the phones are based on the Internet-compatible iMode format. With the spread of wireless LAN access services, mobile phone users now can read or listen to the latest newscasts anytime, anywhere. Mobile phones are now a "lifeline" tool used not only to communicate by voice in a conventional way but to deal with all types of information for daily life, such as pictures, data, news and even personal bank accounts.

News agency Kyodo has developed a new editing/delivery system tailored to needs in the 21st century. It is called HOPE, which stands for Highly Operational Processing and Editing System. This has been an ambitious attempt to update 13 different systems simultaneously. These include the Combined Operation and Control System, the Dissemination Gateway System, the Electronic Editing System, the Picture Image System, the Economic Information System, the Sport System, the Election System, the News Article Search and Retrieval System, the Multimedia Dissemination Server, etc. Apart from this, Kyodo is in the process of developing a new system specifically designed to work in times of disasters such as earthquakes. HOPE system has adopted the NewsML format, which is a news exchange standard, defined by the International Press Telecommunications Council (IPTC). Under the conventional text feed format, computers on the receiving end reject any story once part of the format is changed. But this is not the case with the NewsML format. All format elements are marked with tags and it is quite easy to transform, depending on page layout changes and other purposes. In web applications, NewsML also makes it easy to transform news text into HTML.

Many Kyodo's member newspapers run their own websites and provide news to mobile phone users. According to the Japan Newspaper Publishers & Editors Association, 102 newspapers and news agencies in Japan run a total of 130 Websites. Of these, 59 provide information services; 39 offer information to outside content providers; and 26 make video images available. Kyodo runs its Websites in the Japanese, English and Chinese languages. Kyodo sites are linked to those of member newspapers to provide a news service dubbed Flash 24. Kyodo has also placed digital video recorders at all of its bureaus in Japan and at half its overseas bureaus (21 of 41). Reporters take video images while reporting their news stories and the images taken at regional bureaus are sent to the Tokyo headquarters. They can then be sent on demand to newspapers and broadcasters via broadband services. Kyodo has structured a video image database for constant use by member broadcasters and also puts emphasis on graphics services. Kyodo is making preparations to set up an emergency data center in a place least likely to be hit by an earthquake. This facility will have all necessary equipment to send, by email, news stories, pictures, video images and voices to clients if Tokyo is paralysed by a devastating earthquake.[19]

There are definite savings in communication cost with the use of the Internet. Technological innovations based on the Internet have been found quite useful in agency work. For example, German news agency dpa is using Virtual Private Networks (VPN) technology, which builds a "tunnel" through the Internet. The tunnel is a "point-to-Point" connection through a "firewall" and is secured by sophisticated and standardised encryption. VPN[20] over the Internet is a big money saver and is being used by dpa since 2002 for production sites in Cork (Ireland) Washington D.C. (US), Buenos Aires (Argentine), Madrid (Spain), Bangkok (Thailand), and Cairo (Egypt). It has resulted in savings of over 80 percent compared to conventional leased lines.[21]

There are two ways to profit from the web service or other online news services, One is through Internet advertising and the other is to get content fees for online subscription of data, news articles and photos. In fact, the Internet is a dual world where a large number of very small publishers coexist with a very much smaller number of very large players who take the lion's share of advertising revenue. Because of the widespread perception that information made available on the Internet is free of charge, both newspapers and news agencies even in Japan have not been very successful in making a profit from their Internet-based services.[22]

Some agencies are using their own IT efficiencies to generate revenues. In Austria APA IT is a full subsidiary having qualified technicians and software engineers—a highly profitable enterprise with a share of almost 30 percent in total turnover of the APA group. APA is investing in the development of the "next generation" of its database products, focussed on "relevance search", "similarity search", and "visualisation of results". For that purpose, a completely new, high-powered search engine has been developed by the software engineers of APA IT, which is 10 times faster than TRIP, the most powerful database software.[23]

The Internet is a big copy and paste machine which "invites" to stealing of content, as the content (news) is immediately available by the World Wide Web and machines crawl through the Internet searching for new content. On the Internet, there is a lack of "natural protection" of traditional news publishing as copying and re-purposing can be automated and is inexpensive and it is very difficult to detect and sue violation of copyright. There is no ready-made tool against violation of intellectual property rights. There is no general answer to that question. One possible partial solution is collaboration with customers in Internet projects where news agencies take part as service providers and become part of the (automated) production chain and news agencies as "enabler" for new products, bring parties together.[24]

Copyright is one of the subjects that has attracted attention during the last few years as news agencies around the world are facing a totally new media environment where lot of news is out there for free on the Internet. For news agencies, it is essential to protect the right to get paid by the media companies and non-media companies that are using the news that news agencies invest heavily in collecting, editing and distributing, said Paul Tesselaar, as President of EANA at World Congress of News Agencies in Moscow.[25] Concerning copyright EANA, he said, is in contact with the WIPO in Geneva and the European Union's Commission in Brussels trying to make them understand and respect the interests of news agencies.

Chris Ahearn[26], who represented Reuters at the Moscow Congress, said that protecting both the access to information and the freedom to publish such information as well as protecting the value of content once published is essential to news agency business. This protection (both intellectually and physically) starts with the practice of good journalistic principles, but ends in clear-eyed financial results. "Attempts by third parties to steal, manipulate (whether for political or economic purposes) or to use our content in other unauthorised ways pose significant risk to our brand. Theft and unauthorised usage is not a new problem for any of us. Our agency businesses have been built on creating content for others to use. As such policing and protecting this content has always been important. But the digital world changes the nature and scale of this issue, and calls for a new approach in the way it is managed." About the Internet he said, "There are steps we can take to protect the use of our content. First—Good business practice—Get the contracts right— its essential that business teams understand the copyright challenges posed by emerging technologies and embedded appropriate usage rights. For example, mobile rights. Second—Monitoring (trusting but verifying)—Technologies exist which can help us monitor how and where our content is being used. We use a specially configured web crawling tool that helps us spot unauthorised usage. Legal—serious infringement of copyright, manipulation of imagery or intent and repeated abuses of licenses call for legal action. This is often the last resort, but it is important that when needed we are all prepared to make the strongest defence of our individual and collective rights over our original content."

New businesses like RSiCopyright have also emerged because of this concern for copyright and problems of managing it. In 2003, Reprint Services of St. Paul became RSiCopyright after acquiring the iCopyright Instant Clearance Service customer base and an exclusive worldwide master license from Data Depth Corporation of Seattle. It provides an expansive collection of content marketing tools, custom reprints, digital licensing services and Clip & Copy, an online news clipping service. It helps publishers protect, license and track their intellectual property, and users obtain the proper license to reprint or reuse copyrighted works in the format they desire. Some agencies like AP and UPI have arrangement with RSiCopyright.[27] Some agencies are closely monitoring the development of next-generation DRM (digital rights management) solutions.[28]

Every agency if it is not yet ready with a multimedia offer will have to do it sooner rather than later. At 2004 General Assembly of OANA in

Kuala Lumpur, a declaration to seek a collective commitment to take full advantage of the developments in Information Communication Technology (ICT) was adopted to enhance the flow and exchange of news and information between and among members. In the course of discussions, some delegates mentioned joint efforts are necessary to overcome "digital-divide" problems among news agencies in developing countries. Kyodo has made efforts to cooperate with various Asian news agencies by receiving several IT and system specialists research missions from various news agencies to new headquarters. "We are also now ready to cooperate in exchange of technical experience among news agencies and opinion exchanges in the future in the bilateral relationship with each Asia and Pacific news agency, under the framework of OANA and under the framework of other news agency cooperations such as this forum."[29] Solving common problems by national agencies together seems to make business sense by cost sharing. It can also facilitate co-operation between agencies in other fields. In Europe, cooperation between PAP and DPA is a good example.[30]

The Internet has also created new forms of participatory journalism like bloggers. These interdependent groups connect millions of consumers interested in specific and general news and information. They are mini-publications/editors and "intelligent" sifters of the information overload. To some, they become destinations on the Web and are used as a channel to navigate to relevant content—via links to specific content and other sites posted on the blogging site. These sites are generally run on non-existent budgets and do not represent a direct subscription-based income opportunity for agencies. But they are a key feature of the connected world and represent a powerful audience—one that seeks access to the source material that news agencies provide. Some agencies have opted to embrace evolution and offer readers, bloggers and clients RSS feeds that (whilst allowing for headlines to be exposed) insures that many full stories published to the digital environment can only be legally read in a defined or co-branded environment.

The news agency business that has survived and adapted itself to various communication technologies since the middle of the nineteenth century is in no danger of being extinct. However, the role of news agencies will continue to change and diversify as consumers define the news and information they want, in the ways they want, at the times they want and through the devices that they want. In the world of ever faster and wider flow of information, news agencies can stand out as providers not only fast but reliable and well-organised information. The advent of new technology and new platforms provides a fabulous opportunity for news agencies to grow new profitable revenues from a completely new group of customers. With the huge increase in new outlets for news services, well-run news agencies that focus on their core news activity can look to the future with confidence.

NOTES AND REFERENCES

1. Researchers at Oxford University spent 10 years studying homing pigeons using Global Positioning System (GPS) satellites and were stunned to find the birds often do not navigate by taking bearing from the sun. Instead they fly along motorways, turn at junctions and even go around roundabouts, adding miles to their journeys, British newspapers reported on February 6, 2004.

2. The Internet and the Web are not synonymous. The Internet is a massive network of networks—a networking infrastructure. It connects millions of computers together globally, forming a network in which any computer can communicate with any other computer as long as they are both connected to the Internet.

   Information that travels over the Internet does so via a variety of languages known as protocols.

   World Wide Web, or simply Web, is a way of accessing information over the Internet. It is an information-sharing model that is built on top of the Internet.

   The Web uses the HTTP protocol, only one of the languages spoken over the Internet, to transmit data.

   The Web also utilises browsers, such as Internet Explorer or Netscape, to access web documents called web pages that are linked to each other via hyperlinks. Web documents also contain graphics, sounds, texts and videos. The Web is just one of the ways that information can be disseminated over the Internet. The Internet, not the Web, is also used for email, which relies on SMTP. So the Web is just a portion of the Internet.

3. Klaus Sprick of dpa at World Congress of News Agencies, Moscow, 24 September 2004.

4. Golden Jubilee celebrations of Press Trust of India (March 12 – 13, 1999), Vigyan Bhawan, New Delhi.

5. By the turn of the year 2000, as it was becoming clear that many national news agencies were in crisis, there was a growing concern in Unesco about the gradual commercialisation of news, its implications for the media representation of the poor and rural segments of the society, and for the

ability of these populations to participate in national democratic processes. This concern was reinforced by the collapse of news agencies in some poorer countries and the diminishing of governmental support. To raise attention on this issue, Unesco organised in January 2001 a workshop on News Agencies in the Era of the Internet. Among other issues, this meeting dealt with the Internet challenge and the problem for countries to determine what kind of news collection and distribution they should encourage. It also tried to define the implications of the Internet for competition, quality and accuracy in the supply of news. The report of this workshop can be consulted on the Unesco website. (Unesco Press Release 12 December 2001).

6. Majdi Shawish, Product Manager for Media Solutions, Systems and Electronics Development (SEDCO).

7. Boyd-Barrett, Oliver. (2001) *Final Report of the Workshop on News Agencies in the Era of the Internet*. Paris: Unesco.

8. Vijay S. Satokar, Deputy Editor of Special Services, delivered the PTI presentation.

9. The IPS presentation was delivered by Professor Anthony Giffard of the University of Washington and a member of the IPS board.

10. The CMC presentation was delivered by Richard Cox, Global Services Editor. His was the first of the three presentations under the title *'Should national agencies give way to regional news agencies?'*

11. Speech of Waldemar Siwinski, President of PAP (Poland) at World Congress of News Agencies, Moscow on 24 September 2004.

12. UPI Products on UPI website as seen on 2 February 2005.

13. Ko Yamaguchi, Managing Director of International Department, Kyodo News (Japan) at WCNA, Moscow on 25 September 2004.

14. Clive Marshall, Chief Executive of AAP (Australia) at WCNA, Moscow, 24 September 2004.

15. Wolfgang Vyslozil, General Manager of APA (Austria) at WCNA, Moscow, 24 September 2004.

16. IPTC presentation at World Congress of News Agencies, Moscow (24 – 25 September 2004) by Michael W Steidl, Managing Director. IPTC was founded in 1965 to safeguard the telecommunication interests of the world's press. But as time passed, the focus was adapted to more current needs.

17. Tom Curley promotes the e-AP, 'News Cooperative Faces Cyberage Challenges' by Marc Humbert, Associated Press Writer 27 August 2003.

18. AP press release dated 28 October 2003: Associated Press chief unveils details of 'e-AP' initiative.

19. Ko Yamaguchi, Managing Director of International Department, Kyodo News (Japan) at WCNA, Moscow on 25 September 2004.

20. VPN technology is available in software as "IPSec Client" for users.
21. Klaus Sprick of dpa at World Congress of News Agencies, Moscow, 24 September 2004
22. Ko Yamaguchi, Managing Director of International Department, Kyodo News (Japan) at WCNA, Moscow on 25 September 2004.
23. Wolfgang Vyslozil, General Manager of APA (Austria) at WCNA, Moscow, 24 September 2004.
24. Klaus Sprick, of dpa at World Congress of News Agencies, Moscow, 24 September 2004.
25. Speech of Paul Tesselaar, General Manager of ANP (Netherland) and President of EANA at World Congress of News Agencies in Moscow on 25 September 2004.
26. President of Reuters Media responsible for both News Agency and Consumer News businesses WCNA, Moscow on 25 September 2004.
27. On 3 February 2004 RSiCopyright announced that United Press International will manage reprint and other online content licensing requests with RSiCopyright's Instant Clearance Service and Clip&Copy services. The services will allow readers to easily obtain UPI online content and photographs for Websites, marketing materials and promotional or educational purposes. RSiCopyright's Instant Clearance Service is a web-based content licensing system that will allow UPI to immediately track and fulfill reuse requests.

    RSiCopyright's Clip&Copy service is a free, online news-clipping service that identifies licensable online content. Clip&Copy will offer readers the option to purchase online and print licensing rights for UPI content. By filling out an account profile on www.rsicopyright.com, readers receive news stories that meet their detailed search criteria. RSiCopyright's downstream tracking system will allow UPI to track each request and know which media partner is receiving the request. Because the media partner will be able to license UPI content, the request will generate revenue for both the media partner and UPI.
28. Chris Ahearn, President of Reuters Media, responsible for both News Agency and Consumer News businesses WCNA, Moscow on 25 September 2004.
29. Ko Yamaguchi, Managing Director of International Department, Kyodo News (Japan) at WCNA, Moscow on 25 September 2004.
30. Speech of Waldemar Siwinski, President of PAP (Poland) at World Congress of News Agencies, Moscow on 24 September 2004.

6

CRITICAL ISSUES REVISITED

Reporting truth is the essence of media ethics since ages. In India, one can go back to the ancient Vedas. There were no mass media or Internet then. But there was communication. There was speech. One finds the essence of the Vedas in the Upanishads. And there we find moral pronouncements like *Satyam vada* (speak the truth) *and Satyat na pramaditavyam* (there should be no inadvertence about truth).[1] There is a related statement in Mundaka Upanishad, which has been used in India's national emblem *Satyameva jayate* (Truth alone wins)[2]. In the modern era, under the libertarian concept, the underlying purpose of the media is to discover the truth, to assist in the process of solving social and political problems by presenting all manner of evidence and opinion as the basis for decisions. The essential characteristic of this process was its freedom from government controls or domination. The government, together with its officials, was frequently a party with a direct interest in the outcome of a dispute. Therefore, it should not have the additional advantage of exclusive access to the public, which ultimately makes the decisions. Neither should it have the right or the power to interfere with the presentation of arguments from the opposition. Thus there developed a refinement of the function of the press as a political institution. It was charged with the duty of keeping the government from overstepping its bounds. In the words of Thomas Jefferson, it was to provide that check on the government, which no other institution could provide.[3]

Though initially the news agencies were just a business invented and mastered by clever Jews who made money out of the desire of people to know about events near and far, soon they became powerful tools of nations and empires. One major issue which has cropped up among news agencies from the very beginning was their relationship with the host governments. State-owned agencies were criticised by privates, and among privates the criticism was for taking subsidies from the governments. AP, a newspaper cooperative, and UPI, a private enterprise, both were critical of the European agencies, particularly Reuters and Havas, blaming the respective home governments that subsidised them. Time and again, Reuters complained about the US agencies getting government money for their operations. Together they blamed others for covert or overt control by the government. But either through direct or hidden subsidies, every agency has benefited from its home government; and, in return, has been used.

However, public utterances have been different. At Reuters' Century banquet on 11 July, 1951, in the presence of around 1,100 guests,[4] General Manager of Reuters, Christopher Chancellor said, "I address my final words to the Prime Minister. Some time ago I was sitting in Mr. Kent Cooper's office in New York. Suddenly he said to me: 'Tell me now, does your government really leave you alone? Does it never try to interfere with the news you send abroad?' My answer was as follows: 'I was in charge of Reuters before the present government came into power and I am in charge all through Mr. Attlee's premiership. Never once have I known any pressure or interference with the news that Reuters sent out to the world. (Applause) I recall Mr. Cooper's manifest pleasure when I gave him this answer. Mr. Attlee feels, I believe, just as strongly as Mr. Cooper that governments – all governments – should keep their hands off the news. (Applause) In responding to this toast, the Prime Minster, the Right Honorable Clement R. Attlee, concluded, "I am particularly glad to hear what Mr. Chancellor told us of the conversation with Mr. Kent Cooper. This government has, and in future will, leave Reuters entirely alone." (Applause)[5]

Both Reuters and AP were benefiting from preferential cable tariffs subsidised by their respective governments. When publicly challenged about this, Cooper argued that the United States government, which reduced the cost of news to AP's member newspapers, was subsidising not the news agency, but the newspapers.[6]

News Empires

Lord Palmerston, the British Prime Minister, presented Paul Julius Reuter[7], who had set up on 10 October 1851 his shop in two rooms at I Royal Exchange Buildings, London, at the court of Queen Victoria on

28 March 1861. That was the mark of recognition of the power of news by the British Empire. And even after the end of the empire, the British Government continued to use this power of the news agency Reuters as documented by official biographer of Reuters news agency Donald Read in *Power of News: History of Reuters*. For over a hundred years, Reuters was a national and imperial institution, the news agency of the British Empire, said Read in his introduction[8]. He mentions, "Relations with the British Government remained closer during the 1960s and 1970s than Reuters likes publicly to admit" and discloses some details about negotiations for government payments.

   "Such business, Burgess[9] explained on 9 July 1963 to Leslie Glass of the Foreign Office Information Research Department, was handled within Reuters only by the chairman, general manager, and secretary: 'the files are kept separately.' Glass answered that his department was the only one in the Foreign Office with a separate registry, 'and whose files did not go into the archives.' Burgess expressed himself 'glad to hear this.' The British Government expressly said (21 February 1961) that some of the money on offer was intended to sustain or to start non-economic services. 'Her Majesty's Government also notes your Board's determination to continue to implement the paragraph in your Trust Deed stating: That no effort shall be spared to expand, develop and adapt the business of Reuters in order to maintain in every event its position as the leading world news agency.' This was piquant indeed. The Trust agreement – intended to proclaim independence of Reuters – was being quoted by the Foreign Office in a paragraph relating to payments which amounted to subsidies." By 1967, the Foreign Office was paying Reuters 123,480 pounds per annum on behalf of the overseas departments and 40,000 pounds on behalf of the Central Office of Information (COI). By 1975, Foreign and Commonwealth Office (FCO) and COI increased to 239,000 and 387,000 pounds, respectively.[10]

   Reuters' relationship with the Arab News Agency (ANA) which was subsidised through large subscriptions from the Foreign Office Information Research Department and the BBC has been another interesting case. ANA collected and distributed news for Reuters in the Middle East since 1954. In 1963 its name was changed to Regional News Service (Mid-East) Limited-RNS (ME). On 18 November 1968 there was a meeting between Reuters and the FCO Information

Research Department. "The agreed record (marked secret on every page) explained that Reuters has not yet been able to work out the extent, or annual incidence, of the necessary compensating subsidy, 'diminishing at the end of five years to nil'. In the next paragraph the word 'subvention' took the place of 'subsidy'…In the discussion, it was noted that RNS (ME) would become widely known as 'bought out' by Reuters, and there might be dangers in its continuing to pay a large sum to Reuters for no apparent reasons. An alternative was adroitly found. 'Reuters representative hoped that all the necessary subvention could be channeled through the External Services of the BBC.' These services were themselves funded by the Foreign Office. The idea for this maneuver came from Charles Curran, director general of the BBC." BBC External Services paid to Reuters 20,000 pounds in 1968; 80,000 pounds in 1969 and 1970; 90,000 pounds in 1971 and 100,000 pounds in 1972. Formally, the BBC was paying for the rights 'in such Reuters regional services as are available in London, which the BBC may from time to time require.' From 19 May 1980 the BBC gave up its External Services contract with Reuters entirely. Payment was then running at the rate of 250,000 pounds per annum.[11] With similar covert encouragement by the British Government in 1964, the Regional News Service (Latin America) was formed which from 1964 to 1971 paid generous subscriptions of 25,000 to 30,000 pounds a year to Reuters.[12] Reuters involvement with Agencia Latinoamericana de Informacion (Latin) S.A. also falls in the same category.

Prof. Read was invited by Reuters to write its history in 1987 when Reuters had decided to be a 'supranational' institution and distanced itself from the British Government. Even at the time of floatation of Reuters as a public company in 1984, the Sir Anthony Rawlinson, joint permanent secretary to the Department of Trade and Industry of Her Majesty's Government, lobbied with the insurance companies on grounds of 'public interest'. He wrote on 5 January, 1984, "the proposed share should be made in London, with substantial subscription by British institutions."[13]

Though this was a PR exercise for the "new" Reuters, it confirmed what professionals like Kent Cooper and statesmen like Jawaharlal the Nehru had been saying about Reuters. In fact, Nehru cabinet took a decision that no foreign news agencies should be allowed to directly reach the Indian newspapers; they were required to go through an the

Indian news agency. When PTI was supplying only Reuters as an exception to this rule, the AP was allowed to reach the *Times of India* for a brief period.[14]

In 1942, Kent Cooper, General Manager of the AP published his book, *Barriers Down*.[15] It was full of complaints about how Reuters distorted the American image. Cooper made the grave charge that "international attitudes have developed from the impressions and prejudices aroused by what the news agencies reported. Monopoly made the system of deception work." Cooper even alleged that foreign propaganda carried on through these channels over a hundred years had been one of the causes of wars and these new barriers round Germany had contributed to the cause of Hitler's rise to power and the eventual outbreak of the World War II within the short space of 20 years. Kent Cooper's main complaint was that the Americans were forced to look at the world through the British eyes where as the Americans must look at the world through their own eyes. Indeed, D. R. Mankekar, chairman Press Agency Pool of Non-aligned Countries opened the second meeting of the coordination committee held in Jakarta (Indonesia) on 3 April 1978 by extensively quoting Kent Cooper of AP against Reuters. "I have quoted this interesting episode of 60 years ego to underline the remarkable parallel between the charges leveled by developing countries against the Western media in the 1970s and the American wail against the British news monopoly in the 1920s. Indeed you have to substitute the term, 'USA' with the words, 'the developing countries' and Kent Cooper would appear to be speaking most effectively for the developing countries in the present era."[16]

Significance

But the significance of news agencies was known much before *Barriers Down* or *Power of News*. A document published in December 1938, giving logic for formation of Spanish news agency EFE, has some interesting observations. "The best technique of propaganda is by means of the 'news'; the news is much stronger as a propaganda tool than well-written editorials or signed articles. The news reflects fact and it accomplishes persuasion by subjecting fact 'to different interpretations regarding its meaning, its importance and its occasion.' Hence, the nations have been engaged in battles for 'news domination.' News wars are waged through national news agencies. The news agency, therefore, is no more or no less than a 'national political tool.' "[17] Much before this, Bismarck foiled the attempt of Reuters to buy Wolff in 1869. In June 1869 the Prussian Government signed a secret agreement with the Wolff Bureau, granting it a subsidy and priority for telegrams in return for accepting official control for both its outgoing and incoming news.[18] During World War I, in Germany it was said that the British were using their worldwide cable network to conduct an all-out propaganda campaign and to increasingly pour a flood-of-lies onto the whole world. Reuters was considered "the most powerful weapon in the hands of the English government." By its help alone it had been possible to "arouse anti-German sentiments and even hostility against Germany and its ally Austro-Hungary" among the neutral countries and the US in particular.[19]

Manipulation

On 24 March 2001, the AP put out a story, 'CIA boasts of ability to manipulate news in Bay of Pigs document.' It read : The CIA boasted in a recently declassified section of its propaganda plan for the Bay of Pigs invasion of Cuba 40 years ago that it would be able to place stories about the operation "directly on international wire services." The document said that the placement of news stories on the international wire services "deserves special comment." It said, "For in spite of all elaborate planning to reach the Cuban people and the rest of the world directly, it is the output of the established wire services which most effectively do the job." AP report quoted, "One report on United Press International, for example, will be repeated on nearly every radio station and most of the newspapers of the Caribbean area." The AP report pointed out that the UPI was the only news agency mentioned by name. However, "Because of the importance of this, military planners should be aware of the headquarters' capability of placing items directly on the wire service tickers," the document continued.

In early 1976, there were leaks from the proceedings of the US Congressional Committee on the intelligence activities. William Colby, out-going director of CIA was said to have testified that a number of Reuter correspondents had worked for the CIA by inserting material. Also in a 1981 BBC programme about international intelligence activities, a former CIA office spoke of 'the general assumption of my colleagues that a Reuters journalist is more likely than not to be tied in with British intelligence in some way."[20]

Even this is not new. Kent Cooper, wrote in his autobiography how the Associated Press was used by the US government, "President Wilson and Secretary of State Lancing gave the AP an exclusive, which was a propaganda 'plant'. A German-coded message was intercepted by the British intelligence service, which gave it to President Wilson. It asked Mexico to seek adherence and military support from Japan for a Mexican-Japanese attack on the US from the Southwest if America went to war against Germany. Lancing, in his memoirs written several years later, confirmed that he and Wilson secretly schemed to use the AP solely to incite public demand for a declaration of war. The 'cold-blooded proposition' of Germany's Secretary of Foreign Affairs in one day accomplished a change in sentiment and public opinion that would have required months to accomplish. From the time that telegram was published, the United States entry into the war was assured since it could no longer be doubted that it was desired by the American people from Maine to California and from Michigan to Texas." Kent Cooper's comment on this episode is also revealing, "I never thought that the American Government would ever secretly scheme to plant propaganda for war in the news here at home. I was wrong. In 1912, our own government followed the German lead (Kaiser's government used the Wolff Bureau, its national news agency, by turning news into propaganda to create a jealous rage against anything not German). It was done so effectively that for the first time in history, a Government incited its people by propaganda to ask for a declaration of war before they were ordered headlong into it and became the second in the history successfully to use news to incite the people to demand war."[21] Another important fact about this episode is that the AP agreed not to disclose the source and thus the AP and not the US Government stood sponsor for the accuracy of the fake German message.

War by Media

Since then, the technology and sophistication in news manipulation have increased many fold. In fact, the use of mass media as an additional weapon of war assumed significance during World War I and it reached a level of higher sophistication in World War II. The use of radio, in particular, and news agencies for management of information and disinformation became very significant in the World War II period. The word 'propaganda' assumed its current negative meaning during that period; it was a positive word before that.

Now, war by media is categorised as low intensity warfare alongside subversion, insurgency and psychological sabotage. Propaganda theorists say that in effect the human being should be considered the priority objective in a political war. And conceived as the military target of a guerrilla war, the human being has his most critical point in his mind. Once his mind has been reached, the "political animal" has been defeated, without necessarily receiving bullets. In Central America, the US doctrine of low intensity warfare against Nicaragua was based on the accumulated experience of Germans in World War II, British in Malaya, Kenya and Ireland, the French in Algeria and specially US in Vietnam. Andrew Messing of the National Defense Council of the United States called the region an "accessible laboratory" for the study of low intensity conflict. However, the use of media in Gulf War, Yugoslav War, Afghan War and Iraq War appears to be that of a force multiplier. Coverage of these wars by globalised media like CNN, BBC, AP and Reuters has once again highlighted the importance of media in modern warfare.

The use of propaganda and the disinformation during the Gulf War was widespread and effective in achieving its purpose. The coalition forces succeeded in giving and maintaining the impression that it was a "clean" war in which the use of high-tech weapons resulted in negligible human casualties. For this purpose, wide use was made in press briefings of video films demonstrating the accuracy of the new weapons, military spokesmen avoided discussion on the human cost of the war and a new kind of jargon was introduced (using phrases such as 'collateral damage' for civilian casualties). In spite of the fact that up to 100,000 Iraqi soldiers and unknown number of civilians were killed in the war, there has been little coverage in the media of the unpalatable aspects of the war. There were other uses of media coverage of the Gulf war. It was serving as advertising to promote new weapons. The Patriot missile was advertised and was later sold to the South Koreans who had enough money to pay for the deployment of this new weapon system.

The Kosovo News and Propaganda War published by the International Press Institute, now based in Vienna (September 1999), examines and challenges the media's coverage of the conflict; questions the sources of information; outlines the obstacles that were erected to impede free reporting; asks where and how truth got lost or distorted. In his introduction to this publication, Peter Goff from IPI says, "Officials on both sides pursued their goals of dominating coverage through sheer volume of information, although much of it was inaccurate and of little relevance. Journalists were invited to mounds of propaganda but a dearth of information. Those covering the Nato briefings felt an escalating sense of frustration and irritation that the events were primarily platforms to disseminate sound bites and Nato propaganda aimed at consolidating the alliance. Rhetoric, it was felt, was king and facts the poor relation."

Examples cited in the report: Nato reported on 29 March 1999 that Fehmi Agani and four other well-known Kosovo Albanians had been murdered by Serbian troops. Air Commodore Wilby said the report came from a "very reliable source" in Kosovo, which his department had checked carefully. The reports turned out to be totally false. The "very reliable source" was the London-based Kosovo Information Centre, which is run by Kosovan exiles. They also reported without any basis that Ibrahim Rugova's house had been burned down and that he was in hiding. The Pristina football stadium had been turned into a concentration camp for 100,000 ethnic Albanians; 20 schoolteachers had been killed in front of their pupils; President Slobodan Milosevic's family had fled the country – all false. These false reports, however, received extensive media coverage and helped to strengthen the unity of the 19-member alliance at critical times. It is difficult not to conclude that the alliance used stories – which it knew, were not adequately corroborated and were often coming from sources with a vested interest in intensifying the conflict – to justify the bombings to an unconvinced public. Officials persisted with the line that 'we are not at war with the Yugoslav people,' despite the claims from various sources which say the alliance killed approximately 2,000 civilians and wounded 6,000, destroyed 300 factories, 200 schools and colleges, 20 hospitals, 30 clinics, 60 bridges and 5 airports.

The "embedding" of media persons with US forces is the latest in the use of media in the Iraq war. The public affairs guidance on the embedding of media during possible future operations/deployments in the US Central Command (CENTCOM) area of responsibility were ready on 3 February 2003. The policy paragraph 2.A says, "The Department of Defense (DOD) policy on media coverage of future military operations is that media will have long-term, minimally restrictive access to US air, ground and naval forces through embedding.

Media coverage of any future operation will, to a large extent, shape public perception of the national security environment now and in the years ahead. This holds true of the U. S. public; the public in allied countries whose opinion can affect the durability of our coalition; and publics in countries where we conduct operations whose perceptions of us can affect the cost and duration of our involvement. Our ultimate strategic success in bringing peace and security to this region will come in our long-term commitment to supporting our democratic ideals. We need to tell the factual story—good or bad—before others seed the media with disinformation and distortions, as they most certainly will continue to do. Our people in the field need to tell our story – only commanders can ensure the media get to the story alongside the troops. We must organise for and facilitate access of national and international media to our forces, including those forces engaged in ground operations, with goal of doing so from the start. To accomplish this, we will embed media with our units. These embedded media will live, work and travel as part of the units with which they are embedded to facilitate maximum, in-depth coverage of the US forces in combat and related operations. Commanders and public affairs officers must work together to balance the need for media access with the need for operational security."

The media representative and the organisation he or she represents before embedding sign an agreement. By paragraph 4(a) of this agreement the media employee agrees to "participate in the embedding process and to follow the direction and orders of the Government related to such participation. The media employee further agrees to follow Government regulations. The media employee acknowledges that failure to follow any directions, order, regulation, or ground rules may result in termination of the media employee's participation in the embedding process." In the Iraq war, there were about 500 embedded journalists giving out the US version from different theaters of war and this gave additional support to already established media manipulation practices. It is clear that the news management effort is not to allow media to give the real picture of the war but to give the impression that enough is being told. However, many journalists also became tools of the authorities in making sure that media war was also won by the US-led forces. Because there is so much media today, people tend to believe that they are given more information and they can find the truth. This is not so. The media is managed to the disadvantage of the truth, particularly more so in times of war and to win the war at home and internationally. However, the war is fought in the name of high principles. Naturally media-haves have advantage over the media-have-nots in this area of modern warfare.

The reality is that in all systems different stakeholders, to further their own ends, use the media. Governments are not behind in this race. The Western democracies are no exception. The difference between the Western democracies on one hand and the socialist and totalitarian regimes on the other, in relation to media, has been that of manipulation and direct control. It has been proved that manipulation is more effective than control. Thus the global dominance of Western media serves the interests of their governments and businesses.

NWICO Issues

Many issues that were highlighted during the international debates on New World Information and Communication Order (NWICO) in 1970s and 1980s had a major focus on news agencies. Awareness raised during that period had led to the establishment of many national news agencies where they did not exist. In fact, D. R. Mankekar, Chairman, Press Agency Pool of Non-Aligned Countries, disclosed in a speech, "Indeed I have received a letter from Mr. Stanley M. Swinton, Vice President of the AP expressing support for the Non-aligned News Pool concept and offering to make available AP's more than 125 years of news agency experience to young national agencies on a consultancy basis."[22] It was Cold War period, however, and the US left[23] Unesco, to return[24] after 17 years. In 1989, Unesco abandoned NWICO and has steadfastly resisted attempts to resuscitate it ever since.

The Delhi Declaration as adopted on 12 July 1976 by the plenary session of the ministerial conference of Non-Aligned Countries on Press Agencies Pool noted the following issues:[25]

1. The present global information flows are marked by a serious inadequacy and imbalance. The means of communicating information are concentrated in a few countries. The great majority of countries are reduced to being passive recipients of information which is disseminated from a few centres.

2. This situation perpetuates the colonial era of dependence and domination. It confines judgements and decisions on what should be known, into the hands of a few.

3. The dissemination of information vests at present in the hands of a few agencies located in a few developed countries, and the rest of the peoples of the world are forced to see each other, and even themselves, through the medium of these agencies.

4. Just as political and economic dependence are legacies of the era of colonialism, so is the case of dependence in the field of information, which in turn retards the achievement of political and economic growth.

5. In a situation where the means of information are dominated and monopolised by a few, freedom of information really comes to mean the freedom of these few to propagate information in the manner of their choosing and the virtual denial to the rest of the right to inform and be informed objectively and accurately.

6. Non-aligned countries have, in particular, been the victims of this phenomenon. Their endeavours, individual or collective, for world peace, justice, and for the establishment of an equitable international economic order, have been underplayed or misrepresented by international news media. Their unity has sought to be eroded. Their efforts to safeguard their political and economic independence and stability have even been denigrated.

7. Non-aligned countries have few means, in the present situation, to know about each other, except through the channel of the existing international news media and news centres, their own news media being mainly underdeveloped or undeveloped for want of required resources.

Nobody talks of New World Economic Order or NWICO today, but many of the issues identified above are still relevant, despite vast changes in global polity and major advances in information technology. There has been some progress also, for example, European Alliance of News Agencies (EANA) and Organisation of Asia-Pacific News Agencies (OANA) are doing more effectively what was expected of Non-Aligned News Agencies Pool (NANAP). Despite the digital-divide, the Internet has helped in cutting communication cost which was the major problem for national news agencies of poor countries.

However, President Vladimir Putin, inaugurating the World Congress of News Agencies in 2004, said, "As the workers of news agencies, you transmit realtime information, which is awaited by millions of people. Apart from the printed media and television, this information is welcome in the organisations of state power, diplomatic services, international organisations and financial institutions. In a word, everyone, who needs prompt and truthful reporting and expert analysis of developments, awaits it. Your work exerts direct influence on the globalisation processes that give a boost to markets, accelerate healthy competition, and build up the coordination of international efforts in every sphere of our life. And yet, when we say globalisation, we also mean a common information space. In this sense, the growing inequality of opportunities that different countries have in the field of information policy cannot escape anyone's attention. Far from this, everyone is capable of using the benefits of globalisation with regard to getting objective information these days. We know the reality well. Three-fourths of all the international mass media are concentrated in Europe and North America, the regions the population of which stands at less than a third of the world's total. Hence it is not accidental that the UN, Unesco, and other international forums keep the problem of information imbalances, which really exists, in the focus of their attention."[26]

In Kuala Lumpur at the Thirteenth Summit of the Non-Aligned Movement (February 24-25, 2003) the issue was raised by Indian media activist Suhas Borker[27] who coordinated a statement by 40 media practitioners from NAM countries assembled at Kuala Lumpur to cover the event. It called for, "the struggle for an international information and communication order based on democracy, social justice and pluralism. We are very disturbed at the continuing onslaught of the Western media on the political, economic, social and culture life and values of our citizens and our media institutions. This onslaught by an alien mindset and worldview attempts to enforce a cultural hegemony and uniformity, which is totally antithetical to our paradigm of diversity and pluralism."[28] Prime Minister of Malaysia. Dr Mahathir Bin Mohamad, Chairman NAM took not of it.[29]

Later in November 2005 his successor Abdullah Badawi inaugurated the 6th Conference of Ministers of Information of Non Aligned Countries (COMINAC)[30] and said, "Each country should have the right and freedom to tell its own story from its own perspective, and to have the means to do so," On 22 November 2005 Non Aligned Movement member countries agreed in Kuala Lumpur Declaration on NAM Information and Communication Collaboration to revitalise

Non-Aligned New Agencies Pool by replacing it with a new mechanism called the NAM News Network (NNN).

Post Cold War Issues

The United Nations and Unesco organised a Seminar on Promoting Independent and Pluralistic Arab Media, in Sana'a, Yemen, from 7 – 11 January 1996. The declaration adopted had the following on news agencies: "State-owned broadcasting and news agencies should be granted statutes of journalistic and editorial independence as open public service institutions. Creation of independent news agencies and private and/or community ownership of broadcasting media including rural areas should also be encouraged."

The International Press Institute, Vienna, organised a Round Table on "News Agencies in Transition", in Warsaw, Poland, 29 – 31 August 1996. The Warsaw Declaration on News Agencies adopted at this meeting identified the key issues:

1. Everyone has the right to free access to information needed to exercise their rights and duties as citizens. No laws or regulations should limit this right.

2. News agencies must have the right to gather and distribute information freely. No censorship, direct or indirect, is acceptable; no government authorities at any level, nor economic and other interest groups should interfere with the content of news reports or restrict access to any news source.

3. A free flow of information between news agencies and other media institutions is essential for them to inform the public. Therefore, they must be allowed to act without fear of reprisal, to exchange news with other news agencies and to distribute it to news media, other institutions and subscribers without censorship or any other restraint.

4. All news agencies, regardless of their form of ownership, operating in the same country, should have an equal right to gather, receive and distribute information and to possess facilities and equipment necessary for their operations.

5. No State should restrict the information-gathering and distributing activities of a foreign news agency or of its correspondents. They must enjoy timely and free access to news sources, locations and events.

6. State-owned news agencies must be granted full journalistic independence. Any guidelines for journalistic practices should be developed by the journalists themselves and applied only by the news media organisation, without interference from governments, political parties or other interest groups.

7. Neither government representatives nor any state authority should be allowed to impose an y kind of official judgement on the journalistic performance of a news agency.

8. No news agency or its journalists should be favoured or discriminated against because of what they write or say. They must not be penalised for what they report.

9. News agency journalists should have free access to information from official and other news sources and a right to resist information forced upon them.

10. Authorities should not introduce any legal, technical or tariff constraints which may limit the news agencies' free flow of information and distribution of news. News agencies should have the right to import or export all necessary professional materials and equipment, enabling them to gather and send information. Journalists should be able to obtain visas and accreditation in a timely fashion without any administrative harassment or restrictions.

European Seminar on Promoting Independent and Pluralistic Media held in Sofia, Bulgaria on 10 – 13 September 1997 was organised by the United Nations Department of Public Information (UNDPI) and Unesco. About 200 communication professionals attending the meeting identified the major communication challenges and difficulties in Europe, with a special focus on Central and Eastern Europe. Declaration of Sofia on Promoting Independent and Pluralistic Media has made reference to news agencies as well. "In all media the professional independence and journalistic and editorial freedom should be recognised. State-owned broadcasting and news agencies should be, as a matter of priority, reformed and granted statutes of journalistic and editorial independence as open public service institutions. If supervisory regulatory broadcasting authorities are established, they must be fully independent of government. Creation of independent news agencies as well as private and/or community owned broadcasting media, including in rural areas, should also be encouraged."

There is also an effort to invoke the jurisdiction of World Trade Organisation (WTO) in the case of news agency services. International Press Institute adopted a Resolution on the Free Flow of Information in its General Assembly in Moscow in 1998, where WTO was referred to in relations to news agencies. "Dozens of countries within the World Trade Organisation (WTO) curtail the flow of information channelled through foreign news agencies," said the editors. Within the framework of the World Trade Organisation (WTO), the international community of governments has not only agreed to liberalise trade of goods but also services, including telecommunications services as well as computer/ databases services; however, only 14 of the 132 members of the WTO have committed themselves to liberalisation in the news agency sector. IPI therefore appeals in particular to the governments of mature democracies and advanced societies to fully accept the principles of the free flow of information and to underwrite the commitments of the WTO, Sector 10, Sub-sector New Agency Services (CPC 962). We furthermore appeal to the WTO authorities to promote during the upcoming millennium round of WTO negotiations the full commitment to the free flow of information by as many members as possible."

In 2001 a Workshop on News Agencies in the Era of the Internet organised by Unesco brought together in Amman (Jordan) representatives of 13 news agencies from Africa, Asia, the Caribbean, Eastern and Central Europe, and the Middle East. It was noticed that several national news agencies in Africa had shut down, and others were near closure. The workshop noted that there were new tensions in the relationships between agency executives and owners because of broader changes in the media environment, including the impacts of deregulation and privatisation of previously State-owned or controlled media and greater competition on international media markets. The classical model of news collection and dissemination, at the core of which were the national news agencies, had been undermined by the Internet and other factors. Some agencies had gone closer than ever to governments, at further cost to their credibility; while others were trying to privatise. General remedy suggested was diversification and customisation of services for diverse market with flexible fee structure and with the help of new information technology.

At the APA symposium held in Vienna (13 – 14 May 2002)[31], IPI Director, Johann P. Fritz, presented a research report on East European News Agencies. "The dynamic world of media business and media policies creates considerable difficulties for the news agencies of central and Eastern Europe. In particular, if they remain under governmental influence, they will gradually lose their clients from independent news media. They will also lose their international reputation. They will encounter further economic trouble, since most of the governments have to cut back on budgets, which also effects the subsidies to agencies."[32]

In the same symposium, academicians, Terhi Rantanen[33] and Oliver Boyd-Barrett[34], said there was a role continuation of government-protected national agencies, "if they can be relied upon to provide a consistent and comprehensive view of government priorities, concerns and positions, as well as coverage of entire nation from a public-utility or public interest point of view. Democracy is not necessarily served when commercial or private media and their particularistic interests are allowed to completely drown the voice of government, State and 'Nation'."[35] Whatever the form of ownership, news agency should be independent and should cover the events objectively.

One vs. Many

Another question raised is, should a country have more than one news agency? In India, the decision to breakup Samachar back into four competing agencies in 1978 was criticised by many. T. R. Ramaswami, the president of IFWJ proved prophetic. "In the name of competition, there will be duplication now as has been the case before, frittering away the limited resources. As for foreign coverage, the restoration of *status quo ante* will further increase India's dependence on transnational news agencies."[36]

At the time of that decision, the only country which had two really competing agencies for a reasonable length of time was the US. This situation was seen as ideal. The acquisition of UPI by Douglas F. Ruhe and William E. Geissler in June 1982 was the end of this genuine competition. Edward Wyllis Scripps founded UPI's forerunner, United Press, in 1907, for the express purpose of making a wire service available to all—in defiance of the powerful Associated Press cartel, an exclusive club that could blackball dailies that competed with its members. Scripps offered his service to anyone who could pay for it. The AP was and remains publishers' cooperative that simply bills its members for expenses. UP, by contrast, had clients, not members, and had to suffer many losses. And because UP was much smaller, it had to undersell its rival to stay in the game.

Both wire services flourished through World War II, and then came an event that changed the entire nature of news-agency competition in the US. In 1945, in response to an antitrust suit filed by the Justice Department, the US Supreme Court ruled that the AP could not deny its service to anyone. With every paper now able to get the AP, UP had to fight harder for clients. Still, for more than 15 years, UP continued to show a profit. At its peak in the early 1960s, by which time it had merged with Hearst's faltering International News Service to become UPI, the agency had nearly 6,000 domestic clients, including more than 1,000 newspapers. But faced with a steady decline in the number of US dailies, and with stiff competition from new, supplemental news services, UPI began losing both money and clients. In 1978, the Scripps board of directors voted to reexamine the company's ownership of UPI. "We didn't specify sale as the mandated solution," says Board Chairman Charles E. Scripps, a grandson of the founder. "But we did specify that something be done." The company looked first to the journalistic community. Scripps executives figured that support from a consortium of three dozen news organisations could keep UPI in business, and it won pledges from about two-thirds of the necessary number. But some of the biggest organisations – The New York Times Company, The Times-Mirror Company, and Knight-Ridder Newspapers among them – balked, saying they could not persuade their stockholders to invest in an ailing enterprise. Scripps actually gave the company away to Ruhe and Geissler for want of support to run a competitive news agency from the big ones in the US newspaper industry.[37]

PR Issues

In their bid to diversify the sources of revenue many news agencies, not only work for governments but also for private sector corporations through their own public relations or press release services. For example, the Press Association of UK has been selected by the Government News Network to deliver more than 6,000 releases every year from government departments, official agencies and the Royal Family.[38]

It also offers a wide range of services specifically designed for PR agencies and in-house PR departments. "PA's unique position at the centre of the media industry in the UK enables us to provide support for many PR and marketing campaigns and media-based activities." There is a recent Charter on Media Transparency designed to foster greater transparency in the dealings between public relations professionals and the media that needs a mention here. On 26 July 2004 six global organisations announced[39] their support to this set of principles. The organisations are the International Press Institute[40], the International Federation of Journalists[41], Transparency International[42], the Global Alliance for Public Relations and Communications Management[43], the Institute for Public Relations Research and Education[44], and the International Public Relations Association[45]. The principles in this Charter developed by the International Public Relations Association are:

- News material should appear as a result of the news judgment of journalists and editors, and not as a result of any payment in cash or in kind, or any other inducements.
- Material involving payment should be clearly identified as advertising, sponsorship or promotion.
- No journalist or media representative should ever suggest that news coverage will appear for any reason other than its merit.
- When samples or loans of products or services are necessary for a journalist to render an objective opinion, the length of time should be agreed in advance and loaned products should be returned afterward.
- The media should institute written policies regarding the receipt of gifts or discounted products and services, and journalists should be required to sign the policy.

When many news agencies are becoming part of global public relations activities, it is essential that issues related to that aspect of communication should be kept in mind.

Putin's Point

Different descriptions of similar situations in different parts of the world have been a major issue. President of Russia Vladimir Putin raised it when he opened the World Congress of News Agencies where representatives of more than 100 news agencies of the world had gathered: "Take the word 'terrorism'. Its origin is Latin. And its meaning is similar in all the dictionaries in which I looked it up yesterday. A terrorist is a person who resorts to acts of terror to suppress political opponents by force, English, French and Russian dictionaries give similar concepts and interpretation of the word. So why do we use the word arbitrarily when speaking about the political situation of a specific group in one or another country? How can one describe as "a siege" the horrible tragedy in Beslan, the execution of innocent children, as some of the mass media outlets did? Incidentally, this is a part of an answer to the question about what kind of coverage of events in our country is provided. You know, we recorded the conversations, which the terrorist held through interphone systems. We know what they said to one another and how they did it. Wild beasts do nothing of the kind. And some reporters called it a siege and described as insurgents the people who commit such atrocities. If someone is seeking to reach political ends by such means, everybody should have the same definition of such a person – murderer and terrorist."[46]

Reuters has this question in the Frequently Asked Questions on its website: "Why don't you describe terrorists as terrorists? And the reply is: As part of a long-standing policy to avoid the use of emotive words, we do not use terms like 'terrorist' and 'freedom fighter' unless they are in a direct quote or are otherwise attributable to a third party. We do not characterise the subjects of news stories but instead report their actions, identity and background so that readers can make their own decisions based on the facts."[47]

Ultimately a good agency has to have honest and truthful reporters who should not lie. It is interesting to note what Uzbek scholar Al-Biruni (973 – 1048), author of a book on India wrote in the preface of his book in the year 1030 AD: "The tradition regarding an event which in itself does not contradict either logical or physical laws will invariably depend for its character as true or false upon the character of the reporters, who are influenced by the divergence of interests and all kinds of animosities and antipathies between the various nations. We must distinguish different classes of reporters: One of them tells a lie, as intending to further an interest of his own, either by lauding his family or nation, because he is one of them, or by attacking the family or nation, on the opposite side, thinking that thereby he can gain his ends. In both cases, he acts from motives of objectionable cupidity and animosity. Another one tells a lie regarding a class of people whom he likes, as being under obligations to them, or whom he hates because something disagreeable has happened between them. Such a reporter is near akin to the first-mentioned one, as he too acts from motives of personal predilection and enmity. Another tells a lie because he is of such a base nature as to aim thereby at some profit, or because he is such a coward as to be afraid of telling the truth. Another tells a lie because it is his nature to lie, and he cannot do otherwise, which proceeds from the essential meanness of his character and the depravity of his innermost being.

"Lastly, a man may tell a lie from ignorance, blindly following others who told him. If, now, reporters of this kind become so numerous as to represent a certain body of tradition, or if in the course of time they even come to form a consecutive series of communities or nations, both the first reporter and his followers from the connecting links between the hearer and the inventor of the lie and if the connecting links are eliminated, there remains the originator of the story, one of the various kinds of liars we have enumerated, as the only person with whom we have to deal. That man only is praiseworthy who shrinks from a lie and always adheres to the truth, enjoying credit even among liars, not to mention others."[48]

New agencies, their executives, and journalists should keep in mind this ancient wisdom which is so relevant to their day-to-day work.

NOTES AND REFERENCES

1. Both the phrases are from Taittiriya Upnishad (I-xi-1) as presented in *Eight Upnishads*, Vol. I translated by Swami Gambhiranand and published by Advaita Ashram, Calcutta, 1957 pp. 283 – 284.

2. *Satyameva jayate na anrtam* is from Mundaka Upnishad (III-i-6) as presented in *Eight Upnishads* Vol. II translated by Swami Gambhiranand and published by Advaita Ashram, Calcutta, 1957, pp. 146.

3. Siebert, Fred S. et al. *Four Theories of the Press*, Illinois A. University of Illinois Press, 1963.

4. Read, Donald, (1999) *Power of News: History of Reuters, Oxford*: Oxford University Press, 1999, p. 319.

5. Cooper, *Kent*, (1959) *Kent Cooper and The Associated Press*: *An Autobiography*, New York, Random House, pp. 302 – 303.

6. *Time,* 11 February 1946 quoted in Storey, G. *Reuters' Century*, 1961, p. 250.

7. Born Israel Beer Josaphat in Cassel, Germany, 21 July 1816; came to England as Joseph Josaphat on 29 October 1845; baptised as Paul Julius

Reuter at St George's German Lutheran Chapel, Whitechapel, London on 16 November 1845; married 'Ida Maria Elizabeth Clementine Magnus' at St George's Lutheran Chapel 23 November 1845; became a partner in a Berlin bookshop, 'Reuter & Stargardt' in 1847; fled from Germany and worked in Paris as translator for Havas news agency in 1848. In 1850 Reuter was running a news agency in Aachen. Agreement (24 April) with Heinrich Geller to supply pigeons for service between Brussels and Aachen. Agency operated for over a year, until telegraph gap closed. On 4 June 1851 Reuter arrived in London to open a news agency. On 7 September 1871 Duke of Saxe-Coburg-Gotha conferred barony on Julius Reuter known henceforth as 'Baron de Reuter'. In May 1878 Baron de Reuter retired as managing director – succeeded by his son, Herbert. On 25 February 1899 Baron de Reuter died at the Villa Reuter, Nice.

8. Page 1
9. Sir John Burgess, Chairman, Reuters.
10. Read, Donald (1999) *Power of News: History of Reuters, Oxford*: Oxford University Press, p. 395.
11. Read, Donald (1999) *Power of News: History of Reuters, Oxford*: Oxford University Press, pp. 395 – 397.
12. Read, Donald (1999) *Power of News: History of Reuters, Oxford*: Oxford University Press, p. 373.
13. Read, Donald (1999) *Power of News: History of Reuters, Oxford*: Oxford University Press, p. 398.
14. International Press Institute (1953) *The Flow of the News*, Zurich, p. 178.
15. Roy W. Howard (1883 – 1964), president and general manager of the United Press Associations 1912 – 1920, later chairman of the Scripps-Howard Newspapers, was annoyed with Cooper's book. In his opinion, Cooper and the AP directors had known for years all about the tainted nature of the government-dominated European agencies. The AP nevertheless elected to continue their links with these government agencies because it was cheaper for them to do so and relieved them from the necessity of establishing a newsgathering organisation of their own in Europe, as the United Press had done from its inception in 1907. [Rantanen, Terhi (1998) *After Five O'Clock Friends. Kent Cooper and Roy W. Howard.* Roy H. Howard Monographs in Journalism and Mass Communication Research, No. 4, February 1998. Bloomington: School of Journalism, Indiana University]
16. Press Agency Pool of Non-aligned Countries, Report of the second meeting of the coordination committee held in Jakarta (Indonesia) on April 3 – 5, 1978.
17. Kim, Soon Jin (1989) *EFE: Spain's World Agency*, New York: Greenwood Press, p. 28.

18. Read, Donald (1999) *Power of News: History of Reuters,* Oxford University Press p. 36 – 37.

19. Pensold, Wolfgang (2001) Official Reporting-On the History of Government Policies for News Agencies in Austria medien & zeit 4/2001 p. 23 – 24.

20. Read, Donald (1999) *Power of News: The History of Reuters, Oxford:* Oxford University Press, p. 399.

21. Cooper, Kent (1959) *Kent Cooper and The Associated Press: An Autobiography,* New York: Random House, p. 64 – 65.

22. Press Agency Pool of Non-aligned Countries, Report of the second meeting of the coordination committee held in Jakarta (Indonesia) on April 3 – 5, 1978.

23. US Secretary of State George Shultz confirmed in December 1984 his country's decision to withdraw, citing poor management and advocacy for limitations on free press by promoting the so-called New World Information and Communication Order.

24. Announcing this decision in his speech to the United Nations on 12 September. 2002, President George W. Bush said, "This organisation has been reformed, and America will participate fully in its mission to advance human rights, tolerance and learning."

25. *Times of India,* 13 July 1976. Text of Delhi Declaration, credit-line Samachar.

26. President Vladimir Putin at the World Congress of News Agencies, Moscow, 24 September 2004.

27. *New Straits Times,* Kuala Lumpur, 25 February 2003.

28. Call for NAM Media Convention in Kuala Lumpur, *Mainstream* Vol. XLI No 12, 8 March 2003.

29. Letter from Hashim Makaranuddin, Special Assistant to Prime Minister of Malaysia dated 28 February 2003 promising to call a meeting of senior editors on the subject.

30. Themed "Advancing Information and Communication Collaboration Towards a more Dynamic NAM", the conference was convened nine years after the fifth meeting of information ministers in Abuja, Nigeria in 1996.

31. It was initially planned for 18 September 2001; was postponed because of airline disruptions because of 9/11 events and actually took place on 13 – 14 May 2002. However, papers for this seminar were printed in a special edition of medien & zeit 4/2001 issue, and APA distributed an English translation of it.

32. Fritz, Johann P. (2001) *East European News Agencies and the Transition to Democracy* in medien & zeit 4/2001. p. 43.

33. Since January 2000, Director of the MSc Global Media and Communications Programme of London School of Economics and

Political Science; Docent at the Department of Communication at Helsinki University. Main research interests include global and national news agencies in international communications.

34. Since 2001, Professor at the Department of Communications, California State Polytechnic University, Pomona. Was previously Director of the MA in Mass Communications at the Centre for Communication Research, University of Leicester (U.K.) Main research interests include the globalisation of media, international communications, national and international news agencies.

35. Rantanen, Terhi and Boyd-Barrett, Oliver (2001) *State News Agency: A time for Re-Evaluation?* in medien & zeit 4/2001 p. 40. Final version published (2002) in APA - Austria Presse Agentur (Ed.), *The Various Faces of Reality: Values in News (Agency) Journalism.* Innsbruck: Studien Verlag, pp. 179 – 190.

36. IFWJ (1977) *Slaughter of Samachar,* New Delhi pp. 52 – 53

37. Seelye, K and Roberts, L (1985) 'UPI's Disaster Story: What went on – and what went wrong,' *Columbia Journalism Review,* September/October pp. 25 – 33.

38. PA Mediapoint does this job for UK government.

39. Each one of these organisations issued a press release to that effect.

40. The International Press Institute is a global organisation with members in 115 countries dedicated to the promotion and protection of press freedom and the improvement of the practices of journalism. IPI's membership is made up of editors, media executives and leading journalists working for some of the world's most respected media outlets.

41. The International Federation of Journalists is the world's largest organisation of journalists. The federation represents around 500,000 members in more than 100 countries and promotes international action to defend press freedom and social justice through strong, free and independent trade unions of journalists.

42. Transparency International, founded in Berlin, Germany, is a nonprofit worldwide coalition which is committed exclusively to fighting corruption. It raises public awareness of the damaging impact of corruption on social and economic development, and mobilises the government, private sector and civil society to work together.

43. The Global Alliance is composed of over 50 member organisations, representing more than 150,000 individuals, with a mission to unify the profession and provide a framework for collaboration among the public relations profession and its practitioners throughout the world.

44. The Institute for Public Relations Research and Education, located at the University of Florida, is dedicated to improving the professional practice of public relations through research, education, measurement and evaluation

45. The International Public Relations Association is the premier association for senior international public relations professionals, with over 1000 members worldwide.
46. This was said in reply to a question by President Vladimir Putin at the World Congress of News Agencies, Moscow on 24 September 2004.
47. FAQ on Reuters's corporate website as seen on 31 December 2004.
48. *India by Al-Biruni,* Abridged Edition of Dr. Edward C. Sachsau's English Translation, Edited by Qeyamuddin Ahmed published by National Book Trust, India (1983) pp. 3 – 4.

7

PROFILES

*T*here is wide variety of news agencies that exist in the world today and it is not possible to give details of each one of them for limitations of space. But here are some brief profiles to give a general idea. Indian agencies have been covered in a separate chapter, so they are not here. Major international agencies have been dealt with generally in different contexts, but they find place here for a quick overview. Some exchange arrangements and joint ventures are also here, though not all such entities.

Anadolu Agency (AA)

Anadolu Agency (AA), set up on 6 April 1920 by Mustafa Kemal Ataturk, the founder of the modern Turkish Republic, is the biggest news agency of Turkey. Anadolu Agency went through a structural transformation in 1925 and got the status of company. With its 28 regional offices within the country and 22 bureaus in foreign countries, AA instantly informs its subscribers about the developments in Turkey and in the world with some 700 – 800 news stories and around 200 photographs, daily. AA has also been exchanging news with more than 80 national and international agencies and is the primary and most important news source of press and media organisations in Turkey. It provides news stories to newspapers, TV channels, radios, news portals, GSM operators, magazines, photograph and advertisement agencies, state institutions, local administrations, businesses, entrepreneurs, tourism agencies, hotels, political parties and politicians, unions and educational institutions.

AA delivers more than 200 news photos everyday. There are more than 5 million negatives and more than 100.000 digital images in AA photo archive which includes all significant events since 1969. Leading news reports and photographs are also posted on AA website www.aa.com.tr for surfers who are not subscribers. Features and special news reports are delivered to subscribers through a "Provincial Bulletin" now published in 81 provinces of Turkey.

Agence Algérienne d'Information (AAI)

Agence Algérienne d'Information (AAI), Algerian News Agency, is a private news agency specialised in information on economics and social issues created on 17 January 1996 but began operating on January 1999. It is the first specialised private news agency in Algeria. After the installation of the freedom of the press in 1990, it has succeeded in supplying general interest newspapers and the few specialised journals in economics. There have been attempts to create other news agencies, but their work was rather based on freelance journalism than the proper work usually done by news agencies. AAI services are in French and English. To access its information service, clients are to pay and then receive it through fax or by email. The agency also supplies information on demand.

Australian Associated Press (AAP)

Australian Associated Press (AAP) founded in 1935 as a cooperative, is Australia's national news agency. It is Australia's largest independent originator and aggregator of news and information, serving the media, government, business and financial markets. It is owned by four Australian news organisations—News Ltd, Fairfax, West Australian Newspapers and the Harris Group. AAP is run on a commercial basis and is expected to cover and exceed the cost of its operations by selling its services to media and non-media customers. The primary focus of AAP is to cover Australian news, sports, finance and features relating to and about Australia. In addition, it provides international news to its customers through relationships with major international news agencies like AP, Agence France-Presse, EFE, DPA, Reuters and Xinhua. It employs about 180 journalists and photographers in 13 locations including offices in all the Australian state capitals, Indonesia, Papua New Guinea, New Zealand and the United Kingdom.

The company's core service is the AAP Comprehensive Wire. This contains all of news, sports, business and features output. All major newspapers subscribe to this service. This Comprehensive Wire is also provided to corporate, government and financial markets' subscribers and content aggregators like Lexus Nexus, Factiva and Dialogue. From this comprehensive content feed, AAP then seeks to create new products from sub-sets of the content for ratio and television stations, and 3G mobile phones. AAP provides content to a range of Internet clients such as syndicators, portals, mobile operators, ISPs and websites (such as sports, health, government, corporate and finance sites) as well as database vendors. AAP online database contains over 400,000 photographs from Australia and around the world. The AAP Image collection includes the AAP National Picture wire to the Associated Press (AP), European Pressphoto Agency (EPA) and the Agence France-Presse (AFP) picture wires.

Through its subsidiary, Pagemasters, AAP provides page-ready, TV listings, stocks and shares tables, horse-racing information, and a range of ready-to-publish sports pages highlighting special events. Another subsidiary AAPCS can provide end-to-end prime contractor services covering audit, design, procurement, installation and maintenance services in Desktop, Network, Wireless including Microwave Radio, Cabling and ATM services. Its MediaNet is a leading provider of media communications services. Offering media targeting, news distribution and media management solutions to Australian and international corporate, government and PR organisations wanting to make an impact with their news and information. AAP is also member of AsiaNet[1] and Asia Pulse.[2]

Agencia Centroamericana de Noticias (ACAN-EFE)

Agencia Centroamericana de Noticias (ACAN-EFE), Central American Agency founded in December 1972 with the technical and financial help of EFE is based in Panama has proved to be a successful regional news agency. It is a news cooperative of the newspapers and broadcast stations of seven Isthmian countries (including Belize, formerly British Honduras) It has offices in San Jose, Managua, Tegucigalpa, San Salvador and Guatemala. ACAN provides regional news to its member media and to EFE Madrid, while EFE provides ACAN members major Latin American and world news. It is dominant in Central American news market.

Agence France-Presse (AFP)

Agence France-Presse (AFP), born as Agence Havas in 1835, is the world's oldest established news agency. Today AFP is a worldwide multilingual and multimedia news agency which continues to expand its operations worldwide, reaching thousands of subscribers from its headquarters in Paris and regional centers in Washington D.C., Hong Kong, Nicosia and Montevideo. With more than 2000 staff (900 working outside France) AFP produces 400,000 – 600,000 words in text, 700 photos and 50 news graphics, each day. The agency also offers multimedia products online: text, pictures, graphics, dynamic graphics and video. AFP provides full services in six languages: French, English, German, Spanish, Portuguese and Arabic. It is also available via partner agencies in many other languages, including Chinese, Japanese, Russian, Hindi and Italian.

AFP covers all the news worldwide, from politics and diplomacy to economy and finance, sports and culture to science, technology, health and people. AFP provides content formatted ready-for-use. Its clients include most of the world's major media organisations as well as corporations and government and international agencies.

AFX News Ltd. is a wholly-owned subsidiary of AFP and provides multi-lingual, global news coverage of financial markets, companies and economies to professional and private investor communities both on and off the Internet. AFX itself generates or carries on behalf of third parties some 4,000 business and financial news stories each day.

AFP has a 15-member board of Directors of whom eight represent the French Press, two the French Radio and television, two the staff of the agency and three the public services which take AFP services. The board elects for three years a chairman and managing Director from outside its own members. On 10 January 1957, AFP was given a constitution, which lays down the rules governing its operation and its impartiality. There is a higher council which oversees the strict application of its professional rules.

Agência Brasil

Agência Brasil, the news agency of Radiobrás, Brazilian Communications Enterprise, is linked to the Secretariat of Communications of the Presidency of the Brazilian Republic. Agência Brasil is a freely accessible public news agency with a pluralistic approach that covers acts and facts related to the Federal Government, the State, and citizenship. "Brazilian News" is a service provided by Radiobrás to offer the foreign public information contributing to an understanding of Brazilian reality. The news items in English and Spanish are part of the material produced by reporters and editors of the Agência Brasil, the Radiobrás news agency. The International News Division team selects the day's principal news stories that might be of relevance to the foreign public, develops the context, and translates the texts. All the material, texts and photographs, produced by the Agência Brasil or the foreign language news service can be freely reproduced provided the source is cited.

Agência Estado

Founded in 1970 to offer operational support to the Grupo Estado media units O Estado de S. Paulo (1875), Jornal da Tarde (1966) and Rádio Eldorado (1958).[3] Shortly after it was founded, the agency started supplying news and images to outside clients, usually small and medium-sized newspapers and radio stations. In the late 1980s, anticipating the structural changes about to take place in the Brazilian economy and information market, the company was transformed into an autonomous business unit. The organisation went through changes that aimed at structuring an electronic communication system capable of gathering, selecting, refining, combining and transmitting information of relevance to various productive sectors. In 1991, Agência Estado incorporated Broadcast, a company that transmitted Brazilian and international stock market quotations, and re-designed it to add value for its consumers. The result can be measured by the number of installed terminals: from 200 to over 9,000 in nine years, making Broadcast the market leader in the financial information sector.

In 1991, email started to be used for interviews and special features. In 1992, the agency was chosen by the RNP (National Research Network) to coordinate a list of discussion and news on Eco-92, the United Nations Environment Conference held in Rio de Janeiro. In February 1995, Agência Estado became Brazil's first journalism company with a Web presence. Less than a year later, it founded Brazil Financial Wire, the Internet's first English-language information service on the Brazilian economy. Also launched in 1995 was Agrocast, a realtime information system for the agribusiness community. In mid-1999, Agrocast was made available over the Internet to reach small and medium-sized farmers and the associates of the main agricultural cooperatives.

In 1996, making the most of the availability of new text and image transmission technology, Agência Estado reorganised its media market presence by creating Mídiacast, information service for newspapers, magazines, radio and television stations. Over 200 companies subscribe to the service, which offers via satellite and the Internet a general news service divided into sections, columns by Brazil's most respected writers and information graphs and photos from the agency's Image Bank, which has more than 10 million images covering over a century of Brazilian history. In 1998, the agency created Release On Line. This allows media relations companies and corporate communication departments to send their press releases by email to the service's subscribers.

Agência Estado began testing the market in 1998 for Infocast, an online information service geared toward business management and market prospecting. The information supplied to Infocast's subscribers includes news on the most varied sectors, data and analyses by business organisations, consultancies and business promotion agencies

More than a decade after its restructuring, Agência Estado is the first and only Brazilian company to survive exclusively from the revenues of information sales to the end user.

Agency O Globo

Established in 1974, it is a division of Globo Organisation of Brazil, which includes the leading broadcast television network, a publishing company, a radio network, an Internet division and three newspapers. Our core business is the distribution of information in Brazil with our own structure and abroad with partners. The material distributed by Agency O Globo includes the content of three newspapers—O Globo, Extra and Diario de S. Paulo—as well as real time information produced by the Internet division, Globo Online.

Over 450 professionals work to produce and sell the news distributed to clients all over Brazil and abroad. The team includes 15 correspondents, from the US to China, as well as Europe, Middle East and South America, besides having journalists in all the Brazilian states. The material is distributed to over 100 newspapers in Brazil and covers all the state capitals, which, together, have a population of 40 million people. New ways for increasing results include customisation: delivery to newspapers of edited materials, according to their specific needs and selling solutions through creation of products that unite the journalistic interests and the possibility of attracting advertising. Associated products like books sold first to subscribers of O Globo (with a special discount) and then to other readers or companies.

The strategy for growth also included an increase in sales to other markets such as publishers, recording companies, publicity agencies, government institutions and private companies. An Image Bank was set up to attend exclusively to the needs of these clients. The news pictures service for newspapers has an average of 300 new pictures every day. The Image Bank, with selected photographs especially edited for publicity, publishing and recording companies, contains around 5 million images covering a period of 80 years. Agency O Globo was the first Brazilian agency to have all its photographic department working exclusively with digital cameras and sending the images by wireless transmission using either cell phones (both cdma e gsm) or wi-fi.

Services in partnership with online division include (i) Real time news: distribution of information for financial desks, government institutions and private companies; focuses essentially on politics and economics but allows the client to select other areas as well, and (ii) Intranets: special packages for company intranets, with customised information according to the specific area. Demands from clients can vary from health to tourism, or daily information about investments or education.

A specific site (www.globomais.com.br) has been launched for financial and corporate markets. The site, for subscribers only, focuses on economics (in different areas) and politics. It offers news, analysis, indices, economic indicators, interviews and exclusive special reports.[4]

Agence Haïtienne de Presse (AHP)

Agence Haïtienne de Presse (AHP), Haiti's only news agency was founded in 1989, has a staff of 12 in its main Port-au-Prince office and another 10 correspondents positioned around the country and one each in the Dominican Republic, Canada and the United States. The Haitian Press Agency services are in French and English. All radio and television stations in Haiti, foreign and local press, diplomatic missions and international organisations use AHP services. It represents the principal source of news for the country. In 1992, AHP published a report on attacks directed at the press and Haitian journalists that occurred during the first year of the military coup. Each year, AHP publishes a synopsis of events that have occurred during the calendar year.

Agence d'Information du Burkina (AIB)

Agence d'Information du Burkina (AIB) the Burkina News Agency, national news agency of Burkina Faso was created in 1964. Voltaïque News Agency was its predecessor until the country changed name in 1984. In 1999, AIB and publishing house Sidwaya merged to create the National Information Office. The new structure began operating on 1 January 2000. AIB collects national and international information and provides it to its clients. It serves as Burkina's window to the world. AIB has 45 correspondents in provinces.

Agencia Latinoamericana de Informacion (ALAI)

Agencia Latinoamericana de Informacion (ALAI) was founded in 1976 based in Quito, Ecuador. Its products are in Spanish and English. ALAI is a communications organisation, committed to the full respect of human rights, to gender equality and people's participation in development and policy making in Latin America. It has a website and brings out publications dealing with human rights issues. (Another Agencia Latinoamericana de Informacion-LATIN, founded on January 1970 with 13 newspaper shareholders, was serving about 130 subscribers in 1975 . In May 1981 LATIN ceased trading.)

The Athens News Agency (ANA)

The Athens News Agency (ANA) is the national news agency of Greece. Founded in 1895 as a private company, the Stefanopoli Telegraphic Agency, the Greek State assumed its subsidisation in 1906, and at that time the agency acquired its present name. In 1994 the ANA became a Societe Anonyme with a seven-member Board of directors, three of whom are appointed by the government and one each by the journalist unions of Athens and Thessaloniki, the publishers' union and the ANA employees.

ANA collaborates with the international news agencies Reuters, AFP, DPA, ITAR-TASS and a number of national news agencies, as well as the EPA photograph agency. The ANA employs about 250 persons, of which 180 are journalists, and has offices in Brussels, Istanbul, Nicosia and Berlin and correspondents in Washington, New York, Montreal, Melbourne, London, Paris, Vienna, Rome, Belgrade, Skopje, etc.

All the ANA services are online, with estimated 350 news items in Greek, 60 – 70 items in English and 15 – 20 items in French everyday.

It also publishes English 'Electronic Daily News Bulletin' containing all the Greek news. The ANA has four data banks in Greek—news, biographies of Greek and foreign personalities, election results and sports—and a news bank in English (since 1992). The ANA Photo-Bank contains thousands of photographs covering Greek and international news since 1 January 1996. It also has a press release service in Greek and English.

ANDINA

ANDINA[5] is the leading Peruvian and regional news agency that disseminates the main events in Peru, Latin America and the rest of the world. It compiles, writes, edits and disseminates news of public interest in real time. As a state-run agency, it gives priority to official information. Thirty writers, editors, photographers, reporters and correspondents assigned all over Peru staff ANDINA news agency. The agency supplies information to the country's mass media. Newspapers, magazines, radio stations, TV channels and websites are its main subscribers. The Internet and telephone (in the case of radio stations) are in use for dissemination of its services.

ANEX

The ASEAN News Exchange (ANEX) network established by Bernama, Antara, The Philippines News Agency (PNA) and the Thai News Agency (TNA) in 1980 was meant to be the major source of news on major events in the ASEAN region for the print and electronics media in the ASEAN countries. Brunei Darussalam and Singapore do not have any national news agency. However, news provided by ANEX for the print and/or electronic media have been welcomed by these ASEAN member nations.[6] There is also ASEAN TV News Exchange. At a workshop of ASEAN Photo Editors at Kuala Lumpur (28 November – 1 December 2004), the participants declared their intention to set up an arrangement for the voluntary exchange of news pictures via email and whenever possible. The arrangement was initially coordinated by BERNAMA.

ANGOP

Angola Press Agency (ANGOP) was established in Luanda, on July 1975.[7] It is a public enterprise and enjoys autonomy and editorial independence under the laws.[8] On 2 February 1978, the agency was transformed into a state organ of social communication. In the 1980s

ANGOP employed about 300 persons running a daily 24 hour uninterrupted service, throughout 18 provinces the country of and abroad, with five offices abroad (Portugal, Brazil, UK, Zimbabwe and Congo). A member of the pool of the non-aligned countries news agencies since its foundation, ANGOP took its presidency, between 1989 and 1992. Following UNITA's rejection of the results of the 1992 elections, like other institutions, ANGOP suffered the consequences of the war that started then.

ANGOP offers an uninterrupted 24 hour daily cable service, with an approximate of 250 national and international news items (50,000 words), for local and external distribution to the Angolan state, private and independent media organisations, foreign agencies based in Luanda and other customers. To outside world, ANGOP transmits, through cable, a news service in Portuguese, English and French with 20/25 news items (4,000 words) a day, and some feature articles on the national reality. It prints news bulletins in English, French and Portuguese, for hotels and foreign companies based in Angola. Installation of a news service satellite transmission system and a digital photographic transmission system, interconnection with the data bank of the Portuguese Speaking Community (CPLP) and the creation of a special service for the CPLP are its new ventures.

ANP

ANP (Netherlands national news agency) is the most important news supplier in the Netherlands. Its products and services (news, quote pages, press-support, etc.) are widely used in the Dutch media sector. ANP has various activities: ANP Radio to broadcast news bulletins, ANP Beeld for photographs, ANP News Media for Internet news, and ANP Finance for financial products. ANP's general news service supplies a steady flow of news stories, infographics and photographs from across the country and around the world.

ANP was founded in 1934 by the daily newspapers in the Netherlands. In the last few decades, the market situation has changed rapidly and therefore the foundation was converted into a private company. Since May 2001, ANP operates independently in the media market, allowing the company to increase its commercial activities.

Nowadays, ANP produces some 160,000 news stories and 100,000 photographs a year, tailored to the various needs and styles of the news media. Out of this feedstock, ANP develops marketable products that are being sold by its business lines. With a permanent staff of around 200, ANP is headquartered just outside The Hague in Rijswijk. In addition to a team of correspondents spread throughout the country, ANP operates bureaus in Amsterdam, Rotterdam, The Hague and Brussels (EU).

Agenzia Nazionale Stampa Associata (ANSA)

Agenzia Nazionale Stampa Associata (ANSA), Italian national news agency founded in 1945 as a cooperative of newspapers, today has 22 centers on the national territory and 83 offices distributed in 78 countries and is the biggest Italian and fifth largest news agency in the world. News services include general national and international news coverage (about 250,000 words per day in Italian. Specialised news services in English, Spanish and Portuguese). The writings of the agency produce more than 2000 news items every day that then goes to manufacture a range of the products offered to specialised clients.

Photo service: Member of EPA and has a general picture service from Italy and abroad. Also has radio, TV services and multimedia services for various Italian and international customers.

ANSA has used the opportunity of the multimedia producing audio and video for the Internet, television and mobile phone companies. For a more effective presence in these markets, ANSA in 2002 constituted ANSAWeb, joint stock corporation fully controlled by ANSA.

ANTARA

Indonesia's national news agency—Antara—was founded by Adam Malik, Soemanang, A. M. Sipanhoentar and Pandoe Kartawigoena on 13 December 1937 to serve the struggle for national independence from the Dutch colonisers and Japanese occupation. Antara was the first to announce the proclamation of Indonesia independence on 17 August 1945.

Antara headquarters is in Jakarta. It has 27 provincial bureaus, manned by nearly 200 correspondents who cover news from the provincial down to the district, subdistrict and village levels. The agency also has bureaus in New York, Berlin, The Hague, Canberra, Tokyo, Beijing and Kuala Lumpur and correspondents in Cairo and Sana'a.

Everyday, Antara produces more than 250 news reports and receives more than 3,000 news stories from the AFP, Reuters, DPA, Xinhua, Kyodo, member agencies of the ANEX (ASEAN News

Exchange), OANA (Organisation of Asia Pacific News Agencies), NANAP (Non-Aligned News Agencies Pool) and the news agencies of a number of developing countries. News and photos are distributed to its clients through modern technologies, like VSAT, DVB, the Internet, electronic mail (email) and file transfer protocol (ftp).

ANTARA also offers other services, including realtime data from stock and money markets (Indonesia Market Quote/IMQ) and press release distribution (PRWire). ANTARA also cooperates with well-known information providers, such as Reuters, Bloomberg and Bridge-Telerate. With other news agencies in Asia Pacific, ANTARA runs Asia Pulse in providing Asian business news service and operates Asia Net in global press release distribution.

Associated Press (AP)

Associated Press (AP), born as cooperative of six New York newspapers in 1848, is now an organisation serving more than 1,700 newspapers and 6,000 broadcast outlets in the United States. AP services are printed and broadcast in 121 countries. With more than 240 bureaus worldwide, more than one billion people a day worldwide see or hear news from AP's newspapers and broadcast members and subscribers. Worldwide, the AP serves more than 15,000 news organisations, nearly 100 distributors and over 500 corporations and government agencies. Its multimedia services are distributed by satellite and the Internet to more than 120 nations.

Its fundamental mission is to provide state, national and international news, photos, graphics, broadcast and online services to its domestic owners as economically as it can. The AP is a member-driven company. The AP is the world's largest news gathering organisation with 3,700 employees serving 121 countries.

The Associated Press assumed its modern legal form in 1900 when AP incorporated as a not-for-profit cooperative under the Membership Corporation Law of the New York State. The AP membership elects the Board of directors, AP's governing body. By charter, there are at least 18 and not more than 24 directors. At least three directors must represent newspapers which are published in cities of less than 50,000 population and which are not controlled by or affiliated with papers published in cities of more than 50,000. AP's bylaws authorise the board, by majority vote, to appoint four additional directors for two-year terms.

Representatives of the broadcast membership traditionally hold these seats. The president[9] directs AP operations under powers granted by the Board of directors.

Austrian Press Agency (APA)

Founded in 1946, the Austria Presse Agentur (Austrian Press Agency) is the national news agency owned by 14 different newspapers and the Austrian broadcasting station (ORF). The whole APA Group consists of the news agency and four subsidiaries. The APA editorial office supplies current news, photographs and graphic designs from politics, economics and finance, science, culture and sports. Their headquarters are in Vienna with correspondents' offices in the provinces and in Brussels. More than 100 APA journalists supply about 560 news items a day. The four subsidiaries complete the APA range with distribution, research and knowledge management tools and IT solutions.

APA-MultiMedia provides Austrian advertising portals and mobile services, and current information with multimedia contents in words as well as pictures, graphic designs, flash, audio, and video.

APA Finance Services supply finance information for professional customers from the fields of media, banking and the corporate sector. A team of experts provides current news and company profiles, runs a numeric database with current and historic stock prices, notes and interests and supplies a comprehensive stock of presentation tools.

APA OTS, the Original Text Service of APA is Austria's most important distribution channel for press information. About 380 journalists and press centres with 5,000 users are served through the APA platform. In addition to this, APA OTS provides news portals. APA-IT specialises in the development and the operation of information technology solutions and the supply of the necessary infrastructure, from server hosting to office outsourcing.

APA-DeFacto is the largest media expert database provider of Austria with currently over 30m files in 200 professional databases. It is the expert in the field of information development and knowledge management systems. The Innsbruck-based subsidiary MediaWatch is Austria's leading specialist of media resonance analysis. Tailor-made analyses inform their customers from economics, politics and administration about the success of public relations and establishment of a media image.

The Associated Press of Pakistan (APP)

The Associated Press of Pakistan (APP) began in 1947, with the independence of Pakistan and was initially run by a trust.[10] However, according to Donald Read, from 1 January 1949 the Pakistan part of the Associated Press of India was reconstructed as the Associated Press of Pakistan (APP). In the following year, Reuters gave up its involvement, and APP became Pakistan's independent national news agency. A Pakistani journalist was appointed to Reuters in London, and a separate radio beam was established to transmit news to the Middle East and Pakistan.[11] But owing to financial problems, it was taken over by the Government through an ordinance called; "Associated Press of Pakistan (taking over) Ordinance 1961", on 15 June 1961. The journalists are not regarded as government or semi-government employees. They are governed by labour laws, as is the case with the newspaper industry in Pakistan. APP is administered through a Director General, who is appointed by the Government.

Beginning its life in small buildings in Karachi, Lahore and Rawalpindi, with the reporters relaying news on bulky typewriters and noisy teleprinters, the APP, over the years, has grown into a modern news organisation. Computers have replaced typewriters and the agency's offices are connected through local area networks and wide area networks. From a transmission speed of 50 words per minute, it now provides news at a speed of 1200 words per minute, most of which is directly fed into the computers of the subscribers simultaneously throughout Pakistan and overseas. APP currently has its own buildings at Islamabad and Lahore. APP is a member of OANA, NANAP, ECONA and IINA. APP has also signed bilateral agreements with 27 news agencies for exchange of news.[12]

Algerie Presse Service (APS)

Algerie Presse Service (APS) Algeria's News Agency, was founded on 1 December 1961 in the wake of the national liberation war and its first hand-typed news with the national flag's colours was then taken up by all the foreign media of the time. On 19 November 1985, APS became a public institution with economic missions, endowed with social and cultural dimensions. On 20 April 1991 it became a public institution with an industrial and economic status endowed with the prerogatives of a public organisation.

In January 1993 the agency moved to its new headquarters in Kouba and on 1 January 1994 it launched its first computerised editorial office, and on 25 April 1995 it started delivering its news automatically. On 18 February 1998, APS inaugurated its own Web, having been hosted the previous year by the Research Centre in Scientific and Technical Information (CERIST). On 5 July 1998, both of the pages in Arabic and the agency's online products were launched. In November of the same year, APS started using satellite and from then on, its clients would have the possibility to get remote and real time access to its data banks, its à la carte specialised services, its digital pictures and computer-graphic products.

At the agency's central editorial office, there are 12 editorial divisions: the political, social, cultural, sports, regional, investigations and reporting, business, data banks, international, translation and the Internet. At the regional level, a network of correspondents divided in 12 regional desks covering all of the country collects the news. Overseas, the agency is represented in 12 capitals: Washington DC, Moscow, Paris, London, Brussels, Rome, Madrid, Cairo, Rabat, Tunis, Amman and Dakar.

Armenpress

Armenpress news agency, established in December 1918 is the oldest and biggest agency in Armenia, is currently a closed joint stock company with its shares held by the government of Armenia. Armenpress partners include ITAR-TASS, Reuters, and Xinhua with which it exchanges information. It produces home, international, regional news bulletins, photo news and provides a wide range of analytical stories covering politics, economy, culture and other areas. News items are issued on a daily basis in Armenian, Russian and English. The agency has a rich information and photo archive, which is a unique source of information on Armenian and regional history. Around 100,000 photographs are in its archive. The Armenpress subscribers both in Armenia and abroad include mass media, foreign embassies in Armenia, international organisations, banks, financial institutions, analytical centers and institutes.

Asia Pulse

Formed in 1996, Asia Pulse Pte Ltd is a joint venture company providing realtime commercial intelligence and news service for the

Asian region covering 30 countries and 50 industry categories. It draws on the resources of Asia's major news and information providers, including Australian Associated Press (AAP), LKBN ANTARA (Indonesia), Nihon Keizai Shimbun Inc. (Japan), Oman News Agency, Pakistan Press International Information Services Ltd, The Philippines News Agency, The Press Trust of India Ltd, Vietnam News Agency, Xinhua News Agency (People's Republic of China), Yonhap News Agency (South Korea), Central News Agency (Taiwan), Islamic Republic News Agency (Iran) and sources in Malaysia and Singapore. It creates a continuous flow of updated information that gives a competitive advantage in doing business in Asia and provides an in-depth source for researchers requiring coverage of Asian companies, industries, infrastructure, investments, joint ventures and trade opportunities. Profiles of key industries such as automotive, construction, iron and steel, oil, coal, gold, banking, information technology, textiles, telecommunications, footwear, beverages, chemicals, consumer goods and tourism are continuously updated as major changes in the industry take place. It also produces other products and services, such as the Asia Pulse Business Etiquette Guide to help the business traveller understand subtle cultural protocols and avoid common misunderstandings when conducting business in this region.

Albanian Telegraphic Agency (ATA)

Mihal Sherko founded Albanian Telegraphic Agency (ATA) in 1929, and since the beginning ATA had a network of correspondents in the major towns of the country and relationship with international agencies for foreign news. The basic product is General News Service in Albanian and has about 40 on domestic affairs and 80 on foreign affairs. The subscribers are media, individuals and private companies. ATA's information makes up 40 – 50% of the daily newspapers. The English and French News services provide about 20 news items a day. The main clients are international news agencies, media, banks, and embassies.

For clients who are not online, there are printed newsletters daily with general or business news. ATA's photo service focuses on important home events. ATA has a teletext service, which is used by families and businesses. Foreign subscribers can get the ATA service through the Internet.[13]

Agence Telegraphic Switzerland (ATS)

Agence Telegraphic Switzerland (ATS) or Telegraphic Agency Swiss founded on 25 September 1894 in Bern is the Swiss national agency of information. It diffuses 24 hours a day of information on the political, economic, and social news and sports in French, German and Italian, the three principal national languages. The ATS diffuses on average 180,000 dispatches per year. The ATS is the principal news service of Switzerland and employs 220 employees including 175 journalists. The majority of the Swiss media and a few dozen foreign media outlets are its subscribers. Moreover, some 250 private and public sector customers use its services. In 1983 the ATS entered a new era, abandoning its files on paper to an electronic databank baptised ELSA. All the text diffused by the ATS are stored in ELSA.

Besides its basic service, the ATS also developed special services, oldest being the radio services. [14]

About the middle of the fifties, a new medium was born: television. In 1957, the ATS provided TV bulletins. Since 1965, television gave up the "turn-key" service to use only the general service of the ATS. In 1953, collaboration with the postal and telecommunications authorities created a telephone service of information (SIT). Brought up-to-date several times per day, the bulletins can be listened by composing number 167 (German), 168 (French) or 169 (Italian). The numbers were abandoned in 1996 when in a reorganisation the SIT was integrated into the service of short information (SIC). In 2001 "an in-depth reform" made it service ATS-ONLINE. The ATS does not pursue financial goals for profit but is subjected to the principle of self-financing.

AzerTaj

AzerTaj, the state run news agency of the Republic of Azerbaijan was established in March 1920 as the news agency of the Democratic Republic of Azerbaijan and soon became part of Soviet Tass. In 1991, when the USSR collapsed and Azerbaijan regained independence, AzerTaj was restored its original status of the official state news agency of the republic.[15] Its bureaus operate in Moscow, Ankara, Washington DC., Paris, Berlin, Kiev, the Central Asia, Iran and Georgia. AzerTaj works 24 hours a day dispatching reports and photographs in the

Azerbaijani, Russian and English languages. All these are also uploaded on the website of the news agency.

Bakhtar

Bakhtar Information Agency founded in 1939 is national news agency of Afghanistan. In February 2002 when Unesco launched a project to help it with equipment and training, the news agency had only a few typewriters and two old computers. News was typed on a stencil and run off on a Gestetner machine. The 'international desk' consisted of two people sitting with old short-wave radios writing down the news from overseas. Project includes the digitalisation of Bakhtar's news archive collection going back to the 1950s. Bakhtar is a member of OANA.

Belga

On 20 August 1920, Pierre-Marie Olivier and Maurice Travailleur created the Belgium Telegraphic Press Agency (Agence Belga) with a capital of 5 million Belgian Francs provided by 234 companies and 11 individuals. On 1 January 1921, the agency distributed its first dispatches. Forty-five newspapers, 16 banks, 9 commercial companies and the Government become subscribers. In 1948 Belgium's newspapers become the majority shareholders in the agency. In 1970 the editorial structure was divided into French and Dutch desks. Belga employs 127 people, including 106 editorial staff.

Belga has evolved from a classic press agency into a multimedia information centre by using information technology. Using the Hermes system editorial operations were computerised in 1981 and in 1984 Belga dispatches in real time started reaching the government's Bistel information network. For clients interested in particular sectors or specific subjects, the agency offers a selective distribution service by fax or (later) by email in 1986. From 1993 Belga provides digital transfer of colour photographs through ISDN (Integrated Services Digital Network). In 1998 the BelgaBrief was launched and distribution of Belga "news briefs" for Internet portals was started. SMS, WAP and video service started in 2001.

Belga's customers include the traditional news media (newspapers, magazines, radio and television) as well as the business world, government, the Internet- and Intranet sites and the latest online applications such as SMS and WAP. Belga produces more than 200,000 dispatches a year (French and Dutch), over 50 million words in the two languages. Each year, Belga supplies 25,000 of its own photographs and 75,000 from the European Pressphoto Agency (EPA). Belga also offers a wide range of online products, well as adapted to the Web, intranet, cellular phones (SMS and WAP).

BERNAMA

The Malaysian National News Agency or BERNAMA, a statutory body, was set up by an Act of Parliament in 1967 and began operations in May 1968. A five-member Supervisory Council appointed by the Yang di-Pertuan Agong is created to ensure that BERNAMA is always guided by the provisions of the Act in implementing its objectives. BERNAMA is managed by a board of governors appointed by the Yang di-Pertuan Agong. The board comprises a chairman and six representatives each from the federal government and newspapers that are subscribers of BERNAMA.

The agency has its offices in all the states in Malaysia and correspondents in Singapore and Jakarta and stringers or retainers in Washington DC., London, Manila, New Delhi, Dhaka and Melbourne. Equipped with fully computerised operations, it provides general and economic news services and screen-based real time financial information services to subscribers in Malaysia and Singapore. Previously BERNAMA's news and information were only in the form of text and still photographs but with the launching of its audio-visual unit known as BERNAMA TV in September 1998, news is now available in the form of visuals. BERNAMA products and services include realtime financial information, realtime news, an electronic library, dissemination of press releases, event management, photo and video footage.

BETA

The BETA News Agency is a regional, private, independent news service, established in 1992 to provide full and objective coverage of events in the Federal Republic of Yugoslavia and Southeast Europe. Today its Serbian language general news service moves more than 300 news items each day covering local economic and political issues, as well as those from the neighbouring countries, South-East Europe and the World. This service also contains various trivia from around the world, as well as special services, including culture, ecology, medicine and computer technologies, among others. Its photo service has daily selection of pictures of all major events in Yugoslavia, the neighboring region, and worldwide. Beta Photo includes pictures taken by its own photographers as well as those of the Associated Press. It has services in Albanian, Romanian, Hungarian and English. All can be distributed via the Internet and e-mail.

BETA agency also runs some projects like Clean Hands—a site that deals with corruption in Serbia and Montenegro and its neighbours— originally sponsored by the US-based IREX organisation. There is another project Kriminal Net on organised crime funded by the German government and the Stability Pact for South Eastern Europe. There is also the BETA OTS (Original Text Service) that makes it possible for, press releases to reach, swiftly and entirely unchanged, the agency's users—the media, governmental and non-governmental organisations and companies in Serbia and Montenegro and abroad.

Bloomberg

Michael R. Bloomberg, who had been general partner at Salomon Brothers, head of equity trading, sales and, later, systems development, founded it in 1981. Bloomberg provides the global business community and media with news, data and analysis. It supplies realtime pricing, historical pricing, indicative data, analytics and electronic communications 24 hours a day through the Bloomberg Professional® service. It also has television, radio, publishing and Internet operations worldwide and operates in 126 countries.

The financial newswire service, Bloomberg News®, is comprised of 1,600 reporters in 94 bureaus worldwide, writing more than 4,000 news stories daily.

About 260,000 Bloomberg users can access their Bloomberg Professional service from any computer in the world. Clients can keep an eye on their positions, check email and get the critical information they need whenever and wherever they have Internet access.

A sophisticated 24-hour business and financial news channel, Bloomberg Television® delivers tools for power players and serious investors via 10 networks in seven languages, reaching more than 200 million homes around the world. The Bloomberg Enhanced Channel enables viewers to watch Bloomberg Television while utilising Bloomberg's interactive data screen. Bloomberg Virtual Channel allows viewers to access breaking financial information on demand while watching Bloomberg Television or the programming of their choice.

Other interactive Bloomberg products include video-on-demand and electronic program guide content.

Flagship radio station, Bloomberg 1130 (WBBR-AM), provides 24-hour business news for New York, New Jersey and Connecticut. It is also available in the US through XM and Sirius satellite radio and is distributed as far away as Singapore and Japan. It has two monthly publications — Bloomberg Markets® and Bloomberg Wealth Manager®. Bloomberg is also associated with Bloomberg® Money in the U.K. and Bloomberg® Investimenti in Italy. The strength and diversity of Bloomberg media products allow <u>Bloomberg.com</u> to provide content in any format users require — from around-the-clock access to live, streaming video to archived audio and video coverage.

Baltic News Service (BNS)

Baltic News Service (BNS) was founded in Moscow in April 1990 at the height of the Baltic States' struggle for freedom. BNS is operating in all three Baltic countries of Estonia, Latvia and Lithuania. BNS has its headquarters in Tallinn and larger regional offices situated in Riga and Vilnius. Agency runs reporting bureaus in Moscow, Kaliningrad, Warsaw and Stockholm. With its staff of 160, BNS distributes daily around 1000 news items in five languages Estonian, Latvian, Lithuanian, English and Russian and has around 500 subscribers, among them are the mass media and financial institutions, as well as government institutions and industrial companies. BNS is presenting a new, totally redesigned, functional, unparalleled web-based environment in BNS Terminal. BNS is a member of Alma Media Group, Finland.

Bangladesh Sangbad Sangstha (BSS)

Bangladesh Sangbad Sangstha (BSS), the country's national news agency was launched on 1 January 1972 within days of birth of Bangladesh as an independent country. The Dhaka bureau of the Associated Press of Pakistan (APP) was turned into the national news agency of the new country.

Beginning with a small strength in the head office in Dhaka and a bureau in Chittagong, BSS now has bureaus in Rajshahi, Rangamati and Sylhet also. The national news agency has its correspondents in all the 64 administrative districts of the country. The agency functions almost round-the-clock to disseminate national, international, political, economic, development and other news to nearly 50 subscribers across the country. The subscribers of BSS include all the leading newspapers, radio, television networks, international news agencies having bureaus in Dhaka, banks as well as government ministries.

BSS subscribes to two major international wire services, Reuters and AFP. It also exchanges news with Press Trust of India (PTI), Associated Press of Pakistan (APP), Xinhua, the official news agency of China, Bernama of Malaysia and TransData of Australia. BSS transmits news features including IPS features. BSS has news exchange agreements with a host of other national news agencies. The subscribers of BSS include all the leading newspapers, radio, television networks, international news agencies having bureaus in Dhaka, banks as well as government ministries.

Right from the start its news service was in English. It introduced Bangla news service in 1999 in the backdrop of a swelling number of Bangla newspapers. Recently, it switched over to computerised news network. Earlier it used to depend on teleprinters to disseminate news to clients. With the launching of this website, BSS is planning to go online with clients news and features. There is a subscribers DANIDA-funded human rights desk in the agency.

Bulgarian Telegraph Agency (BTA)

Bulgarian Telegraph Agency (BTA) has over a 100-year history. Under communism, BTA had a market monopoly on wholesale news provision—subject to government control—and on distribution of news from international agencies. BTA still sells to all national media, 60% of regional media and 150 non-media clients. Now BTA faces competition, particularly from international agencies, including Reuters, AP and AFP. The agency is supervised by the democratically elected Parliament, which appoints the director general.

A competing domestic agency was unable to survive as a regular news agency in this relatively small country of about eight million people. With the transition to a market economy, BTA must accommodate to a decline in government subsidy from 100 percent to 25 percent of income, and to restrictions on the categories of expenditure for which the subsidy can be used. One response has been cost reduction: the agency has closed 50 correspondent bureaus abroad, and is now almost fully dependent on the international agencies for foreign news.

BTA first introduced an intranet system for clients to access its internal informational network by means of a local telephone call, but this was dependent on the expensive satellite network of the Bulgarian Telecommunications Company. The Internet, by contrast, has provided cheaper, faster and more reliable communication. BTA has uploaded all of its products onto the Internet, and its site now has 15 news channels. BTA now transmits information only through its Internet network and electronic mail. Internet portals constitute a new category of clients.

Caribbean News Agency (CANA)

Caribbean News Agency (CANA), established in 1976, is owned by a dozen of its subscribing media entities. It serves over 100 clients with wire radio, the Internet and photo services throughout the Caribbean. The Caribbean Media Corporation (CMC) has evolved from the merger of the commercial operations of the Caribbean News Agency Ltd. (CANA) and the Caribbean Broadcasting Union (CBU). It combines traditional news agency, the Internet and audio-visual operations, and is increasingly commercialising its operations. It operates a 24-hour regional, digital satellite network with approximately 50 downlinks.

The CANA online website includes top stories from the CANA Wire Service, which draws on Reuters for international news. Other available online services include an electronic news retrieval (dial-up or email) service; a public relations wire service; CANA Radio, including a daily 15-minute news programme; CANA Business Interactive; and Internet training for government and private sector executives; Caribbean Newspaper Clipping Service; Caribbean News online for websites; and an online photo service for newspapers and websites.

Cyprus News Agency (CNA)

The Cyprus News Agency was officially established on 16 February 1976 at the initiative of the Director General of the Cyprus Broadcasting Corporation (CyBC) Andreas Christofides, who saw the need for a national news agency for Cyprus. Previously, Miltiades Christodoulou had set up a private news service under the same name, in 1957. On his appointment as director of the government Press and Information Office (PIO), he handed over to journalist Christakis Katsambas. The operation closed down in 1967. With the official launching of CNA, Christofides appointed Andreas Hadjipapas, a journalist working for CyBC and correspondent for UPI and AFP in Cyprus, as chief editor of the agency. Technical facilities were provided by the PIO, thus enabling Hadjipapas to dispatch a daily news bulletin in English to Reuters and the Non-Aligned News Agencies Pool. In 1984, CNA expanded its activities, hired journalists and other staff and secured translation and distribution of its dispatches in other languages apart from English

In 1989, the Cyprus House of Representatives approved legislation providing for the operation of the Cyprus News Agency as a "semi-governmental" news organisation with full editorial independence.

In 1996 news in Greek was introduced, the CNA home page was created on the Internet and a cooperation agreement with the Athens News Agency (ANA) provided CNA its first computerised editing system.

In 2002, CNA introduced news in Turkish, a press release service and its own photo service offering local coverage of news events. CAN is a member of Alliance of the Mediterranean News Agencies (AMAN).

CNA (Taiwan)

Founded in Guangzhou (Canton), southern China on 1 April 1924, the Central News Agency (CNA) is Taiwan's national news agency after being relocated to Taipei along with the Nationalist government in October 1949. CNA was transformed into a publicly owned, independently run legal entity in accordance with a statute passed by the Legislative Yuan and promulgated by the president in 1996. CNA's coverage spans the globe, with correspondents in every city and county in Taiwan and in 35 cities overseas.

As Taiwan's national news agency, CNA has been the news provider for the media at home and abroad for many years and is the country's largest information supplier. Its subscribers are in almost all of the country's newspapers, magazines, television and radio stations, Internet service providers and mobile phone operators. Besides serving the media, CNA also provides news to government agencies, academic institutions and private industries. Transmitting news in Chinese, English and Spanish, CNA is Taiwan's only news provider that can offer wide-ranging services.

In November 1990 it began transmitting stories via a computer network. In July 1994, CNA launched a global business information service, and in April 1996, set up its own website to post realtime news in Chinese, English and Spanish, as well as news photos. CNA began offering programs to radio stations and to airplane in-flight entertainment services and the mobile phone industry in January 1994. The agency launched a system in April 2003 to provide overseas Chinese communities with television news abroad daily and also started providing local TV networks with news images of important international events.

The Canadian Press (CP)

The Canadian Press (CP) founded[16] in 1917, its French language service started in 1951, is Canada's multimedia news agency that provides news to broadcasters, newspapers and the Internet. With 99 member newspapers and 500 broadcast partners, CP is the essential ingredient in daily journalism in Canada. CP and its broadcasting division, Broadcast News (BN) provide original reporting, from the desks of more than 300 journalists, is complemented by a news-sharing co-operative of more than 600 Canadian newsrooms and news agencies from around the world. The CP report also includes international coverage, a compilation of material from CP reporters in Washington and London, an extensive network of stringers, reporter-editors on the World Desk in Toronto, and reports from The Associated Press.

The modern-day CP is a computer-driven news service, co-operatively owned by some of Canada's preeminent media companies. Those newspapers voluntarily contribute their own news and pictures to the service, giving CP the distinction of being the only major news agency in the world that relies so heavily on such contributions. CP staff compiles these reports to ensure that the important news of the day is covered and is on the wires in time for deadlines that span six time zones. CP also has its own reporters and photographers based in bureaus across the country. Add into this mix news stories contributed by the hundreds of radio and television stations that are clients of BN. CP also provides powerful multimedia content for websites. CPimages provides a full range of image-related services[17] and has a picture archive with access over 400,000 photos in Canada's top editorial image database.

The Czech News Agency (CTK)

The Czech News Agency (CTK) founded in 1992 is a public corporation gathering, processing, storing, and distributing text and photo information. Since the beginning of 1996, CTK has existed without receiving any state or other subsidy. It covers all its expenses solely from its own commercial activities. Since 1997 it has been moderately profitable. CTK provides its services not only to the vast majority of Czech and major Slovak media, but also to state offices and public institutions, important banks, investment companies, manufacturing companies and individuals. CTK has gone digital since 2001.

Besides general news service, CTK has sports service, business news service, financial news service, news summaries and backgrounders for future events. Detailed information on the most important domestic companies is contained in the PRODATA database. The English-language news service is divided into two parts: Daily News—general news service, and Business News—business news service. CTK also provides photographs and infographics. There is an audio service too. The agency's audio as well as other products are stored in the CTK Infobank and can be retrieved any time. CTK systematically stores all new and relevant information in publicly accessible documentary databases. All the news CTK publishes has been electronically stored since 1988. CTK also offers full texts of several important domestic newspapers, weeklies and other special titles through its media database.

In cooperation with the French company Polycom, CTK transmits via the satellite, independently of fixed lines, written news, current news photos, infographics and audio. Selected and shortened CTK news in SMS form can be received directly in the mobile telephone. Teletext and email can also be used for receiving CTK news. CTK subsidiaries and strategic partners include the Internet and the new media agency Neris;[18] the Czech capital agency Cekia;[19] the specialised information agency NewtonIT[20] and the press releases service Protext.

Dow Jones

Founded in 1882, Dow Jones Newswires is the world's leading independent provider of realtime business/financial, economic and market-moving political news. More than 390,000 (as of September 2004) financial professionals in 66 countries; subscribers include brokers, traders, analysts, fund managers, economists, financial advisers and individual investors; public relations and investor relations executives and many of the world's leading media companies also subscribe to Dow Jones Newswires. Millions of users have access to selected Dow Jones Newswires content via corporate intranets, customer extranets and the Internet. More than 900 realtime editors and reporters are part of the Dow Jones news network of nearly 1,800 business and financial news staff worldwide. Access to an output of more than 3,650 reporters worldwide through a 30-year partnership with the Associated Press and the Dow Jones news network.

Up to 10,000 items daily covering equities, fixed income, foreign exchange, energy, commodities, corporate disclosure, futures and other financial markets — updated 24 hours a day, seven days a week; coverage of more than 37,000 listed companies. Selected services are supplied in 10 languages: Dutch, English, French, German, Italian, Portuguese, Spanish, Chinese, Japanese and Russian. The service includes full content—several Dow Jones publications including the *Wall Street Journal.*

In 2003, Newswires launched Dow Jones NewsPlus, a web-format product enhancement, enabling users to move quickly and efficiently through the 10,000 daily scrolling headlines to a quick, comprehensive review of market-moving stories, market updates, analysis and commentary. Subscribers can choose to receive products and services through data vendors, such as Reuters, Bloomberg and Thomson Financial, via direct digital feed or through the Internet. Dow Jones Newsletters consists of a family of 20 publications) with more than 160,000 readers daily.

dpa

Deutsche Presse-Agentur GmbH (dpa) born in 1949, is now Germany's leading news agency and one of the largest news-gathering organisations in the world. dpa is a limited company with around 200 shareholders (newspaper and magazine publishers, publishing houses, public and private broadcasters). No shareholder may hold more than 1.5 percent of its capital and the broadcasting corporations are limited to a maximum of 25 percent between them. This prevents any one shareholder from exerting an undue influence on the company.

Its network of correspondents reports 24 hours a day from around the globe, providing news stories, photos, graphics and radio reports. The service is backed-up by products from a range of subsidiaries and dpa is also involved with various other companies in the media sector. The dpa logo stands for an international group of companies.

The text services product group covers all of dpa's traditional news services. These provide a constant stream of information and are used as a working basis by daily newspapers, radio and television stations as well as national news agencies. Usage is not confined to the media and among customers for the around-the-clock news service maintained by 1,000 dpa journalists worldwide are organisations, decision-makers, press offices and providers of online news product.

dpa's Picture Service and Archive is supplied with regional, national and international picture material by more than 50 dpa staff photographers and several hundred photojournalists. dpa is a member of the epa European Pressphoto Agency and has full access to the European and international sources of this organisation which is maintained by 14 national European picture agency members. In numerous European countries, the dpa subsidiary gms Global Media Services GmbH is in charge of marketing the photo service of the epa European Pressphoto Agency.

The dpa radio product range is maintained by journalists who are experts in the medium. The dpa subsidiary dpa/RUFA specialises in tailormade audio content for broadcasters, online and TV. The dpa/RUFA headquarters in Berlin can call on a comprehensive network of professional radio correspondents in Germany and around the world whose spoken news bulletins are used by German-language radio clients in Germany, Austria, Belgium, Switzerland and other countries.

The news graphic sector is served by dpa subsidiaries, which specialise in illustrations for online and print applications. The graphics service is linked closely to the content of dpa's news services and virtually all still or animated graphics are supplied with dpa textual information, photos or video footage. Illustrators also place their own emphasis and many complex issues are much easier to understand when tied in with graphics.

dpa's Multimedia products combine quality news content with a complete editorial backup service. The feeds consist of text messages, pictures, spoken news, still graphics and flash animations. All content is supplied in fully structured format (SGML, XML, MPEG, Real, Macromedia) per FTP push. This content feed can be customised to suit the "Look & Feel" of a specific Internet application. The programme components are also all fully compatible with other dpa products and subscribers own content. The turnover of dpa Deutsche Presse-Agentur

GmbH (excluding subsidiaries and holdings) stood at 106 million Euros in 2001.

EFE

EFE, born in 1939, is now the largest Spanish-language news agency and the fourth largest worldwide. With headquarters in Madrid, this Spanish owned and operated entity has offices located in 140 cities in over 100 different countries, reports the news as it happens, providing round-the-clock coverage from five continents with 1,000 full-time journalists and 2,000 correspondents and stringers throughout the world. Its annual output is 1,000,000 news items, 100,000 photographs of current events, 3,000 features, 7,000 radio reports and 4,000 video clips.

EFE maintains a database of news items that is constantly being updated and which is available round-the-clock where 2.5 million documents from the past 10 years can be accessed online. It has 13 million photographic negatives — a visual chronicle of the twentieth century.

EFE has custom-made word processing programs for writing and editing news reports, special software applications allowing subscribers to receive and edit EFE news items and photographs. Over 80 news packages are included in EFE'S product line, ranging from continuous electronic feed to à la carte packages, general news or specialised content (sports, economic, automotive, food and agriculture, health and education), realtime news and archival material (news database, photo library), International news services in Spanish, English and Arabic, specialised services (European Union, Central America) grouped by region or by continent, national services for Latin American countries (Puerto Rico, Bolivia) or those with large Spanish-speaking populations (USA), national service for Spain, a complete range of television services, ranging from news footage to technical assistance, continuous transmission of photographs and feature material for newspapers and magazines, voice tracks, reportage and ongoing coverage of breaking news for radio broadcasts, direct access over the Internet and other interactive networks, complete television production facilities: three studios, editing units, production units, control center, graphic design facilities, and mobile unit. A complete range of services geared to subscribers' specific needs.

ELTA

ELTA, the national news agency of Lithuania, was established on 1 April 1920. In years 1920 – 1940, ELTA had kept in touch with the most prominent foreign agencies—its five teletypes used to "hammer" news from Reuter, Dnb, Havas, Stefani and TASS. When Bolshevik troops had occupied Lithuania in 1940, ELTA was incorporated in TASS and relayed news from Moscow over the period 1940 – 1990. With restoration of the national independence in 1990, ELTA also re-established its direct contacts with leading global agencies. In 1992, ELTA joined the European Union of Press Agencies. On 22 June 1996, the Republic of Lithuania adopted a special law that facilitated ELTA becoming an independent national news agency. Lithuanian News Agency ELTA is a stock company in which 127 owners, holding 68,360 shares, elect a 7-member board, which appoints the director general of the company.

ELTA offers over 350 text and photo news every day. The source of its updated images from abroad is European Photo Agency EPA. Besides, the photo service of ELTA includes more than 100,000 archive photos and negatives, which are also supplied to those interested in them.

ELTA provides its text and photo information to all national dailies, other papers and magazines, TV and radio stations, emigrant publications, state institutions, diplomatic missions in Lithuania and abroad, Lithuanian and joint ventures, organisations, as well as individual consumers.

Ethiopian News Agency (ENA)

Ethiopian News Agency (ENA) was founded in 1942 as Agance Direcsione under Ministry of Pen., to close down in 1947 due to budget cuts, and was re-established in 1954. In October 1965 it was renamed as Ethiopian News Source (ENS), but on 7 June 1968 proclamation providing for the establishment of the Ethiopian News Agency (ENA) was issued. In 1986 the number of regular staff reached 122 and output increased because of sufficient funds provided in the annual budget. Government measures in July 1994 to restructure the country's media have further helped the agency. House of Peoples Representatives proclamation on 13 May 1997, provided for technology upgrade and photo documentation services, among other things.

ENA builds its capacity to receive current world news from a number of international news agencies through latest technologies. The News Manager from Transtel is being used by the agency for processing news and graphics. Besides general news and photographs, it also has Broadcast Monitoring, Business Bulletin and Audiovisual Services. ENA has around 125 journalists to handle the mandate[21] "to gather and distribute balanced and accurate news and news materials, concerning Ethiopia and the rest of the World in accordance with media policies, laws and directives."

epa

epa, the European pressphoto agency was established in 1985, created by Europe's foremost national news and photo agencies just as the landscape of the international news picture industry began to change with new faces replacing old. Its early shareholders ANP, APA, ANSA, belga, dpa, EFE, KEYSTONE and LUSA are still with it and newer shareholders, PAP (Polish agency) and ANA (Greek), continue to provide the most comprehensive photo coverage of Western and Central Europe available.

After almost two decades of documenting the defining moments of recent European history, the epa on 1 May 2003 launched its own, independent world wide picture service. Its worldwide network of 400 photographers are contributing to an average daily epa photo report of 650.

Fides Agency

Founded in 1926 Fides Agency (Faith Agency), earlier called Agenzia Internazionale "Fides"(Fides-AIF), is the news agency of Vatican. It distributes news, features photographs and multimedia material. It maintains Internet presence in several languages: Italian, Spanish, English, French, Portuguese, German and Chinese. Its website provides links to various Vatican institutions.

Ghana News Agency (GNA)

Ghana News Agency (GNA), established in 1957, as the first news agency in Sub-Saharan Africa faced difficulties, due in part to the policy fluctuations of different ministers. Transitioning from government ownership to privatisation, GNA's relationship to government has changed, reducing the potential for political intervention. Previously, the government appointed senior agency executives and the agency's director was part of the presidential entourage. Appointments are now made by the National Media Commission (NMC) representing a broad spectrum of interests (the NMC elects its president from among its members). About 90 percent of agency funding still comes from government, the remainder from sales and advertisements. Computerised in 1989 with aid from Unesco, the computer system broke down in 1996. GNA is designated a subvented institution to be commercialised during the first phase of the public sector reform programme, affecting 217 employees.[22] Main services comprise the Home News Bulletin, and the Foreign News Bulletin (a compilation of news from international agencies). There is a daily summary of major news events, domestic and foreign, available in hard copy. There is also an advertising service that pre-finances and places advertisemens for clients on a commission basis.

HINA

Croatian news agency Hina started its work on 17 August 1990, and transmitted its first news-item, which covered unrest in the Krajina region, which preceded the outbreak of war against Croatia in 1991. Hina was a state agency—50 percent funded from the state budget and 50 percent its own income—until October 2001, when the Croatian parliament passed a new law that enabled the agency to re-structure itself as a media institution. Hina has altogether 159 employees, out of which approximately 75 percent are journalists and editors. It has news desks in Belgrade, Lubiana, Mostar, Sarajevo and Washington D.C. It has correspondents in all major cities throughout Croatia. Services and bulletins are in Croatian and English.

Major services are Croatian: General News Service (over 200 news items from Croatia and the world), Economy service, Information Database Eva[23], and Photo service. Multimedia Service English: English Digest, Brief News Bulletin, Business News Bulletin. Over 400 subscribers, mainly media: radio stations, print media (dailies and weeklies), TV stations (both state and commercial), web portals, major Croatian companies, non-profit organisations, etc. Open Text Service (OTS) is a daily service transmitting original texts of press releases, statements, news advisories, etc. in Croatian, English or German language.

Interfax

The Interfax news agency, an independent news agency started in 1989 by several officials of Moscow Radio (International Broadcasting), is now part of Interfax Information Service Group. The group currently comprises around 30 companies, involves a network of national, regional and branch information agencies working under the Interfax brand name all over Russia, the CIS, China and several countries of Central and Eastern Europe. The group provides international and country-oriented political, economic, financial and business information, coupled with in-depth analysis and research. About 1,000 staff in more than 70 bureau daily produces over 1,500 stories.

The companies incorporated in the Interfax Information Service Group release over 100 special information products designed for various target audiences in the Russian, Ukrainian, Belarussian, Azerbaijani, English, and German languages and offer a number of unique information services based on up-to-date informational technologies. One such service is the System for Professional Analysis of Markets and Companies (SPARK), Russia's major database on companies. The Interfax Group divisions are actively operating in the fields of analysis and special services for financial market players. Interfax Rating Agency, whose partner is a world leader in business rating—Moody's Investors Service, occupies the leading position on the Russian ratings services market. At the end of 2004, the group started actively developing a new business for itself and for the Russian market as a whole by establishing a credit bureau jointly with the global information solutions company Experian. In the middle of October, the two partners set up the company Experian Interfax. Interfax information is integrated with the information systems of world-leading agencies Reuters and Bloomberg, and with all major international databases, including Factiva.

Inter Press Service (IPS)

Inter Press Service (IPS) was set up in 1964 as a non-profit international cooperative of journalists.[24] In its early days, the primary objective of IPS was to fill the information gap between Europe and Latin America after the political turbulence following the Cuban revolution of 1959. The agency's network grew steadily and expanded to include Asia and Africa. The objectives broadened—to cover news from the "Third

World", give a voice to the voiceless, promote information on development issues, and help create a better balance and flow of international news. In 1994, in order to strengthen its non-profit identity, IPS changed its legal status to that of a 'public-benefit organisation for development cooperation', open to journalists, professional communicators and bodies active in the fields of information and communication.

IPS began Internet distribution in 1994, using a website set up by the Norwegian Telecommunications Company, Telenor. The home page (the Global Gateway), based in Rome, was launched in 1996, with a Spanish-language equivalent added in 1997, produced in Montevideo. IPS leverages its Internet presence through arrangements with several web portals, including OneWorld Online. A keyword searchable archive dates from 1994. Visitors see headlines and the first lines of items; only subscribers can access complete texts. A text-based graphic design accommodates users with slow Internet connectivity. Nearly 7,000 hits a day come mainly from the US IPS also sends customised news packages to over 5,000 subscribers, mostly NGOs, UN and EU officials, media and educational institutions and personnel, libraries, trade councils and government ministries. Distributing via Internet portals greatly extends the reach of IPS services.

IPS now calls itself, "civil society's leading news agency". Its flagship World Service presently covers over 120 countries. The service is produced in English and Spanish with selected stories translated into French, German, Finnish, Dutch, Swedish, Japanese, Portuguese, Thai, Mandarin, Nepali and Kiswahili. The daily output is currently around 112000 words.[25]

ITAR-TASS

In existence since 1904, the Information Telegraph Agency of Russia (ITAR-TASS) is one of the world's largest international information agencies. The successor to the Soviet TASS news agency, it was renamed in 1992, when Russia proclaimed its sovereignty following the collapse of the USSR. In 2004, ITAR-TASS marked centennial.

Previously available to only a select few, the agency's resources are now available to anyone who is interested, both within and outside Russia; the mass media, academic institutions, organisations and private individuals.

ITAR-TASS relies on a widespread net of correspondents. It has more than 130 bureaus and offices in Russia and abroad. ITAR-TASS also cooperates with more than 80 foreign news agencies. ITAR-TASS' editorial and other desks process information from correspondents, check and analyze facts, and translate into five foreign languages. ITAR-TASS offers 45 round-the-clock news cycles in six languages and more than 40 information bulletins. The agency also operates a photo service, the largest of its kind in Russia. This offers pictures of the latest developments, available for prompt transmission in digital form. Clients also have access to an extremely rich photo archive dating back to the beginning of the twentieth century. Also available is the INFO-TASS electronic data bank, which contains all agency materials produced since 1987, multimedia products, and unique reference books on Russia and other CIS member states, which are regularly updated. On a daily basis, ITAR-TASS produces and transmits to its subscribers around the world materials that can cover 700 newspaper pages. ITAR-TASS constantly works to expand the list of subscribers and to suit the demands of major national publications, news agencies and TV channels, as well as of small regional media outlets.

Jamahiria News Agency (JANA)

Jamahiria News Agency (JANA) is the official Libyan news agency founded in 1964 by a government decree that was amended in 1970 in the period after the revolution. It has a staff of more than 300 and has 10 overseas offices in London, Paris, Rome, Valetta, Cairo, Tunis, Damascus and Rabat as well as a number of correspondents in different parts of the world. Jana has numerous local bureaus, linked to the head-office in Tripoli. It has correspondents in the *Shabiat* "provincial councils" throughout the Jamahiriya.

Jana has English and French news services in addition to the main Arabic news services. It transmits its services by various means including satellite distribution. It has advanced central communications and computer systems at its head-office in Tripoli. The head office editorial system is linked to all national, regional and international offices and to major international, Arab and African news agencies.

Jana has concluded a number of agreements with Arab, African and international news agencies for the exchange of news, photos and to bolster mutual cooperation in the field of information. It is a member of the Federation of Arab News Agencies (FANA), the Arab Maghreb News Agencies Pool (comprising Libya, Tunisia, Algiers, and Morocco), and the Alliance of Mediterranean News Agencies (AMAN).

Jiji Press

Jiji Press Ltd. is a Japanese news wire established in November 1945, upon the dissolution of the state-owned Domei News Agency at the end of World War II, with independent management—being 100 percent employee-owned. Its main activities are providing news services for newspapers, TV and radio stations, and news agencies in Japan and abroad; business news services for financial and securities houses, government agencies, trading companies and other businesses; and the Internet general news services for the general public. In addition, it publishes books and newsletters, conducts regular public opinion polls and holds seminars both in Japan and abroad. It has 1400 employees; 82 bureaus and branches in Japan and 29 abroad.

Kazinform

Kazinform, national news agency of Kazakhstan, is the direct successor to KazTAG, which was one of the regional branches of TASS and is now a "open joint-stock company with 100 percent state share in statutory capital"[26] and has 80-years traditions of KazTAG (later KazAAG). It has largest network of correspondents in Kazakhstan, covering all regions of the country. It covers activities of the state bodies—the presidential administration, the Government, the senate and the regional authorities, national, financial and industrial institutions. It has a spectrum of services for corporate and individual clients in the field of information consulting, public relations, economic expert reviews and marketing recommendations. It also has Internet presence through sites in three languages—Kazakh, Russian and English—www.inform.kz, www.kazinform.kz, and www.kazinform.com

The Korean Central News Agency (KCNA)

The Korean Central News Agency (KCNA), the state-run agency of the Democratic People's Republic of Korea, (North Korea) was founded on 5 December 1946. It speaks for the Workers' Party of Korea and the DPRK government with headquarters in the capital city of Pyongyang. It announces their stand and viewpoint at home and abroad through official reports and statements and provides information and data on national politics, economy and cultural life and the international situation to national and provincial newspapers, radios and televisions and other media. News is transmitted to other countries in English, Russian, and Spanish. The KCNA is responsible for uniform delivery of news and other information to mass media including newspapers and radios.

Khaosan Pathet Lao (KPL)

Khaosan Pathet Lao (KPL), the Lao news agency was established in 6 January 1968 in Viengsay, northern Houaphanh province, with only a dozen of reporters and technicians. Their task was to collect, process and supply news to the *Pathet Laoradio* and the *Lao Haksat* newspaper, the mouthpieces of the revolutionary movement. To reach the outside world, the news agency transmitted news in English through short wave radio. After the establishment of the Lao People's Democratic Republic on 2 December 1975, KPL, in addition to publishing its bulletin in the Lao language put out daily bulletins in English and French. In April 1979, the agency launched its first issue of the quarterly *Pathet Lao* magazine, and in 1987 its first quarterly English version appeared. Since 1997, the magazine comes out monthly.

At the initial stage, news transmission was done by means of the Morse telegraphic machine. In the 1970s, teleprinter was introduced for news transmission to the outside world. Telegraphic machines still played their role in news transmission within the country. Limited use of the Internet has been introduced and email is used for domestic and international transmission of news and information. KPL has its own branches in all the provinces and sub-branches in all the districts. KPL is the main information source in the country. It collects and supplies news to newspapers, radio and TV stations. KPL as well as other media are state owned institutions.

The Kuwait News Agency (KUNA)

The Kuwait News Agency (KUNA) was founded by an Amiri Decree issued on 6 October 1979. The goals of the agency were gathering news and distributing to individuals and media institutions to provide them with objective news services and to focus on Kuwait's just causes, regionally and internationally. In spite of the Iraqi invasion of Kuwait and the resulting seizure of the KUNA equipment and archives by the Iraqi army, the agency was able to reorganise its structure.

During the Iraqi invasion, the Kuwait News Agency began operating from London on 13 October 1990. From then until November 1991 it transmitted 16,110 news items. After the liberation of Kuwait, KUNA, in November 1991, returned to its head office in Kuwait and on 15 November 1991 KUNA resumed transmission of its news service from Kuwait, with an average of 40 news items daily, which increased to 42000 news items in the year 1999. The number of employees increased from 75 in 1978 to 365 in 1999.

KUNA has bureaus in the following 17 countries: Riyadh, Abu Dhabi, Beirut, Damascus, Amman, Cairo, Tunis, Moscow, London, Paris, Rome, Brussels, Berlin, Geneva, Washington D.C., and New York. KUNA has full-time correspondents stationed in Muscat, Madrid, Sarajevo and Tehran, and part-time correspondents in Algiers, Doha, Islamabad, Khartoum and Vienna. KUNA has recently opened a bureau office in New Delhi.

KUNA also publishes news bulletins on local, territorial, Arabic, and international events. It participates in local and international exhibits and provides political and informative symposia and press conferences for visitors to the State of Kuwait. KUNA is member in the Federation of Arab News Agencies (FANA).

Kyodo

The Kyodo News Service, born in November 1945, is a nonprofit cooperative organisation run on an annual budget, primarily made up of membership dues and revenues from nonmember subscribers.

Kyodo's Japanese-language news service is distributed to almost all newspapers and radio-TV networks in Japan. The combined circulation of newspaper subscribers is about 50 million. Kyodo's English-language news service reaches news agencies, newspapers, radio-TV broadcasters and financial information distributors in various parts of the world as well as international organisations, including the WTO, IMF and IOC.

Kyodo News has an affiliate, K. K. Kyodo News, which was established in 1972 as its business arm. K. K. Kyodo News is an information provider, active not only in Japan but elsewhere in the world. It has at its disposal wide varieties of news, photos and other audio-visual material. Kyodo News has a US subsidiary, Kyodo News International, Inc. (KNI), based in New York. It was founded in 1982 as a marketing and research arm of Kyodo News. KNI now provides major newspapers, TV broadcasters, financial services, online databases and government agencies with more than 200 news reports daily to non-Japanese media.

Recently, KNI has made Kyodo's news pictures available via internet-based online photo database. Kyodo has a huge photo library: 12 million frames, covering three million items. With these resources, Kyodo is able to provide a unique service to magazines, book publishers, newspapers and advertising agencies throughout the world.

Kyodo has some 1,000 journalists and photographers. More than half of them are posted at the Tokyo head office, assigned to political, financial, corporate, city, sports, science and cultural news desks plus various government offices and business organisations. Others work at five regional offices and 48 local bureaus across the country. For international newsgathering, kyodo has some 70 full-time correspondents and 40 stringers posted at 50 places outside Japan. Its news coverage focuses on the Asia-Pacific region, where some 50 staffers, including local employees, are posted at 19 places. It has the second largest concentration of correspondents in North America, followed by Europe, the Middle East, Latin America and Africa. Additional news, amounting to some 1 million words a day, comes from more than 70 foreign news agencies with which Kyodo has news exchange arrangements. Kyodo has been a member of the Organisation of Asia-Pacific News Agencies (OANA) since its founding in 1961.

Lankapuvath

Lankapuvath Limited, the national news agency of Sri Lanka, was established in 1978 as a limited liability company for the twin purpose of receiving news from abroad for distribution to the local media and to send news from Sri Lanka to the outside world. Lankapuvath in mid-1980s transmitted news through IPS to Latin America, Africa and some parts of Asia. Press Trust of India (PTI) used Lankapuvath's service which reaches out to all member countries of the Organisation of Asia-Pacific News Agencies (OANA), and the Non-Aligned News Pool through the Asia-Pacific News Network and the News Pool Links. In 1997 Sri Lankan media minister Mangala Samaraweera announced that Lankapuvath would be scrapped.[27] But one finds Lankapuvath credit line on news reports in 2004.[28] According to the OANA website, it is now located in Sri Lanka Broadcasting Corporation premises, Colombo.[29] As of 2005, there are no plans to do away with it and it is still functioning.

LETA

Founded in 1919, National News Agency of Latvia (LETA) provides complete information solutions to Latvian and foreign enterprises and organisations operating in the Latvian market. Sound reputation in Latvia and abroad, its historical experience, traditions, and the investment of capital through privatisation, all guarantee LETA a stable place in the Baltic information market. LETA is the only full-service information agency in Latvia that, apart from news, also provides periodical and analytical reports, industry analysis, media monitoring, as well as systematised databases for mass media, business enterprises, state institutions, and diplomatic missions. News and reviews are prepared in Latvian, Russian and English.

The daily press review reflects how the Latvian print media cover issues of importance to local news audiences. The Latvian press review is compiled from approximately 40 different publications throughout Latvia. It totals about 4 – 5 pages and is provided by e-mail or fax or the World Wide Web or LETA offers a broad spectrum of databases that include all of LETA's news items in English. The Latvian Economic Bulletin is a monthly analytical review providing wide coverage of Latvia's current macroeconomic reality and individual sectors in order to give a diverse notion of economic activity and future developments. LETA also offers individualised services to its clients, analysing specific sectors, issues or situations.

LUSA

The LUSA, founded in 1986, is a Portuguese news agency jointly owned by the state and subscribers. With its more than 200 journalists, correspondents, photographers and reporters in all the provincial capitals and districts of Portugal and in the metros of Lisbon and Porto and 80 journalists in various points of the globe, it distributes 800 news stories and 250 photographs about Portugal and the world, everyday. It has correspondents in Paris, London, Geneva, Rome, Berlin and Moscow; Washington D.C., Brasilia, S. Paulo and Rio de Janeiro; Rabat and Tel Aviv; and Sidney and offices in Madrid and Brussels. It is also a partner in EPA.

LUSA has a variety of services, that can be received by v-sat or the news agency's website. National service, a comprehensive service of 150 stories per day, also covers events in Macao and Timor-East. Economic service of 70 to 80 news stories deals with the economic, market and corporate coverage and is available via v-sat and the Internet. There are separate sports and international services of similar volume. There is a separate service for Africa as well. Its serves all types of media including websites or online editions of media in Portuguese in Portugal, Brazil and Africa.

MAKFAX

Private news agency Makfax (founded in 1992) began to work May 1993, and it is among the first private media in Macedonia. It claims to be a regional news agency which runs a full coverage of events in Macedonia, Albania, Bulgaria, Greece, Turkey and the states of the Former Yugoslavia and puts out some 90 to 100 news per day. It has about 80 subscribers including international media such as Radio Deutsche Welle, Voice of America and Radio Free Europe. Makfax new agency runs a bulletin service in English language, used by a number of foreign embassies and foreign missions in Skopje, as well as a number of media in the neighbouring states. Makfax has seven employees on full-time basis.

Maghreb Arabe Presse (MAP)

King Mohammed V opened Maghreb Arabe Presse (MAP), the national news agency of Morocco, on 18 November 1959. It started as a private company but was annexed to the State in 1973.[30] It has offices in the various regions and cities of Morocco and several foreign correspondents. It distributes its different news services by satellite and the Internet in four working languages (Arabic, French, English and Spanish), in Morocco and abroad, to meet its users' needs of news and photos. In 1991, MAP was equipped with a data-processing system for the editorial, archiving and management. In MAP 1993 computerised its different editorial services and launched its Website in 1997. MAP uses e-mail in the exchange of correspondences between its central services and its offices abroad, and also in the sending of news bulletins in the working languages of the agency bound for several subscribers in Morocco and abroad.

The agency has a total staff of more than 600 people including 270 journalists who produce 550 to 600 dispatches on average per day. It intends to embark on the promotion of new services such as the SMS, the digital photography, the vocal service, teletext. and offers to the willing organisations and establishments advertising insert in its various publications and spaces available on its website.

Mediafax

Romanian news agency Mediafax, was established in 1991 is the first undertaking of the MediaPro group. Most media outlets subscribe to one or more of its services, including general interest and specialised news, photo services, and business information for companies. Mediafax produces over 450 stories daily, covering society, special events, economy, culture, politics, sport and entertainment. Mediafax employs about 150 reporters in over 40 Romanian cities, as well as in the USA, France, Belgium, Russia, Hungary, Bulgaria and Moldova.

Its business information services, launched in 1994, now cover fields such as: exchange and capital markets, economic and event-related news, opportunities, bids, statistical indexes, companies data (1,100 companies quoted on the capital market).

Middle East News Agency (MENA)

Middle East News Agency (MENA), established on 15 December 1955 as a joint stock company, owned by Egyptian press establishments was nationalised in 1960 along with other press establishments and was affiliated to the Ministry of Information. In 1978, MENA became a national press establishment affiliated to Shura (consultative) council. MENA is now one of strongest regional news agencies and the biggest Arab and African agency, rated eleventh on the list of international news agencies. The network of MENA offices aboard is made up of 38 offices and correspondents—16 in the Arab World, 11 in Europe and the US, 4 in Africa and 5 in Asia.

In 1981 it moved to an independent 13-storey building, and now has staff of more than 1,200, and transmits 250,000 words round-the-clock in Arabic, English, and French and its news services reach via three satellites Africa, Asia, Europe and South and North America. The Internet service gives subscribers a realtime news service with coverage of regional and international news and has a variety of other services for guests.

MENA now has six news services, which are transmitted simultaneously for at least 18 hours daily and could be extended to 24 hours in major events. These services are: Local Arabic News Service, Overseas cast in Arabic, English and French Services, Economic Service, and Special International Service. MENA prepares a variety of photo features covering all aspects of life inside and outside Egypt in sports, culture, arts, science, history, etc. MENA also provides Egyptian and foreign press establishments with photos of important events in Egypt. Publications include: Cairo Press Review (CPR), issued daily in English. It provides non-Arabic-speaking readers a review of important news and commentaries carried by Cairo morning newspapers. This bulletin is distributed to embassies, press offices and foreign organisations in Cairo. Party Press Review (PPR), a biweekly issued in English, offers a comprehensive round up of main news and issues published by party newspapers. MEN, a weekly issued in English, offers a comprehensive review of important economic news to those interested in the field. MENA also issues 10 specialised publications in Arabic on technology, agriculture, environment, medicine, industry, energy, science, computer, culture and arts, woman and children.

Macedonian Information Agency (MIA)

Macedonian Information Agency (MIA) was established by the Macedonian Parliament's decision in 1992. By the decision of the Government of the Republic of Macedonia in 1998, MIA was formed as the public enterprise and became operational on September 30, 1998. MIA is a member of ABNA—the Association of Balkan News Agencies. MIA also co-operates with the German DPA, the Chinese Xinhua, BBC World Service, Deutsche Welle, Radio Free Europe, and the Voice of America.

MIA has fifty journalists and journalists-reporters, and uses the services of forty correspondents form Macedonia and abroad. MIA works 24 hours a day distributing news on Macedonian, (general service) Albanian and English (specialised services) language print and electronic media in the country, the media on Macedonian language abroad, the Macedonian embassies, other organisations, institutions and missions. MIA also provides special thematic sub-services[31] and daily[32] and weekly[33] bulletins. MIA has photo and phono services and a website

MONTSAME

Mongolyn tsakhilgaan medee (MONTSAME), the Mongolian news agency, founded in 1921 by the government as MONTA, the Mongolian telegraph agency, reported in Morse code the victory of the partisan troops of Sukhbaatar over the invaders. Up until 1957,

MONTSAME worked alongside Russian news agencies, and between 1957 and 1990, MONTSAME cooperated with the Mongolian television and radio networks, before becoming fully independent in 1990. MONTSAME, with more than 120 staff, is a critical element in the national media mix and is estimated to account for 80 percent of all news gathered and disseminated in Mongolia. MONTSAME photo news desk provides photographic services—running a special archival information reference service. It has correspondents in Moscow, Beijing, Berlin, Washington D.C., Astana, Praha, Seoul and Hanoi.

MONTSAME publishes the weekly *Human Bichig* newspaper, which is written entirely in the traditional Mongolian script. MONTSAME has published the English language *Mongol Messenger* since 1991, the Russian language *Novosti Mongolia* since 1993 and the Chinese language *Mengu Syao Shibao* since 1998. *MONTSAME News* (urgent evening news) daily magazine has been published since 2001

Human Bichig is MONTSAME'S contribution to preserving Mongolia's intellectual heritage as traditional script usage ebbs away. Foreign news bulletins are issued daily in English and Russian, and provide subscribers with a comprehensive review of up-to-date news gathered from Mongolian daily newspapers. Embassies, press offices and foreign organisations operating in Ulaanbaatar subscribe to the bulletins.

The agency went online in October 1997. The Internet has opened up new opportunities for MONTSAME in disseminating its news directly to the public. Its home page provides an inquiry service, photo service, and domestic news in English and Russian languages.

Magyar Taviati Iroda (MTI)

Magyar Taviati Iroda (MTI), founded in 1880, is the oldest national news agency. It previously had monopoly, and now continues to dominate the market of news agencies in Hungary[34]. Since 1 January 1997, MTI has changed from a state-owned company to a public service corporation, managed by a board of trustees, which is set up from delegates of the political parties in Parliament.

Its entirely new interface via the Internet makes it easy to access its many products efficiently. The old e-mail system for receiving the daily news service was replaced by a brand new, daily real time news service on the Internet beginning 1 January 2003. Besides general news, it has started a number of columns on wine tasting, gastronomy, cigars, art, real estate and travel. International News Desk of MTI informs the international community about Hungary and offers background analysis about current subjects. It provides updated analyses on various subjects related to investments, diplomacy, culture and leisure.

It offers to carry out news surveys for corporations. One can order a daily news summary in a topic of choice in addition to a personally tailored news survey.

NAMPA

The Namibia Press Agency, (NAMPA), was established in 1991 as a national news agency responsible for the distribution of local, regional, and international news as well as picture services to the local and international media organisations, institutions and individuals.

Today it provides its services by utilising Information Technology, as an effective method of distributing both news and pictures from within the country and around the world.

Services include news, sports events, business and economic news, feature articles, and pictures by NAMPA reporters from around the country. It also delivers international news and pictures from Reuters, AFP, and AP, and news items from the South African Press Association (SAPA), Indonesian News Agency (ANTARA) and the Press Trust of India (PTI).

The News Agency of Nigeria (NAN)

The News Agency of Nigeria (NAN) created in May 1976 as a national news agency owned and controlled by the government of Nigeria. In 1981, NAN posted correspondents to London, New York and Harare, in 1982 to Abidjan and Nairobi, in 1984 to Belgrade, Cairo, New Delhi and Washington D.C. and in 1985 to Moscow. The downturn in the nation's economy and the devastating effects of the Foreign Exchange Market (FEM) on the naira forced NAN to close down seven of these offices between 1985 and 1988. In 1988 NAN was listed for partial commercialisation.

In its report, the Implementation Committee of the Technical Committee on Privatisation and Commercialisation (TCPC) supported NAN's diversification proposals. The 1992 agreement between the board and management of the agency and the Federal Government and the TCPC as the monitoring body provides that NAN should "go out and behave like a commercial organisation. . . breaking away from the government structure both in terms of appointments and promotions."

NAN Bizcomm Services, the business and communication services commenced in November 1991, deliver and receive messages for clients throughout the country. NAN ordered Transtel Travellator news display systems for airports, hotels and government establishments.[35] It has also introduced NAN PRWire towards the end of 2004.[36]

The Non-Aligned News Agencies Pool (NANAP)

The Non-Aligned News Agencies Pool (NANAP)[37] is an arrangement for exchange of news among the news agencies of Non-Aligned countries. The Pool came into existence in 1976, with India assuming its first chairmanship (1976 – 79). The Pool is a worldwide operation embracing four continents, viz., Asia, Europe, Africa and Latin America. The Pool news is exchanged in four languages—English, French, Spanish and Arabic. The news is exchanged through a network of satellite/terrestrial/email communication links. Six general conferences and 17 meetings of the coordinating committee have taken place since the inception of the Pool. The last general conference of the Pool was held in Tehran in June 1992, when the Iranian news agency IRNA assumed the chairmanship of the Pool from ANGOP of Angola. NANAP claims membership of over a 100 national news agencies cooperating through 12 satellite and several terrestrial links. Both NAM (Non-Aligned Movement) and NANAP in recent years have faced sensitive and critical times. IRNA had requested Malaysia, the NAM chair to take the NANAP chair also.[38]

Non Aligned Movement member countries on 22 November 2005 unanimously agreed to revitalise their news agencies Pool by replacing it with a new mechanism called the NAM News Network, giving each nation the right and freedom to "tell its own story"

Welcoming Malaysia's proposal to replace the Pool with a new mechanism, information ministers and senior officials of over 70 countries said in a declaration at the end of the 6th Conference of Ministers of Information of Non Aligned Countries (COMINAC) that the network will affect a more sustained and efficient flow of news and information among member nations and other developing countries.

The Ministers noted that despite efforts by the Iranian News Agency's (IRNA) to make the Non Aligned News Agencies Pool a success "it has for many years been inactive due to declining support from member countries."

The Kuala Lumpur Declaration on NAM Information and Communication Collaboration said members should urgently take advantage of the decreasing costs of communications and easy access to internet services worldwide to increase information linkages among them.

NETNEWS

NETNEWS was established in 1998 by a team of journalists led by Sofia Jordaidou, basically as a television news agency with headquarters in Athens. In addition to news reporting services, NETNEWS produces informative programs and special reports for a network of local and regional stations in Greece, the ERT satellite program, and for television channels in the Balkan countries.

The prime news coverage area of NETNEWS is Greece, Cyprus, the Balkan countries and the wider Southeast Mediterranean region. NETNEWS covers the needs of the mass media market in the above regions as well as for the international mass media market current news, informative programs, documentaries and special reports.

NETNEWS activities include journalistic and television coverage, and the distribution of materials of commercial, public and private institutions located in the agency's prime coverage area.

Newsis

Newsis, a private South Korean news agency founded by Choi Hai-un[39], started to provide and distribute overseas news materials to domestic media companies on 1 April 2002 after he won a legal contest[40] to set up a news agency in South Korea. Newsis distributes Reuters, New York Times Syndicate, products with which it has entered into a strategic alliance on overall news distribution. According to Korean media law, foreign news agencies are not allowed to distribute their news material directly in Korea. They are to provide their news only through a domestic news agency. Reuters has been unavailable in South Korea since it ended its partnership with the Yonhap news agency in 1996 due to a contractual disagreement. Newsis is in particular focusing on developing multimedia market comprising mobile service, and contents generation for webcast on the basis of traditional news media market. The agency provides a range of enterprising products, including realtime news, photos, graphics, VOD, multimedia, Web and mobile services.

Nordic News

Nordic News is an English-language news service, developed and delivered in cooperation between the four leading Nordic news bureaus: STT in Finland, TT in Sweden, NTB in Norway, and Ritzaus Bureau in Denmark. English-speaking journalists fluent in the Nordic languages anchor the news service: providing customers with professional quality journalism from throughout the Nordic region.

Approximately 60 stories are delivered daily, with each national bureau delivering 15 stories on average. News telegrams are composed with substantial background information on names, places, political parties, and national affairs, geared toward individuals new to the Nordic region, as well as those keenly in step with current events. The service's editorial content is primarily focused on politics, business news, major regional news stories, EU, and the Nordic countries in the international community.

NOTIMEX

Noticias Mexicanos (Notimex) a state-owned news agency founded in 1968, is Latin America's largest news agency. It has some 800 clients and 740 employees, including more than 100 correspondents in Mexico and another 100 abroad. Notimex provides news in three languages: Spanish, Portuguese, and English. Also has a TV news wing and photo service. Notimex was the propaganda vehicle of the government—the Institutional Revolutionary Party (PRI) and the president. It was forbidden from running news embarrassing to the president, or his clique within the PRI. When Vicente Fox of National Action Party (PAN) was elected in 2000 after 71 years of PRI rule, he tapped Ortiz Pinchetti to run Notimex. Ortiz Pinchetti accepted on the condition of full autonomy and that he be able to shape Notimex into something like England's BBC or Agence France-Presse—government-funded but independent. On 26 November 2001 he was fired.[41] Mexican Notimex news agency is, however, undergoing major transformations aimed at developing it from the current government news agency into a real national news agency enjoying independence and financial autonomy.[42]

In Mexico, there are five regional offices located in the states of Tijuana, Guadalajara, Monterrey, Puebla and Mérida. Similar regional offices are located in Washington D.C., Santiago de Chile, San José de Costa Rica and Madrid, which deal with events and news in North America, Central America, the Caribbean, Europe and Asia. The newscast disseminates an average of 500 daily news items on general information, politics, economics, sports, culture and science. It also includes news analysis, articles, special reports, and interviews, breaking news, previsions and the leads of the front pages of the main Mexican papers. The digital photo service contributes weeklies and magazines with an average of 100 daily pictures. Notimex also offers voice and video service to online publications. It also offers clients unedited official releases by different sources. Its radio and TV service offers the following: News recording and editing, sports, images, radio shows and news cast, advertisements, special projects, music production, digital recording, jingles, remixes, post production, sound effect, documentaries, corporate videos, duplication of copies, direct audio. It also offers a service called "Your correspondent in the world" which puts at the disposal of clients the services of a correspondent to cover any event chosen by the client. It offers its web page for advertisements and links.

Norsk Telegrambyrå AS (NTB)

Norsk Telegrambyrå AS (NTB) was established as a private news service in 1867. Today NTB is Norway's leading news agency and wire service, owned by a Norwegian media. NTB offers broad coverage of national and international affairs, economic news, sports and entertainment. The agency serves more than 40 newspapers, as well as all the major radio and TV stations and Internet sites. NTB cooperates closely with Norway's leading Photo Agency Scanpix Norge AS.

New Zealand Press Association (NZPA)

New Zealand Press Association (NZPA), set up in 1879, is New Zealand's largest national news agency owned by the country's daily newspapers and supplies them with a 24-hour national and international news service

The service is provided by a data link from NZPA's main newsroom in Wellington. The NZPA newsroom sends out about 1000 news items every day, compiled from the news feeds of its own staff, the daily newspapers, overseas wire services and other sources like The New Zealand Stock Exchange. NZPA has more than 40 journalists based in

Sydney, Auckland, in NZ Parliament and at the headquarters in Wellington. NZPA Content Services is the commercial division that provides news and press release products to organisations in the corporate and government sector.

Oman News Agency (ONA)

Oman News Agency (ONA), established by a Royal Decree in 1986, is part of the Oman Establishment for Press, News, Publication and Advertising (OEPNPA) and is the official channel for news about the Sultanate.

Besides transmitting and distributing news, reports and photographs to its subscribers, ONA also prepares a daily bulletin that includes the most important developments in the world. ONA provides its personnel, all of whom are Omanis, with specialist training courses inside the Sultanate and abroad, particularly the ones that it maintains good relations with—several Gulf, Arab and international news agencies. ONA has a number of correspondents in the Sultanate's various regions and *wilayats*, as well as other correspondents in several Gulf Arab and other foreign capitals who enable it to cover local and international developments and events. The headquarters is located in the Governorate of Muscat.

ONA is a member of the Federation of Arab News Agencies (FANA) and the Organisation of Asia Pacific News Agencies (OANA) and a founding member of Asia Pulse. It also takes part in the annual meetings of the News Agencies of the Gulf Cooperation Council states.

PA

The Press Association, founded in 1868, the national news agency of the UK and Ireland, is a private company with 27 shareholders, most of whom are national and regional newspaper publishers.[43] PA's wire service provides breaking news and photographs 24 hours a day, covering UK stories from politics and crime to entertainment and royalty. A network of journalists produce 150,000 words of copy and over 100 photographs each day, setting the news agenda minute by minute. The Press Association supplies one of the most comprehensive sports data and editorial services available, covering major and minor sports in the UK and abroad.

In addition to the core news and pictures operation, PA supplies a wide range of business-to-business services to media, government and commercial organisations. These include weather reporting, audio and video services, TV and event listings and guides, news and photography archives and response and fulfillment services. PA services are designed to help customers in their day-to-day activities, for example, by running a centralised copy-taking service and a growing Page-Ready and Contract Publishing department.

Many non-media customers receive PA's breaking news service via the Internet, use PA press release and picture distribution services and hire photographers or film crews to cover their events.

Pana and Panapress Ltd.

In 1961 in a meeting of media professionals it was agreed to create a continental news agency for Africa. In 1977, the first conference of the information ministers Organisation of African Unity (OAU)[44] was held in Uganda when the debate on NWICO was at its zenith. It was decided to create a Pan-African News Agency with the aim to ensure a wider flow of information among African countries, as well as between Africa and other continents. Its establishment was formally recognised at the second conference in 1979. The Intergovernmental Council of PANA in its 1980 meeting at Dakar, Senegal, decided to make PANA function at the first stage more as a regional pool for national news agencies than as a regional news agency. Sub-regional pools are organised around five centers in Libya, Zaire, Sudan, Nigeria and Zambia.

But due to financial and technical difficulties, PANA was able to start operation only on an experimental basis in 1983. PANA also got Unesco support.

Member states, on who PANA depended for financial contributions, invested about 18 m dollars from 1979 to 1991. In spite of the efforts made, the initial objectives were not achieved. Although it was the only continental network for the distribution of news among African countries, its operations and development were threatened, in 1992, by the accumulation of arrears of governmental contributions. Following the acute crisis of the early 1990s, the Pan-African News agency (PANA) kicked off a structural transformation process spearheaded by Egypt and Nigeria who successively occupied the chair of its board of directors. In 1993, a plan of recovery under the aegis of the OAU Secretary General and Unesco was instituted to professionalise the agency and diversify its services.

Finally, with the backing of Unesco, PANA was liquidated in October 1997. In its place, a company, Panapress Ltd., regrouping public and private shareholders was set up with a capital of 12.9 million dollars. It is now a commercial company with 75 percent ownership by African private investors, 25 percent by African states. The new legal framework guarantees the institution's editorial independence and its management autonomy.

Its recapitalisation led to the creation, from nothing, of a news gathering and dissemination network, which today covers over 180 countries around the world and use the Internet technology. At the editorial level, the news gathering network has increased from 5 correspondents to over 120 correspondents present in 51 African countries. The editorial production was restructured and thus increased from 20,000 to 100,000 words, in 4 languages: French, Arabic, English and Portuguese.

The distribution network takes into account the development of new information and communication technologies in Africa and uses the Internet to distribute news to all subscribers to the agency's services.

Part of the production is placed at the disposal of the general public through the website panapress.com while the rest should be subscribed to. An entirely digitised photo service covering the entire continent was set up in March 2001 and is operational since September 2001. It provides illustrative images of the African news, on a daily basis. It henceforth proposes pictures on Africa to clients established in Africa and outside the continent in co-operation with the MAXPPP photo agency and Getty Images.

The agency's archives contain over 15 years of African news. Panapress also has archives on the most memorable media events of the continent. These archives are available via the Web. Panapress also offers a personalised service based on the needs of the client (content, format, periodicity). Web site editors can have the Panapress content directly integrated into website. To the media, the agency's cast may be continuously supplied by email, the Web, etc. and businesses and other users can get the agency's stories in HTML format. A daily TV news service and radio broadcasting products are being developed.

Specific partnerships have been developed with many international development agencies as well as with civil society networks in Africa. Shares worth 6 dollars are placed in the African market. A board of directors composed of the key shareholders (South Africa, Cameroon, Egypt, Libya, and Senegal) and a Director General administers the agency.[45]

Polskš Agencjê Prasowš (PAP)

Polskš Agencjê Prasowš (PAP), the national Polish Press Agnecy 'Polpress', was organised in Moscow on March 1944 by the Society of Polish Patriots but officially established in Warsaw as state enterprise on 26 October 1945. The lower house of Parliament passed a law on 28 July 1983, transformed PAP into a government agency. In 1991, PAT[46] and the Central Photo Agency[47] were merged into PAP. In 1997, Sejm (lower house of Parliament) passed the PAP Act, transforming it into a stock company with government as the sole shareholder at that time, with provision for other shareholders to join in the future (up to 49 percent in total). The district court registered Stock Company 'Polish Press Agency' "Polska Agencja Prasowa SA" in 1998.

In 1995 PAP services, including its archives, were online and digital technology was introduced for photo services. In 1997 PAP started publishing the country's first online daily. PAP introduced electronic information services as a new product for Internet providers. It started PAP email daily (big part of it is free of charge). PAP started an open Internet service called 'EuroPAP' in 2000, and in 2001 it became a member of European Pressphoto Agency. In 2004 the restructuring plan was initiated, as a result of it, the company would gain a competitive market position. PAP bureaus in London and Paris were reopened, It got photoarchives of 'Interpress' and it opened a modern Press Centre in 2004. Besides printed press, radio and television, Internet portals and mobile telephone companies are also PAP subscribers.

PETRA

The Jordanian news agency (PETRA) established in 1969 is still wholly funded by the government and has been computerised since the 1980s. The first integrated computer system was not introduced until the early 1990s. By 1992, the agency could receive from and transmit to 32 news agencies. An archival system for news and photos was introduced in 1997 that marked the beginning of its news and photos services on the Web. The Internet has become the only distribution mechanism for photos to newspaper clients in Jordan. It has reduced communications costs and extended the agency's reach, both in terms of geography and in terms of categories of client.

PETRA site attracts 500,000 visitors a month (a high percentage of them from the US). There have been improvements in computer connectivity between central and other offices of the agency. The agency currently employs more than 25 correspondents in the major Arab and world capitals.

Prensa Latina (PL)

Prensa Latina (PL), Cuban news agency, was founded on 16 June 1959 by Commander Ernesto Che Guevara and Argentinean journalist Jorge Ricardo Masetti. The key goal in setting up this news agency at the initiative of Fidel Castro was to spread an image of Latin American opposite to that of Western corporate media. Then, Masetti said Prensa Latina should be an objective news agency, though not impartial.

Prensa Latina has several desks according to subject or geographic areas: South America, Central America and the Caribbean, North America, Europe, Asia, and Science and Technology, Economics, Culture and Nacionales (Cuba). By subject: sports, health, economy, computer sciences, electricity, cinema, social security, aviation, gastronomy, tourism, oil industry, communications, constructions, literature, fishing, plant health, sugar, general culture, unions, nutrition, drugs, justice and energy.

Along with the daily news services —key activity of the news agency that presently reaches more than 140 countries— PL transmits daily or weekly more than 100 bulletins, headlines and highlights, news letters, and editorials, all transmitted via email to clients.

Prensa Latina has a Publication Desk. In fact, it is the largest publisher of periodicals (11) in Cuba. Although they are all sold both in the country and throughout the world, 10 are directed to foreign readers. PL also provides other foreign publications with editing services. PL owns a film division that produces documentary films and special works in videotape, TV Latina.

Its publishing house, Editorial Genesis Multimedia, has produced more than 100 books since it was founded in 1997. Its productions consist of computer programs with an editorial profile that range from information to promotional, educational, infant and cultural materials, plus events and incentives. Its productions in CD, video CD, SVCD and DVD formats include "late minute" works compiled, edited and issued few hours prior to the closing of international events in response to the promoter's interest.

Prensa Latina posted its first website in October 1996. It has multiplied its presence since on the Internet, with the number of visitors surpassing two million in 2004. PL also provides photo services available in the site hppt://www.fotospl.com latest offer for clients and visitors.

The Philippines News Agency (PNA)

The Philippines News Agency (PNA), was born on 1 March 1973, some six months after Ferdinand Marcos declared martial law[48] and closed down all private media instruments including Philippine News Service (PNS) organised and financed by privately owned newspapers. PNA was founded by then Information Minister Francisco Tatad who authorised the purchase of the old World War II vintage teletype equipment of the defunct Philippines News Service. In the 13 years of martial rule, PNA's pioneering 13 editors and reporters grew to more than 200. In those years, PNA served as a workplace for professional journalists who were displaced by the closure of the private media.

During its peak, PNA had regional centers and provincial bureaus in Laoag, San Fernando in La Union, Baguio, Dagupan, Tuguegarao, Tabuk, Cabanatuan, San Fernando in Pampanga, Olongapo, Lucena, Legazpi, Tacloban, Cebu, Tagbilaran, Dumaguete, Bacolod, Iloilo, Palawan, Zamboanga, Jolo, Cagayan de Oro, Iligan, Cotabato, Butuan, Davao and Gen. Santos City. PNA stationed regular staff correspondents in major cities like Tokyo, Jakarta, Kuala Lumpur, Bucharest, Sydney, Toronto, Hawaii, Los Angeles, San Francisco, Chicago, Washington D.C., and New York. In the late 70s, PNA launched its own dictation speed broadcast service which included actual broadcasts from a radio booth right inside the agency's central desk at its old headquarters in Intramuros, Manila, using the 50 kilowatts shortwave transmitter of Far East Broadcasting Company located in Karuhatan, Bulacan.

PNA began to lose its clout when its old hands started to move to the reopened private newspapers and similar media organisations. Exodus of professionals followed the EDSA People Power Revolution that ousted Marcos in 1986, which also saw private newspapers sprout like mushrooms after a thunderstorm.

PNA decline became more telling during the Aquino administration. Perceived as a propaganda arm of the Marcos dictatorship, the Aquino government downgraded it to a mere division of the News and Information Bureau and further emasculated it by denying it the support it required.

With computerisation and use of the Internet, PNA has improved its ability to deliver news even in the remotest part of the country. It is a member of two international news exchange networks — the ASEAN News Exchange (ANEX) involving the news agencies or organs of ASEAN's other member countries, and the Organisation of Asia-Pacific News Agencies (OANA).

Reuters

Reuters, founded in October 1851, is now a global information company, providing information tailored for professionals in the financial services, media and corporate markets—a range of information products and transactional solutions, including realtime and historical market data, research and analytics, financial trading platforms, investment data and analytics plus news in text, video, graphics and photographs. It operates in 200 cities in 94 countries. Reuters supplies text in 19 languages. Although it is best known as one of the world's largest international multimedia news agency, more than 90 percent of its revenue is derived from financial services business. Some 427,000 financial market professionals working in the equities, fixed income, foreign exchange, money, commodities and energy markets around the world use Reuters products. Reuters provides financial institutions with specially designed tools to help them reduce risk and distribute and manage the ever-increasing volumes of market data and also offers automated trading products for the treasury market.

It supplies news—text, graphics, video and pictures—to media organisations and websites around the world and provides news to businesses outside financial services. Reuters is incorporated under the name Reuters Group PLC and is registered in England and Wales.

In the latter half of the twentieth century, the introduction of a succession of computerised products for international traders, beginning with Stockmaster service transmitting financial data internationally in 1964, transformed the Reuters business. In 1973 a further innovative development was the launch of the Reuter Monitor which created an electronic marketplace for foreign exchange. This service expanded to carry news and prices covering securities, commodities and money and was further enhanced in 1981 with the launch of the Reuter Monitor Dealing Service.

Following a dramatic increase in profitability, Reuters was floated as a public company in 1984 on the London Stock Exchange and on NASDAQ in the US. On listing, the company had a market capitalisation of some £700 m. Subsequently, Reuters made a series of acquisitions including Visnews (1985 - renamed Reuters Television in 1985), Instinet (1986), TIBCO (formerly Teknekron) and Quotron both in 1994.

Key product launches include Equities 2000 (1987), Dealing 2000-2 (1992), Business Briefing (1994), Reuters Television for the financial markets (1994), 3000 Series (1996) and the Reuters 3000 Xtra service (1999).

In 1995, Reuters established its 'Greenhouse Fund' to take minority investments in a range of start-up technology companies, initially in the US. In July 1999, TIBCO Software completed an IPO on NASDAQ; Reuters retains a substantial proportion of the shares. Reuters announced in early 2000 a range of major initiatives designed to accelerate its use of internet technologies, open new markets and migrate its core business to an internet-based model. In May 2001, Instinet completed an IPO on NASDAQ; Reuters retains the majority of the shares. In October 2001, Reuters completed the largest acquisition in its history, buying most of the assets of Bridge Information Systems. In March 2003, Reuters acquired Multex.com, Inc., a provider of global financial information.

Reuters has 14,500 staff in 91 countries. This includes 2,300 editorial staff in 196 bureaus serving 129 countries, making Reuters the world's largest international multimedia news agency. In 2004, Reuters Group revenues were £2.9 billion.

RIA Novosti

The Russian News & Information Agency RIA Novosti is the successor of Soviet Information Bureau (Sovinformburo), created on 24 June 1941, which became the Novosti Press Agency (APN) in 1961, the leading news and journalistic agency of the Soviet public organisations. APN was transformed into IAN Novosti Information Agency on July

27, 1990. The InfoNovosti news wire service was introduced in 1991. IAN had offices in 120 countries and printed 13 illustrated magazines and newspapers. In September 1991, IAN and the Russian Information Agency merged to create the Russian Information Agency Novosti (RIA Novosti). Since 1993, RIA Novosti has been a state information and analytical agency. The agency has a broad network of correspondents in Russia and the CIS and in more than 40 non-CIS countries. RIA Novosti daily provides sociopolitical, economic, scientific and financial information in Russian, in the main European languages and in Arabic through electronic media and the Internet. Its website www.rianovosti.com publishes the agency's main information services online, while the entire range of the agency's information is available on a subscription basis. RIA Novosti has the country's largest photo service and one of the largest photo banks containing over 600,000 photographs. The agency's translation service has more than 90 highly professional translators working in 12 languages.

The agency organises press tours in Russia for foreign journalists, holds presentations, press functions abroad, and monitors and analyses publications in the foreign media. It has organised ISDN video conferences and Internet press conferences, and held round table meetings and off-the-record functions. The list of RIA Novosti clients includes the Administration of the President, the Russian Government, the Federation Council and the State Duma, the leading ministries and departments, the administrations of constituent members of the Federation, Russian and foreign business circles, diplomatic missions, and public organisations.

Ritzau

Ritzau is the biggest independent Danish news agency supplying news round the clock to the complete Danish press. Several ministries and financial institutions also subscribe to Ritzau's news service.

The name Ritzau traces back to the founder, Erik Nikolai Ritzau. After having fought the war against Germany in 1864, Erik Nikolai Ritzau engaged in journalism. Two years later, inspired by foreign news agencies he founded Ritzaus Bureau.

The core product is the written news, which is distributed online to all Danish media and several media in the remaining part of Scandinavia. Furthermore, Ritzau cooperates with the European news agencies: Reuters in London, DPA in Hamburg, and AFP in Paris. Ritzau also employs special and permanent correspondents in a number of international capitals.

In addition to the written news, Ritzau supplies radio and television stations with a ready-to-use news service and soundbites. Ritzau offers graphics to media, domestically and abroad. Ritzau also provides news in English.

Rompres

Rompres is Romania's state-run news agency, which was known as Agerpres before 1990. It is the official agency of the Romanian government. Rompres claims 90 media (newspapers, radio and TV stations) subscribe to its services. The agency produces over 220 stories on Romania every day, and about 175 – 200 international stories covering all domains. Rompres prepares 14 daily, weekly and monthly news bulletins, offered in print or online. Besides media and governmental organisations, they are distributed to companies, embassies, NGOs in Romania and abroad.

It also puts out about 10,000-word daily news service on Romania, in English and French to the foreign press agencies it cooperates with, as well as to the Bucharest offices of international media, to diplomatic missions and public organisations. It also sends news in Hungarian for the Hungarian-language media in Romania. Most central and local administrations are also subscribed to Rompres. The agency also has a photo service, producing and distributing 25 – 30 images on Romania a day. Rompres also distributes photos from EPA (European Press Photo Agency) and AP.

Rastriya Samachar Samiti (RSS)

Rastriya Samachar Samiti (RSS), founded in 1962, a state-subsidised national news agency of Nepal is the only news agency in the kingdom of Nepal. It has several regional and zonal offices and correspondents in 104 places in Nepal. Its products are National News Service (English and Nepali), International News Service (English and Nepali), Feature News (English and Nepali), RSS photo service 200 high-resolution photos a day. For international news it depends on AFP, AP, Xinhua and PTI. RSS computer network operates in Kathmandu metropolis as well as in Biratinagar. Recently, it has acquired an Internet presence.

Syrian Arab News Agency (SANA)

Syrian Arab News Agency (SANA), established in 24 June 1965, is a body corporate with administrative council chaired by the Information Minister and enjoys financial as well as administrative independence.

SANA has 370 employees, including 200 journalists. It has 16 offices abroad including 10 in the Arab countries and an additional 18 foreign correspondents.

SANA is the main source for news and pictures in Syria and covers local, Arab, as well as international news from their different sources round the clock. The agency transmits at an average of 400 local and 160 foreign news items in Arabic service and 40 items each in English and French services per day. It also has a photo service with an average of 100 local and 60 international news pictures of which about 150 are saved in archives. SANA transmits its news via radio in English and French languages, with an average of 7200 words each per day. This transmission is received in Europe, North Africa, Iran, India, the Arab Homeland, China, Japan, and the US and in Latin America. SANA satellite transmission helps Syrian Embassy staff all over Asia, Europe, and America to receive the Agency News Bulletins. SANA is currently in the process of up-dating its technology, with a data bank that will make services available on demand. It has already introduced Internet bulletins in several languages for clients around the world.

SAPA

SAPA, or the South African Press Association, was established in 1938 by the major South African newspapers of the day to facilitate the sharing of news. Today, the SAPA news agency provides all forms of media (radio, television, newspapers, and the Internet) with breaking news. SAPA is also the prime supplier of global news to the South African media market. With offices in Johannesburg, Cape Town, Durban and Bloemfontein, the focus of 40 editorial staff is on the hard news of the day. Its 'newswire' is a consistent feed of news into the newsrooms around South Africa. SAPA picture service using advanced digital photographic cameras provides newspapers, magazines, and other media with pictures of people, events, and occasions that are significant to the news of the day. SAPA also has a press release service and its PR service is called "link2media". The directors of SAPA are from all the major newspaper groups.

SDA/ATS

The Swiss News Agency (German: Schweizerische Depeschen Agentur—SDA, French: Agence Télégraphique Suisse ATS, Italian: Agenzia Telegrafica Svizzera ATS) is the national news agency in Switzerland founded in 1894. It distributes general news (national/international politics, national/international economics, divers, culture) and sports in German, French and Italian language. There are more than 180,000 messages per year sent to customers. It is the largest news agency in Switzerland with 227 employees (175 journalists). Its headquarters is in Berne. There are 14 regional offices that deliver news to the headquarters. Almost all Swiss news media companies are customers of SDA. More than 250 non-media customers use its news services. SDA is a joint stock company and owned by several Swiss media companies. There are a number of subsidiary companies: Sportinformation Si (Zurich/Geneva) for sports, SDA/AWP (Zurich) for financial and economic news, news aktuell (Zurich) for paid news services.

Smart News Network International (SNNi)

Smart News Network International (SNNi) has been created by the participants of the Global 2000 Southern Africa International Dialogue (SAID) held in Maputo, Mozambique and the Langkawi International Dialogue (LID) meeting in Langkawi, Malaysia. The initial participating members are Daily News of Botswana, BERNAMA, The New Straits Times, The Star, and Utusan Malaysia of Malaysia, Mozambique News Agency of Mozambique, Namibia Today of Namibia, Buanews of South Africa, New Vision of Uganda and The Herald of Zimbabwe. ZIANA, GNA, and NAMPA joined it later. Participating media organisations contribute daily news, features, photographs, video images to the website of SNNi, namely www.snni.org. During the initial stage, the server of the website is located in Malaysia. Anyone is free to use and reproduce such items of news, features, photographs and video image, provided due acknowledgment of the source is made. A link to SNNi is provided on BERNAMA home page.

Saudi Press Agency (SPA)

Saudi Press Agency (SPA), national news agency of Saudi Arabia was established in 1971, to collect and distribute national and international news in the Kingdom of Saudi Arabia and abroad. It is one of the affiliates of the ministry of information, with a staff of nearly 500. It has its head office in Riyadh, regional offices in Jeddah, Dammam, offices in the big Saudi cities, correspondents in governorates and small towns. SPA has offices in Beirut, Cairo, Sanaa, London, Washington D.C., Tunis and Tehran, and maintains correspondents in Islamabad, Jordan, New York, Damascus, Morocco, Mauritania, Palestine, Berlin, Brussels, Paris, Moscow, Beijing and Vienna. Besides, it has arrangements with Reuters, AP, UPI, AFP and DPA.

Since 20 December 1997, SPA began to use computers in all its operations. SPA uses modern digital technology, satellites and the Internet to cover the world in Arabic and English. It also has a French news service, a photo service and uses file transfer protocol (FTP) for distribution. Since 1999, SPA has a website for its Arabic and English news services. Every morning, SPA issues a printed daily bulletin on important news, which are distributed, to all senior officials in the country. It issues about 400 news items of more than 200,000 words in the three languages and more than 150 photographs everyday.

It is a member of FANA and serves as re-transmitting centre for both the international Islamic news agency and the pool of news agencies of the nonaligned countries.

Recently, a royal order has been issued to transform the agency to an independent general organisation. This will be effective soon after the completion of the required regulations. This will assist SPA to cover its operating costs through increasing returns from selling the news services to individual subscribers as well as other organisations and news agencies.

The Slovene Press Agency (STA)

The Slovene Press Agency (STA) was founded on 20 June 1991, five days before Slovenia's declaration of independence and the subsequent aggression of the Yugoslav army. The STA has since become the national press agency, covering events at home and worldwide with its own, as well as foreign sources.

The agency is a member of the European Association of Press Agencies, and exchanges reports with the following press agencies: APA, ANSA, Hina, TANJUG, MTI, DPA, AFP, AP, IRNA, ATA, TASR, ITAR-TASS, Xinhua, MIA, MAKFAX, MINA. The STA has nearly one hundred employees and part-time workers.

It has permanent offices in Brussels, New York, Rome, Vienna, Zagreb, Belgrade, and important events elsewhere in the world are often covered by correspondents who are dispatched to the scene.

The main products of the STA are a daily Slovene language service, abridged service for the Slovene regional media, a daily information service from Slovenia in English and the STA daily bulletin. The agency thus produces around 250 news reports in Slovene and additional 40 reports in English, daily.

The STA also offers an original text service, O-STA, for unedited press releases from subscribers and special service for SMS, WAP and WEB. STA is also a member of CEE—business wire pool of 13 Central European news agencies. The agency is currently planning to expand its range of products with photo and audio services, as well as other services tailored to the needs of users.

STA is a limited liability company, majority owned by the state (96 percent). The agency is planning to undertake a capital expansion, which would involve an external strategic partner or group of partners.

Suomen Tietotoimisto (STT)

Suomen Tietotoimisto (STT), the Finnish News Agency, started as the Finnish Telegram Agency in November 1887 and got its current name in 1915 after merger with a competitor. STT is an independent, national news provider, jointly owned by the leading media establishments in Finland. STT produces top-quality journalism and affiliated services. In addition to supplying subscriber newspapers with news items ready for their pages as well as an array of content for television, radio and the internet, the agency also provides the platform on which these media, including YLE, the public broadcaster, build their own news operations.

STT is headquartered in central Helsinki. The agency has nine branches across Finland and permanent representation in Stockholm, Tallinn, Moscow, Brussels and Washington D.C. STT employs 145 staff, 120 of which are journalists. STT is trilingual: most of the content is produced in Finnish and Swedish—the two official languages in the country—and also in English, including voice news.[49] In addition to the core comprehensive realtime newswire, STT carries a plethora of specialised products aimed at the media and other actors. These include the online and short message news, the Swedish and English services, graphics service, archive, expert articles and political op-ed service, statement and notice service—exclusively from the Finnish ministries—event and sports calendars and radio and television schedules.

In Finland, some 100 newspapers, the Finnish Broadcasting Company (YLE), all nation-wide television channels and around 30 commercial radio stations subscribe to STT services. STT also offers a broad range of news products to companies and public administration.

TANJUG

Telegraphic Agency of New Yugoslavia (TANJUG), founded on 5 November 1943, has passed through different stages of expansion and decline during the past decades. In its "golden times," Tanjug had a network of as many as 48 correspondents all over the world; it was ranked among the world's 10 leading agencies and had the leading role in the pool of news agencies of non-aligned countries. The agency made a large number of interviews with many world leaders and has an extensive collection of historical photographs (four million film negatives). In the late 80s, Tanjug had 1,200 employees, and the tumultuous events in the Balkans affected Tanjug, its editorial and business policies, and its correspondent network.

The General News Service annually transmits about 80,000 news items on the average. It has a photo service and economic service. It transmits the General News Service in the English language, and publishes an English-language Daily News Bulletin, as well as a Serbian-language Selection from Foreign Press and other publications on request. The Daily News Bulletin and the Selection bulletin appear five days a week.

TANJUG has put the General News Service in the Serbian, English and French languages on the Internet.

Radio-TANJUG (88. 1 MHz) broadcasts news and music 24 hours a day, keeping its listeners in Yugoslavia and abroad up-to-date on national and international developments. TANJUG's Data Bank daily files some 400 articles under 12,000 reference headings.

The democratic changes in Yugoslavia on 5 October 2000 reflected on the agency as well, which returned to its original recognisable style of work, carrying out the necessary staff changes and changes in the editorial policy. The agency currently has 375 employees, including about 170 reporters, translators and photojournalists. Tanjug is preparing for an ownership transformation. It will be transformed from an agency under "patronage of the state" into a company of a mixed ownership with an expressed market orientation. The correspondent network will be reorganised and strengthened with the objective to cover about 15 of the most important political and economic centers and seats of international organisations, through permanent correspondents and stringers.

News Agency of the Slovak Republic (TASR)

News Agency of the Slovak Republic (TASR) was established[50] on 30 January 1992 and is based in Bratislava. On 28 April 1999, the general director issued the statutes of News Agency of the Slovak Republic and cancelled the statutes valid since 11 April 1995. TASR is a partially state-funded organisation, that is registered in the Commercial Register of District Court Bratislava 1. The general director of the agency is named and recalled by the Slovak government. Economy of TASR is regulated by rules of the budget economy governing state-funded organisations. TASR gathers, compiles, archives and provides versatile information on events in Slovakia.

Télam

Agencia Telenoticiosa Americana (Télam), founded in 1945, is state owned national news agency of Argentina. The process of growth and consolidation of Télam interrupted in 1955 with the government of the Liberating Revolution making it a mixed limited-liability company and confronted financial crisis. In July 1959 Télam became a joint-stock company, and from 1960 Télam portfolio of clients improved, including the television channels and national newspapers. On 30 May 1963 the agency was closed down by a decree. Télam became a state company on 24 June 1968. After the democratic restoration of 1983, it was possible to know that because of the censorship during the earlier years, important journalistic and photographic files of the agency had disappeared. In the year 2001, the unification of state mass media took place and Télam happened to work within that big organisation, but in the February of 2002 it returned to its independent status and became a Society of the State, whose only shareholder is the Mass media Secretariat.

The journalistic service of Télam is used by about 300 subscribers, and of the 450 workers, about half are journalists. A primitive form of the Internet and email was used by the agency in 1994. First site of Télam was put on line in 1997 and was updated four times a day. Since then, the site has been redesigned in 1999, 2002, 2003 and 2004 to improve the content and navigation and making it a retailer of news services that are updated continuously.

Tidningarnas Telegrambyrå (TT)

Tidningarnas Telegrambyrå (TT), a multi media news provider, is the largest news agency in Scandinavia, and the only nationwide Swedish agency with a complete news service. TT was created through merger of three competing news agencies in 1922. At the start, the news stories were distributed by mail copies and individual telephone calls to the newspapers. Its first radio news broadcast was in 1924.

Most of Sweden's over 100 newspapers, as well as radio and TV stations, government offices and private corporations subscribe to TT's service. In the main office in Stockholm, TT has specialised desks for politics, sports, economy, etc. Bureaus in Gothenburg and Malmö, correspondents in other major cities, and cooperation with local media all over Sweden ensure detailed coverage everywhere. Reporters not only write their stories but also record soundbites for radio service and sometimes make camera interviews for video news clip service.

For international coverage, TT has correspondents and stringers, and subscribes to some of the major international news agencies like Reuters and AFP. For major events and some feature stories, reporters often travel abroad. TT also syndicates stories with news agencies in Denmark, Finland and Norway. All news services are in Swedish.

Apart from well-renowned sports coverage in text, TT provides extensive sports tables, result files, and instant result-SMS goal service for major football events. For graphics and photos, TT cooperates closely with Svenska Grafikbyrån, Pressens Bild and Scanpix.

TT employs around 140 people, most of them reporters and editors. Its subsidiary TT Spektra employs another 40.

TT Spektra provides a wide spectrum of feature stories in special fields like travel or pets and ready-for-print page services for local newspapers with, for instance, international and domestic news or the TV-listings of the papers' own choices. TT prides itself in offering modern, flexible and highly reliable technical solutions for all customers. It is the first agency worldwide to offer a news-MMS service.

Ukrinform

The Ukrainian National News Agency (Ukrinform), successor of the UTA, BUP, UkTa, RATAU, with over its 85-years history, has a network of its own correspondents and photo correspondents in all Ukrainian administrative regions. Its regional news offices are in Donetsk, Lviv, Odesa, Simferopol and Kharkiv.

It has foreign correspondents in Germany, China, Poland, Russia, Serbia and Montenegro, Romania, Hungary, Uzbekistan, and the Baltic countries.

It issues about 500 stories in Ukrainian, Russian, English and German and about 50 photos every day. The agency's informational products are widely represented in the Internet. It had a total of 33 brands of informational products at the end of 2004. Ukrinform is cooperating with many foreign and international news agencies under bipartite agreements. Ukrinform is member of the EANA.

United News of Bangladesh (UNB)

United News of Bangladesh (UNB) is a privately owned national news agency formed in 1988. It has more than 120 journalists including 66 district staff correspondents. The UNB newsroom processes about 250,000 words a day, gathered from a network of local correspondents and reporters covering 54 districts, as well as receiving dispatches from its international partners and overseas correspondents. Subscribers include all leading newspapers, government offices, Bangladesh Television and Radio Bangladesh. In addition to its main service, UNB maintains a Bangla (Bengali) service—translating news from English into Bengali for transmission mostly to newspapers published outside the capital city of Dhaka. UNB is a member of OANA and AsiaNet.

United Press International (UPI)

United Press International (UPI), was born on 21 June 1907 as the United Press Associations because its founder E. W. Scripps believed there should be no restrictions on who could buy news from a news service. It became known as UPI when the UP merged with the International News Service in 1958, which was founded in 1909 by William Randolph Hearst. In 1978 it had more than 7,000 subscribers throughout the world. It is now owned by News World Communications[51], a global multi-media company that owns *Washington Times*.

UPI is a global operation headquartered in Washington D.C. with offices in Beirut, Hong Kong, London, Santiago, Seoul and Tokyo. UPI products include original content in English, Spanish and Arabic. Clients include print publications, websites, multi-media companies, corporations, governments and academic and policy institutions. UPI licenses content directly to print outlets, online media and institutions of all types. In addition, UPI's distribution partners provide its content to thousands of businesses, policy groups and academic institutions worldwide.

Vietnam News Agency (VNA)

Vietnam News Agency (VNA), founded in 1945[52], is the official news service of the Socialist Republic of Vietnam (SRV). VNA provides online information in Vietnamese, English, French and Spanish on a wide range of topics, covering political, economic, social, and scientific and technological issues in Vietnam and the world. VNA news stories reflect the viewpoints of the Communist Party, the State and people of Vietnam on major domestic, regional and international events.

VNA is directed by the Government and is authorised to make official statements reflecting the State's points of view on important national and international issues. Through its news reports, photos, daily bulletins, daily and weekly newspapers, magazines, pictorials, and other publications, VNA provides timely information on current domestic and world events to local and foreign readers, the mass media and research institutions. The agency operates two regional offices in Ho Chi Minh City (Southern Vietnam) and Da Nang City (Central Vietnam) together with a network of 61 local bureaus in 61 provinces and cities throughout the country. It also has 25 overseas offices in Asia, Europe, Africa, America and Oceania.

VNA issues more than 30 publications, including daily bulletins and newspapers: Vietnamese language daily Tin Tuc (News), every afternoon; the English language daily Vietnam News, and the French language daily Le Courier du Vietnam; the weeklies The Thao-Van Hoa (Sports and Culture) and Khoa Hoc & Cong Nghe (Science & Technology) in Vietnamese; monthly magazine Minorities and Highland Regions in Vietnamese and Khmer, the monthly Official Gazette and Vietnam Law and Legal Forum in English, and the

Vietnam Review, monthly in Vietnamese, English and French, and bi-monthly in Lao and Spanish.

VNA issues daily photos on political, economic, cultural, social and scientific activities, and exchanges photos with foreign news agencies and supplies photos at the request of subscribers at home and abroad. Annually, it publishes more than one million photos. VNA National Documentary Photo Service stores more than one million negatives, including 5,000 of President Ho Chi Minh and 1,000 of the country's 54 ethnic groups. VNA recently established an Audio-Visual Centre and a Data Documentation Centre. The VNA Training Centre, established many years ago, has turned out professionally qualified reporters, correspondents, sub-editors and technicians for the agency.

WAFA

Palestine News Agency WAFA was established in 1972 under unique circumstances—the agency of a nation still in the process of emergence through struggle. It was established by fighter correspondents and operated in wartime conditions, and many of its staff members have been killed. The agency does have a website where news is offered free of charge in English, Arabic and Hebrew. Otherwise, the agency has not been able to move towards advanced communications technologies. It has been the beneficiary of a Unesco/Italy grant starting in 1998, to support its international communications activities.

WAM

The Emirates News Agency, Wakalat Anba'a al-Emarat (WAM), was established in November 1976 by a decree of the Minister of Information and Culture of the United Arab Emirates. Transmission of its Arabic language service commenced on 18 June 1977 and of its English language service in December 1978. Its headquarters is in the UAE capital, Abu Dhabi, with other offices in Dubai, Sharjah, Ajman, Umm al-Qaiwain, Ras al-Khaimah, Fujairah, Al Ain and Medinat Zayed. WAM has a total of 180 employees inside the United Arab Emirates and about 25 foreign correspondents. It has offices in the Arab cities of Cairo, Beirut, Rabat, Riyadh, Damascus, Sanaa, Algiers, Jerusalem, Gaza, Khartoum, Amman, Baghdad and Tunis. Other offices and reporters are located in London, Paris, Brussels, Geneva, Moscow, Washington D.C., New York, Tehran, Islamabad, New Delhi, Istanbul and Canberra.

A total of 220 establishments receive the WAM service, including all of the local media, a number of Ministries and UAE corporations and all UAE diplomatic missions abroad, as well as the foreign media.

WAM is a member of the Group of Arab Gulf Co-operation Council news agencies, the Federation of Arab News Agencies, FANA, the Islamic News Agencies Union, the Pool of Non-Aligned News agencies and of OANA. It has also co-operation and news exchange agreements with 20 Arab, Asian and international news agencies.

Women's Feature Service (WFS)

Women's Feature Service (WFS) began in 1978 as a Unesco-UNFPA initiative for the UN Decade for Women. Until 1991, it was a project of Inter Press Service (IPS), based in Rome. WFS became an independent news agency with headquarters in New Delhi, India, where news and features are edited for international release. Today this has become the only link with other bureaus,[53] where each is an independent, registered, non-profit organisation in their country. WFS offices still maintain links, forming a network of editors and writers for its international news service. It is the only independent organisation of its kind. Its revenues come from international donors, sales and projects.

On a weekly basis, the agency produces news, features and opinions on development from a gender perspective. Its original mission was to write on women's issues per se, but its unique selling point today is that it provides a gender perspective on a very broad range of issues related to development. It works with 80 journalists from 35 countries and sells to publications in 11 countries. These correspondents produce some 400 features annually and 500 news-briefs. WFS count many NGOs amongst its clients. Stories are marketed to mainstream newspapers, news agencies, newsletters and journals. As a diversification strategy, the agency offers advice on media strategy; produces and broadcasts radio and video programmes on commission, and produces dailies at international workshops on development issues.

WFS believes that media and communication are critical for women's equality. In 1992, WFS switched from distribution through IPS to electronic mail, and as a result the service reached much greater numbers across a broader geographical spectrum. The Internet has facilitated organisation and networking. The agency's website is online since 2001.

Xinhua

Xinhua News Agency or NCNA (New China News Agency) is the official Press agency of the government of the Peoples' Republic of China. It started in November 1931 as the Red China News Agency and got its current name in 1937. It is the biggest center for collecting information and press conferences in the PRC. It is an institution of the State Council. Xinhua reports directly to the party's Propaganda Department; employs more than 10,000 people, has 107 bureaus worldwide both collecting information on other countries and dispensing information about China; and maintains 31 bureaus in China—one for each province plus a military bureau. People's Daily uses Xinhua material for approximately 25 percent of its stories. Xinhua is a publisher as well as a news agency—it owns more than 20 newspapers and a dozen magazines, and it prints in Chinese, English, and four other languages.

Xinhua has established worldwide networks for news and information gathering, processing, marketing, and transmission, which integrates optical fiber cable with satellite communication technology.

Covering over 100 nations and regions, the news and information transmission network is centered in Beijing with Hong Kong, New York, Paris and London as regional relaying centers.

That network enables Xinhua to release simultaneously news and information round the clock in the forms of text, photos, diagrams, audio and video, and provides other forms of information service across the globe. Xinhua News Agency delivers its news across the world in 7 languages including Chinese, English[54], French, Russian, Spanish, Arabic, as well as news pictures and other kinds of news. It has made contracts to exchange news and news pictures with more than eighty foreign news agency or political news departments.

Xinhua Multi-media Database is a multimedia news and information platform with various media forms and functions. Through it, the agency can supply media and non-media subscribers with their desired multimedia news and information products. It serves as a digital working platform, integrating news and information editing, storage, processing, management, marketing and service. Editors at Xinhua are able to process and release multimedia news and information products using it since 1 July 2003.

Another project Xinhuanet.com, known as an "aircraft carrier" for Chinese websites consists of the Beijing head network, 32 local channels throughout China and 10 subsidiary websites of the Xinhua News Agency. Collecting news and information around the world and covering major events at home and abroad, Xinhuanet.com releases news around the clock in seven languages, namely, Chinese, English, French, Spanish, Russian, Arabic, and Japanese and updates more than 4,500 news items every day. Xinhuanet.com has in fact become a platform and carrier for Xinhua to display its products, which has significantly expanded Xinhua's service scope and influence.[55]

Beijing has been cutting funds to the news agency by an average of seven percent per year over the past three years, and State funds currently cover only about 40 percent of Xinhua's costs. As a result, the agency is raising revenues through involvement in public relations, construction, and information service businesses. In 2001, the Hong Kong-listed media company Global China Technology Group Ltd invested in joint ventures with Xinhua News Agency to set up a market information website and offer audio and visual services planning and consulting.

Yonhap

Yonhap News Agency is the national news agency in the Republic of Korea, founded on 19 December 1980, through the merger of Hapdong News Agency (incorporated on 20 December 1945) and Orient Press (20 April 1952) - bringing Korea's two news agencies under one roof. It was launched on 1 January 1981.

Yonhap clients include government agencies, public and private corporations and portal sites as well as the Korean newspapers and broadcast stations. Yonhap established an electronic system of writing and releasing news to its clients as early as 1988.

Yonhap maintains contracts, news exchange and cooperation agreements and other pacts with 47 foreign news agencies including AP, AFP, Xinhua, Kyodo, Itar Tass, and DPA. The shareholders of Yonhap embrace all of South Korea's broadcasting networks and newspapers.

Yonhap currently has 19 foreign correspondents and over 100 reporters posted in provincial cities. The National Assembly legislated in early 2003 to provide Yonhap with the financial and systemic assistance to reinforce its staff and equipment. Under the law on promotion of news agencies in South Korea, the government is to provide adequate financial support for Yonhap to maintain over 70 foreign correspondents and more than 100 reporters to write articles in English, Chinese, Japanese, Spanish, French and Arabic by 2006.

ZANA

Zambia News Agency, born in 1969, is the only media organisation providing the widest possible news coverage through journalists stationed in regional and district offices in the country. The headquarters of the agency is in Lusaka while regional offices are at Kabwe (Central Province); Ndola (Copperbelt Province); Mansa (Luapula Province); Kasama (Northern Province); Chipata (Eastern Province); Livingstone (Southern Province); Mongu (Western Province) and Solwezi (North-Western Province). It distributes Reuters, Xinhua, DPA and the continental agency Panapress and also co-operates with the Southern African regional news agencies like the Mozambican News Agency (AIM) and the Southern African Broadcasting Association (SABA).

Clients include the national radio and television run by the Zambia National Broadcasting Corporation, the Times of Zambia and the Zambia Daily Mail. It provides news and articles from an African perspective to the Zambians abroad and the international community by the Internet and through Panapress, which has established offices in the USA and Europe. The website, through various links, shows the prominent features of Zambian regions where ZANA reporters cover fields like tourism, business, science and technology, agriculture, sport, environment, culture and gender. Using modern information technology, ZANA is capable of packaging client-tailored content on any subject in English and provides information on past events from its archives.

NOTES AND REFERENCES

1. Formed in 1995, with headquarters in Sydney, to offer a worldwide full-text, translated media release and image distribution service.
2. Formed in 1996, Asia Pulse is a joint venture between six leading Asian news providers: Yonhap News of Korea, Nihon Keizai Shimbun Inc (Nikkei) of Japan, The Press Trust of India, LKBN Antara of Indonesia, Oman News Agency and Australian Associated Press. It is a commercial intelligence news service producing from its pool of dedicated journalists and analysts, regionally relevant, realtime business and market information.

3. Two more units were added in the 1980s: OESP Mídia Direta (1984) and OESP Gráfica (1988).

4. Regina Eleuterio, Executive Manager of *O Globo* (Brazil) gave this information in Moscow in September 2004.

5. The word Andina refers to The Andes Mountain system in South America and it is the name given to all the nations of that region. One of its goals is to strengthen the Peruvian image in the world and that of the Andean region.

6. Brunei Darussalam, Cambodia, Indonesia, Laos, Malaysia, Myanmar, Philippines, Singapore, Thailand, and Vietnam.

7. It was established in July 1975 as Agencia Nacional Angola Press (ANAP), and distributed in the form of bulletins. In October 1975, it became Agencia Angola Press (ANGOP), on proposal of the president Antonio Agostinho Neto, and released, on 28 October, its first dispatch with ANGOP credit line.

8. n° 9/75 of 15 September and the law n° 22/91 of 15 June.

9. Tom Curley is the president and chief executive officer of AP.

10. APP website.

11. Read, Donald, (1999) *Power of News History of Reuters,* Oxford: Oxford University Press, p. 323.

12. Fazalur Rahman Malik, Director General of APP (Pakistan) 25 Sept 2004 at Moscow.

13. Information from agency website as seen on 29 November 2004.

14. In 1922, Radio Lausanne started transmission. The studios of Zurich, Geneva, Basle and Bern functioned since 1926. From the beginning, the journalists of the ATS read the bulletins of news in French and in German and the agency provided bulletins already written to the other radios. In 1931, with the creation of the Swiss Company of broadcasting (SSR), the sorting of the news, drafting and reading with the microphone were centralised in Bern. The ATS assumed the whole responsibility for radio information, since 1932, in French, German and Italian. During the Second World War II, the radio service of information (SIR) of the ATS became one of most listened to in Europe and the ATS reached the top of its fame. After the war, however, the monotonous tone of these bulletins, born at another time, declined. In 1971, the SSR closed the radio operator services of the ATS in French and German language, then in Italian language in 1976. Radio service, baptised Swiss Radio operator News SRN, however reappeared, in 1997, primarily because of the needs for the local radios. In spite of a great popularity with its customers, the SRN folded up at the end of the year 2002 because of lack of profitability.

15. Aslan Aslanov, Director General of AzerTAj (Azerbaijan) at WCNA 24 September 2004.

16. First established as a vehicle to allow distribution of The Associated Press to Canadian newspapers, the press barons of the day quickly came to see the advantages of pooling their own news. The challenges of covering a country like Canada, with six time zones and a small population, were too daunting for each newspaper to shoulder alone.

17. From CP, one can hire the right editorial, commercial or public relations photographer for an assignment. CP can arrange online access and media distribution and turn an event, a static website or a broadcast into an Internet-based multimedia experience (Netcasting) quickly and cost-effectively.

18. Neris, s. r. o. is a 100 percent subsidiary of the Czech News Agency (CTK). Its editorial desk started to create Internet applications in the spring 1996 when it launched the first Czech electronic paper on the Internet—Ceske noviny. It provides information for new media—Internet publishers, mobile operators, audio services, WAP systems and others, It prepares customised World Wide Web applications.

19. Czech capital information agency, a. s. (CEKIA) is a 100 percent subsidiary of the Czech News Agency (CTK) specialising in the Czech capital market and providing information to its participants. The agency has been in operation since 1995.

20. The company NEWTON Information Technology s. r. o. was founded in November 1995 as one of the subsidiaries of the NEWTON Financial Management Group, a. s., and since 1997 it has been a strategic partner of the Czech News Agency (CTK).

21. Article 4 of 13 May 1997, House of Peoples Representatives proclamation.

22. The GNA presentation by Robert Kafui Johnson, General Manager, at Workshop on News Agencies in the Era of the Internet, Amman Jordan 28 – 31 January 2001, Unesco, Paris, 2001

23. Eva contains data from 17 August 1990 in the Croatian and English language.

24. Its founders were Roberto Savio, an Italian freelance journalist, and Pablo Piacentini, an Argentinean political scientist who was then a student in Rome. Savio served as Director General of IPS until 1999 and is now the agency's president emeritus. Piacentini served the organisation in various capacities and is currently editor of the columnist service.

25. IPS website as seen on 17 February 2005.

26. On 8 November 2002 Government resolution #1186 on the reorganisation of the republican state-owned enterprise Kazakh Information Agency (KazTAG) at the Ministry of Culture, Information and Public Accord was passed and created the Kazakh Information Agency (Kazinform) jointstock company.

27. Indian Express Bombay, report dated 5 July 2004.
28. Colombo, (Lankapuvath) - A multi-purpose footwear village is to be set up on 50 acres of under-utilised land obtained from Mahahena Estate in Pitipana, Minister of Rural Economy Bandula Gunawardane told Lankapuvath (Online Edition of Sunday Observer, 18 January 2004).
29. Its earlier address was Transworks House, 54 Chatham St. Colombo 1, Sri Lanka.
30. Farid Ayar, Secretary General, Federation of Arab News Agencies (FANA), in his presentation in 2001 Unesco workshop on News Agencies in the Era of Internet, Amman.
31. MIA SUB-SERVICES: mia FLASH—blocks of short news, mia BOX—short news for direct broadcast, mia 24-HEADLINES—flash news on events during the past 24 hours. SPECIAL SUB-SERVICES: mia BUSINESS Economy, mia INTERVIEW Person & Topic, mia MESSAGE Statement of the day Culture & Arts, mia SKOPJE Skopje themes, mia SPORT Results, mia BALKAN from the region, mia MKD/NATO Integration, mia RETRO MIA archive, mia STORY Foreign press, mia EXPO Science & Technology, mia SUBWAY Bizarre events, mia OOPS!!! Slips, mia MOBIMAK Media support, mia & MIA STOP AIDS, mia IOM Migration
32. Daily Bulletins—Summary of news—Newsletter (English)—Highlights (English).
33. *Weekly* collection of weekly news and information, *Balkan press*- Balkan politics and finance (Macedonian and English)—Balkan defense and security (Macedonian and English).
34. The only challenge so far to the virtual monopoly of MTI as the national supplier of news came from Reuters, which opened its Hungarian language branch but closed it down due to difficulties in the parent company. Reuters continues to be present in Hungary, but not in the Hungarian language market. Other agency services are: Axel Springer—affiliated Europress photo agency and Havaria Press, which was set up by Hungarian journalists and specialises in stories of crime, fire, and accidents. There is also the Roma Press Centre, a small, non-profit news agency dedicated to covering the Roma minority.
35. Transtel press release dated 5 December 2003.
36. NAN Introduces PR Wire Services *By Andrew Ahiante* THISDAYonline 16/11/2004 13:06:38
37. "The formation of the News Agencies Pool of Non-aligned countries was a major act in what we call the decolonisation of information, that is, the effort of the non-aligned countries to dissolve the monopoly on information and to enable them to personally inform the world about themselves. This is a very important contribution to the advancement and democratisation of

the overall world information system."—Josip Broz Tito to the participants of the second conference of the Non-aligned News Agency Pool in Belgrade (20 November 1979)

38. Address by Abdollah Nasiri Taheri, President of IRNA (Chair NANAP, at the world Congress of News Agencies in Moscow, 24 September 2004.)

39. The man who set up South Korea's first trade union for a newspaper company in 1987, when it seemed impossible under the military regime.

40. *Korea Times* 2001/07/05 Former Journalist Breaks News Agency Monopoly: A local would-be news provider's three-year-long legal fight finally ended last Friday when the Supreme Court upheld a lower court ruling ordering the government to withdraw its earlier rejection of an application to set up the nation's second news agency. Also terminated was the monopolised structure for the provision of news that had taken root in Korea for two decades. "The occasion will lead to full-fledged competition in the local news providing business which has been dominated by the de facto state-owned Yonhap News Agency since 1980," said Choi Hai-un, 49, the president of Newsis, syndicate news provider since six years.

41. Internews Network • Mexican Media: The Oral Tradition • 30 July 2002.

42. Speech of. Aranda Enrique Pedroza, Director General of NOTIMEX in Moscow on 24 September 2004.

43. A committee appointed to make arrangements for the formation of the company said: "The Press Association is formed on the principle of co-operation and can never be worked for individual profit, or become exclusive in its character."

44. PanAfricanist Congresses started in London 1890. The important sixth Pan-African conference (Manchester, 1945) included Jomo Kenyatta and Kwame Nkrumah. The first truly intergovernmental conference was held in Accra, Ghana, in 1958, where Patrice Lumumba was a key speaker. The Pan-Africanist Congress (PAC) was founded by Robert M. Sobukwe and others in South Africa in 1959 as a political alternative to the African National Congress, which was seen as contaminated by non-African influences. The founding of the Organisation of African Unity (OAU; now the African Union) by Julius Nyerere and others in 1963 was a milestone, and the OAU soon became the most important Pan-Africanist organisation.

45. Information on Panapressis based on the speech delivered by its Director General Babacar Fall, at World Conference on News Agencies, in Moscow, September 2004 and the website.

46. On 31 October 1918 a group of Polish journalists took over local branches of Viennese Correspondence Bureau in Cracow and Lvov (which were part

of Austro-Hungarian Empire before World War I) and established Polska Agencja Telegraficzna (PAT), the Polish Telgraphic Agency which on 5 December 1918 became Republic of Poland's government press and information agency. In 1921 it got autonomy, and later in 1924 it became a state corporation. PAT left Poland following the evacuated government in September 1939 because of World War II. It reestablished itself first in Paris and later in London, at the side of the Polish emigratory government which was not recognised by the Soviets. Its merger with PAP was rather symbolic as it was never dissolved.

47. Centralna Agencja Fotograficzna (CAF), Central Photographic Agency, was established in Warsaw in 1951.

48. Marcos declared martial law on 21 September 1972.

49. STT radio news was launched as soon as public broadcasting began in 1926.

50. Established by Act 81/1992 from 30 January 1992

51. News World Communications, a global media company, acquired United Press International in May 2000. News World's flagship newspaper, *The Washington Times*, was founded in 1982 and has gained a reputation for hard-hitting investigative reporting and thorough coverage of politics and policy. In addition, News World publishes newspapers and magazines in more than 20 countries and in four languages.

52. Founded on 15 September 1945, the first wire service bulletin released by VNA in Vietnamese, English and French carried the Declaration of Independence of the Democratic Republic of Vietnam (now the SRV) read by President Ho Chi Minh at Ha Noi's Ba Dinh Square on 2 September 1945.

53. The Philippine Bureau started in 1987 by a handful of contributors grew into an independent news agency in 1992. WFS Philippines Inc. is a registered non-stock, non-profit corporation. Today, WFS news and features appear in 13 publications and three websites, including three Indian publications.

54. English service started in 1944.

55. Tian Congming, President of Xinhua News Agency (China) at World Congress of News Agencies, Moscow (24 – 25 September 2004).

8

ALLIANCE, ASSOCIATIONS AND COUNCILS

*L*ike any other business, news agencies also have associations. The first association was Agences Alliees (the allied agencies) and it was born in Bern, Switzerland, in June 1924. By the time the Spanish news agency Agencia EFE S.A was formed in January 1939, the Club of the Allied Agencies had thirty agencies. Its statutes stated that only one agency from each country could be a member of the association. Fabra was its member and EFE replaced it.

European Alliance of News Agencies (EANA)

The present European alliance was founded in 1956 as the European Alliance of Press Agencies. In 2002 its name was changed to European Alliance of News Agencies. This name was more relevant, as these agencies serve a wide variety of media and non-media clients. As a juridical entity, the European Alliance of News Agencies (EANA) is a non-profit membership association registered at the Trade Register in Bern, Switzerland, where it has a bank account and where its books are audited.

The EANA of today comprises 30 European news agencies[1] representing 30 countries with around 750 million inhabitants. EANA serves as a Pan-European professional forum for the establishment of contacts and co-operation as well as exchange of information, experiences and know-how among its members. EANA organises seminars on subjects of common interest to its members. The seminars—normally one in spring and one in autumn—cover subjects such as development of content in news services, marketing, information technology, copyright and other legal matters related to the media, tariff policy, etc.

EANA activities also include various surveys. One of them is a yearly market survey called Country Reports with information from each member country on how the media market has developed, etc.

The major objectives for EANA as described in its mission statement are—

- To secure a business environment where news agencies can fulfil the task of independent and unbiased news reporting. This includes recognition of copyright and related rights for news agencies and access to sources of information.
- To promote co-operation and information exchange between member agencies via our seminars and the EANA Newsletter that is published monthly and distributed exclusively to the EANA members.
- To offer member agencies a pan-European professional forum for discussions and for exchange of experiences and know-how by organising seminars, workshops, etc.

The EANA operations are financed via membership fees to ensure freedom from interference of outside interests. The EANA is formally registered in Bern, Switzerland, and has one employee working full-time as the secretary general from the secretariat based in Stockholm, Sweden. The Swiss colleagues at SDA/ATS assist EANA with bookkeeping, bank contacts, etc. in Switzerland, and the website www.newsalliance.org is hosted by ANA in Athens, Greece.

EANA's annual general assemblies elects a bureau of five persons to supervise the operations of the association. The president of EANA is elected for two years and must be the chief executive of his or her agency. The other four bureau members are elected for three years and are exchanged step-by-step so that not all of them leave at the same time, thereby securing continuity.

Several of the EANA member agencies are also members of other associations for news agencies, for instance, the association for Mediterranean agencies, the Balkan agencies and the Organisation for Asian News Agencies (OANA). With the latter, EANA has signed an agreement for co-operation in 2004.

The statutes say that the annual general assembly should normally be held in Switzerland. But for the year 2004, as an exception, it accepted the invitation by Itar-tass to had the general assembly and a seminar with the title The News Agency Role and Profitability in Moscow in connection with the Itar-tass congress.[2]

EANA mission statement says that it is the interest of EANA to have agencies in transition as members and to assist these member agencies in their ambition to develop unbiased news services based on the principles of freedom of the press.

Statutes

Article 1 Definition

EANA is a non-profit membership association of European News Agencies in the sense of art. 60 ff of the Swiss Civil Code (CC). EANA is registered at the place of its domicile in the trade register of Berne.

Art. 2 Purpose

2.1 The purpose of EANA is to safeguard and promote the common interests of its members in all areas essential to their work and activities.

2.2. EANA serves as a Pan-European, professional forum for the establishment of contacts and co-operation as well as exchange of information, experiences and know-how among its members. EANA shall look after common interests to its members at the European Union and other international organisations. EANA shall organise seminars on subjects of common interest to its members. These seminars shall cover subjects as development of content in news services, marketing, information technology, copyright and other legal matters related to the media.

2.3 EANA can speak and act on behalf of its members, through its President, Secretary General or duly appointed representatives in debates etc on issues of concern to its members.

Art. 3 Membership

3.1 Only the leading news agency from an internationally recognised European country can become a member of EANA. Exceptions can be made by the General Assembly so that EANA has more than one member from a country. If an application for membership is submitted to the Bureau by a news agency other than the member from the same country, this application can be submitted to the General Assembly only if unanimously approved by the Bureau and provided that there is no objection from the agency already being a member from that country. If there is an objection from the current member agency from that country, the Bureau shall inform the General Assembly and postpone decisions for a year at which time the General Assembly decides on the application with a three quarters majority of the membership of EANA.

3.2 Members shall support the principles of freedom of the press and unbiased news.

3.3 Membership fees and exceptional contributions from member agencies shall be the main sources for financing the activities of EANA.

3.4 The size of the membership fee is decided by the General Assembly upon the recommendation from the Bureau and based on the budget submitted. The EANA is only liable for any commitments only with its assets. No unlimited liability of the members beyond their ordinary membership contributions exists.

3.5 Member agencies that have not paid their annual dues within twelve (12) months after having received the first invitation to pay their fee will automatically be excluded from membership, unless the Bureau of EANA decides to make an exception for special circumstances.

3.6 Any member is free to withdraw from EANA at any time provided it has paid all past dues in full, including dues for the year in which it withdraws.

3.7 No individual member agency assumes any liability for EANA and EANA assumes no liability for any individual member agency.

Art. 4 General Assembly

4.1 EANA holds an ordinary General Assembly every year. The General Assembly is the supreme body of EANA. All members are entitled to attend and vote at the annual general meeting. In principle General Assemblies shall be held in Switzerland at a date agreed upon by the members at every annual meeting for the following year.

4.2 The General Assembly:
  • decides on long term objectives for EANA
  • elects President, Bureau members and Secretary General of EANA
  • approves the Secretary General/s annual report

- approves the budget and financial status of EANA
- decides on membership fees - accepts new members
- decides on disqualification of members
- decides on any change in the statutes of EANA
- decides on the dissolving of EANA

  The General Assembly can deal with any other subject that is relevant to the objectives of EANA.

4.3 The member agencies shall be represented by their respective executive heads. If prevented from attending, any such executive can delegate his/her powers in writing to a member of his/her executive staff, who is then to represent the agency. Any official representative is allowed to be accompanied by up to two (2) other members of the executive staff of the agency concerned, the maximum delegation from any agency thus being three (3) persons.

4.4 When voting at the General Assembly each member has one (1) vote. Decisions are taken by a show of hands unless a secret vote is requested by at least five (5) members. For the election of President secret voting is used.

4.5 All draft decisions as well as nominations for office submitted to the General Assembly shall be addressed in written form to the Secretary General at least two (2) months before the opening of the General Assembly.

   All documents for the General Assembly shall be sent from the Secretariat to the member agencies so that all members have received them at least two (2) weeks prior to the General assembly. Any member is free to nominate candidates for the Presidency and members of the Bureau. Such nominations from member agencies shall be supported in writing by at least two (2) other member agencies. It is the Bureau/s duty to see to that there are candidates for the Presidency and the Bureau. Candidates shall have officially represented his/her agency in EANA for at least two (2) years. Candidates for the Presidency shall be the CEO of his/her agency. Candidates for the Presidency shall have served for minimum one (1) year as a Bureau member immediately prior to the election or in the past.

4.6 Decisions will be reached by a simple majority of the votes present except for decisions which must be accepted by three quarters of the votes present. These are as follows:

- disqualification from membership of any agency
- any change in the statutes of EANA
- dissolving of EANA
- admission of new members requires three quarters of the total number of member agencies
  The refusal of a request for membership and the exclusion of members take place without specifying the reasons.

4.7 If considered necessary, the Bureau is empowered to convene an extraordinary General Assembly. The Bureau shall also convene such an extraordinary General Assembly if requested to do so by at least one fifth of the members.

Art. 5. The Bureau

5.1 The Bureau is the executive body of EANA. The Bureau prepares recommendations for submission to ad hoc committees and the General Assembly, is responsible for the implementation of decisions from the General Assembly and takes those decision which are not in the responsibility of the General Assembly. The Bureau prepares the General Assembly and presents the nominations for office to the General Assembly. The Bureau also submits a budget including membership fee to the General Assembly.

The Bureau shall appoint an auditor who shall examine the accounts of EANA and whose report shall be a part of the financial report to the annual General Assembly. The Bureau shall fix the salary and terms of employment for the Secretary General.

5.2 The Bureau consists of five (5) persons; the President, the Secretary General and three (3) other members of the Bureau.

The term of office for the members of the Bureau shall be implemented so that the Bureau is renewed step by step. Members of the Bureau, elected before these statutes were approved, will stay in office till the end of their previously decided term. The President is elected for two (2) years. The three (3) Bureau members and the Secretary General are elected for three (3) years.

5.3 With the exception of the Secretary General, members of the Bureau can not be re-elected within three (3) years after the end of their mandate. The Secretary General can be re-elected for additional three (3) year periods.

5.4 Decisions or recommendations within the Bureau shall be reached by a simple majority of members present. The President has a casting vote in the case of a tie. The quorum for the conduct of business within the Bureau shall be three (3) including the President. If there is no quorum, the meeting is rescheduled with the same agenda, in which case two members of the Bureau shall constitute a quorum. The Bureau can also take decisions in meetings per capsulam if the members agree on such a procedure.

5.5 In the event of a position as Bureau member becoming vacant in between two General Assemblies, the Bureau is authorised to fill the vacancy by co-opting any qualified member. The term of office of the co-opted member shall run only until the next General Assembly. A co-opted member of the Bureau may apply for re-election for a full three-year term at the following General Assembly.

Art. 6. The President

6.1 The President shall be the official representative of EANA and will be vested with its authority. He/she shall preside over the General Assembly and the meetings of the Bureau.

6.2 Should the post as President become vacant in between two General Assemblies, the Bureau elects one of its members to be President until the next General Assembly.

Article 7. The Secretary General

7.1 The Secretary General shall be responsible for the co-ordination of EANA/s activities and its general administration. The Secretary General runs the day to day business of EANA under the supervision of the Bureau. He/she is responsible for the accounts of EANA. He/she shall prepare the meetings of the Bureau as well as all documentation pertaining to the General Assembly. He/she shall submit an annual report to the General Assembly on the activities and the financial status of EANA.

7.2 Should the post as Secretary General become vacant in between two General Assemblies, the Bureau may fill the position in any way it deems fit, pending the next General Assembly.

7.3 The Secretary General is employed by EANA.

7.4 The address used by EANA shall be that of the Secretary General.

Article 8. Committees

8.1 The Bureau can decide to establish working groups on an ad hoc basis as required by the business of EANA.

8.2 Upon the recommendation of the Bureau the General Assembly may decide on the creation of specific committees and appoint chairmen of these committees. Committee Chairmen shall report annually to the General Assembly on the activities of their committees. The Committee Chairmen may if required attend the meetings of the Bureau in an advisory capacity and as such, shall submit interim reports to the Bureau.

Article 9. Finances

9.1 The budget for each year is decided by the General Assembly upon recommendation from the Bureau who will submit a draft budget to that effect to the General Assembly.

Article 10. Language

The working language of EANA is English.

EANA Members: AA. -Anadolu Agency (Turkey), AFP – Agence France-Presse, ANA- Athens New Agency, ATA-Albanian Telegraph Agency, ANP- Algemeen Nederlands Persbureau, ANSA –Agenzia Nazionale Stampa Associata (Italy), APA- Austria Presse Agentur, ATS/SDA Agence Telegraphique Suisse – Schweizerische Depeschenagentur, BNS –Baltic News Service, BTA-Bulgarian News Agency, BELGA- Agence Telegraphique Belge de Presse S. A., CNA- Cyprus News Agency, CTK- Czech News Agency. DPA-Deutsche Presse Agentur (Germany), EFE- Agencia EFE S. A. (Spain). HINA-Croatian News Agency, ITAR-TASS - Russian News Agency, LUSA- Lusa-Agencia De Noticias De Portugal, MTI- Hungarian News Agency Corporation, NTB- Norsk Telegrambyra As, PA- The Press Association Limited (UK), PAP- Polska Agencia Prasowa, RITZAU-Ritzaus Bureau I/S, ROMPRESS- Agentia Nationala de Presa (Romania). STA- Slovenska Tiskovn Agencija, STT/FNB-Oy Suomen Tietotoimisto-Finska Notisbyran AB, TANJUG- News Agency of Serbia-Montenegro, TASR- News Agency of Slovak Republic, TT-Tidningarnas Telegrambyra and Ukrinform- Ukranian National News Agency

Organisation of Asia-Pacific News Agencies (OANA)

The Organisation of Asia-Pacific News Agencies (OANA) was formed in 1961 on the initiative of Unesco to secure direct and free exchange of news between the news agencies of a region inhabited by more than one half of the world's population. OANA brings together 40 news agencies from 33 countries. OANA members are responsible for two-thirds of information circulated throughout the world.

The twelfth OANA General Assembly in 2004 adopted the Kuala Lumpur Declaration, which laid down guidelines for the successful operations of news agencies. The member agencies gathered there reaffirmed their commitment to active cooperation among, and support for, one another in the transborder gathering of news and information as well as the exchange of such news and information.

STATUTES
Preamble

The 7th General Assembly of the Organisation of Asia - Pacific News Agencies in Jakarta agreed to adopt the following Statute (hereinafter referred as the Statute) as revised from the draft proposed at the 5th General Assembly in Kuala Lumpur in November 1981 to be valid from the date of adoption.

Part 1 - Purposes of the Organisation
Article 1

The objectives of the Organisation are:

(a) To increase and facilitate a freer flow of news and information in Asia and the Pacific;

(b) To encourage the removal of discriminatory actions and unnecessary restrictions by governments affecting news agencies engaged in news transmission or distribution so as to promote the availability of news information to people of the world without discriminations, restrictions for purposes of security do not in themselves constitute discrimination, provided that such restrictions are not based on measures designed to restrict the free flow of information in international news transmission or distribution,

(c) To provide machinery for cooperation among news agencies or groups of news agencies in Asia and the Pacific to operate as a news exchange network in or to facilitate news exchange through one or more distribution centres whose function is to relay without editing, news received from other network agencies and to encourage the general adoption of the highest practical standards in matters concerning news exchange and distribution,

(d) To participate actively in correcting the imbalance in information and in improving the flow of news between developed and developing countries,

(e) To concern itself with national, regional and sub - regional efforts at overcoming poverty, hunger, unemployment and disease and at modernisation,

(f) To commit itself to peace and understanding among nations and opposition to all forms of racism, colonialism and neo-colonialism,

(g) To strengthen cooperative relationships among Asia - Pacific news agencies and between them and agencies in other parts of the world to their mutual benefit, and

(h) To study, work together and, when necessary, to take joint action to improve editorial, training, communication and technical facilities in order to implement the above objectives.

Part II - Membership

Article 2

Membership in the Organisation shall be open to all news agencies of Unesco member countries in Asia the Pacific, subject to the provision of part II herein.

Article 3

(a) News agencies of Unesco member countries in Asia and the Pacific may apply for membership in the Organisation by writing to the Executive Board of the Organisation.

(b) The Executive Board may prescribe qualification for membership keeping in view internationally recognised definition of a news agency.

(c) Every applicant should seek endorsement from member agency or members agencies of the country concerned.

(d) The Executive Board has the discretion to admit or reject such application.

Article 4

Any member which fails to conform with this Statute or to any rules and regulations made under this statute may lose its membership on decision of two - thirds of the strength.

Article 5

(a) Newspapers, information agencies, news agency groups, or any international Organisation, former office bearers of OANA or any national or international professional journalist bodies, may on the invitation of the Executive Board be granted observer status in the General Assembly.

(b) Observers may participate in the deliberation of the General Assembly without voting rights.

(c) The number of such observers from any country shall not exceed six at any time.

Part III – Organs

Article 6

The Organisation shall consist of a General Assembly, an Executive Board, and such other subsidiary organs as the Organisation may at any time consider necessary.

Part IV – The General Assembly

Article 7

The Supreme Authority of the Organisation shall be vested in the General Assembly.

Article 8

(a) The General Assembly shall meet once every three years at such time and place as the Executive Board may from time to time determine.

(b) An extraordinary session shall be convened after a notice of 60 days whenever a majority of the members give notice to the Executive Board that they desire a session to be arranged or at any time if deemed necessary by the Executive Board, after a notice of 60 days.

Article 9

A majority of the members shall constitute a quorum for the sessions of the General Assembly.

Article 10

The functions of the General Assembly shall be:

(a) To elect at each regular session from among the members its President, 4 Vice - Presidents and six members of the Executive Board who shall hold office until the next regular session

(b) To determine its own rules of procedure except otherwise provided in the Statute,

(c) To establish any temporary or, upon recommendation of the Executive Board, permanent subsidiary bodies it may consider to be necessary,

(d) To receive and consider the reports of the Executive Board, and to decide upon any question referred to it by the Board,

(e) To determine the financial arrangement of the Organisation in accordance with part IV,

(f) To review the expenditure and approve the accounts of the Organisation.

Article 11

The General Assembly shall have the power to waive an omission or irregularity of any kind arising this statute except in the case of any irregularity in the election of any member to the Executive Board.

Part V - The Executive Board

Article 12

The Executive Board shall be composed of 11 members elected by the General Assembly consisting of the President, 4 Vice-Presidents and 6 ordinary Board members. In electing the members of the Executive Board, the Assembly shall observe that due regard is given to ensure representation from sub - regions within the region of Asia and the Pacific.

Article 13

(a) Members represented on the Executive Board in accordance with Article 17 shall hold office until the of the next regular session of the Assembly. Members shall be eligible for re - election.

(b) No agency shall be eligible to serve as President for more than two (2) successive terms.

Article 14

(a) The President (or in his absence or inability to act as a member of the Executive Board, a Vice - President selected by the other Vice - Presidents or in default of selection chosen by lot) shall during the Organisation's term of office preside over all Executive Board meetings and all sessions of the General Assembly and shall be responsible for the proper conduct of all such sessions. If no Vice - President is present or able to act, a member of the Executive Board elected by the Executive Board's members shall preside.

(b) The Executive Board shall adopt its own rules of procedure unless otherwise provided in the Statute.

(c) The majority of the Executive Board shall constitute a quorum.

(d) Decisions of the Executive Board shall be taken by a majority of the Board members voting person.

(e) The Executive Board shall meet at least once a year. It shall meet at such places as may be convenient.

Article 15

The Executive Board may invite any member agency to participate, without the right to vote in its deliberations on any matter.

Article 16

(a) There shall be a Secretary General appointed to assist the President.

(b) The Executive Board appoints the Secretary - General in consultation with the President.

Article 17

The Executive Board shall submit to the General Assembly the audited financial statements of the organisation together with its comments and recommendations.

Article 18

The Executive Board shall make a report to the General Assembly at each regular session on the work of the Organisation since the previous regular session of the General Assembly.

Article 19

The Executive Board may enter into agreements or arrangements covering the relationship with other organisations as provided for in Part I.

Article 20

The Executive Board may, whenever necessary, consult the members of the Organisation by written communication on any matters relating to the affairs of the Organisation. Any proposal or recommendation circulated in such manner and approved in writing by a majority of the members shall be deemed adopted.

Article 21

The Executive Board may recommend to the General Assembly whenever revision of subscription rates by member's payable is necessary.

Article 22

The Executive Board shall have the power to appoint committees and co - opt any person to perform functions necessary to achieve the Organisation's objective under Part I.

Article 23

A provisional agenda for each General Assembly's session shall be prepared by the Secretary - General and circulated to all members not later than two (2) months before the session. Any members may propose in writing to the Secretary - General matters for insertion in the provisional agenda one month before the session. The Executive Board shall determine the agenda for each session.

Article 24

The Secretary - General shall keep members informed in respect to the activities of the Organisation.

Article 25

The Secretary - General shall perform such other tasks as may be assigned to him by the President from time to time.

Part VI - Finances

Article 26

The general expenses of the Organisation shall be met by dues from the members and by such subsidies and donations as the Organisation may think fit to accept.

Article 27

Any member which fails to discharge its financial obligation to the Organisation within one year from the date on which it is due shall have no voting right in the General Assembly and the Executive Board, unless the General Assembly, at its discretion, waives this provision.

Article 28

The Secretary General shall prepare and submit to the Executive Board the financial statements for each year.

Part VII - Voting
Article 29

The following provisions shall apply to voting in the General Assembly and the Executive Board:

(a) Each member shall have one vote.

(b) Except as otherwise stated in this Statute, decisions of the Executive Board and the General Assembly shall be by majority vote of the members present and voting. In the event of a deadlock, the President or person presiding shall have a casting vote.

Part VIII - Amendments
Article 30

Texts of proposed amendments to the Statute shall be communicated by the Secretary - General to members at least six months in advance of the General Assembly for their consideration. Amendments shall be adopted by a two-thirds majority vote of the members present and voting in the General Assembly or by postal ballot and shall come into force immediately upon adoption.

Article 31

Any amendment adopted under Article 31 shall as soon as possible after the termination of the session be forwarded by the Secretary - General to all members.

Part IX - Withdrawal
Article 32

(a) Any member may withdraw from the Organisation by written notification given to the Secretary - General of the Organisation who will immediately inform the other members of the Organisation of such notification.

(b) The withdrawal shall take effect upon the expiration of three months from the date on which such written notification is received by the Secretary -General.

Part X - Miscellaneous Provisions
Article 33 - Language

The official language of the Organisation for all purposes shall be English or such other language or languages as the General Assembly may determine.

Article 34 - Interpretation

Any question or dispute concerning the interpretation or application of the Statute shall be referred to the Executive Board, whose decision shall be final.

Datuk Syed Jamil Jaafar, General Manager of Bernama (Malaysia) participated on behalf of OANA in the WCNA in Moscow and said:[3]

These are turbulent and even troubling times, for we cover violence, strife, disasters and catastrophes both natural and man-made, among other things, on a daily basis; grim tasks for news agencies and the media in general, but nevertheless a necessary part of our operations.

Much time, energy and efforts are devoted to the coverage of events in Iraq, in the Middle East, in various parts of Africa, and elsewhere, as such events have a bearing on the well-being of mankind as a whole. In this era of instant communication, incidents and events thousands of miles away are brought to us within minutes of their occurrence. It behoves us then to ensure that correct and accurate news and information about such events are disseminated to the world at large.

Bernama maintains OANA website. OANA News Wire - informational product incorporating original articles donated by Asia-Pacific news agencies was initially available for free but after January 15, 2002, one has to fill in and send the form on the website to the OANA Secretariat for determination of optimal conditions of subscription.

OANA Membership: Bakhtar News Agency (Afghanistan); Australian Associated Press Information Services Pty Ltd (AAP), Australia; Azerbaijan State Telegraph Agency – AzerTAj Azerbaijan; Bangladesh Sangbad Sangstha (BSS), United News of Bangladesh (UNB); Agence Khmer de Presse (AKP) Cambodia; Xinhua News Agency (Xinhua), China; Korean Central News Agency (KCNA) of DPR Korea; Emirates News Agency, (WAM) Wakalat Anba'a al-Emarat); Asian News International (ANI) and Press Trust of India (PTI), India; Antara National News Agency/LKBN Antara (Antara), Indonesia; Islamic Republic News Agency (IRNA) Iran; Jiji Press Ltd,, and Kyodo News, Japan; National Company "Kazinform", and Khabar Agency Kazakhstan: Kuwait News Agency (KUNA); Kyrgyz News Agency "Kabar" Lao News Agency (KPL); Bernama News Agency Malaysia; MONTSAME (Mongolyn tsakhilgaan medee) Mongolia; Rastriya Samachar Samati (RSS) Nepal; Oman News Agency (ONA), Associated Press of Pakistan (APP), Pakistan Press International,

Philippines News Agency, Qatar News Agency, Yonhap News Agency (South Korea) ITAR-TASS News Agency, and Russian Information Agency "Novosti", Saudi Press Agency (SPA) Lankapuvath Limited (Sri Lanka) Syrian Arab News Agency, Thailand News Agency, Anadolu News Agency (Turkey) Vietnam News Agency (VNA) Yemen News Agency (SABA)

Alliance of Mediterranean News Agencies (AMAN)

The Alliance of Mediterranean News Agencies is the organisation of Press Agencies of Mediterranean countries, members of which are 20 national news agencies of these countries[4.] It joins together agencies from European continent, countries of Arabia and North Africa and the Peninsula of the Balkan. Through this organisation, the agencies of this region exchange experience in the field of information.

Since 10 years ago, when this organisation was found. AMAN gathers and disseminates the common experience, exchanges information and organises competitions for the best photo and news item. As members of AMAN, from France to Mauritania, from Egypt to Spain, from Italy to Lebanon. During 2004 year, Albania had the honor to host the 13th General Assembly of AMAN.

1991 Tunis declaration to form Alliance of Mediterranean News Agencies (AMAN)

Statutes

Preamble: Tunis Declaration of November 21, 1991 "The General Directors of the Mediterranean countries' news agencies who are participating in an international symposium." Communication in the Mediterranean and the future "in Tunis between 19 and 21 November 1991 as part of a meeting organised because of the 30th anniversary of the Tunisian News Agency (TAP): Conscious of old and omni-directional ties between the two shores of the Mediterranean;

Believing in the future development of closer information in this region between the news agencies of the countries on the shores of the Mediterranean;

Stressing that information and communication will be able to play a basic role in the realisation of the consciousness that it is necessary to strengthen the ties between Mediterranean countries;

Believing that issues like democratisation, human rights, socio-economic, cultural and scientific development, the environment, migration and peace and security in the Mediterranean could be subject to ties and dialogue between these agencies;

Declaring that is necessary to achieve this communication with the desire of contributing to Mediterranean information and in the framework of free transfer of information;

Thinking that meetings between Mediterranean countries' news agencies at predetermined intervals will strengthen dialogue and cooperation among them and direct them to other areas of interest;

Declare their intention to set up a working group constituted of LUSA (Portugal), AA (Turkey) and SANA (Syria) and coordinated by TAP (Tunisia) with the aim of strengthening inter-agency cooperation.

This Committee will be charged with investigating possibilities and ways of achieving the common objectives defined at the Tunis symposium, such as setting up a union or club of Mediterranean news bulletin creating a directory of the Mediterranean news agencies and developing technical relations ". Mindful of these exhortations, the signatory news agencies of the Tunis Declaration met in a Constituent General Assembly in Istanbul on October 2, 1992 and adopted a Statute. On June 7 and 8, 1993, during the General Assembly held in Damascus it was agreed to entrust the Follow-up Committee to revise and enrich the Statutes with the special cooperation of MAP. A draft edition was discussed on April 7, 1994, in Damascus by the Follow-up Committee. The third Alliance's General Assembly, has revised the provisions on June 26-27, 1994, in Rome, as follows:

Chapter One: Definition and Objectives of the Alliance

Article 1: Definition

An association known as the "Alliance of Mediterranean News Agencies is hereby created and called "AMAN".

Article 2: Objectives

The objectives of the Alliance are specified in the Tunis Declaration. The Alliance will be non-political.

Chapter Two: Membership

Article 3: Members

3.1 The founding members are the signatory agencies of the Tunis Declaration, and precisely: Anadolu Ajansi (AA), Agence France-Presse (AFP), Agence Mauritanienne d'Information (AMI),

Agenzia Nazionale Stampa Associata (ANSA), Algerie Presse Service (APS), Agenzia EFE (EFE), Al Jamahiryah News Agency (JANA), Agencia de Informacao (LUSA), Maghreb Arabe Presse (MAP), Middle East News Agency (MENA), Syrian Arab News Agency (SANA), Tunis Afrique Presse (TAP), Palestinian News Agency (WAFA).

3.2 Mediterranean News Agencies which did not take part in the Tunis meeting and consequently were not signatories to the Tunis Declaration can apply to the General Assembly for membership.

3.3 A candidate agency must first fulfil the following requirements:

(a) It shall formally accept and undersign the Tunis Declaration and the Statutes of the Alliance.

(b) It shall be recognised as the agency representative of the country in question.

(c) It shall represent a country belonging to the Mediterranean area or a country having continuous and privileged relations with the Mediterranean basin.

(d) Its Statutes and activity shall not carry any religious or racial contents.

3.4 The Alliance can admit observers. At the time the Statutes were adopted observers were the Federation of Arab News Agencies and the Inter Press Service. New observers can be admitted by a resolution of the General Assembly. Observers can take part in General Assemblies without the right to vote; they cannot be elected to the Follow-up Committee.

3.5 The application for admission must be addressed to the Follow-up Committee, which will proceed to submit it to the next General Assembly.

3.6 A resolution of the General Assembly for the admission of new members and observers requires a three quarter's majority of the members present.

Article 4: Loss of Member Status

Every member can withdraw from the Alliance by addressing a written communication to the Follow-up Committee. The General Assembly, upon request of the Follow-up Committee, can decide to exclude a member or to suspend his member rights in case of: loss of conditions required for admission; serious violation of the Statutes; delayed payment of the membership fee. The relevant resolution of the General Assembly requires a three quarter's majority of the members present.

Article 5: Membership Fees

5.1 The General Assembly, may fix the amount of the annual membership fee according to the different categories of members, as specified in article 3.1.

5.2 The Alliance can accept on approval of the General Assembly donations from member news agencies and international organisations.

5.3 Membership fees and donations will be kept in a bank account opened in the name of the Alliance, in the country of the Secretary General, in a convertible currency.

Chapter Three Structure of the Alliance

Article 6: Structure The structure of the Alliance is the following:

The General Assembly
The President
The two Vice-Presidents
The Secretary General
The Follow-up Committee

Article 7: The General Assembly

7.1 The General Assembly consists of all the members of the Alliance; it is the highest authority to take decisions and define actions.

7.2 The Alliance holds at least one ordinary General Assembly every year, alternatively on the Northern and the Southern shores of the Mediterranean Sea. Within the context of this guideline, each yearly session shall be held in the country of the member agency which, with the consent of the General Assembly, has voluntarily taken the commitment to host it.

7.3 The General Assembly may be convened in extraordinary session upon request of the President, or at least of three member agencies.

7.4 Both the ordinary and the extraordinary sessions are called and chaired by the President or, in case of his incapacity or impediment, by one of the two Vice-Presidents and can be held only in the presence of at least two thirds of the member agencies.

7.5 Each founding or ordinary member agency has one vote.

7.6 The sessions of the General Assembly are open. They may also be convened in camera, without the attendance of the observers, once agreed upon by the majority of those present.

Article 8: Ordinary Session Of The General Assembly

The ordinary session of the General Assembly;

Appoints the President and the two Vice-Presidents of the Alliance

Elects the Secretary General;

Decides on admission, exclusion or suspension of members

Approves the annual budget;

Evaluates the reports proposed by the Follow-up Committee and any other business it may deem necessary;

If necessary, appoints a special committee with the specific task of examining controversies on the interpretation or the enforcement of the Statutes.

Resolutions of the General Assembly in ordinary session are taken by a majority of the members present. 8.3 - However, decisions by the General Assembly on:

Appointment of the President and Vice-Presidents;

Election of the Secretary General requires a qualified majority of two thirds of the members present;

While:

Admission of new member agencies to the Alliance;

Admission of new members to the Alliance Requires a qualified majority of three-quarters of the members present.

Article 9: Extraordinary Session Of The General Assembly

9.1 The General Assembly in extraordinary session decides on:
- Amendment of the Statutes
- Dissolution of the association
- Other questions which do not fall within the scope of the ordinary General Assembly.

9.2 Resolutions of the General Assembly in extraordinary session are taken by a majority of three-quarters of the members present.

Article 10: The President And The Two Vice-presidents

10.1 The President shall be appointed for a term of one year. He shall be the Chief Executive Officer of the member agency which hosts the current General Assembly. He shall stay in office till the opening of the next ordinary General Assembly.

10.2 The President represents the Alliance, calls and presides over meetings of the General Assembly and Follow-up Committee; he has other authority received by the General Assembly.

10.3 The two Vice-Presidents shall be appointed for a term of one year. They shall be the Chief Executive Officers of the two member agencies which have, respectively, (1) assumed the previous presidency (First Vice-President) and (2) proposed to host the following meeting of the General Assembly (Second Vice-President).

10.4 The President and the two Vice-Presidents may delegate their authority to a representative of the same agency.

Article 11: The Follow-up Committee

11.1 The Follow-up Committee is the executive body of the Alliance. It is responsible for the handling of the Alliance's administrative activities.

11.2 The Follow-up Committee consists of the President, the two Vice-Presidents and the Secretary General.

11.3 The competence of the Follow-up Committee is the following:

To implement the General Assembly decisions;

To fix the date and venue of the General Assembly meetings, in accordance with the hosting agency;

To draw up the draft agenda of the meeting and send it to the members at least three weeks prior to the meeting of the General Assembly;

To prepare for the presentation by the President to the General Assembly reports on the activities of the Alliance;

To present to the General Assembly membership and withdrawal applications from the Alliance.

11.4 Resolutions of the Follow-up Committee shall be taken by simple majority of the members present. The President has a casting vote in the case of a tie.

11.5 In the event of resignation of a member from the Follow-up Committee in between two General Assemblies, such member shall be replaced according to the following procedure:

If the vacancy affects the post of President, the new President shall be the first Vice-President;

If the vacancy affects the post of first Vice-President, his position shall remain vacant till the next General Assembly;

If the vacancy affects the post of second Vice-President, who has the task of hosting the next General Assembly, the Follow-up Committee is authorised to fill the vacancy by co-opting the senior Chief Executive Officer of any member agency ready to accept the commitment to host the General Assembly.

11.6 The Follow-up Committee is called and chaired by the President or, in his absence, by the first Vice-President and must meet at least two months before the General Assembly, in order to prepare the agenda well in advance and distribute it to the member agencies at least three weeks prior to the General Assembly. 11. 7 - If considered necessary, the Follow-up Committee may hold an extraordinary meeting.

11.8 The quorum for the conduct of business within the Follow-up Committee is three.

Article 12: The Secretary General

12.1 The Secretary General shall be elected for a term of three years, renewable.

12.2 The applications for the Secretary General position shall be addressed to the Follow-up Committee before being submitted to the General Assembly.

12.3 The responsibilities of the Secretary General are as follows:

To secure the continuity of the management between the General Assemblies.

To secure the coordination between members.

To prepare the necessary documents for decisions to be taken by the ordinary and the extraordinary General Assemblies.

To secure the cooperation with other similar institutions.

To keep the Alliance funds with the written consent of the President and supervise the implementation of the budget within the limits of the authorisation given by the General Assembly.

To present the annual budget to the General Assembly.

Chapter Four General Provisions

Article 13: Representation

13.1 Each member agency will be represented in the Alliance by its Director General. If prevented from attending, he can delegate his power to a representative from his agency.

13.2 In the General Assembly and Follow-up Committee meetings, each Director General may be accompanied by another member of the agency concerned without the right to vote, the maximum from each thus being two persons.

Article 14: Languages

14.1 The working languages of the Alliance are Arabic, English and French. The language of correspondence is English.

14.2 The Statutes are drawn up in three languages: Arabic, English and French. In the event of a dispute over translation, the English text will be the text of reference.

Article 15: Disputes On The Statutes

In case of disagreement in the interpretation of the Statutes, the General Assembly convened either in ordinary, or in extraordinary session appoints a committee formed by three delegates elected within the members, with the task of seeking a solution. The committee shall inform member agencies of its decision within a period of two months. Its decision will be discussed during the following General Assembly.

Article 16: Amendment Of The Statutes

The statutes can be amended only by the General Assembly, convened in extraordinary session, with a resolution taken by a majority of three-quarters of members present, according to articles 7.3 and 9.

Article 17: Dissolution

The Alliance can be dissolved only by the General Assembly convened in extraordinary session with a resolution taken by a majority of three-quarters of members present, according to articles 7.3 and 9.

Article 18: Official Address Of The Alliance

The official address of the Alliance shall be that of the Secretary General.

Article 19: Applicable Law

In cases not expressly covered by this act, the French law will be applied.

Article 20: Enforcement

The Statutes shall come into force once signed by the member agencies.

AMAN Membership: Anadolu Ajansi (AA), Turkey; Agence France-Presse (AFP); Agence Mauritanienne d'Information (AMI); Athens News Agency (ANA) Greece; Agenzia Nazionale Stampa Associata (ANSA) Italy; Algerie Presse Service (APS), Albanian Telegraph Agency (ATA), Cyprus News Agency (CNA); Agencia EFE, S. A. (EFE) Spain; Croatian News Agency- HINA; Al Jamahiryah News Agency (JANA) Libya; Agencia de Noticias de Portugal, S. A. (LUSA), Maghreb Arabe Presse (MAP) Morocco; Middle East News Agency (MENA) Egypt; National News Agency (NNA) Lebanon; Syrian Arab News Agency (SANA), Slovene Press Agency (STA) Slovenia; International Press Center- TANJUG Serbua-Montenegro; Tunis Afrique Presse (TAP), Palestinian News Agency (WAFA).

Federation of Arab News Agencies (FANA)

At present, the Federation of Arab News Agencies (FANA) comprises national news agencies of 18 Arab countries and its aim is to consolidate professional relations between these agencies, to provide more extensive distribution of news within the Arab countries and to disseminate Arab news abroad.

To achieve this goal, the federation endeavours to raise the professional levels of its member-agencies through the provision of consultancy; to encourage exchange of expertise among them; convenes periodical meetings of the directors of these agencies or specialised meetings and works towards the development of information and technical cooperation between its members and the other national news agencies in the world.

Attempts were made in 1964 to establish the Federation of Arab News Agencies and the first conference was held in 1965 in Amman, Jordan. In January 1974 the Arab League called for holding a meeting in its head office in Cairo for the directors of the Arab News Agencies in order to re-study the subject of the federation's constitution. An agreement was reached in this meeting to hold the second conference in Baghdad in April 1974, where decisions were taken toward the actual founding of the federation.

In November 1974 the third FANA conference was held in Beirut during which the first members of the General Secretariat and the

Secretary General were elected. The federation officially started its activities in its head office in Beirut from the beginning of 1975.

Founding members of FANA are news agencies operating at that time in the Arab countries and were the national news agencies of Jordan, Tunisia, Algeria, Saudi Arabia, Iraq, Palestine, Lebanon, Libya, Morocco, Yemen, Egypt, and Sudan. (The national news agency of Kuwait was in the course of constitution in that year). FANA was established within the scope of the Arab League as stipulated in the first article of the FANA statute. The Arab League Council should ratify the statute's articles before their implementation.

The federation has a higher council called the General Assembly, which meets yearly (usually during November) and is attended by the director generals of the member agencies, and the General Secretariat which meets twice each year to discuss the activities of the Federation. It comprises seven members elected by the General Assembly for two years while the Federation's Secretary General is elected for a five-year term and should be a person of vast experience and specialisation in the domain of news agencies work and journalism.

The federation has achieved a unity of opinion among the Arab News Agencies as concerns the professional matters. Its annual conferences and specialised meetings have contributed to the development of cooperation between these agencies and in assisting the emerging Arab News Agencies through providing them with financial and technical aid as well as expertise through the exchange of experts and inter-member visits of officials and technicians. The federation organised two seminars in February 1975 in Tunisia and in March 1977 in Tripoli (Libya) in which participating Arab and African news agencies discussed ways and means of mutual cooperation and studied methods that ensure a better exchange of news between them. These meetings where discontinued after the constitution of the Pan African News Agency (PANA).

The federation also organised three seminars (April 1980 in Damascus, Syria; April 1981 in Acapulco, Mexico; and June 1982 in Tangiers, Morocco). The participants from among the national news agencies in the Arab countries and in the Latin American countries were able to reach a consensus as regards the practical bases for cooperation and the facilitation of the direct exchange of news between them. These seminars were discontinued in view that none of the Latin American news agencies offered to host a follow-up seminar in their countries.

Besides this, the federation organised five meetings between 1976 and 1989 for dialogue between the Arab and European news agencies (Tunis, Istanbul, London, Prague and Tunis). These colloquiums were also discontinued after the dissolution of the USSR and the consequent changes in the international power balance, which led the European agencies to abstain from attending any future meetings. The federation's activities and the meetings it organised led to the opening of centers for news gathering and distribution between the Arab News Agencies from one side and other groupings of news agencies from the other side.

In fact, an Arab center for the distribution of Arab news in Europe was established in Vienna, Austria. The bulletin entitled "FANA-NEWS" in the English was dispatched by federation to this center from the Kuwaiti news agency's head office, containing an average of 40 news items daily concerning the Arab countries. The German news agency DPA was charged with re-dispatching the bulletin to news agencies in Western Europe; and the Czechoslovakian News Agency to news agencies in Eastern Europe. Regretfully, the publication of this bulletin was discontinued in the aftermath of the Gulf War in 1990.

FANA worked towards the establishment of another bureau for the collection and distribution of Arab news to Latin American countries but the intermediary agency, Inter Press Service of Rome, which took upon its charge this mission on behalf of Latin American news agencies, failed to fulfill its obligations.

The federation attends Unesco's meetings and participates in its media conferences as an Observer Member. It participates in the meeting of the Permanent Committee for Arab Media and the Council of Arab Ministers for Information. Besides round-table conferences, the federation organises yearly seminars and training workshops for the Arab news agencies personnel.

FANA Members: Jordan News Agency (PETRA); Emirates News Agency (WAM); Tunis-Afrique Press (TAP); Algerian Press Service (APS); Saudi Press Agency (SPA); Syrian Arab News Agency (SANA) Palestinian News Agency (WAFA); Qatari News Agency (QANA); Kuwaiti News Agency (KUNA); National News Agency, Lebanon (NNA); Jamahiriyah News Agency (JNA); Maghreb Arab Press (MAP); Mauritanian Press Agency (MPA); Yemen News Agency (SABA); Middle East News Agency, Egypt (MENA); Sudan News Agency (SUNA); Oman News Agency (ONA); Bahrain News Agency (BNA).

Association of Balkan News Agencies (ABNA)

The Balkan state news agencies, after an initiative by Macedonian Press Agency[5], established the Association of the Balkan News Agencies (24-26 June 1995) in Thessaloniki. ABNA was founded in as a voluntary, non-profit and professional organisation of the Balkan national news agencies, to improve the flux and exchange of information in the region. Founding charter of Association of Balkans News Agencies was signed in Thessaloniki by representatives of seven Balkan news agencies: Turkey's Anadolu, the Bulgarian Telegraphic Agency (BTA), Balkan Information Pool (BIP)[6], Yugoslavia's Tanjug, Romania's Rompres agency, Greece's Athens News Agency (ANA), and Macedonian Press Agency (MPA). Its first major project was the "Balkan News Bank", financed by the European Union's INTERREG-II. The program started operation in July 1997 with the participation of the news agencies that are members of the ABNA. ANMPA news report[7] to that effect mentioned: FYROM[8] Macedonian Press Bureau (MPB) as ABNA member and "the Slovenian Telegraph Agency (STA) and Bosnia-Herzegovina's B-H Press expressed their wish to participate in ABNA".

The July 2000 meeting chaired by Tanjug was attended by Anadolu Ajansi (Turkey), ANA and MPA (Greece), BTA (Bulgaria), MIA (Macedonia), and ROMPRES (Romania), while guests were officials from the Slovenian STA News Agency, HINA from Croatia, MOLDPRESS from Moldavia[9], Belgrade's BETA News Agency, MINA from Podgorica, as well as FENA[10], SRNA[11], ONASA[12] and Media Plan representatives from Bosnia-Herzegovina.

Macedonian Press Agency with the "concurrent opinion" of the Association of Balkan News Agencies is about to establish a Balkan Data Bank. The Data Bank's servers will be in the facilities of Macedonian Press Agency while offices of correspondents will be operating in all the Balkan state capitals and in the cities where news agencies participating in this cooperation are based. Those offices will supply the Data Bank with news items through an online link up and vice versa: The news items and the information received on a daily 24-hour basis form the Balkan Data Bank and from its system of news exchange will be channeled into all the mass media of the countries where those offices will be based.

In ABNA meeting held in Thessaloniki on 23 June 2003, the participants from national news agencies of Turkey, Greece, Romania, Bulgaria, Macedonia, Serbia, Montenegro, and Albania took part. ABNA discussed the participation of private news agencies in ABNA with observer status. It was also decided to establish an ABNA Internet website, install a press award, and implement an exchange program for the journalists who work in regional agencies.

When the ABNA celebrated its 10 years in December 2004, the members were ANA and MPA from Greece, ATA from Albania, Anadolu from Turkey, BTA from Bulgaria, Rompress from Romania, Tanjug from Serbia-Montenegro, MIA from FYROM, and SRNA from Bosnia-Herzegovina. The Slovenian news agency STA, the news agency FENA from Bosnia-Herzegovina, and the Moldavian MOLDPRES attended the meeting as observers. MPA General Director and ABNA General Secretary Mr. Spiros Kouzinopoulos said that in the 10 years since its founding, ABNA has managed to survive in spite of the difficulties it faced from time to time. He said that ABNA promotes the high goals it has set from the beginning and its basic vision was to erase the boundaries of information and work against nationalism, xenophobia and racism.

The General Assembly in its meeting at Thessaloniki on December 3, 2004 decided the creation of an ABNA portal on the Internet to present all the news agencies in Southeastern Europe and the establishment of annual prizes for journalists who help with their news reports in the efforts for the development of inter-Balkan cooperation, peace and security in the region.

World Council of News Agencies

The formation of a world news agencies association has been proposed in a meeting of representatives from 58 news agencies that took place in Istanbul (Turkey) in April 2003. The final statement adopted at this three-day World News Agencies Summit pledged to cooperate towards ensuring global peace and understanding and to ensure the accuracy of news and recognised importance to just and objective news.

"Free, impartial and independent journalism is the first step towards peace and democracy," it said.

The summit also resolved that news agencies should not be prevented from fulfilling their task of transmitting news in times of peace and even more during conflict as the people need objective and accurate news. "All necessary efforts should be exerted to ensure safety of journalists who have to receive and transmit news under all conditions and in all places," it said.

Some 120 participants from member agencies of the Association of the Balkan News Agencies (ABNA), Alliance of Mediterranean News Agencies (AMAN), European Alliance of News Agencies (EANA) and the Organisation of Asia-Pacific News Agencies (OANA) attended the summit hosted by Anadolu of Turkey. ITAR-TASS of Russia proposed to hold the World News Agencies Congress in Moscow in September, next year.

The first World Congress of News Agencies held in Moscow[13] on 24 – 25 September 2004 decided to create its working body—the World Council of News Agencies.

"Of course, this will be a public council. It apparently will incorporate leaders of regional pools and representatives from news agencies named by them to handle practical work," said Vitaly Ignatenko, Director General of ITAR-TASS, the host news agency.

Uffe Riis Sorensen, managing director of the Danish news agency Ritzaus Bureau and former head of the European Alliance of News Agencies, was invited to head the secretariat of the World Council of News Agencies.

International Press Telecommunications Council (IPTC)

International Press Telecommunications Council (IPTC) was founded in 1965 to safeguard the telecommunication interests of the world's press. But with passage of time, the focus was adapted to more current technological needs.

IPTC is a consortium with members from the world's major news agencies, news publishers, news industry system vendors, and the leading industrial nations worldwide. IPTC revenues come from membership fees. IPTC is based in the United Kingdom but maintains worldwide operation. IPTC's work is focussing on the business of the news industry. IPTC develops and maintains technical standards to improve the free exchange of news which are adopted by virtually every major news provider world wide. IPTC standards are available at no charge.

IPTC members are of two categories:

Nominating Members: Agence France-Presse (AFP), France; ANSA, Italy; Associated Mediabase Limited UK, Austria Presse Agentur (APA),

Austria; BBC Monitoring, United Kingdom; Business Wire, US; Canada NewsWire Ltd, Canada; Canadian Press, Canada; CCNMatthews, Canada; CINTEC, Hong Kong; Deutsche Presse-Agentur (dpa), Germany; Dialog/NewsEdge Inc, USA; Dow Jones & Company, USA; European Alliance of News Agencies; Japan Newspaper Publishers & Editors Association (NSK), Japan; Keystone, Switzerland; Kyodo News Services, Japan; Newspaper Association of America (NAA), USA; PA News Ltd, UK; PR Newswire, UK; Reuters Limited, UK; SDA/ATS, Switzerland; The Associated Press (AP), US; The New York Times Company, US; Tidningarnas Telegrambyra (TT), Sweden; TMNEWS-APCOM, Italy; United Press International (UPI), USA; World Association of Newspapers (WAN)

Associated Members: AFX News Ltd, UK; Agence de Presse Belga, Belgium; Agencia EFE, Spain; Algemeen Nederlands Persbureau (ANP), The Netherlands; ANA (Athens News Agency), Greece; AS Norsk Telegrambyrå, Norway; Atex Media Command, Australia; CCI Europe, Denmark; EAST Co. Ltd, Japan; Eidos Media Srl, Italy; Fingerpost Ltd, UK; Harris and Baseview, USA; HINA, Croatia; IBM, Japan; IFRA, Germany; ITAR-TASS, Russia, La Republica, Italy; Magyar Távirati Iroda Rt (MTI), Hungary; NewsLink, UK; Oy Suomen Tietotoimisto, Finland; RelaxNews, France; Ritzau Bureau, Denmark; RivCom, UK; XML Team Solutions Inc., US.

NOTES AND REFERENCES

1. Baltic News Service (BNS) in Tallinn, Estonia, and Tanjug in Belgrade, Serbia and Montenegro are new members of the European Alliance of News Agencies (EANA) that joined in Geneva on 25 – 26 September 2003. EANA thereby comprises 30 European news agencies.
2. Paul Tesselaar, President of EANA, General Manager of ANP (Nederland) at WCNA, Moscow.
   He also said, "Finally, let me once again thank ITAR-TASS for inviting us to this world forum for news agencies, a meeting that was first announced in 2003 when our colleagues at AA in Ankara, Turkey, had taken the initiative to invite news agencies from all over the world to a conference for news agencies in Istanbul."
3. On 24 September 2004.
4. Frrok Cupi, President of AMAN, Director General of ATA (Albania) at WCNA, Moscow 24 September 2004.

He also said, "We are living a reality when challenges are standing in the way of media all over the world, especially in Eastern and Central Europe, in Arab and Balkan countries.

We are facing, most of all, the challenge of fear. Some political segments and Mafia are posing a real threat to journalists. I like to avail myself of the opportunity, to pay homage to the eight journalists killed in Iraq during 2004 and express my solidarity with the two French colleagues taken hostage not long ago.

Journalism is also confronting the challenge of truth.

The truth is frequently preliminary prepared by media owners or Mafia bosses, while media performs the task of just transmitting this manipulated truth to the public. What's the alternative the journalists must choose under such a situation? Present the truth, or the manipulated truth?

The evil and terrorism have mended fences with the media. Media and terrorism exist because of each other. The media is searching for terrorism, as terrorism exists due to media. Unfortunately, terrorism is gaining ground and threatening millions of people through the media.

Media is in front of the challenge to serve as a political tool, or otherwise suffer from repression. In our Eastern part countries, media has already become more a fighting instrument than an information tool. The political conflict is using media as a fabric on one side and a weapon on the other.

Journalism is suffering from its own faults. Sometimes, it's not a professional and cultural journalism, but it's an "acid" journalism that is scraping the society's values. It is demolishing the values of art, culture, tradition, friendship and good behaviour. The saying that good news isn't news" is applied in practice; which means that nothing is good in this world. Truth is always standing at the focus of challenge. We are now facing the dilemma of helping, or abandoning the truth. We journalists, workers of information, are the only ones that can assist the truth. This is, without doubt, a difficult undertaking, but this is at the same time our mission and challenge. We are confronting the dilemma: "Reveal the truth and start immediately to live after."

5. Founded in 1991.
6. The Balkan Information Pool (BIP), Sofia-based information agency independent from the state institutions and political parties, was established in 1991.
7. Dated 8 June 1997.
8. Former Yugoslav Republic of Macedonia.
9. State run agency.
10. Federation News Agency (FENA) state-run.
11. Sarajevo-based state-run.
12. Bosnian Serb agency private.
13. Representatives of 115 news agencies from more than 100 countries participated in this congress.

CHRONOLOGY

1832 : Charles-Louis Havas set up a foreign newspaper translation agency.

1835 : Havas' agency became the Agence Havas—the first worldwide news agency.

1840 : Using carrier pigeons, Havas landed news in the newsrooms of Paris newspapers about midday from the Belgian morning press and around 3 p.m. news from the same day's British newspapers.

1844 : Morse demonstrated telegraph.

1845 : Agence Havas was the first user of the Paris-Rouen telegraph line.

1848 : Paul Julius, Reuter (born Israel Beer Josaphat in Cassel, Germany on 21 July 1816, baptised as Paul Julius Reuter on 16 November 1845 in London) then partner in a Berlin bookshop, fled Germany after publishing some political pamphlets and worked as a translator in Havas News Agency in Paris.

In May the Associated Press was born as Harbour News Association in New York.

1849 : Wolff'sches Telegraphisches Bureau (WTB) was born—the first, and, until 1933, the most important German news agency.

Joseph Tuwora started the Oesterreichische Correspondenz in Vienna.

Daniel Craig established the AP's first foreign bureau in Halifax, Nova Scotia, the first North American port-of-call for Cunard's liners.

1850 : Paul Julius Reuter used pigeons to fly stock market prices between Aachen and Brussels.

1851 : Reuter opened office in the city of London (I Royal Exchange Buildings on 10 October) that transmitted stock market quotations between London and Paris via Calais-Dover cable.

1853 : The foundation of Telegraphic Notiziario Stefani on 26 January in Italy.

1858 : The first news from Europe arrives directly by transoceanic cable. Addressed to the AP, the cable contained 42 words summarising five stories in headline form and concluded: "Mutiny being quelled, all India becoming tranquil."

1859 : Havas, with Reuter and Wolff, who had set up news agencies in London and Berlin, decided to divide up the world between them for the purpose of gathering and distributing news.

1860 : First State news agency *k. k. Telegraphen Korrespondenz-Bureau* founded by the Austro-Hungarian Government. First news agency in Holland, Delamar, was founded.

1861 : Platoons of AP reporters were dispatched to cover the American Civil War.

1863 : Reuter built telegraph line between Wales and Ireland.

1865 : Reuters Telegram Company went public. WTB was transformed into the joint-stock company Continental Telegraphen Agentur, which provided for fresh capital. The government started to subsidise it and gave it a semiofficial status. Nile Maria Fabra y Deas, a journalist and Catalan industrialist, started Center of Correspondents in Madrid.

1866 : Henry Collins landed in Bombay to set up Reuters operations in India.

Trubnikov, a wealthy merchant with newspaper interests, founded the first Russian news agency Russkoe Telegrafnoe Agentstvo (RTA).

Danish news agency, Ritzau founded by Eric Nikolai Ritzau.

1867 : Fabra met Auguste Havas in Paris while returning from Vienna and turned his Center of Correspondents into Fabra Agency, a subsidiary of Havas.

Norsk Telegrambyrå AS (NTB) was established as a private news service owned by the main newspapers in Norway.

First news agency in Sweden, Svenska telegrambyrå, was founded.

1868 : Press Association (PA) was founded by a group of provincial daily newspaper proprietors in the UK. Reuters' first agreement with UK Press Association (PA) to provide foreign news services.

News agency Telegrafnaja Kontora (the Telegraph Bureau) was founded in Riga.

1869 : Reuter tried to buy Wolff Bureau (WTB); Bismarck ensured that he did not succeed.

WTB agency moved into a wing of the telegraph station building of the post office in Berlin, which must have been an advantage in the working process; remained in the Reichspost until 1877.

1870 : Agreement signed between Havas, Reuters, and Wolff to establish a worldwide news ring (also called cartel) on 17 January. Reuters operated joint news service with UK Press Association.

1872 : Reuters opened agencies in Far East.

Russian news agency Mezhdunarodnoe Telegrafnoe Agentstvo (MTA) was founded by Krajevesky, a rival of Trubnikov.

1873 : Sibirskoe Telegrafnoe Agentstvo (the Siberian Telegraph Agency) was founded in Irkutsk.

1874 : Reuters opened agencies in South America.
Fabra used carrier pigeons to report the ships that cross the Straits of Gibraltar and for that established pigeon houses in Valencia, Barcelona and Palma de Mallorca.

1875 : AP became the first news organisation to secure a leased telegraph wire.

1879 : Agence Havas became a public limited company. In addition to news, Havas launched into advertising.
New Zealand Press Association (NZPA) was founded, owned by 31 daily newspapers.

1880 : Magyar Taviati Iroda (MTI), the state-owned Hungarian News Agency, was founded.
Katkov, the proprietor of a newspaper in Moscow, opened Peterbursko-Moskovskoe Telegrafnoe Agentstvo (the Petersburg-Moscow Telegraph Agency).

1882 : Dow Jones Newswires was founded.
In Russia, Russkoe Telegrafnoe Agentstvo (RTA) and Mezhdunarodnoe Telegrafnoe Agentstvo (MTA) were merged into Severnoe Telegrafnoe Agentstvo (STA).

1886 : First news agency in Japan, Shimbun Yotatsu Kaisha, was founded.

1887 : The Finnish Telegram Agency started to relay news on 1 November in what was then was the Grand Duchy of Finland.

1889 : Stefani detached from Havas (which owned it 50 percent but got its service through Reuters, after intervention of Prime Minister Francisco Crispi).
First news agency in Rumania, Agence de Roumaine; first news agency in Bulgaria, Agence Balkanique, and first news agency in Turkey, Agence de Constantinople were founded.

1893 : The Associated Press was incorporated as national co-operative in the US to replace all various regional press associations. Reuters offered exclusive cartel contract (which was earlier with a private United Press of New York, not the UP founded by E. W. Scripps) to the newly formed Associated Press. It was promptly accepted.

WTB opened its first branch in Cologne.

1894 : Russiiskoe Telegrafnoe Agentstvo (RTA) was started again as a semi-official news agency.

1895 : A private company, the Stefanopoli Telegraphic Agency, started in Greece.

1897 : United Press of New York collapsed.

1898 : The Bulgarian News Agency, Bulgarska Telegrahna Agentsiya (BTA), Bulgaria's national news agency was established by a decree issued by Prince Ferdinand I.

1899 : AP used Guglielmo Marconi's wireless telegraph to cover the America's Cup Yacht Race off Sandy Hook, New Jersey, the first news test of the new telegraph.

1900 : First news agency in Argentina, Agencia Notiociosa Saporiti (ANS) by Carlos Saporiti, founded in Buenos Aires.

Total number of news agencies in the world—29.

Regional AP associations merged and the modern AP was incorporated as a not-for-profit cooperative in New York City with Melville E. Stone as its first general manager.

In Italy, Stefani became the joint stock company of Teodoro Mayer (editor of Piccolo), who possessed half of it, and financier Giuseppe Volpi di Misurata, who possessed the other half.

1901 : Dentsu news agency of Japan was established, having both advertising and news businesses.

1902 : Torgovo Telegrafnoe Agentstvo (TTA) was started to serve financial and commercial interests of the Russian State.

1903 : An agreement with WTB gave AP permission to have a representative in Wolff's Berlin office, who would sort the news material according to its value for the U.S. public.

1904 : The St. Petersburg Telegraph Agency (SPTA), the first official news agency of Russia and the predecessor of ITAR-

TASS began to operate on 1 September. Russiiskoe Telegrafnoe Agentstvo (RTA) was closed down by the Government because of its dependence on the German news agency, Wolff, and using TTA, the new official news agency, Sankt-Peterburskoe Telegrafnoe Agentstvo, the St. Petersburg Telegraph Agency (PTA) was founded.

1905 : Stefanopoli Telegraphic Agency of Greece became Athens News Agency (ANA) and was subsidised by the Government.

1906 : E. W. Scripps purchased control of the Publishers Press, a small news service in the East.

Scripps-McRae Press Association (SMPA) used telephone for delivery of news; Kent Cooper accomplished it for the agency.

1907 : E. W. Scripps founded the United Press (UP) by combining three regional news services, of which, two—Scripps-McRae Press Association in the Middle West and the Scripps News Association on the Pacific Coast—were founded by him, and the Publishers Press, purchased by him.

1909 : International News Service founded by media mogul William Randolph Hearst.

United Press began a cable service to Nippon Dempo Tsushin Sha, the Japanese Telegraph News Agency, which later merged into Domei.

On 31 December the SPTA was subordinated directly to the Russian Council of Ministers.

1910 : Keshab Chandra Roy started a Press Bureau which finally became Associated Press of India (API).

1912 : Foundation of Albanian Telegraphic Agency (ATA)

1913 : German agency Telegraphen Union (TU) was founded. It was largely influenced by the industry and belonged to the conservative right-wing Hugenberg-holding.

1914 : Japanese news agency Kokusai was started, but confined to distribution of foreign news.

AP switched from Morse transmission to teleprinter.

On 19 August one day after Nicholas the Second ruled to rename St. Petersburg into Petrograd, SPTA changed its name accordingly and became the Petrograd Telegraph Agency (PTA).

1915 : Transocean (TO) was founded by the Syndikat Deutscher Überseedienst, a syndicate initiated by the government and financed by the industry and commerce. During World War I, the German foreign ministry used the TO for propagating the German cause.

United Press began its first news file to South America.

Finnish Telegram Agency was merged with a competitor into Suomen Tietotoimisto (STT)—the Finnish News Agency.

1916 : The AP and member newspapers combined resources to cover a national election.

Telegraphic agency Rador replaced Romanian Telegraphic Agency, Roumagence, after Romania entered World War I.

1917 : The Canadian Press (CP), Canada's news agency came into being as a vehicle to allow distribution of The Associated Press to Canadian newspapers.

Bolshevik government (Sovnarkom) decreed PTA to become the central government information agency.

1918 : PTA moved to Moscow where it merged in June with the press bureau of the government. On 7 September the government presidium resolved to rename PTA and the press bureau into the Russian Telegraph Agency (ROSTA) and became the central information agency of the whole Russian Socialist Federative Soviet Republic.

Polska Agencja Telegraficzna (PAT), the Polish Telgraphic Agency; Armenpress news agency in Armenia, and Eesti Teadate Agentuur (ETA), the Estonian Telegraph Agency were founded.

1919 : *La Prensa* of Buenos Aires, started using United Press service.

Associated Press of India (API) became fully-owned subsidiary of Reuters.

On 4 March the Latvian provisional government in Liepaja established the state information agency Latopress. Latopress concluded partnership agreements with the Estonian news agency Estur (now ETA) and Polish news agency PAT (now called PAP). Cooperation with Poland ensured radio news contact between Riga and Warsaw.

1920 : Agence Havas and the Société Générale des Annonces (an advertising company) merged.

The state news agency AzerTAj of the Republic of Azerbaijan was established in March, ELTA national news agency of Lithuania was established on 1 April and Anadolu Ajansi (AA) in Turkey was established on 6 April.

Cabinet of Ministers of the Latvian provisional government established Latvian Telegraph Agency, changing the name from "Latopress" to LETA on 5 May.

Pierre-Marie Olivier and Maurice Travailleur created the Belgium Telegraphic Press Agency (Agence Belga) with a capital of 5 million Belgian Francs provided by 234 companies and 11 individuals on 20 August. On 1 January 1921, the agency distributed its first dispatches.

1921 : Foundation of Mongolian News Agency, MONTSAME by the government as MONTA, the Mongolian Telegraph Agency.

Direct UP service to newspapers in Europe was inaugurated after World War I, to clients in Cologne, Frankfurt and Vienna.

Agerpres took over the assets of the Radio Orient Agency Rador, established on 16 June as an official press institution of the Romanian State, wholly subordinated to the Ministry of Foreign Affairs.

1922 : British United Press Ltd. was organised to serve newspapers throughout the British Empire.

United Press service directed newspapers on the Asian mainland to publications in Peking and Tienstsin.

1923 : Reuters used radio to transmit news internationally.

1924 : Transocean started a daily news service in English.

Polish Telegraphic Agency (PAT) became a state corporation.

The Central News Agency (CNA) Taiwan's national news agency was founded on 1 April.

Agences Alliees, held its first meeting in Bern in Switzerland in June.

Stefani property and the presidency transferred to Manlio Morgagni, former administrative director of the Popolo d'Italia, newspaper founded by Mussolini.

1925 : AP started using by-line.

UK Press Association took majority stake in Reuters Ltd.

Anadolu Agency in Turkey went through a structural transformation and got the status of company with autonomy.

On 10 July 1925 the Telegraph Agency of the Soviet Union (TASS) was founded and took over the main functions of the Russian Telegraph Agency as the central information agency of the country. TASS enjoyed exclusive right to gather and distribute information outside the Soviet Union, as well as the right to distribute foreign and domestic information within the Soviet Union, and manage the news agencies of the Soviet republics. TASS comprised news agencies of all the Soviet republics: RATAU (Ukraine), BELTA (Byelorussia), UZTAG (Uzbekistan), KAZTAG (Kazakhstan), GRUZINFORM (Georgia), AZERINFORM (Azerbaijan), ELTA (Lithuania), ATEM (Moldavia), LATINFORM (Latvia), KIRTAG (Kirghizia), TAJIKTA (Tajikistan), ARMENPRESS (Armenia), TURKMENINFORM (Turkmenia), ETA (Estonia).

Japanese news agency Rengo came into being with the merger of Kokusai (international news service) and domestic news agency Toho (East).

1926 : Agenzia Internazionale Fides (Fides-AIP), the International Agency Faith, of Vatican was founded.

Interviews used by the AP for the first time; first one of Bobby Jones—British and American Open Golf champion.

1927 : Swaminath Sadanand launched Free Press Agency (FPA) in India.

President Janis Cakste signed legislation for establishing by-laws of Latvian Telegraph Agency (LETA) on 17 March.

AP started a news picture service. Reuters introduced teleprinter for sending information to London newspapers.

1930 : UP correspondent Webb Miller was the only correspondent to cover the "salt march" protest organised by Mohandas Gandhi at Dharasana, India, where hundreds of Gandhi's followers were beaten while protesting through nonresistance.

1931 : Xinhua News Agency was established on 7 November.

UP moved its headquarters to offices in the 36-storey news building in New York City.

Havas began using modern teleprinters.

1933 : B. Sen Gupta, who had resigned from the Free Press, started United Press of India from Calcutta.

The Associated Press supplied written news to radio stations owned by newspaper members only when the news was of "transcendent importance."

The "customers" of the AP took the name Associated Press Managing Editors Association (APME).

United Press started supply of news to radio stations.

1934 : Reuters and AP signed a contract allowing AP freedom to distribute its own news all over the world.

IRNA (Iran) was established as PARS.

ANP (Netherlands national news agency) was founded by the daily newspapers in the Netherlands.

1935 : AP WirePhoto network was born; its first photo was a view of an airplane crash in upstate New York.

Bakhtar Information Agency (BIA) established in Kabul.

Foundation of Australian Associated Press (AAP) as a co-operative.

Sadanand went bankrupt through the forfeiture of the heavy securities he had to pay repeatedly for the violation of the imperial code and closed down Free Press Agency (FPA) in India. It was the first Indian news agency, to organise and maintain an efficient world news service to the press of India during the years 1932 – 35.

1936 : Domei News Agency was established with the help of the Japanese government, succeeding Rengo and taking over news and communication operations of Dentsu.

1937 : W. J. Moloney, the General Manager of Reuters, introduced teleprinters in India. Associated Press of India (API) inaugurated its first teleprinter circuit from Bombay to Calcutta.

Antara News Agency (Indonesia) was established on 13 December.

1938 : South African Press Association (SAPA) was founded, jointly owned by newspapers.

1939 : Reuters moved corporate headquarters to 85 Fleet Street, London.

Foundation of Spanish agency EFE.

PAT left Poland, following the evacuated government. It re-established itself first in Paris and later in London, at the side of the Polish emigratory government.

1940 : During the Soviet occupation, the Latvian Telegraph Agency became a subordinate unit of the Soviet information system, TASS.

On 1 August in London, Paul-Louis Bret launched Agence française d'Information (AFI).

In November legislation forced the splitting up of the advertising and newsgathering operations of Agence Havas. The newsgathering operation, now owned by the State, became the Office Français d'Information (OFI, or the French Information Office).

1941 : RIA Novosti came into being on 24 June.

UP provided the first news reports of the Japanese attack on Pearl Harbour.

Reuter Trust was formed to "safeguard the neutrality and independence of Reuters"

On 1 April the AP broadcast wire "officially" signed-on Atlanta station WSB, and New York's WQXR, WOR and WNYC. "Specialists" wrote news stories for the wire in a new kind of style meant for the ear.

1942 : On 15 November in Algiers, Paul-Louis Bret launched the Agence.

1943 : Stefani President Manlio Morgagni shot himself on 25 July.

A decision by Judge Learned Hand opened AP membership to all qualified US newspapers.

Stefani moved to the North of Italy, having finally become property of the State and an organ of the RSI. Foundation of Novinska Agencija Tanjug in Yugoslavia.

1944 : Polska Agencja Prasowa (PAP), the Polish Press Agency, was founded in Moscow.

In Algiers, the provisional government merged the Office Français d'Information and France-Afrique, thus forming Agence Française de Presse (15 March).

Clandestinely, the French National Resistance Committee launched the Agence d'Information et de Documentation (AID) in occupied France (14 April).

On 20 August a group of Resistance fighters traded in their weapons for typewriters, and merged the OFI and the AID, turning them into Agence France-Presse. Martial Bourgeon became its first managing director.

On 30 September a decree conferred to AFP the provisional status of public corporation.

1945 : Agenzia Nazionale Stampa Associata (ANSA) of Italy, Vietnam News Agency (VNA), Kyodo News service and Jiji Press of Japan, American Telenoticiosa –hoy Télam, national news agency of Argentina, and Agjensi Telegrfike Shquiptar (ATS) the Albanian Telegraphic Agency were founded.

The end of Stefani when its last director, Ernesto Daquanno, was shot dead with other Fascists leaders on 28 April.

Polska Agencja Prasowa (PAP), the Polish Press Agency, moved to Warsaw and became a state enterprise.

Domei News Agency stopped its activity at the end of the Pacific War and dissolved in October.

UP launched the first all-sports wire.

1946 : Austria Presse-Agentur (APA), the Austrian Press Agency, was founded, jointly owned by the newspaper publishers' association and the broadcasting service. Started operation on 1 September. Allgemeiner Deutscher Nachrichtendienst (ADN), East German Official news agency and Korean Central News Agency (KCNA), the state-run agency of the Democratic People's Republic of Korea, were founded.

AP established its all-sports wire.

1947 : Australian Associated Press (AAP) and the New Zealand Press Association become co-owners of Reuters with UK Press Association.

Press Trust of India, a non-profit cooperative of newspapers, was established on 27 August. (Operational on 1 February 1949)

AP's Board of Directors elected the first group of radio stations — 456 in all — to associate membership.

1948 : Belgium's newspapers became the majority of shareholders in Belga News Agency.

India's first multilingual agency, the Hindustan Samachar, was set up as a private limited company by S. S. Apte. It was the first multilingual agency in Devnagri script.

United Press of India started its teleprinter service.

Associated Press of Pakistan (APP) was established. (nationalised in 1961).

1949 : Deutsche Presse Agentur (DPA), one of the largest news agencies in Europe, began from scratch with its headquarters in Hamburg. It was formed by the amalgamation of the DENA news agency in the United States zone and the Deutsche Press Dienst (DPD) agency in the British zone.

Romanian Press Agency, Agerpres, was subordinated to the Council of Ministers on May 20.

In February, PTI became partner in Reuters.

The Central News Agency (CNA), Taiwan's national news agency, relocated to Taipei along with the Nationalist government in October.

1950 : UP was first to report the outbreak of the Korean War.

Itonut Isra'el Me'utchedet (ITIM') the Associated Israel Press, owned by four dailies, was founded.

AFP used radioteleprinter.

1951 : United Press and AP launched teletypesetter (TTS) service, enabling newspapers to automatically set and justify type from wire transmissions.

AP Radio Photo Service to Latin America was launched, with El Mercurio of Santiago, Chile, as the first subscriber.

Central Photographic Agency was established in Warsaw.

1952 : United Press acquired Acme News Pictures from Scripps, re-named it United Press Newspictures.

United Press launched the first international television news film service.

1953 : Press Trust of India withdrew from partnership in Reuters in February.

AFP gained international fame for breaking news of Stalin's death (4 March).

1956 : On 14 March a bill on the status of AFP was put forward.

Foundation of Middle East News Agency (MENA) in Egypt.

Pakistan Press International (PPI), a private limited company with Karachi as headquarters was established.

The present European alliance was founded as European Alliance of Press Agencies. In 2002 its name was changed to European Alliance of News Agencies.

Extraordinary shareholders meeting endorsed decision to expand dpa services abroad.

1957 : On 10 January the parliament unanimously adopted AFP status bill. The agency got a new legal structure.

Ghana News Agency (GNA); Mongol Tsahilgaan Medeeniy Agentlag (MONTSAME), the state-owned Mongolian Telegraph Agency; and Agence Zairoise de Presse (AZAP), the Zairian Press Agency were established.

dpa European Service began long wave transmissions. dpa Overseas Service in English began transmissions on five short wave channels.

Hindustan Samachar became a society called the Hindustan Samachar Cooperative Society, with its headquarters in New Delhi. (Workers' Cooperative).

1958 : United Press and International News Service merged on 24 May to become United Press International (UPI).

UPI launched the UPI Audio Network, the first wire service radio network.

United Press of India closed down.

On 1 October 1958 - The Beijing bureau of AFP opened.

dpa Bildfunk picture wire replaced postal distribution with long wave transmission.

1959 : dpa Spanish Service got into operation.

PTI's exclusive partnership with Reuters for the purchase of news ended.

Prensa Latina (PL), Cuba; Agence Maghreb Arabe Presse (MAP), Morocco; Agence de Presse Senegalaisw (APS), Senegalese Press Agency, and Iraqi News Agency (INA) were founded.

1960 : Agence Camerounaise de Press/Cameroon Press Agency; Agence Guineenne de Press, the Guinean Press Agency, Guinea; and Agence Mauritanienne de Press (AMP) (name changed to Agence Mauritanienne de l'Information-AMI in 1990) were founded.

1961 : Agence Tunis Afrique Presse (TAP), Tunisia; Agence Benin-Presse (ABP), Benin; Agence Ivoirienne de Press, the Ivorian Press Agency (API); Algeria's News Agency (APS); Novosti information agency (Agentsvo Pecati Novosti-APN); and United News of India (UNI) were founded.
Organisation of Asian News Agencies (OANA) was set up in December.

1962 : On 1 February the BBC started subscribing to the AFP Rastriya Samachar Samiti (RSS), Nepal; National News Agency (NNA), Lebanon; and Agence Madpress, Madagascar were established.

1963 : Kenya News Agency (KNA); Uganda News Agency (UNA); Myanmar The Din Zin, Myanmar News Agency (MNA); and Agence Burkinabe' de Press (ABP), Burkina Faso were founded.
Syncom 2, the experimental satellite orbiting at a distance of 36, 480 km, was used on 4 August to transmit telephotos and agency stories between Africa and America.

1964 : Stockmaster financial information service was launched by Reuters.
Inter Press Service (IPS); Jamahiriya News Agency (JANA), Libya; and Syrian Arab News Agency (SANA) was started.

1965 : International Press Telecommunications Council (IPTC) was founded to safeguard the telecommunication interests of the world's press.
Jordanian news agency "Petra" was founded as state-owned news agency.

1966 : The second Indian language news agency, the Samachar Bharati and Malawi News Agency (MANA), were founded.

1967 : Using satellites, the AP transmited news photos between Honolulu and London for the first time.

dpa German Service and picture service transmitted round the clock. Middle Eastern Service in Arabic went on the air, Latin American Service expanded from 6 to 12 hours a day and English-language service expanded.

The AP-Dow Jones Economic Report, a joint venture of The Associated Press and Dow Jones & Co., publishers of The Wall Street Journal, was launched to gather financial news from around the world.

BERNAMA (Pertubuhan Barita Nasional Malaysia) was established and operational from 20 May.

1968 : Noticias Mexicanos (Notimex), Mexico, and Khao San Pathet Lao (KPL), Laos, came into being.

Agencia Telenoticiosa Americana (Telam) news agency of Argentina was nationalised.

Computers began to be used to sort and edit news.

1969 : On 1 January - the Arabic language service of AFP was launched.

In October—A consultation structure between trade unions and management was implemented at AFP.

Zambia News Agency (ZANA) was founded in Lusaka.

1970 : The AP entered the age of electronic news transmission when a copy was sent from a computer screen in Columbia, South Carolina, to the main computer in Atlanta and automatically relayed back on the South Carolina broadcast wire.

Eastern News Agency (ENA), a private news agency, was established in Dhaka on 17 March 1970. Its international wing was called Bangladesh News International (BNI).

Agencia Latinoamericana de Informacion (LATIN), Agência Estado, and SABA News Agency, state-owned news agency of Yemen, was founded.

1971 : The Saudi Press Agency (SPA) was established as the first national news agency of Saudi Arabia.

Latvian Telegraph Agency was renamed "LATINFORM"

AP started on a large scale news agency CRT (cathode ray tube) news writing and editing system.

On 1 August AFP used satellites for transmissions.

1972 : Bangladesh Sangbad Sangsths (BSS) and Palestine News Agency WAFA were founded.

Computers were used for writing, editing and filing stories to AP's national news wire, replacing typewriters and teletypesetters.

1973 : Philippines News Agency and Noticias Argentinas (Argentine News) news agency were founded.

First generation of ERNA (electronically steered news switching installation) went into service. dpa journalists began editing texts on computer screens.

The AFP's Board of Directors decided to computerise AFP.

Reuter Monitor foreign exchange electronic marketplace was launched. (Reuter Monitor Money Rate service became gradually operational in London, in June.)

1974 : Agence Centralafricaine de Presse (ACP), the Central African Press Agency was founded after nationalisation of the Bangui office of AFP.

Associated Press Radio went on the air live when Tom Martin fed the first newscast.

Agency O Globo was established as a division of Brazil's Globo Organisation, which included a leading broadcast television network, a publishing company, a radio network, an Internet division and three newspapers.

Initial computerisation of news distribution services of AFP began.

1975 : Agencia Noticiosa N'gola Press (Angop), Angola, Agence Mauritanienne d'Information (AMI). Mauritania, Agence Rwandaise de Presse (ARP), Rwanda Press Agency, Agence Togolaise de Presse (ATOP), Togolese Press Agency, Qatar News Agency (QNA), Cyprus News Agency (CNA) and Federation of Arab News Agencies (FANA) were established. In November, an agreement on computerisation was reached at AFP.

1976 : The four Indian agencies, PTI, UNI, Hindustan Samachar and Samachar Bharati merged their separate identities into Samachar in February and it was registered as a society.

Non-Aligned News Agencies Pool (NANAP) came into existence. Samachar was the Indian partner in the arrangement.

Agencia Latinoamericana de Informacion (ALAI), Quito, Ecuador; Caribbean News Agency (CANA); Emirates News Agency, WAM, (Wakalat Anba'a al-Emarat); and News Agency of Nigeria (NAN) were founded.

The AP introduced LaserPhoto and the first laser-scanned pictures for transmission.

1977 : Thai News Agency (TNA); Agence Malienne de Press (AMAP); Malian Press Agency; and Venpress, the state-owned Venezuela national news agency, were founded.

The Kuldip Nayar Committee was appointed by the Government of India in April to examine the structure of Samachar and suggest its reorganisation. The committee gave its report in August.

1978 : The *status quo ante* was restored. The four Indian agencies resumed functioning separately as before Samachar from 14 April.

Lankapuvath Limited, the National News Agency of Sri Lanka was established as a limited liability company of five shareholders.

1979 : Agencia Nicaraguense de Noticias (ANN), the Nicaraguan News Agency, and Kuwait News Agency (KUNA) were founded.

Standard news item format at dpa was introduced—customers were now able to receive and process news items on screen.

On 19 April 1979, UPI announced an agreement with Telecomputing Corporation of America to make the UPI world news report available to owners of home computers.

APTV wire, the first newswire designed specifically for television stations, was introduced.

The AP was the first news organisation to introduce an "electronic darkroom," a computer that not only transmiteed photos but handled many of the tasks of the conventional chemical darkroom, such as cropping and adjusting brightness and contrasts.

Bombay-New York satellite channel was commissioned on June 6 for reception of AP service by UNI.

1980 :   ANSA headquarters started using its first electronic editorial system, SESR.

European Service of dpa began transmitting 24 hours a day.

AP Radio became the first radio network in the world to be delivered via satellite.

UPI began a strategic relationship with LexusNexus to provide access to UPI stories for readers in the government, academic and corporate markets.

Diversification towards new media and non-media clients began and a special "on-demand' services for sports and economics as well as sound broadcasting and data communication systems was introduced by AFP.

Colprensa, the privately-owned national news agency of Colombia; Sierra Leone News Agency (SLENA), the state-owned national news agency; and Yonhap News Agency, a cooperative of users, were established.

1981 :   Guyana News Agency (GNA), Shihata, Tanzania; Botswana Press Agency (BOPA); and Zimbabwe Inter-African News Agency (ZIANA) were founded.

OANA was renamed as Organisation of Asia-Pacific News Agencies. OANA also set up Asia-Pacific News Network (ANN).

Agora, a databank of AFP news items, was launched on 1 January.

ANSA databank DEA was also created, holding more than 3 million news items transmitted since 1975 and summaries of events in previous years.

Reuter Monitor Dealing Service was launched.

Bloomberg was founded.

dpa's economic desk began operation.

Belga computerised its editorial using the Hermes system.

UNI Bombay-Dubai satellite channel was commissioned on April 1.

1982 :   The AFP Hong-Kong desk was computerised. The Asia-Pacific region now had its own headquarters.

The AP established the first satellite colour photo network with LaserPhoto II, improving the speed and quality of AP photos.

Scripps family sold UPI. Tennessee entrepreneurs, Douglas Ruhe and William Geissler, took over the news service from the owners of the Scripps-Howard newspaper chain. Under their ownership, UPI continued to lose money, eventually filing for Chapter 11-bankruptcy protection. The company's headquarters moved from New York City to Washington D.C.

A group of newspapers of Argentina founded dyN—Diarios y Noticias S.A as an independent private news agency on 15 March.

Hindi service of United News of India, UNIVarta, was started in May.

1983 : Photo Service of dpa was equipped with electronic picture desks.

AP moved its broadcast operations from AP's New York headquarters to AP Broadcast News Center in Washington D.C. On 4 May the AP transmitted the first broadcast from its new location.

Lesotho News Agency (LENA) was launched with the Unesco aid.

Pan-African News Agency (PANA) was founded with headquarters in Dakar, Senegal.

1984 : Reuters floated as a public company, Reuters holdings placed on London Stock Exchange and US NASDAQ.

The AP became the first news organisation to own a satellite transponder.

Information Dissemination, Editing and Switching (IDEAS) software system, installed and maintained by CMC, became operational at PTI.

Reuters contracted with UPI on 25 June to launch its international photo service the next year by acquiring UPI's non-US photo-operations.

On 15 October the audio service of AFP was launched.

dpa Selection Service introduced after extensive trials—

customers receive tailor-made selection of news items. Work began on setting up dpa Databank.

Jampress News Agency was founded in Kingston, Jamaica.

1985 : The international photo service and an audio-visual service by AFP was launched.

Reuters bought Visnews (renamed Reuters Television); also launched its photo-service.

PTI started feeding Doordarshan (Indian television) for its teletext service.

UPI entered bankruptcy for the first time.

epa, European PressPhoto Agency B. V. The Hague/ Frankfurt was launched.

Agence Comres Presse, the Comoros Press Agency, and STP-Press, the state-owned news agency of Sao Tome and Principe, were founded.

1986 : Mexican publisher Mario Vazquez Rana purchased UPI out of bankruptcy.

AFP started transmitting its services on the Minitel.

AFP Photo decided to go "all-colour", with all assignments covered in negative colour film. Photos transmitted in black and white can be provided in colour at the request of subscribers.

PTI launched its Hindi service PTI-Bhasha in April.

Oman News Agency (ONA) was established by Royal decree.

In December there was an eight day strike at AFP. Henri Pigeat resigned on 18 December.

Reuters bought Instinet.

Foundation of Agencia de Noticias de Portugal (LUSA), from the merger of Agencia Noticiosa Portuguesa (ANOP) and Noticias de Portugal (NP), was jointly owned by the state and subscribers.

dpa broadcasting services began operation. gms Global Media Services GmbH was founded as a dpa subsidiary.

Belga offered a selective distribution service by fax or (later) by email to clients interested in particular sectors or specific subjects.

1987 : An independent agency United News of Bangladesh (UNB) was launched in January.

Russian agency Postfactum started as a branch office of information service Fact.

Agence Nigerienne de Press (ANP), state-owned news agency of Niger, was established in Niamey.

The AP introduced PhotoStream, a high-speed collection and delivery network for photos that use satellite circuitry and digital technology.

First Reuter services launched on Integrated Data Network (IDN)—a global highway for data.

On 30 December The AFP Cairo Arabic-language desk moved to Nicosia and became a regional headquarters office.

1988 : dpa bought the Globus Kartendienst GmbH and expanded its range of graphic material. dpa stopped using partner agencies to help supply its international customers. From then on, worldwide coverage was provided exclusively via dpa's own foreign correspondent network.

On 1 October the graphics service of AFP was launched.

Vazquez sold UPI's assets to Earl Brian's Infotech Inc.

1989 : Postfactum was registered as an independent joint stock company.

AP announced that it would install at member newspaper sites the AP Leaf Picture Desk to receive photos.

Interfax started by Mikhail Komissar, with colleagues from Radio Moscow.

Unrestricted reporting started from the German Democratic Republic. dpa and the East German ADN (Allgemeiner Deutscher Nachrichtendienst), Berlin, agreed to cooperate on distribution and technology. dpa and five other agencies set up mecom Medien Communikationsgesellschaft mbH to undertake satellite transmission of their services.

End of privileged position within Reuters for Press Association and Newspaper Publishers Association by conversion of 'A' shares into 'B' ordinary shares on 26 April.

1990 : AP began delivering photos via satellite to AP Leaf Picture Desks, on computer receiving terminals, at newspapers.

AP Information Services, started in 1990, packaged and delivered AP content to corporations and government agencies, and licensed AP content to distributors that provided news to the corporate market.

Romanian Press Agency Agerpres reorganised as Rompres on 8 January.

On 31 May the Cabinet of Ministers of the Latvian Soviet Socialist Republic restored the historic name LETA to its information agency.

Croatian news agency Hina started its work on 17 August.

Baltic News Service (BNS) was founded in Moscow in April at the height of the Baltic states' struggle for freedom.

Interfax was registered as an independent company in September.

The *Thueringer Allgemeine* newspaper in Erfurt became the first paper in East Germany to subscribe directly to the German Service of dpa. By the end of the year, 41 newspapers along with radio stations and television in the new federal states had signed up as customers of dpa. The 100 percent dpa subsidiary "dpa-Agenturdienste GmbH"was set up, Berlin took charge of activities in eastern Germany. Services were set up in the five new federal states with 14 regional bureaus and a central office in Berlin.

ANSA headquarters started using second generation of electronic editing system—SEAN.

The Latvian Telegraph Agency (LETA) changed its legal status and prepared for privatisation.

1991 : Namibia Press Agency, (NAMPA), Slovene Press Agency (STA) and AFX News, an English-language economic subsidiary of AFP, was launched.

The first press private news agency in Romania Mediafax was founded on June 20.

Nega, information service of newspaper *Nezavisimaia gazeta* in Russia, was founded.

The AP launched GraphicsBank, the first online archive of graphics for television news programs.

AP PhotoStream was introduced.

PAT and Central Photo Agency were merged into PAP in Warsaw.

On 15 November 1991 – AFP revenues exceeded one billion francs, while the State's share fell below the 50 percent mark.

Tunis declaration to form Alliance of Mediterranean News Agencies (AMAN), 21 November.

UPI was purchased out of its second bankruptcy by a group of Saudi investors and expanded its involvement in the Middle East.

dpa acquired a 75 percent holding in the ZB-Fotoagentur Zentralbild GmbH, Berlin.

1992 : TASS was reorganised as ITAR (Informatsionnoe Telegrafnoe Agentstvo Rossii) and soon the ITAR-TASS credit line was used to remind customers of the old connection.

News Agency of the Slovak Republic TASR was established on 30 January.

Czech News Agency (CTK) was established as a public corporation.

The independent news agency Makfax was founded and began to work in May 1993. Makfax had the distinction of being the first private news agency to embark after the break up of the old Yugoslav Federation.

ANSA began producing CD-ROM with the full text of news services since 1981.

1993 : In January the whole of AFP was computerised. Emphasis was put on developing the English-language service.

Belga provided digital transfer of colour photographs through ISDN (Integrated Services Digital Network).

1994 : The 40-year era of long wave transmissions ended. DENA closed down its long wave transmitters. Introduction of digital picture transmission via satellite. dpa increased control of "ZB-Fotoagentur Zentralbild GmbH" to 100 percent.

Athens News Agency (ANA) became a Societe Anonyme.

Reuters bought TIBCO (formerly Teknekron), Quotron, and UK radio broadcaster LNR and launched Reuters Television service for financial markets.

The AP introduced the AP News Camera 2000, the first of a series of digital filmless cameras designed for photojournalists.

AP NewsCenter, a newsroom system for television stations, was launched.

APTV, a global video newsgathering agency, was launched.

AP All News Radio, a 24-hour news and information network, was created to provide full-time news programming to radio stations.

AP launched AP AdSEND, a digital ad delivery service that transmitted ads from advertisers and agencies directly to newspapers.

dpa subsidiary Global Media Services GmbH took over "news aktuell GmbH" Hamburg. dpa's English Service established a new editorial office in Washington D.C.

ANSA's English news service got onto the Internet.

1995 : In April AFP-Direct was launched, enabling personalised transmissions of AFP services.

The Balkan state news agencies after an initiative by Macedonian Press Agency established the Association of the Balkan News Agencies (ABNA) in June.

In September AFP ended its agreement with the AP on its provision of American news and set up an autonomous gathering network in the US.

dpa Picture Service changed over to full digital production using databank-based library. gms introduced gms Themenienst.

1996 : Hamburg operation of the international Spanish Service of dpa was transferred to Madrid where the dpa Agencie de Prensa Alemana SL was founded. It produced the Spanish service together with the editorial department already based in Buenos Aires.

Island ECN founded by Reuters. Reuters sold most of LNR to DMG, ITN and GWR.

AP covered a major news event, Super Bowl XXX, without film—by using only digital cameras.

AP launched the Western Regional Service, serving 13 states in the western United States.

AP produced a news desktop computer system for the British Broadcasting Corporation, which combined text, audio and video called the Electronic News Production System (ENPS). AP launched The WIRE, continuously updated online news service on the Internet, which combined text, photos, audio and video news.

APTV, in a joint venture with Trans World International (TWI), launched SNTV, a sports news video agency.

Asia Pulse Pte Ltd was launched as a joint venture company of Asia's major news and information providers.

The Central News Agency (CNA), Taiwan's national news agency, transformed into a publicly owned, independently run legal entity.

Republic of Lithuania adopted a special law that made ELTA an independent national news agency.

1997 : Reuters gave itself a new capital structure by forming Reuters Group PLC and returned 1.5 billion pound sterling to shareholders.

UPI launched Arabia 2000, a collection of Arabic-language news stories from the major government news agencies in the Middle East.

Latvian Telegraph Agency (LETA) was privatised through capital investments under new ownership.

The dpa Agenturdienste GmbH, Berlin was absorbed into dpa as a whole. An editorial department was set up in Nicosia, Cyprus, and began producing the dpa international service in Arabic from January. An editorial desk was established in Bangkok to deal with news from Asia. dpa introduced the dpa-MedienServer (MES), a reception system for dpa's Picture Service, dpa-Online, dpa-Graphic and began the dpa/RUFA broadcasting services. Test phase of dpa-Online began in February. April marked the introduction of dpa's "rapid picture transmission" service which offered all images in colour.

1998 : Reuters bought Lipper Analytical Services (renamed Lipper Inc), and Agence Presse Medicale (APM) and took stake in Datamonitor.

PAP was registered as stock Company 'Polish Press Agency— Polska Agencja Prasowa SA.

APTV became APTN— Associated Press Television News — when AP purchased video agency WTN from its parent companies: ABC News of the United States, ITN of Great Britain and Channel 9 of Australia.

Macedonian Information Agency (MIA) was launched on 30 September.

The BelgaBrief product—Belga news briefs for Internet portals was launched and distributed.

1999 : Fidel Castro, who ordered it shut 30 years ago, allowed AP to reopen a bureau in Havana.

Reuters bought Hardwick Stafford Wright, a supplier of fund performance information to the UK industry, and BOPP ISB AG, a provider of fund performance and analysis to the Swiss industry, and bought majority stake in TowerGroup, US finance sector IT specialists.

dpa's German Service and European Service editorial departments were reorganised and a new general/soft news desk was set up. dpa-AFX-Wirtschaftsnachrichten GmbH was founded. It started work on 1 July (dpa had a share of 50 percent.)

2000 : AP Digital, a new unit, was launched, to concentrate on commercial sales for the Internet, with multimedia production resources and the ability to deliver information on a variety of technology platforms.

In February ALCATEL and AFP teamed up on Mobile Internet Content.

AFP broke new grounds in Japan as it started distributing sports pictures on Third Generation (3G) cellular phones.

In March AFP bought out the Financial Times Group's 50 percent holding in AFX.

In September - Rex Features joined ImageForum of AFP.

Reuters bought CAMRA fund portfolio information and analysis service, BT Alex Brown Investment Trusts data services and ORT corporate information service in France and took major stake in US-based IT forecasters Yankee Group for 72.5m.

News World Communications, a media group founded by the Rev. Sun Myung Moon that included the *Washington Times* newspaper, purchased UPI

dpa's new Berlin central office was inaugurated. Subsidiary dpa-info.com was founded and dpa-Photo Databank contents made available via the Internet.

2001 : Reuters floated part of Instinet and bought Bridge Information Systems, and Diagram, French back-office services agency.

UPI developed and launched a multilingual editorial and distribution system, known as "Bernini," used by all UPI offices around the globe.

Belga developed SMS and WAP services and launched its video service.

2002 : AFP joined forces with Visiware in Interactive television.

Reuters subsidiary Instinet bought rival Island ECN and Reuters sold stake in LNR.

Newsis, news agency launched by Haiun Choi, started to distribute foreign news material to domestic media companies in Korea from 1 April. He had applied for news agency license in October 1997 but had been turned down by the Government and succeeded after a long legal battle.

UPI re-launched its UPI LatAm service to once again provide Spanish-language content focusing on the affairs of Latin America, the United States and the world.

dpa share capital stood at 16.464,750 €, turnover (2001) 106 million €, with 900 employees.

The dpa International Service in English was restructured— from August the main editorial desk was based in Cork/Ireland.

dpa Picture Alliance GmbH was established to distribute via Internet portal images provided by dpa-Bilderdienste and other leading photo agencies.

2003 : Louis D. Boccardi retired as President and CEO of AP after 18 years, succeeded by Thomas Curley, former President and publisher of *USA Today*; "electronic AP" (eAP) a new interactive network of multimedia content was unveiled.

AP established a corporate archives within its corporate communications department for the purpose of preserving AP's valuable historical legacy in journalism.

AP and Ipsos (a publicly listed survey research company) entered into partnership for public opinion polling.

UPI focused its English-language content into two products: short NewsTrack items on current news, and longer-perspectives items providing analysis, commentary and in-depth reports on significant issues.

Reuters acquired Multex.com, Inc., a provider of global financial information.

2004 : AFP released its archives on Liberation of Paris.

UPI re-opened its Beirut bureau as the hub for the Arabic News Service, allowing for more direct coverage of the major issues coming from the Middle East in Arabic.

Reuters launched an interactive TV news channel, offering consumers video news stories from its news bureaus around the world direct to their homes. The service was one of the first video news channels to be available on Microsoft Windows XP Media Center Edition 2005.

Reuters launched a business and financial news and information channel on Vodafone live! It targeted at mobile phone users in the UK.

The OPEC News Agency (OPECNA), based at the organisation's secretariat in Vienna, Austria, transmitted its last bulletin on 30 December.

2005 : CME (Chicago Mercantile Exchange Inc.), the largest US futures exchange and the largest regulated marketplace for foreign exchange (FX) along with Reuters launched CME FX on Reuters.

The "AP and Freedom of Information" web pages in a new section on its corporate website was launched.

NAM agree to revitalise NANAP (pool) by replacing it with Non-Aligned News Network (NNN) on 22 November.

SELECT BIBLIOGRAPHY

Ahmed, Q (1983) *India by Al-Biruni* New Delhi, National Book Trust.

Badikian, Ben H, (1971) *Information Machines Their Impact on Men and the Media*, New York, Harper & Row.

Badikian, Ben H, (1979) More Mergers Mean Less News, *Journalism Studies Review*, No 4, July 1979.

Belfoeld, R, Hied, C, and Kelly, S, (1991) *Murdoch*, London, Macdonald.

Boyd-Barrett O (1979), Theory and Practice: From Cuba to Vietnam, in Boyd-Barrett, *The World-Wide News Agencies: Development, Organisation, Competition, Markets and Product*, Ph. D. thesis, Milton Keynes, Open University, pp. 833-855.

Boyd-Barrett, Oliver (1980). *The International News Agencies*. London: Constable.

Boyd-Barrett, Oliver (1986) 'Political Constraints and Market Opportunities: The Case of the 'Big Four,' pp. 192-204 in.

Boyd-Barrett, Oliver and Thussu, Daya K. (1992) Contra-Flow in Global News, London: John Libbey

Boyd-Barrett, Oliver and Rantanen, Terhi (1998), The Globalisation of News, London: Sage.

Boyd-Barrett, Oliver (2001) *Final Report of the Workshop on News Agencies in the Era of the Internet*. Paris: Unesco.

Brucker, H. (1973) *Communication is Power: Unchanging Values in Changing Journalism* New York: Oxford University Press.

Bures, O (1977) *Towards a New Information Order*, Prague: International Organisation of Journalists (IOJ).

Cardownie, J (1987) News Agency Journalism A Handbook, Bonn: Friedrich Ebert Stiftung.

Cooper, Kent (1942) *Barriers Down. The Story of the News Agency Epoch*. New York: J. J. Little and Ives Company.

Cooper, Kent (1959) *Kent Cooper and The Associated Press An Autobiography*, New York: Random House.

Dreier P. and Weinberg, S. (1979) *Interlocking Directorates, Columbia Journalism Review*, November/December 1979.

Fatoyinbo, Akin (1995) West African News Agencies Development Project (WANAD) Terminal Report, Paris: Unesco.

Fenby J (1986) *The International News Services*, New York: Schocken Books.

Giffard, C. Anthony (1998) Alternative News Agencies, in Boyd-Barrett and Rantanen (eds.), The Globalisation of News, London: Sage, pp. 191-201.

Gordon, G. K. and Cohen, R. E. (1990) *Down to the Wire UPI's Fight for Survival*, New York: McGraw-Hill.

Government of India (1954) *Report of the Press Commission Part I*, New Delhi, Manager of Publications.

Gudykunst W and Bella Mody B. (Eds.) (2001), *Handbook of International and Intercultural Communication. 2nd Edition*. Thousand Oaks: Sage.

Harris P, Malczek H, and Ozkol E (1980) *Flow of News in the Gulf*, Paris: Unesco, New Communication Order series No. 3 (43-63).

Indian Institute of Mass Communication (1979) *A Manual of News Agency Journalism*, New Delhi: Allied Publishers.

International Organisation of Journalists (1969) *Handbook of News Agencies*, Prague: IOJ.

International Press Institute (1953) *The Flow of News*, Zurich: IPI.

International Press Institute (1999) *The Kosovo News and Propaganda War*, Vienna: IPI.

Jaroslav, S. H. (1972) Introduction to News Agency Journalism Prague: International Organisation of Journalists (IOJ).

Jones, Roderick (1935) *World News.* Address, Empire Summer School, Oxford, July 1935. London: Waterlow & Sons.

Kim, Soon Jin (1989) *EFE Spain's World Agency* New York: Greenwood Press.

Kivikuru U. and Varis T (Eds.) (1986) *Textbook on Approaches to International Communication*. Helsinki: Finnish National Commission for Unesco.

Kivikuru, Ullamaija (1998) 'From State Socialism to Deregulation,' pp. 137-153 in Oliver Boyd-Barrett and Terhi Rantanen (Eds.) *The Globalisation of News*, London: Sage.

Mankekar, D. R. (1978) One Way Free Flow Neo-Colonialism via News Media, Delhi: Clarin Books.

Mohammadi, Ali (ed.) (1997) *International Communication and Globalisation*, London: Sage.

Mooney B. and Simpson B. (2003) *Breaking News: How the Wheels Came off at Reuters* Capstone, John Wiley.

Mowlana, Hamid (1997) Global Information and World Communication, London: Sage.

Palmer Michael (1998) 'What Makes News,' in Oliver Boyd-Barrett and Terhi Rantanen (Eds.) *The Globalisation of News*, London: Sage pp. 177-190.

Raghavan, G. N. S. (1987) PTI Story, Bombay: Press Trust of India.

Rantanen, Terhi (1990) *Foreign News in Imperial Russia: The Relationship between International and Russian News Agencies, 1856-1914*. Helsinki:

Federation of Finnish Scientific Societies.

Rantanen, Terhi (1992) *Mr. Howard Goes to South America. The United Press Associations and Foreign Expansion.* Roy W. Howard Monographs in Journalism and Mass Communication Research, No 2. Bloomington: School of Journalism, Indiana University.

Rantanen, Terhi (1994) *Howard Interviews Stalin. How the AP, UP and TASS Smashed the International News Cartel.* Roy W. Howard Monographs in Journalism and Mass Communication Research, No 3, 1994. Bloomington: School of Journalism, Indiana University.

Rantanen, Terhi (1998) *After Five O'clock Friends. Kent Cooper and Roy W. Howard.* Roy H. Howard Monographs in Journalism and Mass Communication Research, No 4, February 1998. Bloomington: School of Journalism, Indiana University.

Rantanen, Terhi (2002) *The Global and the National. Media and Communications in Post-Communist Russia.* Lanham: Rowman & Littlefield.

Rantanen, Terhi and Vartanova, Elena (1995) News Agencies in Post-Communist Russia: From State Monopoly to State Dominance," in *European Journal of Communication*, Vol. 10, No 2, June 1995, 207-220.

Rantanen, Terhi (2004) Media and Globalisation, London: Sage.

Read, Donald (1992) *The Power of News The History of Reuters* Oxford: Oxford University Press.

Read, Donald (1999) *The Power of News The History of Reuters* Oxford: Oxford University Press.

Reston, James (1967) *The Artillery of the Press: Its Influence on American Foreign Policy*, New York, Harper & Row.

Robinson, G. J. (1977) *Tito's Maverick Media: The Politics of Mass Communication in Yugoslavia*, Urbana, University of Illinois Press.

Robinson, G. J. (1981) *News Agencies and World News* Fribourg: University Press of Fribourg, Switzerland.

Rosenblum, M (1979) Coups & Earthquakes Reporting the World for America New York: Harper and Row.

Rosewater, V (1930) *History of Cooperative News Gathering in the United States.*

Salinas, Raquel (1977) News Agencies and the New Information Order, in Varis et al (eds.), *International News and the New Information Order*, Institute of Journalism and Mass Communication, University of Tampere.

Schiller H (1976) *Communication and Cultural Domination*, New York, International Arts and Sciences Press, Inc.

Shrivastava, K. . M. (1991) *New Reporting and Editing*, New Delhi: Sterling Publishers Pvt. Ltd.

Shrivastava, K. M. (1992) *Media Issues*, New Delhi: Sterling Publishers Pvt. Ltd.

Shrivastava, K. M. (1995) *Recent Trends in News Agency Journalism*. Paper presented at Seminar on Deontology of Journalism in the Countries in Transition to Market Economy, Moscow. (September 20-24).

Shrivastava, K. M. (1995) *Practices of Big Media and News Selectivity*. Paper presented at 33rd World Congress of Sociology of The International Institute of Sociology University of Cologne (July 7-11 1997) Working Group #3. 5 The Selectivity of International Knowledge.

Shrivastava, K. M (1998) *Media towards 21ˢᵗ Century*. New Delhi: Sterling Publishers Pvt. Ltd.

Shrivastava, K. M. (2000) *International News: Should it be Redefined?* Paper presented at Conference on International News in the Twenty-First Century organised by Centre for Mass Communication Research, University of Leicester (16-17 March 2000).

Shrivastava, K. M. (2003) *Media and War* in online *Global Media Journal* hosted by Prudue University Calumet, Hammond, Indiana, USA (Fall 2003).

Siebert, Fred S. et. al (1963) *Four Theories of the Press*, University of Illinois Press.

Sreberny-Mohammadi A (1991) The Global and the Local in International Communications, in Curran J and Gurevitch M (eds), *Mass Media and Society*, London, Edward Arnold.

Storey, G. (1961) *Reuters' Century, 1851-1951* London Reuters.

Thussu, Daya K (1995), Development News, Unit 38b of the MA in Mass Communications, Center for Mass Communication Research, University of Leicester.

Tomlinson (1991), *Cultural Imperialism*, London, Pinter.

Unesco (1953) *News Agencies Their Structure and Operation*, Paris: Unipub.

Unesco (1964) *World Press, Newspapers and News Agencies*, New York: Unesco Publications Center.

Unesco (1978-79) The International Commission for the Study of Communication Problems Papers 1-73, Paris Unesco.

Unesco (1980) *Many Voices, One World: towards a new, more just and more efficient world information and communication order* (The McBride Report), The International Commission for the Study of Communication Problems, Paris, Unesco; London, Kogan Page.

Unesco (1989) World Communication Report, Paris: Unesco.

Unesco (1993) Project Document, PANA, Paris: Unesco.

Unesco (1994) Transfer of SEANAD. Handing-Over Notes from Project CTA, Paris: Unesco.

Villard O (1930) *The Associated Press*, The Nation, April 16/April 23.

Vyslozil, Wolfgang (2002) Aspects of news agency typology. An unpublished memo.

INDEX

□□□